an
ARYAN
Journey

Harsh Mahaan Cairae is a student of philosophy and religion, who has studied the scriptures of several religions. The Veds have been his special interest, as their meaning and linkages to later Indian philosophy are subject to a lot of speculations. He was trying to decipher the code in which they have been written when he stumbled on the history of the Indo-Aryans.

an ARYAN Journey

Harsh Mahaan Cairae

REVISED AND UPDATED EDITION

RUPA

Published by
Rupa Publications India Pvt. Ltd 2014, 2019
7/16, Ansari Road, Daryaganj
New Delhi 110002

Sales centres:
Allahabad Bengaluru Chennai
Hyderabad Jaipur Kathmandu
Kolkata Mumbai

ISBN: 978-81-291-3258-1

Second impression 2019

10 9 8 7 6 5 4 3 2

The moral right of the author has been asserted.

Printed at Gopsons Papers Ltd, Noida

Dedicated to my Guru,
His Divine Grace Sri Swatmaram Swami,
the author of
Hatyog Pradeepika

Contents

begins—emergence of new gods—level of development.

Preface

As India did not have a tradition of recording history, a lot of difficulties have been faced by historians in reconstructing it. Somehow they have been able to reconstruct it from the sixth century BC onwards. For the period before that historical facts are not very clear. Two things, however, are known, one that there was a flourishing urban civilization which has been named as the Indus Valley Civilization and two that the Aryans came to India sometime in the past. As people in North India believe that they are descendants of Aryans, a conclusion was drawn that the Aryans had invaded India and destroyed the Indus Valley Civilization and had driven its people towards the south. A lot of Aryan literature has survived, all of which comes in the category of Vedic literature. No attempt has been made to reconstruct the history of the Aryans on the basis of this and, all that has been done is only to speculate the place of their origin. Several theories have been propounded, including one, which insists that the Aryans were indigenous to India.

Apart from the scriptures of the Indo-Aryans, scriptures of another ancient Aryan religion, the Zoroastrianism have survived as well. The present work is an effort to reconstruct the history of the Aryans on the basis of the evidence that emerges from the scriptures of these two religions—the Vedic religion and Zoroastrianism. The Veds have references to a large number of wars fought between the Devs and the Asurs. A study of these scriptures shows that the Vedic people called themselves 'devs', a term used for them by the Zoroastrians also, whose scriptures too report of a lot of wars fought against them. Evidently, Zoroastrianism is the religion of people who have been called Asurs in the *Veds*. Information emerging from both these scriptures is confirmatory to each other which makes it possible to trace the journey of this remarkable group of people, the Aryans. It also brings to light significant historical events, especially those that led to the break-up of one tribal group into two mutually hostile entities leading to the emergence of two different religions. Though it is not possible to bring out the dates of these events but the places where events in their histories occurred are identifiable. The reasons as to why a small group from amongst them came to India, to be called the Indo-Aryans, also emerge distinctly.

This study establishes that the Aryans did not come to India as invaders to destroy the Indus Valley Civilization, but as refugees seeking shelter in the wake of religious persecution in Persia. They came in Indian trade ships and with the help of their hosts, settled down in the Indian cities to start life afresh.

The study also brings out the reasons for the disappearance of the Indus Valley Civilization and proceeds to look for evidence within western sources concerning Indians of that period as it had emerged from the *Veds* that India had a flourishing trade with West Asia and beyond since remote past. A study of the Greek and Roman sources brings out a startling information that the people, who have been called the Phoenicians in the Mediterranean, were people of the Indus Valley Civilization. They had, initially, established a widespread trade network and, later, when the prosperity of the Indus Valley Civilization came to an end, they migrated to the Mediterranean and established colonies and finally the Carthaginian Empire. The impact of the coming of these Indians on Greek and world civilization is well-known, only their link with India has been lost. Evidence to establish this has also been brought out in this study.

What has been stated in this book stands to contradict a large number of historical theories but evidence has been brought out for what has been propounded. It is true that this evidence is from literary sources only, but the same is strong enough to require a study by other sources, especially genetics. In the end, this book would be of interest to committed students of history as well as to readers in general.

1
The Early Days

THE STORY OF MAN HAS always been a fascinating subject. Whenever something noteworthy has been done by someone, it has found reflection in several facets of the society. It is seen in folklore, scriptures, coins, paintings, designs on clothes and pottery, sculptures, artifacts and so on. Reading this story from each of these source requires a different approach. Two ancient Aryan religions, the Vedic and the Zoroastrian, have left behind a rich collection of scriptures, which have a lot of stories of wars. An initial reading of these gives an impression that they are stories of wars between gods and demons. A closer look, however, shows that these are not stories of gods and demons, but of men fighting each other. A still closer look reveals that both religions are telling the story of the same people, who at one time lived in perfect harmony as a group, but at some stage developed differences over religious practices and they fought each other as enemies over them.

With both sides telling the same story, the fights between gods and demons emerge out of mythology and knock at the doors of history. However, as the authors of these works were writing scriptures and not history, the story, as it emerges, has its shortcomings. Firstly, they do not tell the story in a continuous sequence because their main concern was religion and only events that had some significance in their view were taken note of. Secondly, being scriptures, they have mentioned the events as instances of the grace of God. The style of writing being such, setbacks and defeats have not been mentioned or have been referred to in an oblique manner. Reading them gives an impression that on all occasions only the other side was the loser.

Thirdly, they do not give the dates. If, at all, the length of someone's reign is mentioned, it is exaggerated. Fourthly, additional difficulties have been created by using several names for the same person and at times shortening or twisting those of the opponents, to make them derogatory. This difficulty caused by the twisting and turning is over and above what is due to the language being different. Despite all shortcomings, the story that emerges is still very fascinating and needs to be heard, as a story of men who were driven by the same passions that lead us to do the same things today. Once it is brought out of the realm of mythology it would help also in understanding the real message of the scriptures, and perhaps at some stage other sources of information would remove the shortcomings left.

Since the scriptures are the source, the religion of this Aryan group remains the pivotal point around which everything else is told. They tell us that in the beginning these Aryans believed in one God. Belief in God is something seen in all people. It seems to be a part of the process of evolution. It seems that when humans reach a certain level of evolution and try to understand things around them, there are many phenomena beyond their comprehension, all of which they place in one category and call them either God or due to the wish of God. Perhaps one aspect that would have puzzled the early humans the most, was the uncertainties of life. They must have been baffled to see that one day in hunt, within a very short time and without much effort, they are able to kill an animal and get food, while on another even after toiling for the entire day, they got hardly anything. Many such uncertainties must have been faced by them, which could not be understood because they saw that the person was the same, his capabilities were the same, and despite that one day, a little effort gave all the results, while on another even much more proved futile. They would have concluded that there was some other factor also, which made all the difference. This unknown factor has been created as God by humans across the globe. As God was created by man as the unknown factor working with him in his endeavours, he created Him in his own image. God, when pleased, gave everything and when angry, punished people in the manner they saw evils coming upon themselves. Since He could

dispense reward and punishment on everyone, even on the high and mighty, He had to be all powerful, the ultimate sovereign. This God had to be pleased so as to have the wishes fulfilled. Here too, God was created in the image of man. As we like good people and dislike the bad, the same was applied to God, with which ethics emerged and received the sanction of religion. Similarly, as we like people who are submissive, praise on every possible occasion and are liberal with gifts, the same attributes were put on God, with which all rituals of religion have emerged. Since it was the non-comprehension of things around, especially the uncertainties of life, that led to the emergence of God and the development of religion, the level of man's faith in God gets linked to the level of his understanding of natural phenomena and the level of uncertainties in his life. The need for divine support is not felt in societies where the basic requirements are met in the normal course and there is no uncertainty attached to them. In such societies, people know that food is there on the shelf in the store next door and they do not need God for it. In such societies, unless there are reasons other than the primary causes for which God had emerged, religion loses its relevance.

Like all people, the Aryans were leading a simple life with limited requirements. Gradually, they moved forward and reached a stage wherein agriculture emerged. This was something new and initially its uncertainties were not understood. They needed help from the unknown factor for the new development. For this, they decided to have four gods instead of one. The *Veds* tell us that this was done by the Ribhus. These events are of a remote period and have found expression in a concrete form only in the *Veds*. The Avesta provides only supportive evidence. The Ribhus and the changes they brought about emerge from these passages of the *Veds*.

1. When, Ribhus, you who were amongst my ancestors, yet immature but desirous of enjoying (the Som libations), retired to the forest to perform (penance), then sons of Sudhanvan, through the plentitude of your complete (devotion), you came to the (sacrificial) hall of the worshipper Savita.

2. Then Savita bestowed upon you immortality, when you came to him, who is not concealed, and represented (your desire) to partake of the libations and that ladle for the sacrificial viands which the Asur had formed single, you made fourfold.

(M-1, S-110, R-2 and 3)

3. Ribhus, you covered the cow with a hide, and reunited the mother with the calf, sons of Sudhanvan, leaders (of sacrifice), through your good works you rendered your aged parents young.

(*Rig Ved.* M-1, S-110, R-8)

4. Make fourfold the single ladle, so the gods command you, and for that purpose am I come, sons of Sudhanvan; if you accomplish this, you will be entitled to sacrifices along with the gods.

5. Then said they, in answer to Agni, the messenger (of the gods). Whatever is to be done, whether a horse is to be made, or a car is to be made, or a cow is to be made, or the two (old parents) are to be made young, having done all these (acts), brother Agni, we are then ready to do (what you desire) to be done.

(*Rig Ved.* M-1, S-161, R-2 and 3)

6. When Tvasta said, let us slay those who have profaned the ladle (designed) for the drinking of gods, then they made use of other names for one another as the libation was poured out and the maiden (mother) propitiated them by different appellations.

(*Rig Ved.* M-1, S-161, R-5)

7. Sons of Sudhanvan, from a skinless (cow) you have formed a living one, by your marvellous acts you have made your aged parents young, from one horse you have fabricated another, harness now your chariot and repair unto the gods.

(*Rig Ved.* M-1, S-161, R-7)

8. Water are [sic] the most excellent said one (of them), Agni is the most excellent said another, the third declared to many 'Vardhayanti Bahubhya' (to be the most excellent), and thus speaking true things the Ribhus divided the ladle.

(*Rig Ved.* M-1, S-161, R-9)

9. Ribhus, leaders (of the sacrifice) you have caused the grass to grow upon the high places, you have caused the water to flow over the

low places, for (the promotion of) good works, as you have reposed for a while in the dwelling of the inapprehensible (Sun), so desist not today from this.

(*Rig Ved*. M-1, S-161, R-11)

10. In as much as for a year, the Ribhus preserved the cow, in as much as for a year, they invested it with flesh, in as much as a year they continued its beauty, they obtained by their acts immortality.

11. The eldest said, let us make two ladles; the younger said, let us make three. Tvasta, Ribhus has applauded your proposal.

12. The men (Ribhus) spoke the truth, for such (ladles) they made and thereupon the Ribhus partook of that libation. Tvasta, beholding the four ladles, brilliant as day, was content.

13. The Ribhus, reposing for twelve days, remained in the hospitality of the unconcealable (Sun). They rendered the fields fertile, they led forth the rivers, plants sprung upon the waste, and waters (spread over) the low (places).

(*Rig Ved*. M-4, S-33, R-4 to 7)

14. The gods first generated the words of the hymn, then Agni, then the oblation. He is the (object of the) sacrifice of these deities, the protector of the body; him the earth and the waters, know.

(*Rig Ved*. M-10, S-88, R-8)

The Ribhus, like the Rudras and Vasus, are a separate category of divinities in the Vedic concept of gods. These Richas state that they were ancestors of the Aryans and were deified, because of their role in the initiation of new religious practices that became the order of the day. Their names were Vaja, Vibhavan and Ribhu, all called the sons of Sudhanvan, though Sudhanvan seems to be an ancient progenitor of the entire tribe or tribes that were involved in the exercise and not the immediate father of the three as these changes had been accepted widely, for which it appears to have been an exercise with widespread consultations and not as a family affair. The main theme of these Richas is that the Ribhus divided one ladle into four. A ladle is a spoon with which an offering is made to God. Saying that one ladle was divided into four means that four gods were formed instead of the

existing one by creating three new divinities. The sixth Richa speaks of
new names being used. Though the language gives the meaning that
new names were used by the Ribhus for themselves, it means that a
new name was brought in for the earlier single God, who was Tvasta.
The new name could have been totally new or one of his lesser used
names. What new purposes for which these gods had been created is
best seen in the eighth Richa which states that one suggested water,
the second suggested Agni and the third suggested 'Vardhayanti
Bahubhya'. These are the requirements of agriculture. Water needs
no explanation. Agni in the *Veds* is believed to have three forms, fire
on earth, lightning in the sky and the sun in the heavens. The sun had
initially not been conceptualized as an independent god, though over
the ages it emerged in various forms and did become an independent
deity. Fire in this Richa represents the sun with its links to seasons.
The third element is 'Vardhayanti Bahubhya' in the text. This has
been translated by the translators as the 'earth', which is incorrect,
not only because it does not go with the spirit of the Richa but also
because the earth has been separately deified with Dyau or heaven and
has been treated as the mother of all gods. The literal meaning of the
term is 'multiplier of many'. It refers to that quality of a seed which
produces a good crop. Evidently, the Aryans had started agriculture
but had not been able to understand its intricacies. They must have
noticed that despite all factors remaining the same, like tilling the
soil, good rain, good sunshine and the same land, on one occasion the
crop was good while on the next it was not so. This uncertainty in the
behaviour of the seed must have led them to have a god on this count
also, though very soon they seem to have understood that this was
because of the loss of fertility of the soil that needed to be restored by
manure, because the god that they created for this purpose soon lost
importance. For these people who kept cattle, it would not have been
very difficult to notice that manure and fertility have a link because
they would have seen that the grass grew healthier where there had
been cow dung. The gods that were created by the Ribhus have to be
there in the Veds, as well as the Avesta because this event is earlier to
the split that took place, which in course of time led to the creation

of two separate religious identities. For fire, the clarity is total. The *Veds* have called him Agni, while the *Avesta* has Atar. The god for water has to be Varun, who happens to be on both sides with the same name. In the *Veds,* his association with water is beyond doubt. The *Avesta* does not give information of his attributes to say anything conclusive. The element linked to productivity has been deified as Pushan in the *Veds*, while in the *Avesta*, he is Peshan. His links to agriculture are clear in the *Veds* while again in the *Avesta* references are scanty. The fourth god is Tvasta with his old functions of overall superintendence, but with a new name Mitra in the *Veds* and Mithra in the *Avesta*. He is repeatedly mentioned in the *Avesta* as Mithra, the lord of wide pastures, signifying his stature during the pastoral days. Though all four of these were created together, Pushan in the *Veds* appears to be an antiquated deity giving an impression that he was worshipped in the past only, while the other three appear living and vibrant. There are very few Richas addressed to him. Apparently, once the Aryans understood more about agriculture and saw what factors went into having a good crop Pushan, who had been created for the productivity of the seed, lost importance and was not remembered very often, while Varun and Agni, being forces of nature still needed to be appeased.

The main thrust of the exercise undertaken by the Ribhus to seek assistance for agriculture from the divine forces is further confirmed by the ninth and thirteenth Richas. The ninth says that the Ribhus caused the grass to grow upon the high places and water to flow over low places, as they reposed in the dwelling of the sun for a while. Grass here means agricultural crops, which the Richa says have now come up well. These hymns have been composed at a later stage when the Aryans had begun to make water channels to irrigate their fields on the slopes of hills where they dwelt, something which will emerge in their journey ahead, because of which they are talking of flowing waters here. At the time of the Ribhus, when they had just begun to practise agriculture, they could not have had irrigation channels. This Richa also speaks of the sun having provided all the desired bounties because of the Ribhus, a reference to the role of weather in agriculture.

The thirteenth Richa states that the Ribhus rendered the fields fertile, they led forth the rivers, plants sprung upon the waste and waters spread over the low places. Leading the rivers is again a reference to irrigation channels that they had started digging later. As agriculture involved new uncertainties, new gods with specific purposes, were thus created as people were unsure that the existing God would be able to provide for the new bounties.

The second thing mentioned in these hymns is that the Ribhus covered the dead cow with skin and made it alive. It seems that the religious practices of the Aryans were very simple at that stage and the Ribhus brought in some rituals, which made them lively. Cow here means religion. The fourteenth Richa, though from a Sukta not addressed to the Ribhus, gives an idea of how the religious practices gradually evolved amongst them. It states that the gods first generated the words of the hymns, then Agni, then the oblation. This shows that to start with, the religious practices involved just the singing of hymns. Next, this singing of hymns was begun in the presence of fire. This could have been a sheer accident, as fire may have been initially brought in either for illumination or for warmth and over a period of time became a mandatory element to be present when the hymns were being sung. The Ribhus seem to have brought in the concept of oblations in the religious practices. This was an offering of food and other desirable items to the gods as a token of gratitude, making the rituals elaborate and governed by a set of rules, which could be understood better by those specialized in the task, bringing in the concept of a priest. The scriptures of the two sides show that it involved making of a seat for the gods at the place of worship suitable to his stature, summoning him to receive the things that had been prepared and with due praises making of an application of things being sought. For people with deep faith in what was being done, it would have been of utmost importance to do everything carefully without error because the presence of the god was felt right there. Any reason for annoyance could make him angry with adverse consequences. In a situation wherein the people felt the direct connection between pleasing god and receiving bounties, making religious practices elaborate would have made them convincing. Instead of just singing hymns in front of fire, the priest could now claim that the god had been summoned and was seated right there. They could offer gifts and seek what they desired, though only through the medium of the priests, who alone knew the rules which had to be observed to ensure that He does not take offence. As the exercise became more convincing, it has been expressed in the *Veds* by saying that the Ribhus covered a dead cow with skin and made it alive again.

The third thing which has been said about the Ribhus is that they made their old parents young again. The Ribhus have been deified, and as they have become gods, the parents that are being spoken of are the parents of the gods. The single God that was there before this exercise and has been named Tvasta, seems to have had more than one name. Mitra apparently was one while another appears to have been Dyau. It is with the second that he has been mentioned very often in the *Veds* identifying him as heaven, with earth as his wife and all gods as their children. Tvasta or Dyau was not conceptualized having a consort before the Ribhus but was a single entity. The need for imagining a wife would have emerged only when new gods were created and some link had to be established with the earlier one. As the new gods were treated to be the children of the earlier God, Tvasta or Dyau emerged as the universal father and with him Prithvi or the earth was brought in as their mother. She has also been called Aditi. Tvasta, a single entity, was now with a wife and children.

Though the fourth and fifth Richas give an impression that it was a divine ordain for the Ribhus to divide the ladle into four but the subsequent references show that there was an assembly of leaders, wherein the matter was debated upon and only thereafter these decisions were taken. The eleventh Richa says that the eldest said, let us make two ladles, the younger said, let us make three which shows that there was a debate on the subject and various aspects of agriculture were examined to cover the areas where divine assistance was needed and a conclusion arrived thereafter. The thirteenth Richa gives an impression that the leaders, who were either only religious leaders or exercised temporal authority also, had assembled for twelve days. It says that the Ribhus, reposing for twelve days remained in the hospitality of the unconcealable (sun). Though the Ribhus have been named as three, Vaja, Vibhavan and Ribhu, the assembly in which all these decisions were taken seems to have been attended by thirty-three persons. The *Veds* repeatedly speak of thirty-three gods. A few instances are here.

1. Come, Nasatyas, with the thrice eleven divinities, come Ashwins to drink the oblation. Prolong our lives, efface our faults, restrain our enemies and be ever with us.

    (Rig Ved. M-1, S-34, R-11)

2. With all these in one chariot, Agni, or in many (chariots) come to our presence, for your horses are able; bring the three and thirty divinities with their wives, for the sake of (the sacrificial) food and exhilarate them (all) with Som libation.

    (Rig Ved. M-3, S-6, R-9)

3. Destroyers of foes, adored by Manu, who are three and thirty and are thus hymned.

    (Rig Ved. M-8, S-30, R-2)

The identity of these thirty-three divinities has not been given anywhere in the *Veds*. This being a matter of speculation amongst the Aryans from very ancient times is borne out from the following passage of the *Aitarey Brahman*.

For there are thirty-three gods, viz. eight Vasus, eleven Rudras, twelve Adityas, one Prajapati and one Vashatkar.

(Aitarey Brahman. Chapter II)

This shows that even at this early a stage, when the Brahman was written, the identity of these thirty-three gods was not known. What has been stated is an incorrect speculation because these thirty-three divinities find mention in the *Avesta* also for which they have to be of a period earlier to the split between the two groups, while Rudras and Vasus emerged much later. The third Richa too indicates that these were of a period before the split because it states that they were adored by Manu and the split took place in his times. In the *Avesta*, these thirty-three divine entities are mentioned at several places. A few are given here.

1. To thee come all the performers (of holiness), all the masters of holiness, who to the number of three and thirty stand next to Havani, being masters of holiness.

    (Vistasp Yast XVIII)

2. And I announce and complete (my Yasna) to all those who are the thirty and three lords of the ritual order, which, coming the nearest, are around about the Havani.

    (Yasna I)

The identity of these thirty-three holy beings is not given anywhere in the *Avesta* either. As both sides speak of the same number in the same manner, it appears that the religious assembly of the Ribhus was attended, not by three, but by thirty-three persons, all of whom were deified and perhaps up to a time the names of all were remembered, after which only the numbers remained and the *Veds* have mentioned names of the three prominent persons. The *Avesta* does not provide much information about the happenings of this period. Apart from mentioning the thirty-three divinities, it mentions the name of Haoshyangha, which has become Hoshang in the Pahlavi language. He is said to be associated with the primitive law and appears to be the counterpart of the Ribhus, despite being mentioned as a single individual only as against three in the *Veds*. A few passages about him are given here.

1. To her did Haoshyangha, the Paradhata offer up a sacrifice on the enclosure of the Hara. He begged of her a boon saying, 'Grant me this, O good, most beneficent Ardvi Sura Anahita! That I may become the sovereign lord of all countries, of the Daevas and men, of the Yatu and Parika, of the oppressors, the blind and the deaf, and that I may smite down two thirds of the Daevas of Mazana and of the fiends of Varena.'

    (Aban Yast VI)

2. The most powerful amongst the Fravarshis of the faithful, O
    Spitama! Are those of the men of the primitive law or those of
    the Saoshyants not yet born, who are to restore the world.

    (Farvardin Yast I)

3. To her did Haoshyangha, the Paradhata offer up a sacrifice, upon
    the enclosure of the Hara, the beautiful height made by Mazda. He
    begged her a boon saying, 'Grant me this, O great Ashi Vanguhi!
    That I may overcome all the Daevas of Mazana that I may never
    fear and bow through terror before the Daevas but that all the
    Daevas may fear and bow in spite of themselves before me, that
    they may fear and flee down to darkness.'

    (Ashi Yast III)

4. At another time it came to Vaegered and Hoshang of the early
    law, for providing in the world the law of husbandry or cultivation
    of the world, and of sovereignty or protection of the world. And
    through their companionship and united force, given by religion,
    the sovereignty and cultivation of the world were prepared through
    progress and a succession of provisions of Auharmazd's creatures,
    as well as the religion appointed by Auharmazd. And through that
    glory of destiny two-third of the demons of Mazano and the seven
    evil-instructed ones of Aeshm were destroyed by Hoshang.

    (Dinkard. Book VII, Chapter I)

5. Among the children of Fravak, were for Haoshang and Vaegared,
    as Haoshang through superior glory was ruler of the world and
    Vaegared through provincial government became the cultivator
    and cherisher of the world, and their well-destined descendants
    aggrandized the race of the monarchs among the well-born
    provincial governors.

    (Dinkard. Book V, Chapter IV)

In the first and third passage, Haoshyangha is shown as offering a
sacrifice and seeking a boon from certain divinities. The *Avesta* has
such passages where important personalities have been shown as
seeking a boon of what they have done. This is the style of the *Avesta*
of narrating events. In all such passages the *Avesta* has followed the

sequence in which the events occurred. In all cases, Haoshyangha has come before all the rest, except in one where Ahur Mazda himself has come before him seeking a boon from Ardvi Sura Anahita. In this sequence, Haoshyangha is mentioned before Val and Yam, who are yet to come in the journey. Apart from the fact that he has been called 'the Men of Primitive Law', this sequence shows the antiquity of Haoshyangha and brings him to the times of the Ribhus of the *Veds*. It is noteworthy here that Haoshyangha though named as a single person, has always been called as 'the Men of the Primitive Law', giving an indication that more than one person is being referred to though only one was being named. The fourth and fifth passages are of interest. These are from the Dinkard, which is in Pahlavi language and is of a later time. It mentions Vaegered as a brother of Hoshang. The *Avesta* at all places has mentioned Haoshyangha only and has not mentioned Vaegered anywhere nor a brother or associate of Haoshyangha by any other name. There will be an occasion ahead to dwell in greater detail on the point that some very important priests and families of the Zoroastrian religion were followers of the Vedic religion for a very long time and on their conversion, carried several Vedic mythologies to incorporate them in the Zoroastrian traditions. This seems to be one such instance. Vaegered has been brought into the Zoroastrian traditions at a later date because of which he does not find mention in any of the earlier scriptures and it is only the Dinkard, which is of the ninth century AD, that does so. More than one single entity seems to have become necessary as in the *Veds*, the Ribhus have been shown as three brothers. Though a later incorporation, it firstly goes to show that the identification of Haoshyangha with the Ribhus is correct and secondly, agriculture was what was being talked of all along in connection with these personalities because Vaegered has been stated to be a cultivator. The mention in all these passages of killing of two-thirds of the Daevas is due to the later trend. Once the two sides split and started fighting each other, praying and wishing for the other side to be killed had become an overpowering obsession for both. However, at the time when the Ribhus or Haoshyangha established the primitive law, both sides were one and lived in harmony. There were no Devs, just as there were no Asurs. Both were one and remained so for very long even after this.

The exact location of the place where the Aryans started agriculture and the Ribhus brought in changes in the prevailing religious beliefs and practices cannot be found from the *Veds* and the *Avesta*. However, an outer limit, with a wide margin, can be placed for the same on the basis of the descriptions that emerge from the *Veds* about the Ashwins who are believed to be twins and are linked to the early morning sun. The Aryans, initially, had not conceptualized the sun as a god. The Ribhus had given this status to Agni only, and sun was deemed to be Agni in heaven. It would have taken some time for the sun to emerge out of the shadow of Agni and develop an independent identity for itself. Once the sun had emerged as a god, again some time would have elapsed for the early morning sun to emerge with a separate identity and with distinctive features. At a later stage, the early morning sun has been named Savita and is a male deity, but to start with, it was called Suryaa, the daughter of the sun. Ashwins are shown as her consorts and drive her chariot. It would have taken quite some time for mythology to grow from a simple Agni to the sun, to the sun's daughter Suryaa and then to her consorts, the Ashwins. It could have been several centuries. There is no indication in the *Veds* whether the Aryans were moving during this period or had remained static, because of which a wide margin to this outer limit has to be conceded. The location of these people when the Ashwins had emerged as deities can be stated with a reasonable amount of clarity on the basis of the following hymns of the *Veds* addressed to them.

1. Who are divine, of pleasing appearance, children of the sea, willing dispensers of wealth, and granters of dwellings (in recompense of) pious acts.

    (*Rig Ved*. M-1, S-46, R-2)

2. Children of ocean, mighty ones, discoverers of riches, Gods, finders of treasures through our prayers.

    (*Saam Ved*. Part II, Book VIII, Chapter III)

In both the expression, 'Children of the Sea' has been used for the Ashwins. This poetic expression for something linked to the early morning sun can come only from people who were watching sunrise from the seashore. These passages show that the Aryans were on the western shore of a sea and developed the imagery of the Ashwins being the children of the sea watching the sun emerge from the sea. Next emerges the question of the identity of this sea, the western shore of which was the homeland of these people. The sea has to be close to Central Asia as these Aryans were in that area later. There are two seas in this region, the Caspian and the Aral Sea. It appears that they were on the western shore of the Caspian Sea as the sea which is being referred to is not small, but big enough to witness storms in which small ships could capsize and survivors could remain lost for days. This is brought out by the legend of Bhujyu, son of Tugra, which appears to be of this period, because Indra as a protector from calamities had not yet emerged and Ashwins have been assigned that role. After the emergence of Indra, the Ashwins developed the role of the gods of medicine and are not to be seen as protectors in danger. The references to Bhujyu in the *Rig Ved* are given here.

1. Tugra, verily, Ashwins, sent (his son) Bhujyu to sea, as a dying man parts with his riches, but you brought him back in vessels of your own, floating over the ocean, and keeping out the waters.

2. Three nights and three days, Nasatyas, have you conveyed Bhujyu in three rapid, revolving cars, having a hundred wheels, and drawn by six horses, along the dry bed of the ocean to the shore of the sea.

3. These exploits you achieved, Ashwins, in the ocean, where there is nothing to give support, nothing to rest upon, nothing to cling to, that you brought Bhujyu, sailing in a hundred-oared ship to his father's house.

                                                (*Rig Ved*. M-1, S-116, R-3 to 5)

4. Dissipaters of affliction, as you were praised with former praises by Tugra, so were you again adored (by him), when you brought

Bhujyu back safe from the tossing ocean, with the swift ships and
rapid horses.

5. The son of Tugra, brought back by you, Ashwins (to his father)
    glorified you when he had crossed the ocean in safety and you bore
    him, showerers (of benefits), with your well-harnessed car, swift
    as thought, to safety.

                                    (*Rig Ved.* M-1, S-117, R-14 and 15)

6. Four ships launched into the midst of the receptacle (of the waters)
    sent by the Ashwins, brought safe to shore the son of Tugra, who
    had been cast headlong into the waters and plunged in inextricable
    darkness.

                                          (*Rig Ved.* M-1, S-182, R-6)

These Richas show that Tugra was a man of importance of his time
who sent his son Bhujyu on an exploratory expedition into the sea. It
appears exploratory as no purpose has been mentioned and the disaster
left nothing unaccomplished and his safe return was enough to be
happy about. The boats seem to be rowboats, as in the salvage mission
a hundred-oared boat is mentioned, but at no stage have sails been
referred to. They must have been sufficiently large to carry provisions
for the crew and have been called ships. The mission encountered a
storm in which all boats were wrecked and everyone except Bhujyu
perished. Bhujyu survived for three days and was rescued by the rescue
party on the fourth, clinging on to the wreckage of a boat. Though in
the general area where these Aryans were later, the Aral Sea is also
there, but as this account of Bhujyu's sea journey and his survival in
a storm shows the sea to be bigger than the Aral Sea, the western
shore of the Caspian Sea appears to be the homeland of these Aryans,
according to the accounts of the *Veds.* The *Avesta* has no mention of
any location for this period.

    Some idea about the level of material development of the Aryans
when they were living on the western shore of the Caspian Sea
emerges from the references. The cow had been domesticated by
them very early in their journey. Apart from the frequent references
to it, this emerges from the use of the word 'duhitri' for daughter in

their language from a very early stage. Literally, this means 'one who milks the cattle'. This shows that the daughter of the family had the task of milking cows, with which the word got coined and came in usage. The word has gone to so many Aryan languages that its early origin has to be believed. The horse had also been domesticated by this time. There are repeated references to the horses of the sun as well as those drawing the chariot of the Ashwins. It seems to have been an important item of food also. The chariot has been referred to with no ambiguity. This is with reference to the Ashwins as well as for other deities and so had been designed and was in use at this stage. The wheel, the invention with which the civilization is said to have started, would have come in earlier, though it cannot be said when, but by now horse-drawn carriages were certainly in use. The sea journey of Bhujyu, shows that they had boats though these were not seaworthy as they could not survive a storm in the Caspian Sea. This is understandable as they were not seafaring people. The size of these boats, however, was big enough to carry sufficient provisions to last for several days for the crew, who would have been in a good number as rowboats would have needed them. Iron was in use by this time as can be seen from this Richa.

> One (Tvasta) immovably stationed among the gods, holds his
> iron axe in his hand.
>
> (Rig Ved. M-8, S-29, R-3)

Iron is specifically mentioned. Conceptualizing Tvasta's weapon as an iron axe goes well with his role as the god of a stage when woods were cleared to make way for agriculture. Use of iron this early would have been a great advantage for clearing vast areas of forests for agriculture, which, was a new entrant in the life of these people needing all the exercise carried out by the Ribhus for divine assistance in new areas. The references of the Ribhus show that they had understood sunshine, water and fertility to be important elements for agriculture. To start with, they seem to have thought that fertility was linked to the seed, but soon realized that it was the soil which needed to be treated and very soon found solutions for it. Issues relating to irrigation seem to have been understood by them fairly early because by the time we find them at their next place of stay, they had channels for carrying water to their fields. With uncertainties relating to water getting reduced, a change in the nature of Varun, the god created for the purpose, is visible. While on the shores of the Caspian Sea, Varun was linked to water for the purposes of agriculture only. He was not the lord of the sea because in the legend of Bhujyu, it is the Ashwins who have been stated to have saved him and not Varun. Ashwins would have been remembered for this purpose because they were thought to be living somewhere there, being the sons of the sea, to emerge each morning. Much later, when another sea journey was undertaken by these Aryans, this time in the Arabian Sea, it would be Varun who would be called for assistance because by then he had become the god of waters that were not linked to agriculture, though in between his role seems to have become the same as that of Mitra as the upholder of the righteous order.

Though the first major activity of the Aryans seen in the *Veds* is that of the Ribhus and for that the outer limit of their location appears to be the western coast of the Caspian Sea, this is not the place from where the journey started. They had certain things in their memory that have been mentioned at random, which give information of the place from where it began. This information is contained in the following Richas of the *Rig Ved*.

1. The divine Usha dawned continually in former times, the source of wealth. She still rises on this (world), so will she give light hereafter through future days, for exempt from decay or death, she goes on in her splendour.

    (Rig Ved. M-1, S-113, R-13)

2. Many are the days that have dawned before the rising of the Sun, on which you, Usha, have been beheld like a wife repairing to an inconstant husband and not like one deserting him.

    (Rig Ved. M-7, S-76, R-3)

3. I now glorify his vast and Asur destroying (vigour), those exploits that he has determined (to achieve) no one can resist; (by him)

the Sun was made daily visible, and he, the doer of great deeds, spread out the spacious regions (of the universe).

(*Rig Ved*. M-6, S-30, R-2)

4. The milch cow (the dawn) yields the desired milk to the ancient (Agni), the son of south passes within the sky, the bright-houred (day) brings the illuminative (Sun), the praiser awakes (to glorify) the Ashwins preceding the dawn.

(*Rig Ved*. M-3, S-58, R-1)

Usha is the deification of dawn. The first Richa states that now we have dawn every day, but there was a time when it used to dawn continually, an indication that earlier the Aryans were at a place where the sun rose only once a year and so dawn was for a long period, though again only once a year. The second Richa confirms this point. It states that the dawn continued for many days before the rising of the sun. Days here are a reference to time and are not linked to the rising and setting of the sun because in it the dawn is waiting for the sun to rise. Poetically, dawn has been compared to a dutiful wife, who waits for her late coming husband and does not desert him. The third Richa is in praise of Indra, who though a later deity is eulogized here as being an all-powerful entity because of which it has been stated that he made the sun visible daily. It does not state that he makes the sun visible daily. The use of past tense is a reference to an earlier happening and shows that the Aryans were at a place where the sun did not rise daily and when they moved to a place where it rose so, they have given the credit for it to the all-powerful entity they were worshipping. The fourth Richa has metaphorically called the sun 'the son of the south'. The emergence of this imagination is possible only from the Arctic Circle. At all other places the rising of the sun remains linked to the east because of its rising and setting daily. In the Arctic Circle, the sun rises after six months from the far end of the southern horizon, while the sky above keeps rotating like a wheel every twenty-four hours. In this situation the initial lights of dawn and later the sun emerge at a point which revolves all around, completing a full circle in twenty four hours. This point of emergence can be linked only to the south. As it moves in its six-monthly journey, the sun appears to come closer till it is over the Tropic of Cancer, and then recedes back to set when it is over the Equator, circumambulating every twenty-four hours. Its link to the east or west is thus not apparent. It is only this image of the sun that can lead to a poetic expression of calling it the son of the south. This term seems to have survived in their language from the Arctic days and has been used here.

In the *Avesta*, indications of the memory of the Arctic days surviving are hinted in a legend associated with Yim. There are distortions in this because of a long time having elapsed. As the story is long, an abridged version is given here.

The fair Yim, the good shepherd of high renown in the Airyana Vaego, by the good river Daitya, called together a meeting of the excellent mortals. To that meeting came Ahur Mazda. And Ahur Mazda spake unto Yim, saying, 'O fair Yim, son of Vivanghat! Upon the material world the fatal winters are going to fall, that shall bring the fierce, foul frost; upon the material world the fatal winters are going to fall, that shall make snow-flakes fall thick, even an Ardvi deep on the highest tops of mountains. And all the three sorts of beasts shall perish. Therefore make thee a Vara to be an abode for men, to be a fold for flocks. Then Yim said within himself, 'How shall I manage to make that Vara which Ahur Mazda has commanded me to make?' And Ahur Mazda said unto Yim, 'O fair Yim, son of Vivanghat! Crush the earth with a stamp of thy heel, and then knead it with thy hands, as the potter does when kneading the potter's clay.' And Yim did as Ahur Mazda wished. And Yim made a Vara. O Maker of the material world, thou Holy One! What (lights are there to give light) in the Vara which Yim made? Ahur Mazda answered, 'There are uncreated lights and created lights. There the stars, the moon, and the Sun are once seen to rise and set and a year seems only as a day.'

(Vendidad. Fargarad I)

The distortions in the legend are apparent. First, the location stated is Airyana Vaego, which, as would emerge ahead, is further south on the migration route of these Aryans. This belief appears to have come in as Airyana Vaego is the earliest place, the name of which has survived in the *Avesta* as well as the *Veds*. No place earlier to this has been named anywhere. This would have led to a belief that Airyana Vaego was the original homeland, for which the earliest legends have been linked to it. Secondly, Yim has been mentioned, though he, again was of a later period, being the king of Arjika. This could have emerged because of the storytellers repeatedly projecting Yim as a redeemer, who defeated the Devs and took back Airyana Vaego. If these distortions are ignored, the description appears to be of the Ice Age, wherein everything went under the cover of snow and most of the creatures and plants perished. In terms of natural lights also, the passage states that the stars, the moon and the sun, rise and set once a year and the year seems like a day. The mention of the moon creates a problem, as the moon does not follow this pattern in the Arctic. This could, however, again be a distortion as the legend would have been based on a story that had survived several thousand years from generation to generation. The distortion could have crept in as the original storytellers would have mentioned only a day and night of one year while people later would have tried to elaborate this by mentioning all the features of night, including the moon and the distinction that the moon maintains its cycle and its visibility does not change in the Arctic with the sun not being visible for six months, would have been lost. The *Veds* have no passage which would indicate a reference to the Ice Age, but this long and catastrophic winter had been faced by every species in the north that lived to survive it. The Aryans were in the north and so there can be no question of they not having faced it. The absence of any reference to it in the *Veds* cannot be a reason for doubting the information given by the passage of the *Avesta*, to be a reflection of the memory of the catastrophic snow.

These Richa from the *Rig Ved* and the passage from the *Avesta* establish that the Aryans were in the Arctic Circle initially. This is the earliest homeland of these people which can be stated on the basis of what the scriptures tell us. Apart from what emerges from these passages, the level of their knowledge of astrology and astronomy from very early times gives an impression that it was gathered by them during their stay in this part of the globe. There will be an occasion ahead to dwell on this point in greater detail.

Two very important facts emerge from the reading of the *Veds* which lead to very significant inferences. One, that the Aryans were living in the Arctic Circle and two, in their journey south, they did not come across any other human race till they reached the fringes of the Arabian Sea. Since they were at the Arctic Circle, they could have gone there only before the onset of the last Ice Age, because during the Ice Age, conditions there would have been too severe for anyone to come and adjust, and after the Ice Age there would have been no necessity to do so. This shows that before the Ice Age, the entire land mass, from Europe to at least Central Asia, was home to some very dangerous animals. It must have been very difficult for man to survive with them. To escape, some humans moved away to the north and kept moving till they reached a place where these animals were not present. This was the Arctic Circle. Very soon they would have adjusted to the conditions of the Arctic Circle and made it their homeland. With the onset of the Ice Age, all humans and most of the animals that were on land perished, but these humans who were living over ice in the Arctic Circle survived. At first glance this sounds a miracle that humans should have survived only at a place which should be the coldest, but on closer scrutiny, it appears that this was the only place in the north where humans could have survived. To survive an Ice Age, apart from having the capacity to withstand the cold, food is essential. People living on land were dependent on land for food. Whether it was plants, fruits, roots or meat, everything came from land. With the Ice Age setting in, the entire land mass went under a thick blanket of ice. Food would have just vanished for them. All vegetation getting covered by ice would have led to a drastic fall in the population of herbivorous animals, making it extremely difficult for humans and carnivorous animals to get food. Nobody could have survived such starving conditions for fifteen thousand years, because of which all of them perished. On the other hand, in the Arctic Circle, firstly the humans would already be used to Ice Age conditions for being able to withstand the cold. Secondly, they were not dependent on land for food. Like the present-day Eskimos, they would have dug a hole in the ice and would have waited near it with a sharp weapon for food. The light passing through the hole would have attracted fishes, which they would have hunted for six months in which the sun was up, to consume its flesh as food and oil as fuel for the entire year. The Ice Age would have only made the ice surface thicker, for which they could have either moved to the periphery where it would have been thinner or would have dug deeper. Either way food was available where they knew it was and was obtainable in the manner in which they had always been able to. The deep blue sea would have remained as bountiful as it always was. It was not like the situation on land where food was just not available where the people always found it, and was not obtainable in the manner in which they knew to do so. The brutal cold of the Ice Age did not give anyone the luxury to learn new lessons from the situation and to find new solutions. Since the existing levels of competencies of the people on land were inadequate to get food in those trying conditions, this was the only fate that they could have met. For this reason when the Aryans started trickling south after the end of the Ice Age, they found neither the dangerous animals that had driven them north, nor the brave hearts who had stayed behind to face their challenge.

2
The Break Up

THE NAME OF THE NEXT landmark in this journey, which remained the homeland of these Aryans for quite some time, has survived in the scriptures of both sides. The *Veds* give it as Arjika, while the *Avesta* calls it Airyana Vaego, which, in Pahlavi, has become Airen Vej. This was also the last homeland that was completely abandoned and contact with the place lost. Lot of things have been written about it reflecting their fond and revered memories. Their stay here was very eventful and shaped the history of Central Asia for very long. To start with, the *Veds* report of religious persecution at the hands of fellow Aryans. Though there were several Aryan tribes in the area, the report of persecution is from a very close quarter, in fact from within the same habitation and in one case, from within the same family, which shows that the schism was within a single group. The Aryans who have given the *Veds* to us have called themselves Devs at this stage and have called the other side Asurs. In the *Avesta* too, these Aryans have been called Devs at this stage and either Devs or Dev worshippers later. The reports of religious persecution of the Devs are on the following lines in the *Rig Ved*.

1. With those aids by which you raised up from the water, Rebha, who had been cast bound, and also Vandan (similarly circumstanced) to behold the sky, by which you protected Kanva, when longing to see the light, with them, Ashwins come willingly hither.

2. With those aids by which you rescued Antak, (when cast into) a deep (pool) and about to be destroyed, by which, inflicting no distress, you preserved Bhujyu, and by which you relieved

Karkandhu and Vayya, with them Ashwins come willingly hither.
(*Rig Ved.* M-1, S-112, R-5 and 6)

3. You quenched with cold (water) the blazing flames (that encompassed Atri) and supplied him with food-supported strength, you extricated him Ashwins, from the dark (cavern) into which he had been thrown headlong, and restored him to every kind of welfare.
(*Rig Ved.* M-1, S-116, R-8)

4. When his father caused Rjrasva, as he was giving to a she-wolf a hundred sheep cut up in pieces, to become blind, you Dasras, the physicians (of the gods) gave him eyes, (that had been) unable to find their way, with which he might see.
(*Rig Ved.* M-1, S-116, R- 16)

5. Undecaying Nasatyas, you bore away by night in your foe-overwhelming car, Jahush, surrounded on every side by (enemies) through practicable road and went to mountains.
(*Rig Ved.* M-1, S-116, R-20)

6. Ashwins, you raised up like Som in a ladle, Rebha, who for ten nights and nine days had lain (in a well), bound with tight bonds, wounded, immersed, and suffering distress from the water.
(*Rig Ved.* M-1, S-116, R-24)

7. You restored eyes to Rjrasva, who, on presenting a hundred sheep to the she-wolf had been condemned to darkness by his indignant father, and gave light to the blind wherewith to behold all things.

8. (Desiring) that the enjoyment (arising from the perfection) of the senses (should be restored to the blind), the she-wolf invoked you, (saying), 'Ashwins, showerers (of benefits) leaders, Rjrasva (lavish), as a youthful gallant, (has given me) a hundred and one sheep, cutting them in fragments.'
(*Rig Ved.* M-1, S-117, R-17 and 18)

9. You gave (relief) to the imprisoned Atri (quenching) the scorching heat, and fed him with grateful food, solicitous of worthy praise, you gave sight to Kanva, blinded (by darkness).
(*Rig Ved.* M-1, S-118, R-7)

10. This Atri, whom the irresistible (Asurs) dragged bound like a

swift horse, you unloosened like a strong knot (setting him) free.
Youngest born upon earth.

(*Rig Ved.* M-10, S-143, R-2)

It is significant that in all these hymns the deity invoked and who is
credited to have saved the worshippers are the Ashwins. This is because
Indra had not yet emerged and only the Ashwins had a legend of
protecting someone earlier, Bhujyu, the son of Tugra. Richas at four,
seven and eight are significant as they give the case of Rjrasva, who
was blinded by his father for presenting a hundred sheep to the she-
wolf. It establishes that this schism cut through even families, and also
gives an idea of the changes made that caused it. The term she-wolf
has been used for the sacrifice. It is evidently a term the Asurs used in
ridiculing the Devs for consigning meat and other edible commodities
into fire. They must have asked whether the sacrifice was a he-wolf or
a she-wolf that needed to be fed with meat.

The scriptures of both religions following a common pattern of
ignoring reverses, the cases reported, have to be limited to only the
persons surviving. Those not surviving would not find mention. The
things that were done would have caused death in many cases. Atri is
reported bound, dragged and kept without food or water in a pit with
a fire burning. He had every reason to be grateful to the Ashwins for
surviving. In the case of Rebha also, the account reports him injured,
bound and cast in a well. Surviving such tortures would have been a
miracle and only a few would have been in a position to thank the
Ashwins for it.

The *Avesta* has references which show that the Asurs did bind the
Devs and cast them in some sort of a prison. We have this passage.

And he who should set that man at liberty, when bound in
prison, does no better deed than if he should flay a man alive
and cut off his head.

(Vendidad. Fargard XVIII)

Persecution being from within, as people of the same village did this
to others who were believed to be practising and preaching heresy,

would have been with the approval of the political authority of the place. These incidents show that the new practices started by the Devs did not have the approval of the king and the cases of violence against them were with his consent. The *Veds* as well as the *Avesta* indicate that monarchy was the prevalent political system amongst them. The *Veds* repeatedly use the term 'Kavi'. In later Sanskrit this means a poet and has been thought to be so in the *Veds* also. In the *Avesta* 'Kavi' means a king, which in Pahlavi is 'Kai'. It seems that in the *Veds* also 'Kavi' means a king. As most of these 'Kavis' were leaders of men in the intellectual field also and are credited with the composition of several hymns of the *Veds*, the word gradually got linked to the composers of poetry and the original meaning appears to have been lost. This would explain the use of the word 'Kavya' in the *Veds*, which has been used for the son of 'Kavi' or prince. In later Sanskrit this word means poetry or the creation of the 'Kavi', but this meaning to Kavya was not so in the *Veds* as the references are for individuals. The specific use of the word Kavya or prince in the text indicates that monarchy was hereditary. Though loosely called a king, the Kavi was essentially just a leader of men. Exclusive territorial jurisdiction was not a necessary precondition for being a Kavi in those days. Land was not an issue as it was abundantly available. Many people were on the move and migration was the order of the day. In such a situation, the existence of exclusive territorial control for a Kaviship would have been an impossible situation and would have led to war with every passing migratory group violating such a domain. The Kavi, therefore, only exercised authority over his people, whether living in fixed habitations or on the move. In the same area there could have been more than one group of people because of which there would have been more than one Kavi exercising sovereign powers over his people within the same territorial boundaries. His powers may not have been dictatorial at such an early stage, but he being the chief cannot be doubted.

The accounts do not give a clear picture of the separation of temporal and religious leadership. At places it appears to be combined. A large number of hymns of the *Veds* have been composed by Kavis and Kavyas. Like the political leadership, the religious leadership too does not seem to have been absolute. Religious ceremonies required a large number of priests who could gain in stature and occupy positions of respect in the hierarchy. In this background of a monarchy, that was not dictatorial and religious leadership which allowed space to others, a group of seven priests, who have been called the Angiras Rishis in the *Veds*, decided to introduce certain new practices in the religion. Of the tribe, some agreed with them while some, which included the Kavi, disagreed and considered it to be a heresy. As political authority was with the disagreeing side, it decided to stamp these practices out by use of force, with which, the history of these Aryans who had come a long way, living in peace, becomes the history of fratricide. Blood that now flowed was of brothers, shed to decide which ritual was correct. There are references in the *Rig Ved* to show that the quarrel was over the following of different rituals by the two sides. These are mentioned here.

1. May your friends, parvat, hurl down from heaven him who follows other rites, the enemy of men, him who offers not sacrifice and who worships not gods; may Parvat hurl the Dasyu down to the stern smiter (death).

    (*Rig Ved*. M-8, S-7,R-11)

2. The Dasyu practicing no religious rites, not knowing as thoroughly, following other observances, obeying no human laws, baffle, destroyer of enemies, the weapon of that slave.

    (*Rig Ved*. M–10, S–22, R-8)

Unlike the occasion of the Ribhus, where the *Rig Ved* speaks of the changes made, the changes brought in by the Angiras Rishis have not been spelt out. This could have been because it was thought to be obvious and needing no elaboration. To know what exactly was done that led to all the bloodshed, it is necessary to know the religious practices followed earlier. As the *Avesta* is the scripture of the group that continued with the earlier rituals, the practices that emerge from the *Avesta* have to be the benchmark for the purpose.

Both scriptures show that fire was an essential feature of the sacrifice. It was kindled by the priest, who has been called an Atharvan by both sides. Evidently, this is a very old term and was in use before the split occurred. By the side of the fire, bundles of a particular grass were placed in a certain manner so as to make a seat. It was believed that the god invoked, was seated there to receive the oblation. The Veds have called this grass Barhi, while the Avesta has called it Baresma. A few extracts from the *Veds* and the *Avesta* which provide the relevant information about this are below.

1. We worship Sraosha, who first spread forth the Baresma, and the three bundles, and the five bundles and the seven bundles and the nine, till it was heaped for us knee-high, for the Bountiful Immortals, for their worship.

    (Yasna LVII, the Srosh Yast)

2. Agni, generated (by attrition) bring hither the gods to the clipped sacred grass (Barhi), you are the invoker for us, and are to be adored.

3. As you discharge the duty of messenger, arouse them, desirous of the oblation sit down with them on the Barhi.

    (*Rig Ved*. M-I, S-12, R-3 and 4)

Having seated the invoked god on the seat so prepared, hymns were sung in their praise. Several priests were involved in the process, which could have initially been a choir. Later, when the ritual became more detailed, specific tasks were assigned to each of them. There seem to have been seven or eight priests as a requirement for the sacrifice. This roll call of the priests as given in the *Avesta*, gives the names for each.

(The Zaotar speaks) (I call for) the Havanan, and would have him here.
(The Ratu answers) I will come (and fulfil his duties).
(The Zaotar speaks) I would have the Atarevaksha here.
(The Ratu answers) I will come (and fulfil the services which fall to his charge).
(The Zaotar) I would have the Frabaretar.
(The Ratu) I will come (and do his duty).
(The Zaotar) I would have the Aberet present.

(The Ratu) I will come (for him).

(The Zaotar) I would have the Asnatar.

(The Ratu) I will come (for him).

(The Zaotar) I will have the Raethwiskar to be here.

(The Ratu) I will come (for him).

(The Zaotar) I will have the Sraoshavereza present, the wisest one, the most correct and veracious in his speech.

(The Ratu) I will come.

(Visparad III)

The *Veds* also talk of seven priests. Some of the names of the two sides have a marked resemblance. A few instances where the priests have been referred to in the Vedic literature are given here.

1. I worship with oblations that Agni whom the seven invoking priests invite as the invoker of the gods, who is most worthy of worship at sacrifices and who is the donor of all riches. I solicit of him wealth.

(*Rig Ved*. M-1, S-58, R-7)

2. Yours Agni is the office of the Hota, of the Pota, of the Ritvij, of the Nesta, you are the Agnidhra of the devout, yours is the function of the Prashasta you are the Adhvaryu and the Brahma; and the householder in our dwelling.

(*Rig Ved*. M-2, S-1, R-2)

Though the *Rig Ved* gives the names of these priests in the second Richa, the names given in the Shat Path Brahman have some variations and are given as Adhvaryu, Brahman, Udgatri, Hotri, Pratiprasthatri, Neshtri and Potri.

The religious practices of the two sides show a marked degree of similarity up to this point with the fire kindled, a seat of bundles of grass prepared for gods to sit and seven or eight priests being present. A difference is seen at the next stage which was of offering the oblation to the gods. The *Avesta* shows that only wood and fragrance were put into the fire, while food and drinks were offered to the gods only as a token by lifting them up. These were thereafter eaten by the faithful.

In the Vedic practices, the edible material offered to the gods was consigned to the flames. Some accounts of the *Avesta* that reflect that libation was eaten by the worshippers after a token offering to the gods are given here.

1. Of this libation of mine thou shalt drink, thou who are an Athravan, who hast asked and learnt the revealed law.

   (Aban Yast XXI)

2. Ahur Mazda answered, 'Let the Aryan nation bring libation unto him, let the Aryan nations tie the bundles of Baresma for him, let the Aryan nations cook for him a head of cattle. Let not a murderer take of these offerings nor a person who does not sing the Gathas, who spreads death in the world and withstands the law of Mazda, the law of Zarathustra.'

   (Tir Yast XVI)

3. (The Ratu speaks) Eat, Oye men, of this Myazda the meat offering, ye who have deserved it, by your righteousness and correctness.

   (Yasna VIII)

The Vedic literature has references which confirm that the Asurs used to eat the libation. Some are given here.

1. You Indra, by your devices have humbled the deceivers who presented oblations to their own mouths, propitious to men, you have destroyed the cities of Pipru, and have well defended Rijishvan in robber-destroying (contest).

   (*Rig Ved.* M-1, S-51, R-5)

2. Once upon a time the Devs and the Asurs, both of them sprung from Prajapati, strove together. And the Asurs, even through arrogance thinking, 'Unto whom forsooth, should we make offering?' went on offering it into their own mouth.

   (Shat Path Brahman. Kand V, Adhyay I)

Though these references in the *Rig Ved* and the Shat Path Brahman have stated the eating of the libation by the Asurs, there are a few Richas in the *Rig Ved* which seem to be of a period when the changes had not been brought in by the Devs and the oblations were eaten even by the Aryans who have given the *Veds* to us. The Sukta, from which these Richas have been taken, is of a later period and at places shows that the libation was consigned to the fire, but these Richas appear to be older and seem to have survived to creep into the Sukta. These are mentioned here.

1. Let their exertions be for our good who watch the cooking of the horse, who said, it is fragrant, therefore give us some, who solicit the flesh of the horse as alms.

2. The stick that is dipped into the caldron in which the flesh is boiled, the vessels that distribute the broth, the covers of the dishes, the skewers, the knives, all do honour (to the horse).

    (*Rig Ved*. M-1, S-162, R-12 and 13)

3. Let not the smoke-smelling Agni cause you (horse) to utter sound, let not the glowing caldron odoriferous (with its contents) be overturned, the gods accept a horse that has been selected for sacrifice that has been led (round the fire), that has been devoutly offered and has been consecrated by (the exclamation) Vashat.

    (*Rig Ved*. M-1, S-162, R-15)

The first two Richas show that the meat of the animal sacrificed was eaten by the worshippers. There is mention of even the vessels used for its distribution to the persons performing the sacrifice who were now to participate in a religious feast. The third Richa speaks of making the exclamation 'Vashat' for the consecration of the sacrifice. In the *Veds* it is noticeable that the Aryans used the exclamation 'Vashat' up to a certain point of time and thereafter used the exclamation 'Swaha'. Evidently, 'Vashat' was the exclamation used for offering the food to the gods when this was done as a token and thereafter eaten by the worshippers. Swaha came in when it was being consigned to the flames. For some time both exclamations seem to have been in use and gradually 'Vashat' became obsolete. Vashat appears in the *Avesta* also, though in a corrupted form as 'Usta' in the language. The passage that mentions it follows.

We worship Ahur Mazda with the usta. And we worship the
Amesha Spenta with the usta. And we worship the prior world
of the holy (and of the clean) with an usta.

(Visparad XVIII)

On the face of it, the change introduced by the Angiras Rishis seems
to be insignificant. The Aryans were already offering meat and Som
to the gods as a token and were thereafter eating and drinking them.
Instead of this, these Rishis decided that the share of gods should be
put into fire. It was believed that fire would play the role of a messenger
for the gods and would convey it to them after burning. Though
apparently, not a very big departure from the prevailing practices,
this had its implications. Firstly, the fire that was so far kindled, was
only to be there. It had no specific task to perform for which its size
was not material and could be small if the situation so demanded.
With food and Som being consigned to it, things other than fuel were
being put which had to be fully burnt because only then they could
be conveyed to the gods by fire. For this the size of the fire had to be
bigger. Depending on how much food was being offered, the size of
fire and the fuel required had to increase. It could not have remained
the small fire that was enough in the earlier practices. So far as food
and drinks are concerned, the earlier practices did not involve any
extra spending. Food and drinks, as much as were required for the
consumption of the worshippers, were prepared and brought into the
place of sacrifice. After making a token offering to the gods, these
were consumed by the worshippers. It would have been just a feast
with singing of hymns and a few rituals to precede it. With the share
of gods being consigned to fire, the sacrifice would have added a cost,
because that portion would get burnt. If the worshippers were also to
be fed in a feast, it would have to be in addition. This cost too had
no limit attached to it. In the earlier practice as the entire food being
offered had to be eaten by the worshippers, this would have always
remained limited to the quantity required for their consumption. The
smaller the number, lesser would have been the food. Now as the
sacrificed portion was to be consigned to fire, there was no such limit.

Any number of animals could be sacrificed. The *Veds*, at times, speak of hundreds and thousands of animals sacrificed by someone on some occasion. Even if these are exaggerated accounts, they would still be in a very large number, much more than what would have been sacrificed if they had to be eaten by the worshippers.

Though to start with cooked food was offered, but very soon raw flesh took its place in the sacrifices of the Devs. The account of the *Veds* and the Brahmans show that a pole was fixed close to the fire, which was called the 'Yup'. The animal to be sacrificed was tied to it, to be immolated, skinned and dismembered there itself, before specific body parts were given in offering to specific gods, after blood had been offered to the evil spirits. This would have made the sacrifices extremely gruesome to watch, as compared to the earlier practices where, even if meat was being offered, it came to the place of worship cooked as food and in proper containers. It is not a surprise that contemporary Greek observers have called them 'Blood Sacrifices'. The *Avesta* has also mentioned them on these lines.

> There Verethraghna, made by Ahur proclaimed thus, 'The Soul of the Bull, the wise creature does not receive from man due sacrifice and prayer, for now the Daevas and the worshippers of the Daevas make blood flow and spill it like water.'
>
> (Bahram Yast XVII)

The excessive slaughtering of animals has also been noticed in the context of new converts to the Mazda faith where the following advice is given in the Dinkard.

> The Ashavahisto calls out to the Mazda worshippers, 'You are for the worship of Mazda, let no one of you become such a slaughterer of the cattle as the slaughterer you have been before.'
>
> 'Contentedly, the Mazda worshippers slaughter the cattle, contentedly, the cattle of the Mazda worshippers let them butcher.'
>
> (Dinkard. Book VII, Chapter IX)

It appears that because of the cost and other associated difficulties involved in the new method, very soon animal sacrifice got replaced by agricultural produce. Animal sacrifice got limited to only a few occasions and it seems that it was performed only by the rich. The rituals required three libations to be offered each day. It is impossible that animals could have been used in these sacrifices. In the *Veds*, there are a larger number of references to barley cakes or fried barley being offered as compared to animals. The gradual change in the animal being used for sacrifice, till a stage was reached when agricultural produce was used for the purpose, can be seen in certain passages of the *Aitarey Brahman* and the Shat Path Brahman. The passage from the latter is here.

> At first the gods offered up a man as a victim. When he was offered up, the sacrificial essence went out of him. It entered into the horse. They offered up the horse. When it was offered up, the sacrificial essence went out of it. It entered into the ox. They offered up the ox. When it was offered up, the sacrificial essence went out of it. It entered the sheep. They offered up the sheep. When it was offered up, the sacrificial essence went out of it. It entered into the goat. They offered up the goat. When it was offered up, the sacrificial essence went out of it. It entered into this earth. They searched for it by digging. They found it (in the shape of) those two (substances) rice and barley. As much efficacy as all those animal victims would have for him, so much efficacy has this oblation (of rice and barley). And thus there is in this oblation also that completeness which they call 'the fivefold animal sacrifice'.
>
> (Shat Path Brahman. Kand 1, Adhyay 2, Brahman 3)

This passage, apart from showing the gradual change in the animal being used for the sacrifice till a stage was reached when rice and barley were used, also mentions that in the beginning humans were sacrificed. In the *Veds*, there is no real reference of human sacrifice. Two instances are often quoted in this regard, one, the legend of Shunah Shepa and other, the Purush Sukta. The legend of Shunah Shepa would come up for a closer examination ahead, wherein it would be clear that it has been understood incorrectly to be a case of human sacrifice. The Purush Sukta refers to the cosmic Purush or the universal man, from whose body the entire creation was believed to have originated. It cannot be taken to be meaning a human being. References to man being a victim in the sacrifice in the above passage of the Shat Path Brahman appears to be symbolic. The religion does not at any stage appear to have approved of human sacrifice. This is evident from the fact that making an offering into the fire was introduced later. To start with they used to only sing hymns in front of a fire and the libation was only of the food that they were about to eat which was lifted as a token and was believed to have been offered to the gods. Human sacrifice would have made them cannibals. There is not even the faintest possible trace of cannibalism in the two scriptures. The reference to sacrifice of man here is the sacrifice of oneself to God. This spirit is brought out in this passage of the *Avesta*.

> And to you, O Ye Bountiful Immortals! Ye who rule aright and dispose (of all) aright, I offer the flesh of my very frame, and all the blessings of my life.

> (Yasna XIII)

It appears that sacrifice amongst the Devs was not a ritual that was performed on all occasions of worship. Usually it seems to have been only the singing of hymns in a group in which, to add to the fervour, perhaps some dancing was also involved. The *Avesta* has said this in the following passage.

> Then Zaruthustra asked Ardvi Sura Anahita, 'O Ardvi Sura Anahita! What becomes of those libations which the wicked worshippers of the Daevas bring unto thee after the sun has set?' Ardvi Sura Anahita answered, 'O pure, holy Spitama Zarathrustra! Howling, clapping, hopping and shouting, six hundred and a thousand Daevas, who ought not to receive that sacrifice, receive those libations that men bring unto me after (the sun has set).'

> (Aban Yast XXI)

It appears that the changes introduced by the Angiras Rishis were opposed by the Asurs on two counts, one, the sacred fire had been polluted and two, it was causing wastage of food. On both these points, perhaps to do the opposite of what the opponent was doing, the Asurs went to the other extreme. Maintaining the sanctity of fire and gradually of all other elements, like earth and water, seems to have been taken to a level of obsession. Cases of even accidental incidents where these elements got polluted, had detailed rituals for purification and repentance. On the question of wastage also, they seem to have moved to the other extreme and made a law for thrift. It must have started as a reaction to what the Devs were doing, but soon became a general command for everything in life. The *Avesta* has this passage which shows their disapproval of the pollution caused by the Devs to the fire.

> We would approach You Two, O (ye) primeval ones in the house of this Thy holy Fire, O Ahur Mazda, Thou most bounteous spirit! Who brings pollution to this (Thy flame) him wilt Thou cover with pollutions (in his turn).
>
> (Yasna XXXVI)

On the issue of avoiding wastage and thrift, there are a very large number of references. The preponderance of passages where wastage is considered to be sinful, gives an impression that this was the prime objection. The issue of maintaing the sanctity of fire may have come in later, just to add to the argument. The *Veds* too have reacted only to the charge of wastage and have called the Asurs 'niggards' very frequently. They have not responded to the charge of polluting the fire at any place. A few passages from the *Avesta* advocating thrift are here.

1. Ahur Mazda, indeed does not allow us to waste anything of value that we may have, not even so much as a maid lets fall in spinning.
    (Vendidad. Fargard V)

2. (And they cry aloud to Thee, O Mazda! I speaking with them and in their name): Where is the (promised) lord of our thrift (the

embodied law saving us from the most dreaded dangers that we fear, the thrift-lord) of (our) ready zeal.

(Yasna LI)

The reaction of the Devs to this, was to ridicule the Asurs. They seem to have felt how someone could be miserly in making an offering even to gods. With an evident contempt they have used the word niggard. Sayan, the famous fourteenth-century commentator and several others after him, have taken this to be a reference to a person, who does not give a proper dakshina or gift to the priest for having performed the sacrifice. This would have been the obvious meaning so long as it was not known that there was an external entity with which there was a dispute on this issue. With the *Avesta* giving the additional information, it can be said with certainty that the commentators have made an error. This is not a reference to a worshipper who was not liberal with his purse, while sending off the priest, but to the Asurs, who had objected to the practice of consigning the share of the gods to fire on the ground that this was wastage and had further proceeded to advocate thrift as a desirable virtue.

In the *Avesta* too, at a few places, they have used the term niggard for their adversaries. These appear to be only to return the compliment and do not seem to have been meant seriously. A few instances from the *Rig Ved* on this point are given here.

1. We are not evil who worship him, nor too poor not to offer gifts, nor destitute of sacred fires, since assembled together, when the Som is effused, we make Indra, the showerer, our friend.

    (*Rig Ved*. M-8, S-61, R-11)
2. Agni, do you protect us by great wealth from every niggard and mortal foe.

    (*Rig Ved*. M-8, S-71, R-1)
3. May Agni utterly confound those Dasyus who perform no (sacred) rites, who are babblers defective in speech, niggards, unbelievers, not honouring (Agni) offering no sacrifice. Agni preceding has degraded those who institute no sacred ceremonies.

    (*Rig Ved*. M-7, S-6, R-3)
4. When a wicked (man) with twofold (malignity) obstructing

our offerings and refraining from gifts (himself) reviles us, may his prayers be heavy on him and involve his person (in the consequences of) his evil words.

(*Rig Ved.* M-1, S-147, R-4)

5. Worship the two who come first (of the gods) at dawn, let them drink before the greedy withholders (of the offerings) for the Ashwins verily claim the morning sacrifice; the ancient sages praised them (at dawn).

(*Rig Ved.* M-5, S-77, R-1)

Apart from calling the Asurs niggards and misers, these Richas give a further confirmation of the issue over which the two sides had differences that led to the dispute. The first Richa states that we are not too poor not to give gifts to gods, an indication that the Asurs felt it to be an act of wastage. The third Richa calls them not only niggards and unbelievers but also babblers with a defective speech. This Richa is of a slightly later time when the language of the Asurs had not remained as chaste as it used to be, something which can be seen from the language of the *Avesta*. The fourth Richa talks of the twofold evils being done by the Asurs, on the one hand they do not offer the offerings themselves and on the other, they obstruct the Devs from doing so. The fifth confirms the same point. It says, be bountiful to the liberal giver and shun him who gives not. All Richas have a rebuttal of the point, that the Asurs objected to the offering being consigned to the flames because they felt it to be wastage.

The response of the Asurs to being called niggards even in the matter of making an offering to God can be seen in the *Avesta*. This is reflected from the following passage.

The law of Mazda will not deliver thee unto pain. Thou art entreated for charity by the whole of the living world, and she is ever standing at thy door in the person of thy brethren in the faith. Beggars are ever standing at the door of the stranger, amongst them who beg for bread. Ever will that bread be burning coal upon thy head.

(Vistasp Yast V)

The information in the *Veds* about the persons who brought about this change is very scant and scattered. The Angiras Rishis with Bhrigu as their chief are said to have done it, for which at places the Angiras Rishis have been called Bhrigus also. Manu was Bhrigu's son and by far the most important person responsible for the survival of these practices. The passages from the *Veds* that speak of the Angiras Rishis and the institution of new rites are here.

1. The Angiras first prepared (for Indra) the sacrificial food and then, with kindled fire (worshipped him) with a most holy rite. They the institutors (of the ceremony) acquired all the wealth of Pani, comprising horses, cows and (other) animals.

2. Atharvan first by sacrifices discovered the path, then the bright sun, the cherisher of pious acts, was born. Atharvan regained cattle. Kavya (Ushana) was associated with him. Let us worship the immortal (Indra) who was born to restrain (the Asurs).

    (*Rig Ved*. M-1, S-83, R-4 and 5)

3. Matarisvan brought, as a friend to Bhrigu, the celebrated Vahni, the illuminator of sacrifices, the careful protector (of his votaries), the swift moving messenger (of the gods) the offering of two parents, (to be to him) as it were a precious treasure.

    (*Rig Ved*. M-1, S-60, R-1)

4. Our forefathers, the Angiras, by their praises (of Agni) terrified the strong and daring devourer, by the sound, they made for us a path to the vast heaven, and obtained accessible day, the ensign of day (Aditya) and the cows.

5. They secured him (Agni, in the sacrificial chamber), they made his worship the source of wealth, whence opulent votaries preserve his fires and practise his rites. Free from all (other) desires, assiduous in his adoration and sustaining gods and men, by their offerings, they come into his presence.

6. When the diffusive vital air excites Agni, he becomes bright and manifest in every mansion, and the institutor of the rite, imitating Bhrigu, prevails on him to perform the function of messenger, as a prince who has become a friend sends an

ambassador to his more powerful (neighbour).

(*Rig Ved.* M-1, S-71, R-2 to 4)

7. Address, worshippers, after the manner of the Angiras, a new (hymn) to that Indra, whose withering (energies) were developed of old, who in the exhilaration of the Som, forced open the obstructed and solid clouds.

(*Rig Ved.* M-2, S-17, R-1)

8. May we seven priests first in order engender from the maternal dawn the worshippers of the creator (Agni). May we Angiras be the sons of heaven and radiant, divide the wealth-containing mountain.

(*Rig Ved.* M-4,S-2,R-15)

9. This invoker of the gods and minister of frequent worship, who is glorified at sacrifices, has been placed first (of the gods) by the performers of the rite, the Agni whom Apnavan and other Bhrigus lighted in the woods for the sake of all men, marvellous and sovereign.

(*Rig Ved.* M-4, S-7, R-1)

10. Holy Agni, to whom oblations are offered, we worship you in like manner (as you have been worshipped) by Bhrigu, by Manu, by the Angiras.

(*Rig Ved.* M-8, S-43, R-13)

11. O Agni, the Angiras discovered you when you lay hidden, fleeing back from wood to wood. You by attrition are produced as conquering might, and men, O Angiras, call you the Son of Strength.

(*Saam Ved.* Part II, Book III, Chapter I)

12. They who were versed in ritual and metre, in hymns and rules, were the seven godlike Rishis. Viewing the path of those old, the sages have taken up the reins like chariot drivers.

(*Yajur Ved.* Adhyay-34, Yajush-49)

These passages show that the Angiras Rishis were seven in number. The Sukta 107 of the Ninth Mandal of the *Rig Ved* is attributed to all seven of them. The names given are Bhardwaj, Atri, Kashyap,

Gotam, Vishwmitra, Bhrigu and Vashisht. In some of these passages an impression is given that they discovered fire or brought in fire as an essential part of the sacrifice. From all accounts, fire was occupying a place of prominence in the religious practices of the Aryans at least from the times of the Ribhus, if not earlier. This is borne out from the accounts relating to the Ribhus and the reference to fire as a messenger from the gods. The prominence given to fire in the *Avesta* confirms this. All such references mean that the Angiras Rishis discovered a new role for Agni, that of a carrier of oblation, apart from being a god. Though Bhrigu was their leader nothing is mentioned in the *Veds* about what happened to him. The *Avesta* has taken no notice of Bhrigu or the Angiras Rishis and has confined its blame on Manu. There is only a vague reference to seven persons who have been called 'the evil instructed ones', which could be a reference to the Seven Rishis of the *Veds*. This is mentioned here.

> And through that glory of destiny two third of the demons of Mazano and the seven evil-instructed ones of Aeshm were destroyed by Hoshang.
>
> (Dinkard. Book VIII. Chapter I)

In a situation where Atri, Rebha and others have been reported to have been tortured, Bhrigu, being the leader, should have been the prime target of persecution. Absence of any mention of what happened to him, as per the style of the *Veds*, is ominous. He seems to have been killed. There is a fleeting reference to this in the *Atharv Ved*, which is given here.

> They grew excessively, they did not quite touch up to the sky, having injured Bhrigu, the Srinijayas, Vaitahavyas, perished.
>
> (*Atharv Ved*. Kand-5, Sukt-19, Richa-1)

It seems that the Asurs, in their initial reaction to the changes brought about by the Angiras Rishis, were successful in completely stamping them out in Arjika. The Devs were either killed or forced to leave. The war that followed and the accounts of Manu in the *Avesta* show that the surviving Devs went away and returned with a vengeance only after thirty years. There is a vague passage in the Shat Path Brahman which says that the Devs went away.

> The gods and Asurs, both of them sprung from Prajapati, were contending. The gods drove about on wheels and the Asurs stayed at home.
> (Shat Path Brahman. Kand VI, Adyay-8, Brahman-I)

The reference is vague and cannot be conclusively linked with this occasion when the Angiras Rishis and their initial followers were being persecuted, because there were other occasions too, wherein the Devs had been driven away. The total silence of the *Avesta* for Bhrigu and the Angiras Rishis shows that they were of no real consequence in their perception, because what they had sought to do was wiped out in the first rush of reaction. A full thirty years elapsed, wherein all memory of the events of the time would have become hazy, if not totally lost. It was with Manu coming with an army and inflicting a defeat on the Asurs that the teachings of the Angiras Rishis resurfaced in Arjika. So far as the Asurs were concerned, the blame for it was on Manu, for which the entire focus of the *Avesta* is on Manu alone and the real founders, the seven Angiras Rishis find no mention.

3

War Breaks Out

ARJIKA IS SHAKEN BY WAR, the first war in the world to be recorded, a war between the Devs and the Asurs. This Dev, Asur Sangram is at the centre of much of Indian mythology, although often with stories, which have been woven much later with Asurs that are not Vedic, fighting divinities which too are not Vedic. The *Veds* have projected the Asurs and the *Avesta* the Devs as demons, some supernatural creatures who were the epitome of evil. They were, however, not only fellow human beings, but fellow Aryans of the same tribe with the same forefathers, who had disagreed on a certain point and had opted to decide it by war. Apart from the several references in the Brahmans which state 'Devs and Asurs, children of the same father, Prajapati, were contending', there are several passages in the *Veds* and the *Avesta* that confirm this. Some of them are mentioned here.

1. Go not ever, Agni to the sacrifice of anyone who injures us; nor to that of a malevolent neighbour, nor to that of a relation. Accept not the due (oblation) from an insincere brother. Let us not derive enjoyment from the enemy of a friend.

   (*Rig Ved*. M-4, S-3, R-13)

2. Annihilate, Indra, the strength of those who, whether kinsmen or unrelated, present themselves before us, exerting themselves as adversaries. Enfeeble their prowess, put them to flight.

   (*Rig Ved*. M-6, S-25, R-3)

3. When the libation is effused, I celebrate Indra and Agni, your heroic exploits. The Pitra, the enemies of gods, have been slain

by you, and you survive.

(Rig Ved. M-6,S-59,R-1)

4. O Lord of heroes, you slay our Aryan Vritras; you slay the Dasas. You drive all our enemies away.

(Saam Ved. Part II, Book II, Chapter II)

5. When purified, he sits enthroned as king over the warring clans. What time the sages spread him on.

(Saam Ved. Part II, Book IV, Chapter II)

6. You are daughter of the Asurs, the same, are the sisters of the Devs, arisen from the sky, from the earth, you have made the poison sapless.

(Atharv Ved. Kand 6, Sukt-101, Richa-3)

7. (And I beseech for Thine instruction), I who will abjure all disobedience (towards Thee, praying that others likewise may withhold it) from Thee; I who abjure the Evil Mind as well, the lordly kinsman's arrogance and that lying sin which is (alas!) the next thing to the people (their most familiar fault), and from the kine the worst care of her meadows (the crime of stint in labour).

(Yasna XXXIII)

8. Aye, let us send that petition forth for the encounter with, and for the dislodgement of the Kahvaredhas, of the Zandas, and the sorcerers, of the covenant breakers and those who tamper with the covenants.

(Yasna LXI)

In the third Richa, the term 'Pitra' is used for Asurs. This word means forefathers. The Devs are extolling the earlier exploits of Indra and Agni when they killed those of their forefathers, who were inimical to the Devs. Despite the enmity, the relationship has not been lost in this Richa. The fourth Richa calls Vritras as Aryans. The fifth speaks of the warring clans. This leaves no scope for doubt that the two sides at war, were not just Aryans, but were from the same tribe. The sixth Richa calls the daughters of the Asurs, sisters of the Devs, confirming the same relationship between the two sides. The passages from the *Avesta* confirm this. The adversaries have been called kinsmen and those who tamper with the covenants. The two sides being from the same tribe emerges also from a reference in the *Veds* which shows that at some stage the Vedic people also followed funeral rites similar to those of the Zoroastrians. This emerges from the following Richa.

> They that are buried, and they that are scattered away, they that are burned and they that are set up raised—all those Fathers, O Agni, bring you to eat the oblation.
>
> (*Atharv Ved*. Kand-18, S-2, R-34)

This is a prayer for the forefathers, who have been divided on the basis of the manner in which their funeral had been conducted. 'Scattered away' seems to be a reference to the immersion of the dead in a river, while 'they that are set up raised' appears to be a reference to a funeral on the pattern of that of the Zoroastrians.

The first war reported was between Indra and Vritra. This finds mention at several places, being retold at different times with the perception of new authors. As a result, several versions emerge in the *Veds* and the Brahmans, which have variations. Because of the significance of this victory, Indra is often addressed as Vritrahan or slayer of Vritra. Its importance to the Devs was immense as with it they regained their homeland, abandoned due to persecution. To understand this war as an event of history, it is necessary to identify Indra as well as Vritra, because neither of them were the real names of the warriors. The *Veds* show that Indra was born in this war. Evidently, he is the deification of the Dev who led their army. The passages stating that Indra was born for this war are given here.

1. At the birth of you who are resplendent, trembled the heaven (and) trembled the earth through fear of your wrath, the mighty clouds were confined, the destroyer (of distress), spreading water over the dry places.

2. Heaven, your, progenitor, conceived (I have obtained) a worthy son, the maker of Indra was the accomplisher of a most excellent work. He who begot the adorable (Indra), armed with the thunderbolt

irremovable from his station and endowed with greatness.

(Rig Ved. M-4, S-17, R-2 and 4)

3. As soon as generated, Indra, you have made your mind resolved, you have gone alone to contend against numerous (foes), you have rent asunder the rock by your strength, you have rescued the herd of milk-yielding kine.

4. When you have been born, most excellent and supreme, bearing a name widely renowned, then the gods have been in dread of Indra, and he has subjugated all the waters, the brides of the Das (Vritra).

(Rig Ved. M-5, S-30, R-4 and 5)

5. The slayer of Vritra, as soon as he was born, seized his arrow and asked his mother, 'who are the terrible, who are the renowned.'

6. Your strong mother answered you, 'he who wishes your enmity fights as the elephant in the mountain.'

(Rig Ved. M-8, S-45, R-4 and 5)

These Richas give the message that Indra as a god, emerged for the war with Vritra. This warrior who led the Dev army and is deified as Indra, appears to be Manu, not only because of the importance assigned to Manu in laying down the laws in Indian mythology and the repeated statement of the subsequent Devs that they were descendents of Manu, but also due to various hints that are found scattered in the *Veds*. It is also confirmed by the fact that Manu is found to have become the Kavi of Arjika, after dethroning the defeated king. Some of the references which give this information are given here.

1. He, who was formerly subject to a superior, having been protected, Agni, by you, now stands in your presence as an offerer (of oblations) without bashfulness, and supplied with food.

(Rig Ved. M-1, S-74, R-8)

2. Indra, friend of man, mount the horses whom you cherish, who are fleet as the wind, are easily yoked, and who bear (their burden) well, you have sharpened the foe-destroying thunderbolt, the slayer of Vritra, which inspiring (weapon) Ushana, the son of Kavi, gave you.

(Rig Ved. M-1, S-121, R-12)

3.   Maghvan, who are glorified by us, assailing with the thunderbolt
     the antagonist (of the gods), you have slain those who were ever
     hostile (to you) from your birth, desiring to do good to Manu,
     you have bruised the head of the Das Namuchi.

                                           (*Rig Ved.* M-5, S-30, R-7)
4.   Ushana, the son of Kavi, has established you, Jatved, as the
     ministrant priest, you as the offerer of sacrifice, for Manu.

                                          (*Rig Ved.* M-8, S-23, R-17)
5.   Indra, victorious, Mitra-like, smote like a Yati, Vritra dead. As
     Bhrigu quelled his foes, he cleft Val in Som's rapturous joy.

                            (*Saam Ved.* Part II, Book III, Chapter I)
6.   Now will I glorify great strength's upholder, food. By whose
     invigorating might Trita rent Vritra limb from limb.

                                  (*Yajur Ved.* Adhyay-34, Yajush-7)

The first Richa speaks of a changed situation wherein the Devs, who
were subject to a superior, were now masters. The second Richa speaks
of Ushana, as the son of Kavi. Ushana was the son of Manu, as would
emerge ahead. He being the son of Kavi shows that Manu had become
the Kavi. This could have happened only after the defeat of the existing
Asur Kavi and dethroning him. In this Richa, Ushana is also said to
have given the weapon to Indra for the fight establishing that this was
for this war. The third Richa speaks of Manu. Indra is being glorified
for assailing the antagonists of Devs, desiring to do good to Manu.
This style of expression is seen at several places in the *Veds*, where a
particular Dev or a warrior has done something, it is reported by stating
that Indra had done it for him. This Richa stating that Indra killed
Namuchi and several other Asurs with the intentions of doing good
to Manu means that Manu killed these Asurs in this war. The fourth
Richa, while speaking of Ushana as the son of Kavi, hints of Manu
being the father of Ushana as in it Ushana has established a fire for
Manu. The fifth, a Saam and sixth, a Yajush remove all possible doubt
that Manu is being referred to when Indra is named in this war. The
Saam says that Bhrigu quelled his foes and cleft Val. The Yajush says
that Trita killed Vritra. Bhrigu and Trita both are terms used for Manu,

as Bhrigu was his father and Trita, one of his illustrious forefathers after whom an entire clan was named Tritsu. At many places Manu has been called Trita.

Another indication that Indra is the deification of Manu comes from the weapon Vajra. This is the weapon of Indra alone in the entire Indian mythology and is not found to be used by anyone else. The term has been translated as the thunderbolt and is often pictured in a zig-zag shape, like that of lightning. Evidently, this is a later imagination, when Indra became a rain god instead of a war god. As a rain god, it was believed that the cloud is Vritra, holding back the waters and the thunderbolt, seen as lightning, is the Vajra with which Indra pierces him to release it. This is an adaptation of the original story of a war god to suit a rain god. Vajra appears to be the first weapon of war to emerge. Before this the Aryans had either agricultural implements or hunting weapons. A zig-zag weapon, as the Vajra is shown to be, cannot be a weapon of war, as it cannot be effective. Normally innovations take place by improving on the existing. Vritra is reported to have been cut limb by limb with this weapon. As an axe was already there, this appears to be a battleaxe. Manu seems to have improvised upon the axe to make it lighter to be handled with a single hand, with a wider and curved blade. In an encounter, where the other side had heavy axes, needing both hands, this would have been of great advantage to Manu because of which it came in for special notice. A battleaxe in Sanskrit is called Parshu. It appears that Vajra was the name of Indra's Parshu. In Indian traditions, weapons of several gods and heroes have had names, like the bow of Lord Shiv is Pinak, while that of Lord Vishnu is Sharang and of Arjun is Gandiv. It seems that Vajra was the proper noun of Indra's weapon, which was a Parshu, because of which this term as a weapon is not found for any other warrior. There are a few references in the *Veds* to show that Manu designed the Parshu. These are mentioned here.

1. The daughter of Manu, Parshu by name, bore twenty children at once; may good fortune, O arrow of Indra, befall her whose belly was so prolific. Indra is above all (the world).

                                          (*Rig Ved*. M-10, S-86, R-23)

2. The golden-bearded (Indra), lord of bay horses, who made the
    Vajra for the easy destruction of the Dasyu, who has irresistible
    jaws like the vast sky.

                                        (*Rig Ved*. M-10, S-105, R-7)

The first Richa calls Parshu, the daughter of Manu, who gave birth to
twenty children at the same time. It appears that Manu killed twenty
Asurs in this war, which has been expressed peotically. The first Richa
calls the Parshu of Manu to be the arrow of Indra to confirm that this
was the weapon with which all persons killed by Indra had died. The
second Richa, instead of figuratively saying that Parshu was fabricated
by Manu, says it directly, but uses the terms Vajra and Indra in it.
Evidently this was a new weapon of war that had come in use.

    Another factor which points to Manu being Indra is that a few
personalities of this period have been deified. Manu was the Kavi or
the king while these were his subject. On the same lines Indra is treated
as the king of gods. The equation as it existed in Arjika was imagined
for gods also. Initially, this must have been for the newly deified ones
only but soon all gods, even those who existed before Indra, came
within the ambit.

    For Vritra, very frequently, the epithets Dasyu and Ahi are found
used. Dasyu or Das in later Sanskrit came to mean a slave. At this stage
it could not have been so, as slavery could not have been there in such
remote times. In all likelihood it meant an uncultured person. Apart
from Dasyu, another word 'Simyu' has been used in the *Rig Ved* for
the Asurs. Both of these could have simply been derogatory terms of
the time. Here is a Richa calling them Simyus.

    Indra, who is invoked by many, attended by the moving
    (Maruts), having attacked the Dasyus and Simyus, slew them
    with his thunderbolt. The thunderer then divided the fields
    with his white-complexioned friends, and rescued the sun
    and set free the waters.

                                        (*Rig Ved*. M-1, S-100, R-18)

Ahi means a snake. In the *Avesta* language it has become Azi and has been used at many places for Devs, especially for Dahak, who is always referred to as Azi Dahak. In the *Veds* too, Ahi has been used for other Asurs also. As both sides have used this term for each other, this also appears to be a derogatory term of its time. It could have been an abuse. This Richa from the *Rig Ved* shows that all Asurs were called serpents or Ahi and Vritras.

> You Som, who like Indra perform mighty acts, are the slayer of Vritras, the destroyer of those who are called serpents, you are the destroyer of every Dasyu.
>
> (*Rig Ved*. M-9, S-88, R-4)

The term Vritra has been a subject of speculation from early times. It appears that even when the Brahmans were written, the identity of Vritra and the reasons why he was called so had been lost. In the Brahmans, more than one speculation about Vritra can be seen. The Shat Path Brahman has this passage on him.

> Vritra in truth lay covering all this (space) which here extends between heaven and earth. And because he lay covering (vri) all this, therefore his name is Vritra.
>
> (Kand I, Adhyay-3, Brahman-7)

The same Brahman at another place has given a long story about the birth of Vritra, which is here.

> Tvasta had a three-headed, six-eyed son. Because he was thus shaped his name was Vishwarup (all shapes). Indra hated him and cut off those heads of his. Tvasta was furious: 'Has he indeed slain my son?' he exclaimed. He brought Som juice from which Indra was excluded. Indra thought to himself, 'They are now excluding me from Som,' and though uninvited, he consumed what pure (Som) there was in the tub, just as the stronger consumes that of a weaker.
>
> Tvasta was furious and exclaimed, 'Has he indeed consumed my Som uninvited?' He let flow (into the fire) saying, 'Grow thou, having Indra for thy foe.' The moment it reached

the fire, it developed (into human shape). It became possessed of
Agni and Som of all sciences. And since it so developed whilst
rolling onwards it became Vritra, and since he sprang forth
footless, he was a serpent. Danu and Danayu received him like
mother and father whence they call him Danav.

(Kand I, Adhyay-6, Brahman-3)

This speculation has emerged perhaps because the *Rig Ved* has passages
stating that Indra killed Vishwarup, the son of Tvasta. They are given
here.

1. Indra, hero, keep up the strength where with you have crushed
    Vritra, the spider-like son of Danu, and let open the light to the
    Arya. The Dasyu has been set aside on your left hand.
2. Let us honour those men, who, through your protection, surpass
    all their rivals, as the Dasyus (are surpassed) by the Aryas. This
    (have you wrought) for us. You have slain Vishwarup, the son of
    Tvasta, through the friendship of Trita.

(*Rig Ved.* M-2, S-11, R-18 and 19)

These Richas give no indication of the birth of Vritra as given in the
Shat Path Brahman. By referring to Trita, the second Richa gives
an impression that Vishwarup could be another name of Vritra or
of a warrior who fought on his side, because Trita is Manu. In any
case the speculation of the Brahman, apart from disclosing that
even then the identity of Vritra had been lost, does not lead to any
realistic conclusion. In this war with Indra, Vritra has been used in the
singular, but at many other places the term has been used in plural. The
commentators have stated that this was a reference to the followers of
Vritra. The use of the word is, however, seen to be very wide ranging
amongst the two sides. We have references in the *Avesta* using this
term for the Devs, which may be seen below.

1. I invoke Verethraghna, made by Ahur, who wears the glory made
    by Mazda.

(Vendidad. Fargard XIX)

2. To the well-shapen, tall-formed, Strength to Verethraghna, made

by Ahur, to the crushing Ascendant.

(Sirozah I)

3. Zarathustra asked Ahur Mazda, 'Ahur Mazda! Who is the best-armed of the heavenly gods?' Ahur Mazda answered, 'It is Verethraghna made by Ahur, O Spitma Zarathustra.'

(Bahram Yast I)

Like the Vedic Vritraghan or Vritrahan used for Indra meaning the slayer of Vritra, the *Avesta* too has a Verethraghna with the same meaning. This has led some historians to believe that Indra was once worshipped by the Zoroastrian also under this name. Verethraghna of the Avesta is not Indra, as he shares none of his attributes, except being well-armed and of slaying Vritras. He is a separate entity believed in the *Avesta* to be a counter to the war god of the Devs. Being called the slayer of Vritras, the Devs are being called Vritras.

Since both sides have called each other Vritra, this term too, like Ahi, appears to be an abuse. Vrit means a circle in Sanskrit. It seems that amongst these people a prominent chin was considered to be a sign of beauty. In the *Veds*, Indra is repeatedly called Sushipra or one with a good or prominent chin. A round face would be its opposite, someone with an indistinct chin, something considered ugly by them. With usage over time, Vrit for a round face seems to have become Vritra. In the *Rig Ved*, two names appear for the warrior who seems to have been killed on this occasion by Manu which are close to this. The relevant Richas are given here.

1. Come friends, let us celebrate that solemn rite which was effectual in setting open the (secret) stalls of the (stolen) cattle; by which Manu overcame Vishishipra; by which the merchant, going to the wood (for it) obtained the water.

(*Rig Ved*. M-5, S-45, R-6)

2. You too, Indra and Vishnu, have made the spacious world for the sake of sacrifice, generating the sun, the dawn, Agni; you leaders (of rites) have baffled the devices of the slave Vrshashipra in the conflicts of hosts.

(*Rig Ved*. M-7, S-99, R-4)

In the first Richa, Manu has been named and the Asur is called Vishishipra. The meaning is a person without a chin. It would be a person with a round face but does not give the correct name which could have been something close to be twisted as Vishishipra to make it derogatory. The second Richa calls him Vrshashipra, a person with a bull's chin. Again the same twisting, but with a shipra or chin at the end. These Richas give an impression that the real name of Vritra perhaps ended with shipra.

The information available in the *Avesta* about this war is scanty, as in the usual style defeats were not mentioned. It, however, does provide a confirmation of what is told by the *Veds*. Airyana Vaego or Arjika was ruled by Takma Urupa at that time. In the Pahlavi language he is called Takhmorup. His realm was invaded by Angra Mainyu who is Ahriman in Pahlavi. The relevant passages which provide information about them are here.

1. To him did Takhma Urupa, the well-armed offer up a sacrifice on a golden throne. He begged him of a boon saying, 'Grant me this, O Vayu! that I may conquer all Daevas and men, and that I may ride Angra Mainyu turned into the shape of a horse, all around the earth from one end to the other, for thirty years.'

    (Ram Yast III)

2. That clave unto Takma Urupa, while he ruled the seven Karshvares of the earth, over the Daevas and men. When he conquered all Daevas and men, and rode Angra Mainyu turned into the shape of a horse, all around the earth from one end to the other for thirty years.

    (Zamyad Yast VI)

3. The advantage from Takhmorup, the well-armed was this, that the accursed evil one, the wicked was kept by him for thirty years as a charger. And the writing of penmanship of seven kinds, which that wicked one kept in concealment, he brought out to public.

    (Dina-i Mainog-i Khirad. Chapter XXVII)

4. When Angra Mainyu broke into the creation of the good holiness, then came in across Vohu Mano and Atar. They destroyed the

malice of the fiend Angra Mainyu, so that the waters did not stop flowing nor the plants stop growing.

(Farvardin Yast XXII)

5. I am speaking in accordance with it, O Spitma and therefore I shall rule as sovereign over the creatures which are mine, I who am Ahur Mazda. Let no one rule as Angra Mainyu over realms that are his own, O Zarathustra Spitma. Let Angra Mainyu be hid beneath the earth. Let the Daevas likewise disappear.

(Miscellaneous fragments)

6. I invoke the ancient and sovereign Merezu the greatest seat of battle in the creation of the two spirits.

(Vendidad. Fargard XIX)

7. And when the great struggle shall have been fought out which began when the Daevas first seized the Demon of Wrath as their ally and when the just vengeance shall have come upon these wretches, then, O Mazda, the kingdom shall have been gained for Thee.

(The Gathas. Yasna XXX)

8. And that keenness, that deciding satisfaction, which Thou hast given by Thy Spirit and Thy Fire and by Thy Righteousness to the two battling sides, do Thou declare unto us, O Ahur.

(The Gathas. Yasna XXXI)

9. Full of crime (your leader) has desired to destroy us, wherefore he is famed and his doctrine is declared, but if this be so of these, then in the same manner, O Ahur! Thou possesses (because Thou knowest) the true teachings in Thy memory.

(The Gathas. Yasna XXXII)

The first passage shows that Takhma Urupa was the Kavi. It also states that he rode Angra Mainyu as a horse around the earth from one end to the other for thirty years. He being a king is stated by several passages after that also. As he was the Kavi of a place, he could not have been away from his realm for thirty years riding a horse. It shows that Angra Mainyu was sent away from his kingdom and he wandered all over the place for thirty years. The fourth passage states that Angra

Mainyu invaded the country. The next passage prescribes that no one should rule as Angra Mainyu, which shows that Angra Mainyu was a ruler over a kingdom once. This would mean that, when he invaded the realm, after being away for thirty years, he defeated Takhma Urupa and after dethroning him, became the Kavi. This sequence of events matches with Manu. It can be said with certainty that Angra Mainyu who is pictured as the very epitome of evil, to the extent that several commentators have treated him as a Zoroastrian equivalent of the devil and have considered the principles put forward in the said religion to be Dualism, is none other but a vilification of Manu. The sixth passage states the place of the battle to be Mount Merezu. This mountain is the same as Mount Meru of Hindu mythology. In both scriptures this is stated to be the highest mountain. Arjika, the Aryan homeland at this point of time, was at its foothills. The seventh passage states that the great struggle started when the Daevas first seized the Demon of Wrath as their ally. The Demon of Wrath is a reference found at several places in the Zoroastrian scriptures for Angra Mainyu. Because of the lapse of time the exact position seems to have become hazy because of which it was not remembered that Angra Mainyu himself was a Dev. It has been stated that he came into the fight as an ally for them. The eighth passage shows that the two battling sides were of the same stock. They had been provided with the same keenness and the same deciding satisfaction by Ahur's Spirit. The ninth passage shows that the leader of the Devs had come up with a different doctrine and he had tried to destroy the Asurs. All the events confirm that Angra Mainyu of the *Avesta* is none other than Manu, deified as Indra in the *Veds*.

The *Veds* too have references to show that Indra was born of wrath or is the personification of wrath. Some from the *Rig Ved* are here.

1. Although (some) say he came from the horse, I know that he is the offspring of strength. He came from wrath. He stands in the homes (of his enemies). Indra knows whence he was born.

   (*Rig Ved*.M-10, S-73, R-10)

2. He who worships Manyu (wrath), the thunderbolt, the destroyer (of enemies), enjoys all might and strength, combined. May we

overcome the Das and the Arya with you for our ally, invigorating, strong and vigorous.

(*Rig Ved.* M-10, S-83, R-1)

Apart from wrath being the common feature described by both sides, as the cause for which Indra in the *Veds* and Angra Mainyu in the *Avesta* emerged, the references to the divinities of the opposite side in the *Avesta* also show that Angra Mainyu is none other than Manu. Some are given here.

1. They run about to and fro, their minds waver to and fro, Angra Mainyu, the deadly, the Daeva of the Daevas, Indra the Daeva, Sauru the Daeva, Naunghaithya the Daeva, Tauri and Zairi, Aeshma of the wounding spear, Akatasha the Daeva, Zaura the baneful to the fathers, Buiti the Daeva, Driwi the Daeva, Daiwi the Daeva, Kasvi the Daeva, Paitisha the most Daeva-like amongst the Daevas.

    (Vendidad. Fargard XIX)

2. And after thou hast twice said those words thou shalt say aloud these fiend-smitting and most-healing words: 'I drive away Indra, I drive away Sauru, I drive away the Daeva Naunghaithya from this house, from this borough, from this town, from this land...'

    (Vendidad. Fargard X)

3. He it is who smites me that brood of the two-legged, and who might smite these Daevas by thousands. Angra Mainyu, who is all death, the worst-lying of all Daevas, rushed from before him.

    (Ardibehist Yast II)

To be a counterpart of what the devil is in the *Bible*, it would be necessary for Angra Mainyu to be an integral part of the Zoroastrian religion. These passages show that Angra Mainyu was the main deity of the religion of the Devs, which was a rival religion, considered a heresy by the Zoroastrians. The first passage calls Angra Mainyu, the chief of the Daevas. This confirms that Angra Mainyu was the personification of Manu, who was the chief of the Devs and had become their first Kavi. It also shows that the Asurs knew that

Manu had been deified by the Devs and was treated as their most important deity. The passage, however, names Indra next. It shows that the Asurs knew about Indra and that he was worshipped by the Devs, but it had been forgotten by then that Indra was the deification of the same person by the Devs, who had been vilified by them as Angra Mainyu. Naunghaithya is Nasatya of the *Veds*, another name for the Ashwins. Though Ashwins had emerged before the split, it seems that memory regarding them had not remained distinct and the Asurs accepted only the divinities that were of the time of Ribhus. Ashwins, being a later creation, were perhaps confused to have been created by the Devs when Indra, Vishnu etc. emerged, because of which they were rejected as divinities. The other Daevas mentioned in the passage are not identifiable with Vedic names. The third passage repeats Angra Mainyu to be the worst of the Daevas by calling him the worst lying amongst them. The Devs and Angra Mainyu not being an integral part of the Zoroastrian religion, but of a rival creed, which was considered heretic, is also seen from an oath that a Mazda worshipper took and which is found repeated at many places in the *Avesta*. One from the Ormazd Yast is given here.

> May Ahur Mazda be rejoiced, may Angra Mainyu be destroyed, by those who do truly what is the foremost wish (of God). I confess myself a worshipper of Mazda, a follower of Zarathustra, one who hates the Daevas and obeys the laws of Ahur.
>
> (Ormazd Yast I)

This repeated affirmation to be made by a Mazda worshipper, that he is a follower of Zarathustra, obeys the laws of Ahur and hates the Daevas, shows that the Devs were not the followers of Zarathustra and did not obey the law of Ahur. The Devs and their chief Angra Mainyu were thus external factors, an external threat to the Asurs and their religion. As they were from the same ethnic group, the threat became graver, because continuously there was an effort from both sides to bring over more and more people of their race and tribe to their religion, as the real area of dispute was very thin. In such a situation the expansion of one religion would have been at the expense of the other, so far as the same group of people is concerned. This made the struggle between the two a struggle for survival, with all its associated intensity to the extent of wars and killings.

Though the *Avesta* gives information about Manu, even if it is by way of vilification, there is no mention of the warrior that fought against him and has been called Vritra in the *Veds*. However, the history of the subsequent period shows that several important persons in Persia and amongst the Zoroastrians had the name 'Ardshir'. The repeated use of this name gives an impression that it originated from a legendary hero. If this is the name of Vritra it would be the name of the first martyr of their religion. The word 'Ardshir' of the *Avesta* language would be 'Ardhshipra' in Sanskrit, which means a person with half a chin, making it a person with a round face. Though there is nothing in the two scriptures to say so, it appears very likely that the real name of Vritra was Ardhshipra, which was distorted to Vishishipra and Vrshashipra to make it derogatory, and also became Vrit and finally Vritra.

The war between Indra and Vritra has been mentioned at several places in the *Veds*. With the identity of Manu being clear on both sides, the description of this war and the chain of events give the identity of the Kavi Takma Urupa in the *Veds*. The passages about this war from the *Veds* are mentioned here.

1. You, wielder of the thunderbolt, did open the cave of Val, who had there concealed the cattle, and the Devs whom he had oppressed, no longer feared when they had obtained you (for their ally).

    (*Rig Ved.* M-1, S-11, R-5)

2. I declare the former valorous deeds of Indra, which the thunderer has achieved. He clove the cloud, he cast the waters down (to earth), he broke (a way) for the torrents of the mountain.

3. He clove the clouds seeking refuge on the mountain. Tvasta sharpened his far-whirling bolt. The flowing waters quickly hastened to the ocean, like cows (hastening) to their calves.

4. Impetuous as a bull, he quaffed the Som juice, he drank of

the libation at the triple sacrifice. Maghvan took his shaft, the thunderbolt, and with it struck the first born of the serpents.

5. Inasmuch, Indra as you have divided the first-born of the serpents, you have destroyed the delusions of the deluders, and then engendering the sun, the dawn, the sky, you have not left an enemy (to oppose you).

(*Rig Ved*. M-1, S-32, R- 1 to 4)

6. When the single resplendent Vritra returned the blow (which had been inflicted), Indra, by your thunderbolt, you became (furious), like a horse's tail. You have rescued the kine, you have won, Hero, the Som juice; you have let loose the seven rivers to flow.

(*Rig Ved*. M-1, S-32, R-12)

7. When fear entered, Indra, into your heart, when about to slay Ahi, what other destroyer of him did you look for, that, alarmed, you did traverse ninety and nine streams like a (swift) hawk?

8. Then Indra, the wielder of the thunderbolt, became the sovereign of all that is moveable or immoveable, of hornless and horned animals, and as he abides the monarch of men, he comprehends all things (within him), as the circumference comprehends the spokes of a wheel.

(*Rig Ved*. M-1, S-32, R-14 and 15)

9. When Indra, who delights in sacrificial food, had slain the stream-obstructing Vritra, and was pouring down the waters, he stood firm amid the torrents, like a mountain, and endowed with a thousand means of protecting (his votaries) increased in vigour.

(*Rig Ved*. M-1, S-52, R-2)

10. Indra, performer of holy acts, desirous of going to men, you with your steeds, have slain Vritra (having set free) the waters, have taken in your hands your thunderbolt of iron, and have made the sun visible in the sky.

(*Rig Ved*. M-1, S-52, R-8)

11. Behold this, the vast and extensive (might) of Indra; have confidence in his prowess; he has recovered the cattle, he has recovered the horses, the plants, the waters, the woods.

(*Rig Ved*. M-1, S-103, R-5)

12. He, who having destroyed Ahi, set free the seven rivers, who recovered the cows detained by Val, who generated fire in the sky, who is invincible in battle, he men, is Indra.

(*Rig Ved.* M-2, S-12, R- 3)

13. Priests offer this libation, which like the wind in the sky (is the cause of rain) to him who slew Drbhik, destroyed Val and liberated the cows; heap Indra with Som juice, as an old man (is covered) with garments.

(*Rig Ved.* M-2, S-14, R- 3)

14. That was the exploit (performed) for the most divine of the gods, by which the firm (shut gates) were thrown open, the strong (barriers) were relaxed (by him) who set the cows at liberty, who, by the (force of the) sacred prayers, destroyed Val, who dispersed the darkness and displayed the light.

(*Rig Ved.* M-2, S-24, R-3)

15. Vyamsa, exulting and striking hard blows, smote you Maghvan, upon the jaw, whereupon, being so smitten, you proved the stronger, and did crush the head of the Dasyu with the thunderbolt.

(*Rig Ved.* M-4, S-18, R-9)

16. As elders (send forth the young), so the Devs have sent you (against Vritra) thence you became, Indra, who is the abode of truth, the sovereign of the world, you have slain the slumbering Ahi for the waters and have marked out (channels) for the delighting rivers.

17. On the day of full moon you have slain with the thunderbolt the insatiable, unnerved, ignorant, unapprehending, slumbering Ahi, obstructing the gliding-downward-flowing (streams).

(*Rig Ved.* M-4, S-19, R-2 and 3)

18. They have come to the aid of the warring Trita, invigorating his strength and (animating) his acts; they have come to the aid of Indra, for the destruction of Vritra.

(*Rig Ved.* M-8, S-7, R- 24)

19. He liberated the cows for the Angiras Rishis, making manifest those that had been hidden in the cave, hurling Val headlong down.

(*Rig Ved.* M-8, S-14, R- 8)

20. Let him overthrow the mighty with powerful (weapons), he destroyed Sushna for the sake of the liberal Kutsa, he humiliated Kavi, who praised him, who was the giver of form to Indra and his men.

(*Rig Ved.* M-10, S-99, R-9)

21. What time you cast from his seat and punish the riteless man; strengthen for opulence, O Indra Maghvan, our plant desired by many.

(*Saam Ved.* Part I, Book IV, Chapter I)

22. You in your battles, Indra, are subduer of all hostile bands. Father are you, all-conquering, cancelling the curse, you victor of the vanquisher.

(*Saam Ved.* Part I, Book IV, Chapter I)

23. O Lord Indra! You had made to appear the undisclosed rays thrown captivated in a cave in the form of the sun and accessed them to all the Angiras Rishis. The illicitly withholding Val was made to depart after a bitter defeat.

(*Atharv Ved.* Kand 20, Sukt-40, R-3)

From these passages the objectives achieved give the cause of war. The original dispute over new religious practices remaining in the background, the atrocities committed by the Asurs on the Devs to suppress them that led to the war, can be seen from what has been stated to have been achieved by Indra in this victory. Three things have been stated, he released light that had been confined, he released the cows that had been kept in an enclosure and he released the waters that had been arrested. All these are references to what the Asurs did thirty years ago, when the Devs were living with them and were yet to leave the place. They have to be understood as a part of the persecution that was perpetuated then and not something that could have continued for thirty years when Manu came with an army to avenge it.

At places in the *Veds* and the Brahman, the release of light has been stated in a way to mean that the Asurs had confined the sun in a cave which caused darkness and Indra, defeating Vritra, set it free. The fifth Richa states that Indra has engendered the sun, the dawn and the sky. The tenth Richa says that 'you have made the sun visible in the sky'. The twenty-third Richa says that he had made to appear the undisclosed rays thrown captivated in a cave in the form of the sun. These passages stating that the sun had been captured and confined in a cave, are of a later period when facts had become hazy and instead of remembering it as a conflict of humans, it was believed to be of two supernatural powers. As these descriptions show what the Asurs did to the leading Devs thirty years ago they have to be seen alongside the persecutions that had been reported earlier. In describing the persecution of Atri and others, it has been reported that they were tied and kept in a pit or a cave, which would have been dark. The end of the Asur rule meant that the sovereign would no longer do this. No Dev now faced the danger of being confined, in a dark prison for his beliefs. It cannot mean that the sun and light were confined in a cave by the Asurs but only that people who had the risk of being confined in a cave or a dark place were relieved from this danger. The tenth Richa gives the clearest meaning of what was intended. It says that you made the sun visible in the sky. The fourteenth Richa is also close as it says that you dispersed the darkness and displayed the light. As it was a conflict between two groups of humans imputing anything, which on the face of it is not possible, would be a distortion, though it has to be admitted that because of later events and the moving out of the Aryans from Arjika, a situation was created in which many things poetically stated, could not have been understood in their correct perspective, leaving people with little choice, but to find an explanation even if it was fanciful.

The second objective achieved by the victory is that cows confined in an enclosure were released. This again is with reference to what the Asurs did thirty years ago because the cows could not have been left in an enclosure for that long a period. The first Richa states that Indra opened the cave of Val who had concealed the cattle there. The sixth and several other Richas say the same. It shows that this was the next item of persecution by the Asurs. Killing and confining people in a prison, has its limitations and cannot be done for all. Evidently, the Asurs had limited it only to the leaders. For the rest, economic pressure was applied. With the decision of the sovereign, the cattle of all who followed the unacceptable practices seem to have been seized and kept in an enclosure. This, after the Devs had left, would have ended with the Asurs distributing the cows amongst themselves. It has been symbolically mentioned in the *Veds* to show that this threat no longer remained and the Devs were free to follow their religious practices, without fearing it.

The third objective achieved is that the waters, that were obstructed, were released. A very large number of Richas have stated this in different ways. This poetical expression has caused a lot of difficulties leading to a lot of speculations from very early times. On the one hand, it has been understood to mean that the Asurs built dams over rivers in such remote times, by which they used to stop the flow of water and, on the other it has been explained to mean that Vritra is the cloud and had detained water in the sky. Before trying to understand, what is meant by these Richas, it is first necessary to be clear what waters are stated to have been held back by the Asurs, whether river or rainwater. The sixth Richa says that he has let loose the seven rivers to flow. The ninth Richa says that he had slain the stream-obstructing Vritra. The twelfth Richa says that he set free the seven rivers. The sixteenth Richa says that he has slain Vritra for the waters and has marked out channels for the rivers. The seventeenth Richa says that he has killed Ahi who was obstructing the gliding downward flowing streams. All these references show that river water had been obstructed by Vritra.

There are, however, some passages which give the meaning that rain is being referred to and that water had been obstructed by Vritra in the clouds. The second Richa says that Indra clove the cloud and cast the waters down to the earth and broke a way for the torrents of the mountain. The third Richa makes a similar statement. These passages indicate rain and that Vritra was obstructing water in the clouds. Accepting this version would require accepting a supernatural identity for Vritra and Indra. Such a supernatural identity for Devs and Asurs has emerged at a later stage, but to start with, this was not so. It is a story of men, which got blurred into mythology to become the story of gods and demons. Indra's identity as a god has also witnessed a change from being a war god to a rain god. It cannot be said whether this description of the war with Vritra that Indra released the waters, led to his becoming a rain god in the course of time or after his acquiring an identity of a rain god, the Richas relating to this feat saw a change to depict Vritra as an entity in the clouds. It is, however, evident that after a certain period Indra ceased to be a war god and became a rain god. The passages in the *Veds* relating to the war with Vritra, which depict Indra piercing the clouds to release water are of a period when history had moved into mythology wherein Indra was a rain god. The water that Vritra had obstructed should be understood to mean flowing river waters.

It would not be reasonable to say that people at that level of material development could have built dams to check the flow of rivers. To understand what is meant by Vritra obstructing the waters of the rivers, the topography of the area where the Aryans were living at this stage, has to be seen. Arjika, as would emerge ahead, was in the foot hills of a mountain. The place has several streams and these people were living on slopes. The number of these streams being seven, the references to them has been confused with the seven rivers of Sapt Sindhu of India. In these Richas too, in the sixth and twelfth, seven rivers are mentioned. People practising settled agriculture on hills often have fields in terraces. They also make small water channels to carry water to these terraces. The Aryans were apparently doing the same. They were practising settled agriculture in which they had water channels from the rivers going to their fields. There is evidence in the *Veds* as well as the *Avesta* to show that they were having water channels, if not bigger canals. The Richa from the *Rig Ved* mentioning them is given here:

> May the waters that are in the sky, or those that flow (on the earth), those (whose channels) have been dug, or those that have sprung up on the ground spontaneously, and those that seek the ocean, all pure and purifying, may those divine waters protect me here (on earth).
>
> (*Rig Ved*. M-7, S-49, R-2)

Similar references are found in the *Avesta* and other Zoroastrian scriptures. Some of them are mentioned here.

1. We sacrifice to thee, O thou Ahurian one! And we sacrifice to the sea Vouru Kasha and to all waters upon earth, whether standing, or running, or waters of the well or spring-waters which perennially flow, or the dripping of the rains, or the irrigations of canals.

    (Yasna LXVIII)

2. Even Frasiyav of Tur was especially mighty by causing the construction of channels there where it is mountainous and also in low lands in which there is no mountain.

    (Dadistan-i Dinik. Chapter LXX)

These water channels running from the river or a stream on a slope to the agricultural fields are what is meant in the Vritra war. It seems that the Asurs, thirty years ago, had blocked the water channels going to the fields of the Devs to put economic pressure to give up their newly started religious practices. The *Veds* saying that Indra removed the obstruction and the waters started flowing again, means that this impediment in the practice of their religion for the Devs was removed. There are references in the *Avesta* to show that stopping the water flowing to the fields of the other side was quite common on both sides and often led to some sort of a fight. A few are given here.

1. They fight in the battles that are fought in their own place and land. And those of them who win bring waters to their own kindred, to their own borough, to their own country.

    (Farvardin Yast XXII)

2. Let not our waters be for the man of ill intent, of evil speech, or deeds, or conscience; not for an insulter of a Magian, nor for one who hates his kindred. And let not our good waters, help on the man who strives to mar our settlements which are not corrupted, nor a burier of dead bodies, nor the jealous, nor the niggard.

    (Yasna LXV)

The objectives achieved in this victory by Indra show the circumstances in which the Devs had left Arjika. Their leaders were either killed or put in some sort of a prison which was dark. The rest faced an economic blockade with their means of livelihood taken away, their cows seized and kept in an enclosure and water channels to their fields blocked. Nobody could have survived this situation. Some must have succumbed and given up their religious practices while others must have gone away. Thirty years had elapsed and the Asurs must have felt the issue settled for which there is no mention in the *Avesta* of the original founders of the new practices, the seven Angiras Rishis, led by Bhrigu. Their entire anger is on this one person, who brought it all back with a vengeance, Manu.

A few passages give a glimpse of the events in the battle. The fourth Richa says that Indra, with his thunderbolt, struck the first born of the serpents. The first born means the eldest son of the Kavi. It refers to Vritra, who, by this statement was the eldest son of the Kavi, the crown prince. The fifth and several other Richas mention that Vritra's body was mutilated after being killed. His limbs were dismembered. This shows a certain amount of personal vengeance on the part of Manu and could be an evidence of Bhrigu having been killed and with Vritra having some role in it, when the Asurs were persecuting the Devs. The battle has been fought with all its bitterness and ferocity. The sixth and fifteenth Richas report that Manu received a blow on his face. This must have been from a blunt weapon, as Manu survived it. The seventh Richa says that at one stage fear entered Indra's heart before he killed Vritra and he ran away, which shows the fortunes of the two sides fluctuating with the Asurs winning at one stage. A number of rivers and streams have been mentioned and Vritra's body was thrown into one, which shows that the battlefield was at a place having several streams, possibly close to a hill feature from where several tributaries were emerging or in a delta, where several distributaries had been formed.

Names of a few Asurs, who fought, have also been mentioned. The thirteenth Richa says that Drbhik was killed. The fifteenth says that Vyamsa struck a blow that hit Manu on his jaw and in return, was killed. A few warriors on the side of Manu have been deified along with him. In the *Veds* there are several passages, which name a divinity who along with Indra, killed Vritra. Amongst these are Agni, Varun, Mitra, Pushan, Brahmanaspati and Vishnu. The rest were gods from before but Brahmanaspati and Vishnu are new names that appeared now. These were warriors, who fought alongside Manu and have been deified. Another group of divinities mentioned in the *Veds*, as 'Constant Auxiliaries of Indra' in the fights, are the Maruts. In Hindu mythology, the Maruts are a group of divinities who are not at the same level as the Devs. At most places they are stated to be forty-nine in number, seven troops of seven each, all of equal strength. At a few places, they are said to be sixty-three, which would be nine troops of seven each. Often they are referred to as the troops of Maruts or the army of Maruts. This looks like a military formation and seems to have been the army of Manu. They were the constant auxiliaries of Indra in the war with Vritra and were with him even when all Devs had fled. The entire army seems to have been deified as Maruts just as on the earlier occasion of the Ribhus all the thirty-three participants of the religious assembly were deified.

Val emerges as the name of the Kavi at the time of this war and also when the Devs were being persecuted thirty years ago. This can be said as several Richas state, that the cows, the wealth and light had been withheld by Val. As this was being done under the directions of the sovereign authority, Val has been named for it. At several places the enclosure, in which the seized cows were kept has been called the enclosure of Val, a reference to the sovereign. Takma Urupa of the *Avesta* is evidently Val of the *Veds*. Vritra would be his son. Manu seems to have dethroned Val to become the Kavi after this war. The eighth Richa states that Indra had become the sovereign of all that is moveable or immoveable, of horned and hornless animals. The eleventh Richa says that Indra has recovered the cattle, he has recovered the horses, the plants, the waters, the woods, a clear indication that the entire realm had been taken over from the Asurs. The twenty-first says that he cast from his seat and punished the riteless man, again an affirmation of dethroning the Asur Kavi. The twenty-second repeats the same, as it says that he is the victor of the vanquisher, a reference to the atrocities committed by the Asurs in the earlier days. The twenty-third Richa is significant as it states, that the illicitly withholding Val was made to depart after a bitter defeat. This shows that Val was not killed but was only dethroned and made to leave the place though at several places an impression emerges that Val was killed. At places, Indra is said to have thrown him headlong down the mountain, while elsewhere he is said to have destroyed him. These appear to be later versions when the memory had faded. The first Richa also gives a hint that Val remained alive, but was not to be feared any longer. It says that Indra opened the cave of Val, who had there concealed the cattle, and the Devs, whom he had oppressed, no longer feared when they obtained him (Indra) as an ally. The twentieth Richa says that Indra humiliated the Kavi who was the giver of form to Indra and his men. This confirms Indra's identification with Manu as it was Val's decisions as a sovereign which had led to this war of revenge. The eighteenth Richa, too, gives the same confirmation as, speaking of the Maruts, in the first line it states that they have come to the aid of the warring Trita, while in the next it states that they have come to the aid of Indra, making Indra and Trita the same person.

Closely linked to the war with Vritra, is the legend of the three steps of Vishnu, which has the story of taking away of the possessions of the Asurs. In the *Purans*, the legend of Vishnu as a dwarf taking three steps is not the same as is found in the Vedic literature. Val has become Bali in the *Purans*. The story there is that he was a king performing a sacrifice. At the stage when gifts are given to priests, a dwarf Brahman appeared and sought a gift of land equivalent to his three steps. King Bali readily agreed. This dwarf Brahman was Vishnu, who in two steps covered the earth, heaven and sky. As there was no place left to place the foot for a third time, King Bali lay down before him to enable him to place his foot. Vishnu placed his foot on Bali's head and pushed it down to send him to the world below, to become the king of serpents. This story confirms that Val was the Kavi and remained so even after Vishnu had intervened, but only that of the serpents, a term used for Asurs, but differs in its contents with what the Brahmans state or the limited references that are there in the *Veds*. The *Aitarey Brahman* has this story.

For both (Indra and Vishnu) had been victorious. After they
had defeated them, they said to them, 'Let us divide.' The
Asurs accepted the offer. Indra then said, 'All through which
Vishnu makes his three steps is ours, the other part is yours.'
Then Vishnu stepped through these (three worlds), then over
the *Veds* and lastly over Vach.

(Book VI, Chapter III)

In this, the Asurs appear to have agreed after being defeated in a war
that whatever is covered by Vishnu's three steps would be conceded
to the Devs. The three worlds have been covered in a single step. In
the second step, the *Veds* had been covered. A study of the *Avesta*
shows that unlike the Devs, who started the tradition of retaining the
existent texts and adding to it from the time of the war with Vritra,
the Asurs started very late. In their case, the prayers and all related
text were compiled and preserved only from the time of Zoroaster.
As a result, the earlier literature, which has been called the *Veds* by
the other side, was lost to them. The third step covered Vach or
speech. This also emerges from a study of the *Avesta*. The Asurs were
not able to retain the Sanskrit language or the language which these
Aryans had at the time of the split. This is also linked to the *Veds*. The
Devs had started memorizing and retaining the hymns that were in
existence at that time. In doing so, this text remained at the centre of
their language because of which it remained the same, atleast for the
educated class. As the Asurs had not done so, their language changed
over a period of time and did not remain the same. This legend in
the *Aitarey Brahman* is evidently of a period when the difference in
the language of the Devs and Asurs had become perceptible. Vishnu,
having covered Vach, or speech by his third step means that the
language, in its chaste form remained with the Devs only while to
the Asurs this was lost. The legend does tell us that this exercise was
a part of an agreement between the Devs and Asurs after a war in
which the Asurs had been defeated. It seems to be referring to the
Vritra war. The references to Vishnu's three steps in the *Veds* are not
very elaborate. These are mentioned here.

1. Vishnu traversed this (world); three times he planted his foot and the whole (world) was collected in the dust of his (footsteps).
2. Vishnu, the preserver, the uninjurable, stepped three steps, upholding thereby righteous acts.

   (*Rig Ved.* M-1, S-22, R-17 and 18)
3. Vishnu is therefore glorified, that by his prowess, he is like a fearful, ravenous and mountain-haunting wild beast, and because of that, in his three paces all worlds abide.
4. May acceptable vigour attend Vishnu, who abides in prayer, the hymned of many, the showerer who alone made, by three steps, the spacious and durable aggregate (of the three worlds).

   (*Rig Ved.* M-1, S-154, R-2 and 3)
5. May we be happy in a home, in riches, in persons, in children, bestowed upon us by you, Vishnu, who with three (steps) made the terrestrial regions for Manu when harassed (by the Asurs).

   (*Rig Ved.* M-6, S-49, R-13)

Of these, the fifth Richa is very significant, as it says that Vishnu, with three steps made the terrestrial regions for Manu when harassed by the Asurs. Apart from supporting the view that Indra is the deification of Manu, this Richa perhaps gives the correct historical position. It appears that after the war, the victorious Devs, led by Manu approached Val, who was the Kavi, but had not fought perhaps because of old age. They asked for the restoration of all their properties that had been taken away thirty years ago. A defeated Kavi Val had no option before him. He offered that whatever lands were required by the Devs may be taken by them, and the Asurs would relinquish and live in whatever is left. Vishnu seems to have been given the task of making an assessment of the requirements of the Devs. He did so taking into account the three requirements of the people for land, for dwellings, agriculture and pastures. In doing so, he covered the entire area, which was being used in Arjika for these purposes. A helpless Kavi Val was left with no choice, but to leave the place along with the surviving Asurs. All lands were distributed by the Devs amongst themselves. It has been expressed poetically in the *Veds* that Vishnu took up the task of assessing the requirements for the three purposes step by step.

With the victory over Vritra and the agreement with Val, the Devs came to occupy all the lands that were in use in Arjika till then. The Asurs left their habitations, but continued to be in Arjika in the nearby areas. This had the seeds of future conflicts as the Asurs were aggrieved now and had all the reasons to feel injured. Asurs having been driven out of Arjika is reflected from these passages.

1. Stop, Surya, your yellow horses, for this Etasha, Indra, drags the wheel: having driven those who offer no sacrifice to the opposite bank of the ninety rivers, you compel them (to do) what is to be done.

    (Rig Ved. M-1, S-121, R-13)

2. Whose great deeds his worshippers now celebrate, who is clothed with light, radiant as the sun, exempt from decay, the purifier, he illumes (all things), and destroys the ancient cities of the dispersed (evil beings).

    (Rig Ved. M-6, S- 4, R-3)

3. By Jagati metre in the sky strode Vishnu. There, excluded, is the man who hates us and whom we detest.

    (Yajur Ved. Adhyay-2, Yajush-25)

Meanwhile, the Devs seem to have taken up missionary activities for the spread of their religion. This must have started from the time they had been driven away from Arjika and, led by Manu, were wandering about for thirty years. Manu seems to have had the support of some other Aryan tribes in his conflict with Vritra because without such support, he may not have been in a position to come up with an army and fight the Asurs, who were well settled and seem to have been in a larger number. This support for Manu from people of other tribes would have been the result of these missionary activities by which the Devs would have succeeded in converting people to their religion. Indications of missionary activities by the Devs can be seen in these passages of the *Veds*.

1. Who clove for Trishok, the broad womb-like cloud (and made) a path for the cows to issue forth.

(Rig Ved. M-8, S-45, R-30)

2. May we be prosperous at the coming of the present or of any future dawn (through the adoration) of you, the chief leader of men; through your favour Trishok obtained a hundred followers; the chariot which was common to him and you was acquired by Kutsa.

(Rig Ved. M-10, S-29, R-2)

3. O the leader of all men! May our superiority be rejuvenated by virtue of your worship in these as also in other dawns. O lord Indra! The Rishi Trishok had obtained the cooperation of one hundred people by your prayer and the chariot, on which the Saint Kutsa rode, too is an outcome of your assistance.

(Atharv Ved. Kand-20, Sukta-76, Richa-2)

Trishok seems to have been a preacher, either of the time when Arjika was taken over by Manu or earlier, because Kutsa is said to have proceeded in his footsteps. Kutsa, as would soon emerge, was the grandson of Manu. The beginning of missionary activities by the Devs so early, for the spread of their religion had a significant bearing on the conflict between the two sides, because it created a much wider support base for them. The Asurs, on the other hand, do not seem to have taken up any such activity because of which when finally Zoroaster took up the issue of the spread of his religion, he had to start from a very desperate position and needed the support of the sovereign authority.

In the continuing fight between the two sides, the next round of the war took place between the successors of Manu and Val. In the *Veds*, Ushana is named as Manu's son, who seems to have succeeded him as Kavi though in the entire Vedic text Ushana is not called a Kavi anywhere. He has been called a Kavya only, which means a son of the Kavi or prince. This seems to be because Ushana is credited to have composed a lot of hymns of the *Veds*. He was a Kavya to start with, when his father Manu was the Kavi. He seems to have continued to use the same title in the works relating to the composition and compilation of the *Veds* because of which he is found to have been called only Kavya Ushana and not Kavi Ushana. The other Rishis too called him Kavya Ushana because of the same reason. The Asur who emerges against him, is Shushna. There is nothing in the *Veds* to show the relationship of Shushna with Val or Vritra, but as Kaviship was hereditary, he has to be in the bloodline. He could be either another son of Val or a grandson, being the son of Vritra. The references in the *Veds* relating to their conflicts are stated here.

1. You have defended Kutsa in fatal fights with Shushna, you have destroyed Shambar in defence of Atithigva; you have trodden with your foot upon the great Arbud; from remote times were you born for the destruction of oppressors.

    (*Rig Ved.* M-1, S-51, R-6)

2. He is quick in action and mighty; his faultless and destructive prowess shines in manly (conflict) like the peak of a mountain (afar), with which, clothed in iron (armour), he, the suppressor of malignant, when exhilarated (by the Som juice), cast the wily Shushna into prison and into bonds.

    (*Rig Ved.* M-1, S-56, R-3)

3. You, Indra, the best of all beings, the assailer and humiliator (of your foes), the chief of the Ribhus, the friend of man, the subduer of enemies, did aid the young and illustrious Kutsa and slew Shushna in the deadly and close-fought fight.

    (*Rig Ved.* M-1, S-63, R-3)

4. When, Indra, you and Ushana with vigorous and rapid coursers went to the dwelling of Kutsa, then destroying his foes, you went in one chariot with Kutsa and the gods, and verily you have slain Shushna.

    (*Rig Ved.* M-5, S-29, R-9)

5. You, Indra (abiding on the further bank), have rendered the fertilizing waters agreeable to Yadu and Turvash; you two, have assailed the fierce (Shushna) and (having slain him) you have conveyed Kutsa (to his dwelling), and Ushana and the Devs have honoured you both.

    (*Rig Ved.* M-5, S-31, R-8)

6. The wielder of the thunderbolt, the render of the rain cloud, has destroyed with his bolt, the mighty Shushna, the wrath-born (son) of the Danav, the walker in darkness, the protector of the showering cloud, exhilarating himself with the food (offered in sacrifice).

(*Rig Ved.* M-5, S-32, R-4)

7. Desirous of opulence, you, Indra, have been an ancient benefactor of Ushana, the son of Kavi, having slain Navavastva, you have given back his own grandson, who was (fit) to be restored to the grandfather.

(*Rig Ved.* M-6, S-20, R-11)

8. O Lord Indra! You had given wealth to Kutsa, the son of Arjuni and killed the slaves, namely Shushna and Kuyav in course of the war when you did protect Kutsa by serving him yourself.

(*Atharv Ved.* Kand 20, S-37, R-2)

In these passages the sixth Richa calls Shushna the wrath-born son of the Danav giving an indication that Shushna was the son of Vritra and had before him the issue of avenging the killing of his father. A similar epithet was used for Indra at the time of his emergence, by which Bhrigu's killing has been hinted for Manu. It seems that Shushna made several attempts to recover the land that had been lost to the Devs. Apparently, he was very young at the time of the Vritra war and had started his campaigns only after coming of age, because most of his fights have been with Kutsa, at whose hands he was finally killed. Kutsa appears to be the son of Ushana, who would have been the Kavi initially and perhaps died before Shushna was killed, leaving the succession to Kutsa. The fourth Richa hints at the relationship of Ushana and Kutsa. It states, that Indra and Ushana went to the dwelling of Kutsa, who was then engaged in destroying his foes and Indra killed Shushna. The fifth Richa, too, gives the same information as it says that Indra assailed Shushna and conveyed Kutsa to his dwelling for which Ushana honoured him. The eighth Richa gives Arjuni as the name of Kutsa's mother.

So far as the conflict is concerned, the second Richa says that

Shushna was cast into a prison and into bonds. This shows that in one of the fights Shushna was taken alive and made a prisoner. The seventh Richa says that Indra killed Navavastva and restored the grandson of Ushana to his grandfather. This shows that on one occasion the Asurs had taken the grandson of Ushana into their custody. This could have been a case of kidnapping, which led to a war, in which the Asur Navavastva was killed. The identity of this Asur and his relationship with Shushna cannot be found with the information given about him. The third Richa, which like several others, speaks of the killing of Shushna states that it was a deadly and close fought fight. Apparently, some of the conflicts may not have been full-blown wars. They may have been minor fights between two antagonistic neighbours over water for irrigation or demarcation of territory. However, finally there seems to have been a full-fledged war between the two sides, which was very closely fought and in which Kutsa won and Shushna was killed, bringing to close the second round of the Dev Asur Sangram.

In these passages Kutsa emerges as a warrior, fighting the Asurs led by Shushna, while in those relating to Trishok he appears to be a preacher of religion. It appears that he started as a prince, leading the army on behalf of his father and after being successful for a long time, in which he defeated and killed Shushna, he finally lost to the Asurs. This would have led to the loss of the sovereign authority on his part, whereafter he became a preacher. Apparently, he was equally illustrious as a preacher.

The *Avesta* has no mention of these wars, perhaps because they were reverses for the Asurs. However, it seems that the stories about them had survived in the folklore in Iran at least till the eleventh century AD because Firdausi seems to have had access to them. He has recorded certain things in the *Shahnama*, which match the narrative of the *Veds* about these wars. Having come from folklore, however, Firdausi's accounts have many facts mixed up. At places, the events that were connected to one personality have been linked to some other. Such things do happen in folklore, when they survive for so long. If certain corrections are made in Firdausi's account on the basis of the information available in the *Veds* and *Avesta*, it gives a fair picture to support the evidence emerging from the scriptures and provides some additional information. The relevant passages from the *Shahnama* are given here.

When eloquent Dehkan first to record brought,
The name of him on earth who greatness sought?
None from of old has brought the memory down,
But he to whom his father told, the son,
Who tells his father's stories one by one,
He who the Bastan-namah searched of old,
That stories of the Pahlavans has told.
He said, 'The customs of the throne and crown,
First Kayumurs when he was king laid down.
When Kayumurs was master of the land,
In the hill country first he took his stand.
His throne and fortune overtopped the hill.
Yet all of panther skins wore clothing still,
For all advancement give to him the mead,
Men knew not how to dress or how to feed.
For thirty years, when he the crown had won.

One son, Siamak, fair of face and name,
Sought virtuously, like his father, fame.
Handsome in face, of genial temper too,
Kayumurs heart rejoiced with him in view.
Of enemies upon the earth he'd none,
But secretly the impure Ahriman,
And Ahriman, on evil deed intent,
To seize upon him envy's counsel lent.
He had one son, as a fierce wolf he grew,
And he was brave, with a large army, too,
Gathered his host, he took towards him the way,
As for Kay's throne and crown in wait he lay.
To that Div child the world was very black,
Of King Siamak's fortune for the lack.
And Kayumurs, how knew he of the thing,

For his great throne there was another king?
A heavenly messenger came sudden in,
In Paris' form, clothed in a panther skin,
And said, 'From door to door let all man know,
What towards thy son now contemplates thy foe?'
When to Siamak's ear the word was brought,
Of deeds done by foul Div of evil thought,
The prince's heart grew hot such things to hear,
He gathered troops and opened wide his ear.
Now when the armies face to face were set,
Eager to fight, the aspiring Div he met.
Naked in body, Siamak came on,
And held on to that son of Ahriman.
The black Div's claw struck him a backward blow,
The two together fell, the prince below.
Down to the earth that princely form he bent,
And with his claw his royal loins were rent.
Siamak of his life, by Div bereft,
Died, and his host without a lord was left.
Of his son's death the monarch was aware,
And black to him became the world through care.
He beat his back and hands, with wailing moan,
Tearing his side he came down from his throne,
With bleeding cheeks his heart with sorrow burned.
Hard on himself he thought his fate had turned.
Up from the host arose a wailing shout,
At the king's gate they close their ranks about.
Their garments all were stained with purple dye,
Wine-hued their cheek, and full of blood their eye.
Mourning, in pain, in sorrow for their woes,
From the king's palace a great dust arose.
A year they sat, their hearts with grief aflame,
Until a message from their Maker came.
Propitious greeting then an angel brought,
'Recall your senses, do not wail for naught,

From now an army, my command obey,
From that assembly raise a dust this day,
Clear ye from off the earth that demon base,
And from your hearts these thoughts of wrath efface.'
To the sky raised his head the noble king,
And vented curses on that evil thing.
By the great name of God on him he cried,
From the king's eyelash then the tear was dried,
Siamak to avenge he went in haste,
And sought not day or night repose and rest.
Happy Siamak had an only son,
Dastur's place to his grandsire who had won,
Of sterling worth, now Hushang was his name.
When he set war with vengeance in his heart,
Worthy Hushang he summoned then, apart,
Repeated to him all he had to tell,
His secrets all revealed to him as well.
'An army will I draw now me around,
And raise a war-cry that shall far resound.
And thou wilt have to go before them all,
For I must go, thou the new general.'
Then Kayumurs behind to move began,
His grandson marching forward in the van.
The black Div came on with a trembling cry.

As to each other the two hosts drew near,
At the wild beasts the Divs drew back in fear.
As lion fierce, Hoshang stretched out his hand,
The world grew small for those brave Divs to stand.
From head to foot the general him flayed,
And severed from his form his monstrous head.
When thus he had exacted vengeance meet,
The days of Kayumurs became complete.
He went, the earth remaining of him bare.
Hushang, of right, and with good counsel' grace,

Assumed the crown in his grandparent's place.
For forty years the sphere turned in his reign.
These words he uttered from the royal throne,
'Over all seven climates is my kingly sway,
    As ruler me they everywhere obey.'

Water to use a plan did he device,
Drawn from the streams, the plain to fertilize,
Rivers to join to streams the access gave.
For with this knowledge when mankind were filled,
Spreading the seed, they harvested, they tilled,
Thus all preparing for themselves their bread,
Each knew and for himself provision made.
Above all, God he'd worship and adore,
As was his grandsire's custom heretofore.
And when there came for him a better day,
As destiny no longer would delay,
King Hushang, wise and prudent passed away.
One only son he dying left behind,
Worthy Tehmuras, who the Divs confined.
He came and sat upon his father's throne.

A vazir pure and perfect, too, had he,
Whose mind from evil thoughts was far and free,
In every place Shidasp was of renown,
And nowhere but for good his foot set down
He showed the monarch naught but what was true,
And ranks' road only in his virtue knew,
Thus from all ill the king was purified.
With a vazir of knowledge so possessed,
The monarch you may know was greatly blessed.
In bonds of magic Ahriman he tied,
And as a courser swift on him would ride,
From time to time on him a saddle bound,
He drove him wildly the whole world around.
When Tehmuras of their tricks became aware,

Enraged, he closed their little market there.
Girding his loins up in his kingly grace,
He on his shoulder laid his heavy mace.
Magician demons there, a mighty force,
Came sweeping onwards in their magic course,
Came on the black Div, too, the host before,
As to the heavens they raised their thundering roar.
The earth was darkened and grew black the sky,
And dimmed became to him the monarch's eye.
On came Tehmuras then in his lordly might,
His loins grit for vengeance in the fight.
On one side demons' smoke, as fire, there roared,
On that side warriors round the world its lord.
With the Divs suddenly the battle raged,
But not for long was either side engaged.
Two parts of them with magic spells he bound,
His heavy mace cast others to the ground.

Some wounded he contemptuously tied,
Others to save their lives for quarter cried.
And said, 'Slay not, from us that thou mays't learn,
A novel art thou may'st to profit turn.'
The Kai them quarter gave on their appeal,
That what was hidden they might clear reveal.
The monarch they instruct then how to write.
And after this for thirty years and more,
The king of every art acquired a store.
He passed away. Time was for him complete.

Usually in folklore, significant events relating to a prominent
personality remain linked to him. Prominent events too survive with
little or no aberrations. However, often personalities, places, time and
their relationships get mixed up. The same features can be seen in
Firdausi's account also. Hoshang, who is Hoshyangha in the *Avesta* and
represents the Ribhus of the *Veds*, has been linked to the development
of agriculture, a correct projection of what the scriptures have said

about the Ribhus. He has, however, been shown as the grandson of Kayumurs, who is attacked by the son of Ahriman. The identity of Kayumurs cannot be linked to anyone in the *Veds* or the *Avesta*, unless that is what has become of Sudhanvan, who in the *Veds* emerges as an ancient progenitor of the Ribhus. Manu, who is Angra Mainyu in the *Avesta*, appears as Ahriman with Firdausi, but the attack in this version has been launched by his son and not by Ahriman himself, which is a departure from what was stated in the *Avesta*. This could be an impact of Islam, wherein there is a concept of Satan or Iblis, who is an eternal evil entity. Ahriman would have been considered to be the Zoroastrian version of Iblis, in which case it would have been difficult to conceptualize an eternal entity launching a war on a human king, forcing the storytellers to find a solution by calling him the son of Ahriman. The attack has been launched and has been met, not by the king, but by his son who gets killed in battle. This adds to the information given by the *Veds* and shows the relationship between Val and Vritra. The victorious Devs, who are called Divs here, assemble at the king's palace and create a lot of noise, after which dust rises from the said palace, indicating that the king left the place after being dethroned. The story proceeds to say that a war of revenge was launched, which was led by the king's grandson Hoshang. As all folk tales have a happy ending, the story concludes with Hoshang killing the son of Ahriman and Kayumurs dying a satisfied man. The killing of this son of Ahriman is of course not true, because if any such thing had happened, the *Avesta* would have mentioned it.

This story matches with the events of the war between Manu and Vritra, after which Val left his realm, with Shushna launching attacks to avenge the defeat and killing of Vritra. Shushna thus emerges as the son of Vritra and the grandson of Val. The first war should, however, have been with the son of Tehmuras, the name of Takma Urupa in the Pahlavi works and the counterpart of Val of the *Veds*. Instead of that, the *Shahnama* has shown this to be a war fought by the son of Kayumurus, who is Haoshyangha of the *Avesta* and the Ribhus of the *Veds*. Though this distortion has taken place, the significant events about Tehmuras have been correctly remembered. He has been stated to have made Ahriman a horse and used him to ride all over the world for thirty years. This is what has been stated in the *Avesta* for Takma Urupa. A war with the Divs in his time has also been remembered, but as the information of it had already gone to the war attributed to the times of Kayumurs, there was nothing eventful left, because of which it has been shown to be just a war with Divs, in which the Black Div and many other Divs were killed, while the rest sought mercy. Distortion has crept in to show victory in this war, which would have happened over the ages in the folklore to show the heroes in a positive light.

Independently, the information provided by Firdausi, with so many distortions, would not have had any historical worth and would have been taken to be a record of just a few folk tales. However, once the story emerges from the *Veds* and is supported by the *Avesta*, even this account, despite its flaws, has immense value in confirming the authenticity of the information coming from the scriptures.

4
The War Continues

THE NEXT PERSONALITY OF HISTORICAL significance that emerges in the *Veds* is Dadhich. He has been called by three names Dadhich, Dadhyanga and Dadhichanga. In the *Purans* and later literature, he has been called Dadhichi. The story about him in the *Purans* differs from that of the Vedic literature. The Puranic story says that he was an eminent Rishi, who had undergone a lot of austerities for which his bones were very strong. Indra, in his battle with Vritra was unable to defeat him. In consultations, it emerged that only if Indra fights with a Vajra made of Dadhichi's bones would he be able to kill Vritra. Indra approached Dadhichi and begged for his bones with which a Vajra was made and Indra proceeded to kill Vritra with it. The story in the Brahmans differs from this. Its version from the Shat Path Brahman is given here.

> Now, Dadhyanch Atharvan knew this pure essence, how this sacrifice becomes complete. He then was spoken to by Indra saying, 'If thou teachest this (sacrificial mystery) to anyone else, I shall cut off thy head.' Now this was heard by the Ashwins—'Verily, Dadhyanch Atharvan knows this pure essence, how this sacrifice becomes complete.' They two went up to him and said, 'We two will become thy pupils.' 'What are ye wishing to learn?' he asked. 'This pure essence of this sacrifice. How this sacrifice becomes complete,' they replied. He said, 'I was spoken to by Indra, saying, "If thou teachest this to anyone else I shall cut off thy head," therefore I am afraid lest he should indeed cut off my head. I cannot take

you as my pupils.' They said, 'We two shall protect thee from him.' 'How will ye protect me?' he replied. They said, 'When thou wilt have received us as thy pupils, we shall cut off thy head and put it aside elsewhere; then we shall fetch the head of a horse, and put it on thee, therewith thou wilt teach us; and when thou wilt have taught us, then Indra will cut off that head of thine; and we shall fetch thine own head and put it on again.' 'So be it,' he replied. He then received them (as his pupils), and when he had received them, they cut off his head, and put it aside elsewhere; and having fetched the head of a horse, they put it on him, therewith he taught them. Indra cut off that head of his, and having fetched his own head, they put it on him again.

(Kand XIV, Adhyay I, Brahman I)

The *Veds* are very cryptic on this. Though a hint is there that Indra cut off the head of Dadhich, the emphasis is more on saying that to avenge his bones Indra defeated the Asurs and destroyed their habitations. These events are of a time after the war with Vritra, which was fought by Manu and now Vritra has been used in plural. The passages about Dadhich in the *Veds* are here.

1. Indra, with the bones of Dadhich, slew ninety times nine Vritras.
2. Wishing for the horse's head hidden in the mountains, he found it at Sharyanavat.

(*Rig Ved*. M-1, S-84, R-13 and 14)

3. You replaced, Ashwins, with the head of a horse (the head of) Dadhich, the son of Atharvan, and, true to his promise, he revealed to you the mystic knowledge which he had learned from Tvasta, and which was a ligature of the waist to you.

(*Rig Ved*. M-1, S-117, R-22)

4. (You) through whom Dadhyanga, the offerer of the nine days' rites opened, through whom the Rishi recovered, through whom under the protection of the gods, the worshippers obtained the sustenance of the delicious water.

(*Rig Ved*. M-9, S-108, R-4)

5. I, Indra, am the striker off of the head of the son of Atharvan, I generated the waters from above the cloud for the sake of Trita. I carried off their wealth from the Dasyus, taming the clouds for Dadhich, the son of Matarisvan.

(*Rig Ved*. M-10, S-48, R-2)

6. The most victorious Lord Indra had killed ninety and nine Vritras with the blows of the thunderbolt made of the bones donated by Dadhich.

7. When Lord Indra had known the fact that the head of that horse existed in the lake, namely Sharyanavat behind the mountains, he then made a thunderbolt of that head and killed the Dasyus.

(*Atharv Ved*. Kand 20, S-41, R-1 and 2)

These Richas support stories from both the scriptures, Vedic, as well as Puranic. From a historical perspective, however, they have to be understood differently. Before examining them, a major error in the translation of the *Veds* needs to be corrected. There are references here, as well as elsewhere of Indra destroying the cities and forts of the Asurs. This has given an impression that the Asurs were city-dwellers, while the Devs or Aryans were rural people. This view received further credence, when archeological remains of the cities of the Indus Valley Civilization were found. The Dev Asur Sangram was understood to be a war between the invading Aryans and the non-Aryan city-dwelling population of India. This is not correct as this war was a fight between two groups of Aryans belonging to the same tribe in Central Asia, much before some from one side came to India. They were both at the same level of development and lived in the same conditions, with no such distinction as urban or rural. In fact, there is no sign of urban habitations being in existence at the places where these Aryans were living and fighting. The word used in the texts is 'Pur', which has been translated as cities and forts by the translators. It is true that in later Sanskrit 'Pur' means a city. This, however, seems to be a later development. In the *Veds*, it does not seem to be carrying this meaning, but only that of a habitation, because in the following Richa there is a reference to moveable 'Purs'.

You have broken to pieces the moveable cities of Shushna with
your weapons; you who are light have followed him, wherefore
Indra, you are in two ways to be worshipped.

(*Rig Ved.* M-8, S-1, R-28)

The translation of 'Pur' as city, has led the imagination of some
commentators to a level of absurdity, wherein they have explained
that the Asurs had cities with wings with which they could take
them wherever they wanted. If this word is translated as habitation, a
moveable 'Pur' would simply mean a camp or a temporary habitation
with dwellings made of make-shift materials, which may be shifted
according to the need. This is the meaning of moveable 'Purs' of
Shushna, who, as has already emerged, was the grandson of Val and
after the Vritra war, would have been living with the other Asurs in
make-shift structures in the vicinity of the earlier regular villages from
where Val and his followers had been driven out in consequence of
Vishnu's assessment of land required by the Devs. In their turn, when
the Devs got dislodged from Arjika, they too lived in similar conditions.
Their moveable dwellings have been mentioned in the following Richa.

Fasten you not to us the fetters, a heavy burden; become you
light like a bride, O dwelling, we carry you where we will.

(*Atharv Ved.* Kand-9, Sukt-3, Richa-24)

Next the figures ninety, ninety-nine and ninety times nine appear here
as well as at several places in the *Veds.* These Aryans had something
associated with the number nine and its repetition. It seems to be
meaning either all or just a very large number and had nothing to
do with the actual figure that it represented because similar usage is
seen in the *Avesta* also. A passage showing this from the Vendidad
is given here.

Then the ruffian looked at me; the ruffian Angra Mainyu, the
deadly, wrought by his witchcraft nine diseases, and ninety
and nine hundred, and nine thousand, and nine times ten
thousand diseases.

(Vendidad. Fargard XXII)

Viewing Dadhich as a historical person, the first thing that emerges is that he was a Rishi and not a warrior. He has not been shown to have fought any war, yet the fourth Richa says that 'he recovered'. The commentators have explained that he recovered cows, but this is not what seems to be meant. It appears to mean that he recovered Arjika, the country, for the Devs. If he had recovered Arjika, the same should have been lost by the Devs before that. The *Veds* have no mention of this loss, which is a part of the pattern wherein reverses are not mentioned. This loss by the Devs means a victory for the Asurs, because of which details about it would be in the *Avesta*. Lost Dev country has been recovered by Dadhich, who is a Rishi and not a warrior, shows that he was a preacher and was able to convert the Asur Kavi, who had defeated the Devs and established his rule. After that, he has been killed. If the legends of the Shat Path Brahman and the *Purans* are left out, in the *Veds*, it is only in the fifth Richa that a mention is found which hints that Indra killed Dadhich. Here he has been called the son of Atharvan. Though this could mean even Shambar, the Richa and the entire Sukt from which it has been taken, projects Indra as the Almighty God and not just a Dev fighting the Asurs. In the entire Sukt, Indra says that he is the principal lord of wealth; conqueror of treasures of adversaries; father of all living beings etc. It is evident that this is an idea of God as the Creator, Preserver and Destroyer. This being the case, he has to be responsible for everything that has happened or happens. Dadhich's head has been struck off. Whosoever may have done it, the Supreme Being has to be ultimately responsible for it. Evidently, it was with this intention that the Richa has Indra saying, 'I, Indra, am the striker of the head of the son of the Atharvan,' if he meant Dadhich. Later commentators and composers seem to have taken it literally, creating the problem of explaining why Indra struck off the head of Dadhich, who was a Rishi and his worshipper. This led them to create the legends to give a valid reason. Who killed Dadhich becomes clear when it emerges who was killed in revenge. It is the Asur Shambar, who is repeatedly mentioned in the *Veds*, as having nine and ninety cities, which Indra destroyed. In the fifth Richa itself, which in the beginning states that Indra struck off the head of the son of Atharvan, it is further stated that, 'I carried off their wealth from the Dasyus, taming the cloud for Dadhich, the son of Matarisvan.' The repeated mention of killing the Vritras with the bones of Dadhich means that the war that was fought, in which a large number of Vritras were killed, was a war to avenge the killing of Dadhich, though it seems that Dadhich was beheaded and his head thrown in the Sharyanavat.

Dadhich can be located in the *Avesta* on the basis of what the *Veds* have said he did, what happened to him and with what consequences. He emerges as a preacher, who succeeded in converting the Asur king to the religion of the Devs, whereafter he was killed, as a revenge for which the Asurs were attacked, a large number of them got killed and all, or a very large number of their habitations were destroyed. This description matches perfectly with Dahak in the *Avesta*. With Dadhich getting identified as Dahak, the Asur king or Kavi, who defeated the Devs and took away Arjika from them to be later converted, is Yim of the *Avesta* and Yam of the *Veds* and the Asur who killed Dadhich is Thraetaoma of the *Avesta* and Shambar of the *Veds*. Yam is the only person, after the split, who commands respect from both sides. In the *Avesta* and later Zoroastrian scriptures he is called Yim, the great shepherd, Yim the son of Vivanghat, Yim Khshaeta (splendid), and finally Jamshed. In the *Veds*, Yam as well as Manu have been called sons of Vivasvat. Some references from the *Veds* on this are given here.

1. As you, Shakra, did drink the effused Som from Manu Vivasvat, as you did accept the hymn from Trita, so do you gladden yourself with Ayu.

    (*Rig Ved.* M-8, S-52, R-1)

2. Worship with oblations Yam, king, the son of Vivasvat, the aggregation of mankind, who conducts those who are virtuous over earth, and opens to many the path (of heaven).

    (*Rig Ved.* M-10, S-14, R-1)

3. Come hither, Yam, with the venerable and multiform Angiras Rishis and be exhilarated, I invoke Vivasvat, who is your father, to this sacrifice; may be seated on the sacred grass.

    (*Rig Ved.* M-10, S-14, R-5)

4.   What that was Yam's the Karshivans made, digging down in the
     beginning, food-acquiring, not with knowledge, that I make an
     oblation unto the king, Vivasvan's son, so let our food be fit for
     the sacrifice, rich and sweet.

                                   (*Atharv Ved*. Kand 6, S-116, R-1)

These Richas show that Manu and Yam had a common ancestor
Vivasvat. In the Brahmans and in the later commentaries on the *Veds*,
Vivasvat is said to be a name of the sun and these two, along with
others, are said to be the sons of the sun. Treating them as having a
common ancestor would mean that both Manu and Yam were from
the same clan or perhaps even a sub-clan of this Aryan tribe. In the
Avesta, Yim has been called the good shepherd, which shows that he
was not from the royal family of Val, whose dynasty seems to have
ended with Shushna. The information available about Yim from the
Avesta is in these passages.

1.   Ahur Mazda answered: The fair Yim, the great shepherd, O holy
     Zarathustra, he was the first mortal, before thee, with whom did
     I converse, to whom I taught the law of Ahur. Unto him I spake,
     saying, 'Well fair Yim, son of Vivanghat, be thou the preacher
     and bearer of my law.' And fair Yim replied unto me saying, 'I
     was not born to be the preacher and the bearer of thy law.' Then
     I, Ahur Mazda, said thus unto him, 'Since thou wantest not to be
     the preacher and the bearer of my law, then make thou my worlds
     thrive, undertake thou to rule over my world.' And the fair Yim
     replied unto me saying, 'Yes, I will rule over thy world.' Then I,
     Ahur Mazda, brought two implements unto him, a golden ring
     and a poniard inlaid with gold. Behold, here Yim bears the royal
     sway. Thus under Yim, three hundred winters passed away, and
     the earth was replenished and there was no more room for flocks,
     herds and men. Then I warned the fair Yim saying, 'O fair Yim,
     the son of Vivanghat, the earth has become full, there is no more
     room for flocks, herds and men.' Then Yim stepped forward,
     towards the luminous space, southwards he pressed the earth with
     the golden ring and bored it with the poniard, speaking thus, 'O

Spenta Armaiti, kindly open asunder and stretch thyself afar, to bear the flocks, herds and men.'

And Yim made the earth grow larger by one-third than it was before. Thus under the sway of Yim, six hundred winters passed away and there was no more room for flocks, herds and men. And I warned Yim saying, 'There is no more room for flocks and herds and men.' Then Yim stepped forward southward and pressed the earth. And Yim made the earth grow larger by two-thirds than it was before. Thus under the sway of Yim nine hundred winters passed away and the earth was full of flocks and herds and men. And I warned Yim saying, 'There is no more room for flocks and herds and men.' Then Yim stepped forward southward to meet the sun and pressed the earth. And Yim made the earth grow larger by three-thirds than it was before.

(Vendidad. Fargard II)

2. To her did Yim Khshaeta, the good shepherd offer up a sacrifice from the height Hukairya. He begged of her a boon saying, 'Grant me this, O good, most beneficent Ardvi Sura Anahita! That I may become the sovereign lord of all countries, of the Daevas and men; that I may take from the Daevas both riches and welfare, both fatness and flocks, both weal and glory.'

(Aban Yast VII)

3. We worship the Fravashi of the holy Yim, the son of Vivanghat; the valiant Yim, who had flocks at his wish, to stand against the oppression caused by the Daevas.

(Farvardin Yast XXIX)

4. To him did the bright Yim, the good shepherd, sacrifice from the height Hukairya. He begged of him a boon saying, 'Grant me this, O Vayu, that I may become the most glorious of the men born to behold the sun, that I may make in my reign both animals and men undying.' In the reign of the valiant Yim there was neither cold wind nor hot wind, neither old age nor death nor envy made by the Daevas.

(Ram Yast IV)

These passages show that Yim became the sovereign after ending the rule of the Devs. In the second passage, he has been granted the boon of becoming the sovereign lord of all countries, of Devs and men and to take away from the Devs both riches and welfare, both fatness and flocks, both weal and glory. He has evidently fought the Devs and defeated them as the third passage says that he stood up against the oppression caused by the Devs. The name of the Dev Kavi defeated by him is not mentioned, but it has to be Ushana, if he was alive till then or Kutsa, if Ushana was no more. In any case, the war in all certainty would have been fought by Kutsa, as he was already leading the Devs in the wars with Shushna. The *Avesta* does not mention that the Dev Kavi was killed by Yim. Evidence from the *Veds* also shows that Kutsa had survived to become a preacher, in the footsteps of Trishok.

The first passage is significant as it states that Yim enlarged the world three times. This shows that after the defeat, the Devs had vacated the original habitation of Arjika, which would have been taken over by the Asurs. The Devs would have moved to the neighbouring areas like the Asurs had done under Val and Shushna. Yim seems to have driven them away farther and farther three times, perhaps till they were totally cleared of Arjika and did not have access to the water of the river flowing there, which has been called Ardvi Sura Anahita in the *Avesta* and Parushni in the *Veds*. Once they had no access to water, it would have been impossible for the Devs to survive in Arjika. This would have been the occasion when the Devs left this homeland forever, Arjika, called Airyana Vaego in the *Avesta*. The Asurs continued to stay on till their turn came to leave. Hereafter, whatever were their places of stay were not totally abandoned by the entire tribe. Some branches did migrate in different directions. Some lost contact with the rest and with the homeland, but the place was never again totally abandoned by the entire tribe. Arjika or Airyana Vaego was fondly remembered by both sides for very long, but contact with the place was totally snapped.

In the *Veds* there are some Richas which show that the Devs had left Arjika in distress and did not know where to go. They seem to have wandered around for some time, before they found their next homeland. These passages are stated here.

1. The Ashmanvati flows along; be alert, rise up, cross over, my friends; here let us leave those who are unhappy, so that we may cross over to auspicious sacrificial viands.

(*Rig Ved.* M-10, S-53, R-8)

2. May the gods help and favour us out of the place whence Vishnu strode. Over the back and ridge of earth.

(*Saam Ved.* Part II, Book VIII, Chapter II)

3. We have wandered, gods, into a desert where there is no track of cattle; the vast extant earth has become the protectress of murderers, direct us, Brahaspati, in our search for cattle, show the path, Indra, to your votary being they astray.

(*Rig Ved.* M-6, S-47, R-20)

The second passage leaves no element of doubt about the place that the Devs were fleeing from. It is where Vishnu had placed his three steps, the land taken over by Manu from Val. Even for getting out of that place help and favour of the gods has been sought, an indication of the dangers being faced. The first Richa speaks of the Ashmanvati river. Arjika, as would soon emerge, had seven streams flowing. Though distributaries of the same river, it appears that the Aryans had a name for each of these streams. Ashmanvati seems to be the westernmost stream. With the crossing of this, the Devs would have been left with no natural barrier in fleeing. Evidently, they were fleeing in panic. Whosoever had been able to get away, fled without waiting for the rest to join. The third Richa shows them lost. Their cattle seem to have been seized by the Asurs and they were not able to catch new ones in the wilderness, because they had reached a place where there were no pastures. The mention of the earth becoming the protectress of murderers is a reference to Arjika which had been left behind. Murderers is a reference to Asurs, who had taken it over. As they are being called murderers at this juncture, it shows that not only in the war, but also on the three occasions when Yim drove the Devs farther away, killings were involved. He was successful in creating conditions wherein the Devs had no option but to flee for their lives, even if they did not know where to go.

It appears that after defeating the Kavi of the Devs, ending the rule of Manu's dynasty and driving the Devs out of Arjika, Yim got converted to the religion of the Devs and so became a Dev. This seems to have happened after a long time, because the Devs, who had fled Arjika do not seem to have come back, despite Yim becoming Yam. It seems that they had reached their new homeland by then, which was far away and had a more comfortable winter. Yim was converted by Dahak. In the *Avesta*, there is a reference which supports the image of Dadhich as a Rishi and preacher of the religion of the Devs. In the Afrin Paighambar Zartust Yast, where Zoroaster is blessing Vistasp, apart from several other things, he blesses him saying, 'Mayest thou be instructed with a thousand senses, like Azi Dahak, of the evil law.' Passages from the Zoroastrian scriptures, which show that Yim was converted, are stated here.

1. That clove unto the bright Yim, the good shepherd, while he ruled over the seven Karshvares, over the Daevas and men. He who took from the Daevas both riches and welfare. In whose reign there was neither old age nor death, nor envy made by the Daevas; in the times before his lie, before he began to have delight in words of falsehood and untruth. But when he began to find delight in words of falsehood and untruth, the Glory was seen to flee away from him in the shape of a bird. When his Glory had disappeared, then the great Yim Khshaeta, the good shepherd, trembled and was in sorrow before his foes.

    (Zamyad Yast VII)

2. The Evil Spirit flung a dart, and so did Akem-Mono and Aeshma of the wounding spear, and Azi Dahak and Spityura, he who sawed Yim in twain.

    Then came forward Atar, the son of Ahur Mazda, thinking thus in his heart, 'I want to seize that Glory that cannot be forcibly seized, but Azi Dahak, the three-mouthed, he of the evil law, rushed on his back thinking of extinguishing it.

    (Zamyad Yast VIII)

3. Of these wretched beings Yim, Vivanghusha was famed to be. He

eeling that he is God and there is no other God. His going away from religion is, therefore, shown to be not due to any external influence of a preacher, but because of his own arrogance. Once astray, the glory of God left him and made him vulnerable to attack. Zuhak has been portrayed as a capable Arab chieftain, who was accepted by the Persian army as their king. On being crowned as king of Iran, he removed Jamshed and with a saw divided him in two.

The *Veds* mention no achievements of Yam. This could be because, except for being converted to their religion at a later stage, all he did was to kill, harass and uproot the Devs from Arjika, which was always remembered by them as a very dear homeland. It will always remain a mystery, how Yam got deified in the *Veds*. Though as a god of death and as a king of the dead forefathers, yet to have received the honour of being a divinity from the very Devs who had suffered at his hands, would remain a puzzle difficult to unravel. These Richas from the *Rig Ved* show that he was deified in the Vedic period itself.

1. Yam, the chief (of all) knows our well-being, this pasture no one can take from us. By the roads by which our forefathers have gone, all who are born (proceed) along the paths they have made for themselves.

   (*Rig Ved*. M-10, S-14, R-2)

2. Yam, who are associated with the Angiras Pitrs, sit down at this sacrifice, many the prayers recited by the priests bring you hither, be exhilarated, Sovereign (Yam), by this oblation.

   (*Rig Ved*. M-10, S-14, R-4)

3. Depart, depart, by the former paths by which our forefathers have departed. There shall you behold the two monarchs Yam and the divine Varun, rejoicing in the Svadha.

4. Be united with the Pitrs, with Yam and with the fulfilment of your wishes in the highest heaven, discarding iniquity, return to your abode, and unite yourself to a luminous body.

   (*Rig Ved*. M-10, S-14, R-7 and 8)

5. Pass by a secure path beyond the two spotted four-eyed dogs, the progeny of Sarama, and join the wise Pitrs who rejoice joyfully with Yam.

who, desiring to content our men, was eating kine's flesh in its pieces. But from (such as) these, O Ahur Mazda, in Thy discerning discrimination, am I (to be seen as distinct).

(The Gathas. Yasna XXXII)

4. On the nature of the ape and bear they say, that Yim, when reason departed from him, for fear of the demons took a demoness as wife and gave Yimak, who was his sister, to a demon as wife; and from them have originated the tailed ape and bear and other species of degeneracy.

(Bundahis. Chapter XXIII)

5. One is this, that Yim the splendid, the son of Vivangha, who in his worldly career was most prosperous in worldly affairs, when he was deceived by the fiend and was thereby made eager for supreme sovereignty instead of the service of Auharmazd. And about his administration of the creatures it is said he himself became cut away from radiant glory by the fiendishness and their cause of wandering is the demon and mankind perishes in that wandering from plain and hill side.

(Dadistan-i Dinik. Chapter XXXIX)

These passages show that Yim was converted to the Dev religion. The first says that Glory was with him till the time before his lie, before he began to have delight in words of falsehood and untruth, when he began to find delight in words of falsehood, Glory fled away from him and Yim was in sorrow before his foes. The second says that Azi Dahak sawed Yim in twain, an indication that Yim was converted by Azi Dahak. Azi would be Ahi of the *Veds*, meaning a serpent. The third passage counts Yim amongst the wretched beings, as he left the law of Ahur Mazda. The fourth says that after a time, reason departed from Yim and he married a demoness and gave his sister Yimak in marriage to a demon. Demon here means Dev. The fifth passage states, that Yim at a certain stage, after a long and glorious career as a king, was deceived by the fiend and was no longer in the service of Auharmazd. This leaves no scope for doubt that Dadhich, who is Dahak in the *Avesta*, had converted Yim. The Zoroastrian scriptures at certain places, speak of the reign of Dahak after Yim. This does not seem to be true, because if Dadhich had become a Kavi after Yim, the *Veds* would have mentioned it. In all likelihood, Yim, after being converted, was ruling as per the advice of Dahak, because of which that part of Yim's reign has been mentioned as the reign of Dahak. This, however, seems to have become a popular tale, because Firdausi treats Dahak as a regular ruler and states that he, after defeating Yim, sawed him into two and then ruled for nine hundred and ninety-nine years. Extracts from the *Shahnama* on Dahak are mentioned here.

When passed away this monarch of renown,
His son assumed his father's place and crown.
Worthy, his son Jamshed embraced the part,
He sat upon his father's glorious throne.
The world knew never such enquiring king.
From trouble and all ill were they preserved,
And them the Divs with girded loins served.
Jamshed as Kai would on his throne recline,
Within his hand a royal bowl of wine.
Suddenly he looked upon his mighty throne,
And saw himself on earth the only one.
From faith in God then changing in his mood,
He from his God turned in ingratitude.
To those great men of many years he cried,
'None in the world I know myself beside.
Like me none possessed the royal throne.
And this that I have done as ye know all,
Ye should me now the world's Creator call.'
God's light forsook him when these words were said.
From the Creator when he turned in pride,
He found defeat, and fortune left his side.
There was a man once in those days of old,
This pious man an only son possessed,
Who of affection with no share was blessed.
His name Zuhak, and most ambitious he,

Light-headed, brave and fearless could be.
Now it so happened Iblis on a day,
Came him to visit in a friendly way,
The chief's heart from the right path led astray,
The youth his ears bent to his words that day.
There rose on this from all Iran a shout,
On all sides war and tumult raged about,
The white and brilliant day to darkness turned,
And men of Jamshed the connection spurned.
Armies collected, all prepared for war,
The love of Jamshed from all hearts afar.
In Iran suddenly arose a force,
Directing towards Arab's land its course,
For they had heard there was a chieftain there,
Full of all dread, a dragon's form that bare.

And Iran's horsemen, searching for a king,
Towards Zuhak their face together bring.
With blessings him their monarch they proclaimed,
And of the Persian land the ruler named.
Towards the throne of Jamshed turned their face.
And when from Jamshed fortune turned away,
Him did the new king quickly bring to bay.
And when at last Zuhak him brought to bay,
He granted him to live no long delay,
But with a saw divided him in two.

The folklore compiled by Firdausi has its elements of facts as well as distortions. It correctly remembers that Jamshed, who is Yim Khshaeta of the *Avesta*, was an illustrious king who ruled for a very long time. After a stage he left the ways of the religion and Dahak, who has become Zuhak now, was responsible for his end. The distortions are such that the story has become almost unrecognizable. Jamshed has been made the son of Tehmuras, who is Takma Urupa in the *Avesta* and Val in the *Veds*. He is shown to have succeeded him to the throne and ruled for very long, keeping the Divs in servitude, till he started

6.   Entrust him, O king to your two dogs, which are your protectors,
     Yam, the four-eyed guardians of the roads, renowned by men, and
     grant him prosperity and health.

                              (*Rig Ved*. M-10, S-14, R-10 and 11)

Evidently, Varun was the god of death earlier, as can be seen from the
third Richa here and also elsewhere in the *Veds*. He was the upholder of
truth and virtue, keeping an account of what a person did in his lifetime,
based on which he delivered his judgment, the sovereign of the realm
of the dead. This Richa shows that a second king had been added and
this was Yam. In the course of time, Varun receded into the background
and faded away from this role and only Yam has remained as the god
of death and as the sole sovereign of the realm of the dead. The *Veds*
provide no clue to Yam's good fortune. He remains a much respected
figure in the *Avesta* and has also been made a god in the *Veds*. If the
events and their sequence are not understood, he would be mistaken to
be a deity of the times before the split took place, who has survived in
the scriptures of both. If his conversion to the religion of the Devs was
so important that it could erase everything else that he did and pave the
way for him to be elevated to the status of a divinity, it is again surprising
that Dadhich, who was the person responsible for it, has been passed
over in just a few Richas. The *Avesta* and later Zoroastrian scriptures
have given far more importance to Dahak than the *Veds*. He emerges
as the most hated person of his times, only after Manu, who, as Angra
Mainyu is evil incarnate. In later times when the worst sinners have
been counted, he is one of the three in the company of Arjasp, who
killed Zoroaster and Alexander, who destroyed the Persian kingdom
which was the mainstay of Zoroastrian religion and burnt the library
which stored all the scriptures. This has been stated here.

> 'Of these nine thousand years' support which during its
> beginning produced Dahak of evil religion, Frasiyav of Tur
> and Alexander the Ruman, the period of a thousand years of
> those leather-belted demons with dishevelled hair is a more
> than moderate reign to produce.'
>
>   (Bahman Yast. Chapter III)

Dadhich was only a Rishi and a preacher. He was not a warrior and fought no war, killed nobody but got killed himself. Yet the Zoroastrian scriptures have equated him in evil with persons like Alexander and Arjasp, who has been named Frasiyav in later literature. This seems to be because of the impact he had on the fortunes of the Asurs at Arjika. The Asurs had lost Arjika to the Devs in the times of Val. They were living in the neighbourhood in make-shift dwellings and made several unsuccessful attempts to dislodge the Devs under Val's grandson Shushna. After Shushna had been killed, Yim, who was simply a shepherd with no claim to royalty, emerged as their leader. He was able to consolidate his position and give a fight to the Devs and succeeded in defeating them. Arjika was taken back by the Asurs. The Devs lived in the neighbouring areas in the same manner as the Asurs had, in moveable 'Purs'. Yim with the earlier experience realized that the Devs staying in the vicinity of Arjika would make attempts to take it back, just as the Asurs had done. In such a struggle, whenever the Asurs were weak and a capable leader emerged on the other side, they would be defeated. The best guarantee against it would be to drive the Devs away while they were weak. With this strategy Yim took up a campaign to drive them away and in three attempts pushed them out of the basin of the river, which was the lifeline. Being deprived of all means of livelihood in the neighbourhood of Arjika, the Devs left the place. Everything looked good for the Asurs. It seemed that the good old days had returned and they were comfortable in their homeland, with the enemy not even in sight and no possibility of his returning, when suddenly, this single soul comes up. He was no warrior, had no weapons, except for his wisdom and intellectual capabilities. He succeeded in converting Yim, the very person who had accomplished all this for them. Yim was now guided in his rule by the person of the evil religion, Dahak. After Yim was dead, his successor killed Dahak. Again the conversion of Yim turned out to be only a small interruption. Things were the same now as Thraetaona, who is Shambar in the *Veds*, after killing Dahak, ruled for forty long years. The Asurs in Arjika were without anyone to create problems for them. But Dahak was a preacher. It seems that he was a very respected preacher and had a lot of following. In such a situation, a dead Dahak proved to be as deadly, if not more, than the living. His followers decided to avenge his death. Indra, with the bones of Dadhich, comes to war. This had devastating consequences for the Asurs. They not only lost, but were uprooted completely from the place and, like the Devs, were compelled to leave Arjika for good.

The impact of Dahak on the fortunes of the Asurs being decisive, he occupies a very important place in the literature of the Zoroastrians. On the other hand, the fortunes of the Devs seem to have remained unaffected by his achievements. The Devs had left Arjika much before Dahak converted Yim. By the time Yim was favourably disposed, they had already gone far away and had more or less settled comfortably in their new homeland. Their getting information of Yim's conversion did not result in their going back, which would have involved a long, difficult and hazardous journey. It is also possible that they may not have been sure of the future to take the risk of going back. In such a situation, Yim's conversion to their religion remained only a matter of theoretical interest to the Devs. To an extent, they were right, as the course of events showed that Yim's conversion did not result in the conversion of the Asurs. They remained with their religion and with the death of Yim his successor beheaded Dahak and threw his head in the Sharyanavat lake.

The second historical event linked to Dadhich, of the Asurs being defeated in the war of revenge, would have happened after another half a century, because Shambar ruled for forty years. On this occasion, Arjika was completely abandoned by the Asurs and was open to the Devs to come back and occupy, without the fear of being harassed by them. The Devs did not opt to do so shows that by then, which was about eighty years later, they were well-settled and comfortable in their new homeland. Being south of their earlier homeland, this new place would have had a less severe winter. For the Devs, in such a situation, the conversion of Yim to their faith and the later defeat of the Asurs and their annihilation from Arjika was only a matter of academic interest. It made them happy, but did not directly change their fortunes.

The story of Dahak and his getting killed, is unfolded by the *Avesta* and subsequent Zoroastrian scriptures in these passages.

1.   To her did Thraetaona, the heir of the valiant Athwya clan, offer up a sacrifice. He begged of her a boon saying, 'Grant me this, O Ardvi Sura Anahita! That I may overcome Azi Dahak, that most powerful, fiendish Drug, the strongest Drug that Angra Mainyu created against the material world; and that I may deliver his two wives, Savanghavak and Erenavak.'

(Aban Yast IX)

2.   Then Thraetaona seized that Glory, he, the heir of the valiant Athwya clan; who smote Ahi Dahak, that most powerful, fiendish Drug, that demon, baleful to the world, the strongest Drug that Angra Mainyu created against the material world.

(Zamyad Yast VII)

3.   Who was the second man, O Hom, who prepared thee for the corporeal world? What gain did he acquire? Thereupon gave Hom answer, 'Athwya was the second who prepared me. This gain did he acquire, that to him a son was born, Thraetaona, who smote the dragon Dahak, a lie-demon of the Daevas, whom Angra Mainyu made to slay the homes of Asha.'

(Yasna IX)

4.   The twentieth Fargard, Vahu-Khshathrem, is about the sovereignty which Dahak exercised over the earth of seven regions. About Dahak's enquiry of the members of the assembly, regarding the reason of the affliction, after the cutting up of Yim and the accession of Dahak, and the people saying in reply to Dahak, that Yim had kept away want and destitution from the world.

And Audak, who made Yim the splendid and rich in flocks— who was struck down by you through violent assault—produced want and destitution, and the sacrificer of Wrath the wounding assailant, and the seven arch-demons. About the smiting by Fredun, for the sake of killing Dahak. The striking of his club upon the nape of his neck, the heart, and even the skull, and Dahak not dying from that beating. Then smiting him with a sword, and the formation of noxious creatures of many kinds, from the body of Dahak. The exclamation of Auharmazd to Fredun thus, 'Thou shouldst not cut him who is Dahak, because if thou shouldst cut him, Dahak would be making this earth full of serpents,' with the mode of binding him with awful fetters, in the most grievous punishment of confinement. This too, that when Azi Dahak was bound, the report of the same proceeded thus through all the regions, which are seven, that down-stricken is Azi Dahak, but he who smote him is Fredun. This too, that though he who smote him were his brother, or descendant or kinsman, it did not seem to them as that which is grievous.

(Dinkard. Book IX. Sudkar Nask)

These passages have called Thraetaona to be of the Athwya clan, which shows he was an Atharwan and this is what could be meant of what has been understood to be the killing of Dadhich in the *Veds* where Atharwan is reported to have been killed by Indra. The first passage is repeated at several places in the *Avesta*, with Thraetaona seeking the same boon from different divinities. In this, apart from smiting Dahak, mention is made of delivering his two wives Savanghavak and Erenavak. Their mention is apparently because they were Asur women married to a Dev. Firdausi tells us that they were Yim's sisters. In his version they are named Shehr-i-Naz and Arnavaz. In the Asur traditions, Yim marrying his sisters to Dahak would have been very objectionable. The fourth passage from the Dinkard shows that Dahak and Thraetaona were of the same clan. They were related to each other and were descendants of the same ancestor. It also shows that the legends that grew around Dahak said that he was not killed by Thraetaona, but was bound with awful fetters. This is a reflection of the hatred for Dahak, because people seem to have wanted to believe that even death could not relieve him of pain.

After Dahak's death comes the revenge. Thraetaona is Shambar in the *Veds*, whose ninety-nine cities have been reported at several places as destroyed by Indra. The persons for whom this is reported in the *Veds* to have been done, are Divodas and his son Sudas. The relevant extract about these wars between Shambar and Divodas and later with his son Sudas from the *Veds* are stated here.

1. You have shaken the summit of the spacious heaven, you have slain Shambar by your resolute self; you have hurled with exulting and determined mind the sharp and bright-rayed thunderbolt against the assembled Asurs.

    (*Rig Ved*. M-1, S-54, R-4)

2. Indra, wielder of the thunderbolt, warring on behalf of Purukutsa, you did overturn the seven cities, you did cut off for Sudas wealth of Asurs, as if (it was a tuft) of sacred grass, and did give it to him, O king, ever satiating you (with oblations).

    (*Rig Ved*. M-1, S-63, R-7)

3. With those aids by which you defended the mighty and hospitable Divodas, (when having undertaken) the death of Shambar, he hid himself in the water; by which you protected Trasadasyu in war; with them, Ashwins come willingly hither.

    (*Rig Ved*. M-1, S-112, R-14)

4. For Puru, the giver of offerings, for the mighty Divodas you Indra the dancer (with delight in battle), have destroyed ninety cities, dancer, you have destroyed them with (your thunderbolt), for (the sake of) the giver of offerings. For (the sake of) Atithigva the fierce (Indra) hurled Shambar from off the mountain bestowing (upon the prince) immense treasure, (acquired) by (his) prowess; all kinds of wealth (acquired) by (his) prowess.

5. Indra the manifold protector in battles defends his Arya worshipper in all conflicts; in conflicts that confer heaven. He punished for (the benefit of) the descendants of Manu the neglecters of the religious rites. He tore off the black skin (of the aggressors) as if burning (with flame). He consumes the malignant. He utterly consumes him who delights in cruelty.

    (*Rig Ved*. M-1, S-130, R-7 and 8)

6. You have humbled the people, suing for pardon when you have destroyed the seven new cities; you the irreproachable have dispersed the flowing waters; you have destroyed Vritra for the sake of the youthful Purukutsa.

    (*Rig Ved*. M-1, S-174, R-2)

7. He, who discovered Shambar dwelling in the mountains for forty

years; who slew the Ahi, growing in strength, and the sleeping son of Danu; he, men, is Indra.

(Rig Ved. M-2, S-12, R-11)

8. Exhilarated (by the Som beverage) I have destroyed the ninety and nine cities of Shambar, the hundredth I gave to be occupied by Divodas when I protected him, Atithigva at his sacrifice.

(Rig Ved. M-4, S-26, R-3)

9. You have slain the Das Shambar, the son of Kulitar hurling him from off the huge mountain.

(Rig Ved. M-4, S-30, R-14)

10. Indra has overturned a hundred stone-built cities for Divodas, the donor of oblations.

(Rig Ved. M-4, S-30, R-20)

11. Indra, who are the subduer (of foes), you have achieved a glorious (deed), inasmuch as you have, hero scattered the hundreds and thousands (of the hosts of Shambar), have slain the Das Shambar (when issuing) from the mountain and have protected Divodas with marvellous protections.

(Rig Ved. M-6, S-26, R-5)

12. You have destroyed the hundred impregnable cities of the Dasyu Shambar, when sagacious Indra, you, who are brought by the libation, have bestowed in your liberality riches upon Divodas presenting to you libation, and upon Bharadvaj hymning your praise.

(Rig Ved. M-6, S-31, R-4)

13. Prastak has given to your worshipper, Indra, ten purses of gold, and ten horses and we have accepted this treasure from Divodas, the spoil won by Atithigva from Shambar.

14. I have received ten horses, ten purses, clothes and ample food and ten lumps of gold from Divodas.

(Rig Ved. M-6, S 47, R-22 and 23)

15. She gave to the donor of oblations, Vadhryashwa, a son Divodas endowed with speed, and acquitting the debt. She who destroyed the churlish niggard (thinking) only of himself, such are your great bounties, Saraswati.

(Rig Ved. M-6, S-61, R-1)

16. The adorable Indra made the well-known deep waters fordable for Sudas and converted the vehement awakening imprecation of the sacrificer into the calumniation of the rivers.

17. Turvash, who was preceding, diligent in sacrifice (went) for wealth; but like fishes restricted (to the element of water), the Bhrigus and Druhyus, quickly assailed them. Of these two everywhere going the friend (Indra) rescued his friend (Sudas).

(*Rig Ved.* M-7, S-18, R-5 and 6)

18. The waters followed their regular course to the Parushni, nor (wandered) beyond it; the quick courser (of the king) came to the accessible places and Indra made the idly talking enemies, with their numerous progeny, subject among men (to Sudas).

(*Rig Ved.* M-7, S-18, R- 9)

19. The hero Indra created the Maruts (for the assistance of the Raja) who, ambitious of fame, slew one and twenty of the men on the two banks (of the Parushni), as a well-looking priest lops the sacred grass in the chamber of sacrifice.

20. You the bearer of the thunderbolt didst drown Shrut, Kavash, Vridh and afterwards, Druhyu in the waters; for they Indra, who are devoted to you and glorify you, preferring your friendship, enjoy it.

21. Indra in his might quickly demolished all their strongholds and their seven cities, he has given the dwelling of the son of Anu to Tritsu; may we (by propitiating Indra) conquer in battle, the ill-speaking man.

22. The warriors of the Anus and Druhyus, intended (to carry off the) cattle (hostile) to the pious (Sudas) perished to the number of sixty-six thousand six hundred and sixty; such are the glorious acts of Indra.

23. These hostile Tritsus, ignorantly contending with Indra, fled, routed as rapidly as rivers on a downward course, and being discomfited, abandoned all their possessions to Sudas.

24. Indra has scattered over the earth the hostile rival of the hero (Sudas), the senior of Indra, the appropriator of oblations Indra has baffled the wrath of the wrathful enemy, and the (foe) advancing on the way (against Sudas) has taken the path of flight.

25. Indra has effected a valuable (donation) by a pauper; he has slain an old lion by a goat; he has cut the angles of the sacrificial post with a needle; he has given all the spoils (of the enemy) to Sudas.

26. Your numerous enemies, Indra had been reduced to subjection. Effect at some time or other subjugation of the turbulent Bhed, who holds men praising you as guilty of wickedness. Hurl Indra your sharp thunderbolt against him.

(Rig Ved. M-7, S-18, R-11 to 18)

27. In the same manner was he (Sudas) enabled by them easily to cross the Sindhu river, in the same manner, through them he slew his foe, so in like manner, Vashisht, through your prayers, did Indra defend Sudas in the war of ten kings.

(Rig Ved. M-7, S-33, R-3)

28. Suffering from thirst, soliciting (water), supported (by the Tritsus) in the war with the ten kings (Vashisht), made Indra radiant as the sun; Indra heard (the praises) of Vashisht glorifying him and bestowed a spacious region on the Tritsus.

(Rig Ved. M-7, S-33, R-5)

29. Indra and Varun, you protected Sudas, overwhelming the yet unassailed Bhed with your fatal weapons, hear the prayers of these Tritsus in time of battle, so that my ministration may have borne them fruit.

(Rig Ved. M-7, S-83, R-4)

30. Both (Sudas and Tritsus) call upon you two (Indra and Varun) in combat for the acquirement of wealth, when you defend Sudas, together with the Tritsus when attacked by the ten kings.

31. The ten confederated irreligious Rajas did not prevail Indra and Varun, against Sudas; the praise of the leaders (of rites), the officers of sacrificial food, was fruitful; the gods were present at their sacrifice.

32. You gave vigour, Indra and Varun, to Sudas when surrounded on all sides by the ten Rajas (in the country) where the pious Tritsus, walking in whiteness and wearing braided hair, worshipped with oblations and praise.

(Rig Ved. M-7, S-83, R-6 to 8)

33. Agni of Divodas, comes forth like Indra in his might. Rapidly has he moved along his mother earth; he stands in high heaven's dwelling-place.

(*Saam Ved.* Part II, Book VII, Chapter I)

34. O people! Lord Indra is he who detected the Asur Shambar who had remained concealed within the cave of a mountain for forty years and further who killed the Ahi, growing in strength, the sleeping son of Danu.

(*Atharv Ved.* Kand 20, Sukt-34, Richa-11)

35. O Lord Indra! You had churned the men by participating in the war of the Ten Kings; by reason of this valour you revealed, you became honourable to all. You had appeared in the company of the Yaksh.

(*Atharv Ved.* Kand 20, Sukt-128, Richa-12)

After the war between Indra and Vritra, this has received the attention of the *Veds* the most. The last Richa gives an idea of the identity of Divodas and his son Sudas. It says that Indra had appeared in the company of the Yaksh. Divodas and Sudas were evidently Yakshs. In Indian mythology, Yakshs are demi-gods, portrayed as powerful entities, friends of the Devs. They seem to be an Aryan tribe, which was different from that of the Devs and Asurs. Unlike the Panis, who were the immediate neighbours and were sharing the same homeland, the Yakshs appear to be living at a distance. As they took up the issue of the killing of Dadhich and waged a war of revenge against the Asurs, evidently they were followers of the religion of the Devs and held Dadhich in high esteem. Land, water, cattle or wealth was not the cause of their aggression, as they made no attempt to occupy the land after dislodging the Asurs. Cattle and other wealth coming as spoils of war seem to be incidental. The cause of attack was revenge and revenge alone. The bones of Dadhich were the only issue.

Apart from the Yakshs, some Richas show that the Tritsu were fighting alongside. In the twenty-first Richa, it is stated, that Indra gave the dwelling of the son of Anu to Tritsu. The twenty-eighth Richa, too, says something similar, that he gave a spacious region to the Tritsus. The thirtieth Richa speaks of two entities fighting from the side of the Yakshs, Sudas and the Tritsus. It further says that Indra defended Sudas together with the Tritsus when attacked by the ten kings. On the other hand, the twenty-third Richa places the Tritsus on the side of the Asurs. It says that those hostile Tritsus ignorantly contending with Indra were routed and fled, abandoning all their possessions to Sudas. Apparently, Tritsu was a clans of this Aryan group. As the divide went through clans and families, some Tritsus were Asurs, while some were Devs, because of which we find mention of them on both sides of the combat. Though the Devs had left Arjika, when they were driven away by Yim, it appears, some of them from the Tritsu clan got separated from the main body. They seem to have moved to the Yaksh country and were preaching there and came along to avenge the killing of Dadhich. The word Tritsu originates from Trita, which would make it the same clan to which Manu and Yam belonged. Trita appears to be an earlier forefather, the common progenitor of the clan.

The relationship of Manu with these Tritsus is hinted in some of the Richas where some names have been mentioned. The second Richas says that Indra was warring on behalf of Purukutsa, when he overturned the seven cities. This evidently is the name of Kutsa's son, the grandson of Ushana. Kutsa, after being defeated by Yim had moved away to become a preacher. This shows that he had moved to the Yaksh territory and was preaching there. The third Richa has the name Trasadasyu, which appears to be a reference to Purukutsa only. The fourth Richa calls him Puru and says that Indra destroyed the ninety-nine cities of Shambar for him and Divodas. The eighth Richa says that while the ninety-nine cities were destroyed, one was given to Divodas to occupy. Divodas and the Yakshs had no interest in the land in Arjika. They had not come to war with the Asurs to take away their land for themselves, because they were already settled comfortably in their home territory and did not need to do so. It appears, that after Shambar had been defeated by Divodas, in the first war that took place on this occasion, the lands in Arjika were given to the Tritsus to occupy.

It seems that these Tritsus, living with the Yakshs were all along nurturing the desire to take back Arjika from the Asurs. Though the *Veds* have given the credit of the destruction of the ninety-nine cities of Shambar, to the bones of Dadhich, these Tritsus appear to have played a very important role in instigating the Yakshs for the war. As some of them were preachers, they could have used the killing of Dadhich to show the evil disposition of the Asurs. By saying that the Tritsus were also fighting, only some credit for the victory is being claimed. They could not have been of any consequence in the actual engagement, which would have been won by the Yakshs. After having their dwellings ravaged in the next war of this sequence of the Dev Asur Sangram, these Tritsus would have realized the non-viability of reviving Arjika and would have left it to join the main body of the Dev migration carrying the stories of these wars for which they became a part of the *Veds*, because otherwise, the Devs had gone so far away that it would not have been possible for them to know what had happened in their abandoned homeland almost a century later.

So far as the wars are concerned, the first war was led by Divodas and was an attack on the Asur territory. The first Richa states that the summit of the spacious heaven has been shaken. This reference to heaven is to Arjika. The Richa is of a later period, by when Arjika and heaven had been fused into one. This is confirmed by the fifth Richa, which says that Indra defends his Arya worshipper in all conflicts, in conflicts that confer heaven. The attack that was launched by Divodas was forty years after Shambar had become the Kavi. This is revealed by the seventh Richa, which says that Indra discovered Shambar dwelling in the mountains for forty years. This is confirmed by the thirty-fourth Richa, which states that Shambar had remained concealed in the cave of a mountain for forty years and was detected by Indra.

The third Richa gives an account of the attack. It says that Divodas, when he had undertaken to kill Shambar, hid himself in water. The war between Indra and Vritra has given the information that Arjika had a river in which the body of Vritra had been thrown. Divodas with his army seems to have reached there and kept his movements concealed to take the enemy by surprise. The fourth Richa says that Indra destroyed the ninety cities of the Asurs and hurled Shambar down from the mountain. It shows that the main habitation in Arjika, where the Kavi lived, was on a hill feature. The number ninety and at some places, ninety-nine appear to mean all. The real number appears to be seven. This is reflected from the second Richa, which states that Indra overturned the seven cities of Asurs on behalf of Sudas. This is confirmed by the twenty first Richa, which states, that Indra demolished all their strongholds and their seven cities. The information available from the *Avesta* also gives credence to this being the actual number of the habitations in Arjika, as it repeatedly speaks of the 'seven Karshvare'. The word 'Karshvare' could have emerged from the Sanskrit word 'Kshetra,' which means an area. As it would emerge soon, these seven Karshvares were seven flat lands in the delta of a river and so were islands. Each of these islands seems to have had a habitation, which has been called a 'Pur' in the *Veds*. The tenth Richa speaks of the stone-built cities of Shambar. This is only making a distinction between the habitations having permanent dwellings and make-shift camps. Both sides had been rendered homeless at different times. In such a situation both sides would have lived in temporary structures or camps, which have found mention as 'moveable Purs'. The mention of stone-built cities in such a situation is a reference to regular houses which were of stone.

Kulitar has been named as the father of Shambar in the ninth Richa. No mention of him is found elsewhere. The eleventh Richa shows that Shambar was on an elevated feature, when the war began. This shows that Divodas had approached the main habitation in Arjika, where the Kavi lived and the war took place close to it. This would have given Shambar an advantage of the topography, as Divodas was approaching uphill, which in terms of military tactics is a very difficult attack. No wonder, the twelfth Richa calls it an impregnable city. Shambar appears to have fled after the defeat and does not seem to have been killed in this war, though some Richas do say so. Varchin appears as the name of an important Asur warrior killed. The thirty-third Richa is significant. It states, that Agni of Divodas, comes forth like Indra in his might. It has rapidly moved along its mother, the earth and stands in high heaven's dwelling-place. It shows that Divodas burnt all the habitations of the Asurs. Agni, the fire, has destroyed everything, just like Indra destroys the enemies with his might. It reached even the highest habitation, where the Kavi lived and has burnt everything there too, standing in the high heaven's dwelling-place. The dwelling of the Kavi Shambar appears to have been burnt down, along with all the rest.

Having defeated the Asurs and destroyed their habitations, Divodas seems to have given Arjika over to the Tritsus, led by Purukutsa and extended his protection to them. He also performed a sacrifice, either at Arjika itself or back in his homeland. The location is not clear, but the priests were Bharadwajs, who received as gifts the spoils of war from Divodas, who is also called Atithigva. The thirteenth and fourteenth Richas speak of the gifts, the priests received on this occasion. The fifteenth Richa gives the name of the father of Divodas as Vadhryashwa.

The Asurs after this defeat at the hands of Divodas remained in the vicinity of Arjika, just as they had done after the defeat of Vritra. A small hamlet of the limited Devs, belonging to the Tritsu clan, occupied the lands. These Tritsus, though under the protection of the Yakshs seem to have been scared of the Asurs. Shambar had grown old by then and Bhed appears as the name of the Asur, who was in control, though the old Kavi Shambar, remained king. The twenty-sixth Richa shows the Devs praying for the subjugation of Bhed, as he held the worshipper of Indra to be wicked. In the twenty-ninth Richa, Bhed is reported killed by Sudas, which would have happened in the second war that was fought in this sequence.

The second war was fought after an interval. By then Divodas appears to have died to be succeeded by his son Sudas. On the other side Shambar was old. This appears to have been an attempt on the part of the Asurs to take back the lost territory in alliance with all possible Kavis that were favourably disposed towards them. The *Veds* have reported this as a confederation of ten kings fighting Sudas. The twenty-seventh Richa says that Indra defended Sudas in the war of ten kings. The same Richa in the first part states, that Sudas was enabled to easily cross the Sindhu river. Evidently, this is a Richa of a later period, when the Aryans had come to India. The story was remembered and it was remembered that there was a river which was crossed before the attack, but the identity of the river had been lost. As a result, whichever river was known has been named. The thirtieth Richa and a few after that repeat that ten kings attacked Sudas.

The Devs seem to have abandoned Arjika and taken shelter with the Yakshs before this war. This is reflected from the seventeenth Richa, wherein the Devs appear to be doing their bit in the war. It shows Turvash advancing, but is restricted in the zone with water, by the enemies. The Bhrigus and the Druhyus have come to his assistance and kept the enemies away. The Asurs seem to have crossed the Parushni river and the war has been fought on its banks. Sudas seems to have come after them and also crossed Parushni. The sixteenth Richa says that Indra made the deep waters fordable for Sudas. The eighteenth Richa repeats the same. It says that the waters flowed on their regular course in the Parushni, but his horse came quickly to the place that was accessible. The war was fought on the eastern bank of the Parushni, after the same had been crossed by both sides. This appears to be a cavalry attack by Sudas, perhaps the first in the world to be recorded, as the earlier fights of Manu etc. were infantry combats. The nineteenth Richa states that Sudas killed twenty-one Asurs on the two banks of the Parushni. The twentieth Richa shows that Shrut, Kavash, Vridh and Druhyu got drowned in the river, apparently while attempting to run away on being defeated. The twenty-second Richa gives the names of the clans to which the main warriors from the side of the Asurs belonged. They have been called the Anus and the Druhyus. The twenty-fifth Richa speaks of the killing of Shambar again. Here Shambar has been called an old lion and Sudas a goat, reflecting the age of the two. Shambar was old by then, while Sudas had just begun his career. It also shows, that Shambar was a very brave man because even his adversaries have called him a lion. Shambar being old, Bhed was the main leader, who too got killed in this war.

Since the war has been fought in Arjika, where the Asurs reached first after crossing the Parushni river and Sudas followed with his cavalry, evidently the Asurs did not attack Sudas. They collected their forces and with the ten kings moved to occupy Arjika. The few Devs from the Tritsus, who were in occupation of the place would have abandoned it to wait for the Yakshs to come, as they were assured of protection. Sudas has crossed the Parushni river to fight the war, despite the Asurs using this river as a defence feature. In terms of war strategy again the Asurs were defending their position, while Sudas was attacking. His task would have been all the more difficult because a river was in between, which the Asurs defended to prevent him from crossing. This is evident from the nineteenth Richa, which says that Sudas killed Asurs on both side of the river and other Richas, where Asurs have been stated to have been drowned.

After the defeat at the hands of Sudas and the killing of Shambar and Bhed, the Asurs were in no position to stay at Arjika to continue the struggle. They appear to have abandoned the place for good, just like the Devs had done on being driven away by Yim. The twenty-fourth Richa says that the hostile rivals were scattered all over the earth and the wrath of this wrathful enemy was baffled and the foe who was advancing on the way towards Sudas, took the path of flight. The Devs too, the limited number that was left, seem to have felt the difficulties in being there in such short numbers. They had the option of occupying Arjika again after the Asurs had been driven away, but this option does not appear to have been exercised by them because Arjika was totally abandoned after this war and no contact of either side remained for which its location was forgotten, though both remembered it very fondly. The Yakshs, in any case, had no interest in this land. They had been instigated for the fight by their religious leaders to avenge the death of Dadhich and to ensure Dev control over the territory. The Tritsus, at this stage, were essentially preachers and people devoted to religion is reflected from the thirty-second Richa, which says that Indra gave vigour to Sudas when surrounded by the ten Rajas in the country where the pious Tritsus, walking in whiteness and wearing braided hair, worshipped with oblations and praise.

Though in these wars, the Asurs suffered reverses and were uprooted from Arjika, they find mention in the Zoroastrian scriptures.

In the course of the war, there were fluctuation of fortunes which
have been highlighted and some changes made to make them look
like a victory for the Asurs. The passage from the Dinkard on this is
given here.

About those of the Mazendaran country having consulted,
after the smiting of Dahak, as to turning to Khvaniras, and
driving out Fredun; also, on account of their tallness, there
are parts of the wide formed ocean that come up to their
mid-thigh. And, when they have come to this region, their
producing grievous harm and destruction to the poor, and the
coming of the people to Fredun with complaints and their
speaking thus, 'Why didst thou smite Az-i Dahak, who was a
good ruler as to prerogative so that danger was kept away by
him, and an inquisitor from him protected this region from
those of the Mazendaran country?'

About the encountering of Fredun with those of the
Mazendaran country on the plain of Pesanigas and disputing
with them thus, 'You are of the Mazendar country and I
have destroyed Az-i Dahak by the swiftest ruin; for that
smiting of him, I am produced by Auharmazd, and then
you destroyed this country of mine.' And the Mazendarans
thought slightingly of Fredun and spoken in a tone of derision
thus, 'Should it be so, that thou destroyed Az-i Dahak by
the swiftest ruin, him who was a good sovereign of both
demons and men, and thou art produced by Auharmazd for
that smiting of him, even then we will settle in this place and
will stay in this place; and it is not thou that are exalted, who
art an overgrown huge sheep, and we would not admit thee
here.' This too, that nevertheless they afterwards fled and the
victorious Fredun pursued them to the foremost upland, and
his nostrils flamed upon it so that they split it through. And he
made it rush on the ascent and they who are of the Mazendar
country are destroyed by him.

(Dinkard. Book IX. Sudkar Nask)

Thraetaona of the *Avesta* is Fredun in Pahlavi. The people who have attacked to avenge the killing of Dahak have been called the people of the Mazendaran country. If the identity of these people is known in Persia from other literary sources, it will give the identity of the Yakshs of the *Veds*. The account started correctly stating that these people attacked the Khvaniras, which are the Karshvares of the *Avesta*, and drove out Fredun from there. It also says that they caused massive harm and destruction to the people, confirming the information given by the *Veds* that Divodas burnt the ninety-nine cities of Shambar. To make the defeat palatable, the people of the Mazendaran country have been projected as giants, who were so tall that even the ocean came up to certain parts of their bodies. It also states that Fredun after the defeat remained close by though a great number of his men had fallen. The Khvaniras is reported to have been occupied by the Mazendaran people. This could be an error in the reporting of the story over the ages because it was the Tritsus who had occupied Arjika and not the Yakshs. The attempt on the part of Fredun to take back the territory and the second war is also reflected. Its end result is also correctly given, that the other side vacated the Karshvares never to return again, but to make the story on the pattern of folklores, Fredun has been shown the victor, as the story could not have possibly ended with the hero losing for which changes have been made, though a hint is there that he died in the engagement though not at the hands of the enemy, but because of exhaustion as his nostrils flamed and split while chasing them uphill.

The Asurs abandoning Arjika is reflected in one of the passages of the Bundahis which is here.

> In the region of the Khvaniras are many places, from which, in this evil time of violent struggling with the adversary, a passage is constructed by the power of the spiritual world and one calls them the beaten tracks of Khvaniras.
>
> (Bundahis. Chapter XXIX)

5
Locating Arjika
❧❧❧

T HE STAY AT ARJIKA WAS very eventful. A lot has been
mentioned with these events, which provide information about
the geographical features of the place. This was also a homeland,
which both sides were forced to abandon and not a place from where
they voluntarily migrated out. Something lost is often missed and
remembered more dearly than something left by choice. Possibly,
because of this, Arjika is the only homeland, which is found to
have been remembered with a lot of fondness and nostalgia in the
scriptures of both religions. Due to this evident nostalgia several
things mentioned provide an accurate account of the place making it
possible to locate it.

First, the information from the *Veds*. In the war with Vritra,
as well as Shambar, a river has been prominently mentioned. It has
been called Parushni. In the context of the war of Sudas, this river
has been mentioned as deep and difficult to cross. Some Asurs got
drowned during the combat. Evidently, it is a major river. Along
with the river, a mountain is mentioned in connection with the cave
of Val as well as with the sending away of Val from Arjika. The river
and mountain being together, the river has to be swift-flowing. Apart
from the river and mountain, there is a huge water body, which has
been called Sharyanavat in the *Veds*. The head of Dadhich is reported
to have been found in it. Some of the passages from the *Veds* which
provide information about Arjika, the Parushni river and Sharyanavat
lake are mentioned here.

1. The leaders of the rites have proceeded with downward chariot-wheels to the Arjika country, where lies the Sharyanavat, abounding in dwellings and where Som is plentiful.

(*Rig Ved.* M-8, S-7, R-29)

2. This is your beloved most exhilarating Som, which grows in the Sharyanavat lake by the Sushoma river in the Arjika country.

(*Rig Ved.* M-8, S-64, R-11)

3. Accept this, my praise, Ganga, Yamuna, Saraswati, Shutudri, Parushni, Marudvridh with Askini and Vitasta, listen Arjikiya with Sushoma.

(*Rig Ved.* M-10, S-75, R-5)

4. There where the mountains downward slope, there at the meeting of the streams, the sage was manifest by song.

(*Saam Ved.* Part I, Book II, Chapter I)

5. With honey I mix the streams; the rugged mountains are honey, honey is the Parushni river, the Shipala; weal be to your mouth, weal to your heart.

(*Atharv Ved.* Kand 6, Sukt-13, Richa-3)

These accounts of Arjika show that Sharyanavat, whether lake or sea, is a very prominent feature and Som grew in plenty near it. It also shows that the place is in the foothills, as the fourth passage says that the sage was manifest where the mountains downward slope. For the river, the information is significant, as this account shows that there are several rivers in Arjika and not just Parushni alone as it says, 'there at the meeting points of the streams'. These rivers are meeting at some places, either joining each other, or disintegrating. Apart from the Parushni, Sushoma in the second Richa and Shipala in the fifth seem to be names of the rivers in Arjika. The third Richa names ten rivers, of which some are in India while some seem to be names of the rivers of this place.

The *Avesta* too provides information about the geographical features of Airyana Vaego. The extracts relating to this are here.

1. The first of the good lands and countries, which I, Ahur Mazda, created, was Airyana Vaego, by the good river Daitya. Thereupon

came Angra Mainyu, who is all death, and he counter-created the serpent in the river and winter, a work of the Daevas. There are ten winter months there, two summer months; and those are cold for the waters, cold for the earth, cold for the trees. Winter falls there, with the worst of its plagues.

(Vendidad. Fargard I)

2. Ahur Mazda spake unto Spitama Zarathustra, saying, 'Offer up a sacrifice, O Spitama Zarathustra! Unto this spring of mine, Ardvi Sura Anahita, who hates the Daevas. The large river, known afar, that is as large as the whole of the waters that run along the earth; that runs powerfully from the height Hukairya down to the sea Vouru Kasha. All the shores of the sea, Vouru Kasha, are boiling over, all the middle of it is boiling over, when she runs down there, who has a thousand cells and a thousand channels, the extent of each of those channels is as much as a man can ride in forty days. From this river of mine alone flow all the waters that spread all over the seven Karshvares, this river of mine alone goes on bringing waters, both in summer and in winter.

(Aban Yast I)

3. I will worship the height Hukairya, wherefrom this mine Ardvi Sura Anahita leaps, from a hundred times the height of man, as the whole of the waters that run along the earth, and she runs powerfully.

(Aban Yast XXVIII)

4. We sacrifice unto Tistrya, the bright and glorious star, who fly between the earth and the heavens, in the sea Vouru Kasha, the powerful sea, and the deep sea of salt waters. He goes to its lake in the shape of a horse and down there he makes the waters boil over, and the winds flow above powerfully all around. Then Satavaesa makes those waters flow down to the seven Karshvares of the earth.

(Tir Yast V)

5. Ardvi Sura Anahita with a volume sounding from afar, which is alone equal in its bulk to all the waters which flow forth upon earth, which flows down with mighty volume from high Hukairya

to the sea Vouru Kasha. And all the gulfs in Vouru Kasha are
stirred (when it falls down). And the (chief) outlet of this one
water (Ardvi Sura Anahita) goes apart, dividing to all the seven
Karshvares.

(Yasna LXV)

These passages show that there is a major mountain in Airyana Vaego
which has been called Hukairya here. In speaking about the war
between Manu and Vritra, the name mentioned was Meruzu. Both
seem to be the same mountain, with Meru being mentioned in Indian
mythology too. The second feature is the sea Vouru Kasha. It has been
reported to be a large-sized deep sea of salt water. The fourth passage
should not create confusion, when it says that the Satavaesa makes
the waters of the Vouru Kasha flow down to the seven Karshvares of
the earth. It does not mean that the rivers are originating from Vouru
Kasha and flowing to the seven Karshvares. This is a Yast addressed
to the Star Tistrya, which rises at the time when rains were expected.
The first part says that the Star makes the waters boil over and the
winds flow above powerfully all around. It is talking of rain, in which
the vapours rise from the sea Vouru Kasha and are taken by the winds
to the seven Karshvares to fall over them after precipitation. The river
is flowing down from the mountain with all the force of a hill stream
and the sea Vouru Kasha is not very far from the mountain, because
it retains its force when it falls into the sea and causes turbulence in it,
which has been expressed by saying, that the sea boils all over, when
she runs down there. The sea Vouru Kasha would be to the north of
the mountain and Arjika, because in the context of Yim's expansion
of the earth three times, it had been stated that he did it towards the
south. As the space for expansion was towards the south, the position
of the sea has to be to the north.

The description of the river as it emerges from these passages,
is very important. In the first passage, the river has been named
as Daitya, while elsewhere it is Ardvi Sura Anahita. The second
passage, apart from saying that this river runs down powerfully
from the height Hukairya down to the sea, Vouru Kasha also says
that all the waters that spread over the seven Karshvares come from

this river. This point has been further elaborated in the fifth passage which states that the chief outlet goes apart, dividing to all the seven Karshvares. This is the description of a delta. The river Ardvi Sura Anahita is getting divided into seven distributaries soon after it has descended from the hills. It is small, but a very diffused delta. Small, because the distance from the mountain to the sea is not much as the river retains the force of its flow when it falls into the sea. This is a very unique geographical feature which helps in identifying the location with precision.

The *Veds* are full of references to seven rivers, seven sister streams and the land of seven rivers. The number being the same, this has been taken to mean the seven rivers of the Sapt Sindhu, which is the region falling in western India. There could have been no dispute with this understanding till the *Avesta* provided the input that Arjika had a river disintegrating into seven streams. If the Richas of the *Veds* with reference to the seven rivers are re-examined with this information, it would emerge that a very large number of them are speaking of these seven distributaries of Ardvi Sura Anahita, which is Parushni in the *Veds*, and not of the seven rivers of Sapt Sindhu. This one Richa is extremely close.

> Agni everywhere repairs to the undevouring, the undevoured (waters); the vast (offspring) of the firmament, not clothed, yet not naked, seven eternal ever youthful rivers, sprung from the same source, received Agni as their common embryo.
>
> (*Rig Ved*. M-3, S-1, R-6)

Sayan has explained the common source of the seven rivers to be the Himalayas. The other commentators have agreed with him. He could not have been faulted till the *Avesta* was also added to the information, but with the *Avesta* saying that one river broke into seven, this Richa appears to be saying the same thing. It is not a reference to the Himalayas. The reference in *Veds* where the seven rivers appear to be of Arjika and not Sapt Sindhu, are very large, a few are given here.

1. You, Chitrabhanu, are the distributer of riches, as the waves of

the river are parted by interjacent (islets); you ever pour (rewards) upon the giver (of oblations).

(*Rig Ved*. M-1, S-27, R-6)

2. The seven pure rivers that flow from heaven (are directed, Agni, by you; by you the priests), skilled in sacrifices, knew the doors of the (cave where) the treasure, (their cattle), were concealed, for you Sarama discovered the abundant milk of the kine with which man, the progeny of Manu, still is nourished.

(*Rig Ved*. M-1, S-72, R-8)

3. Through that friendship, Som, which has united you with your (friend) Indra, he has made the waters flow for man; he has slain Ahi, he has sent forth the seven rivers, and has opened the shut-up sources (of the streams).

(*Rig Ved*. M-4, S-28, R-1)

4. The summits of the firmament are measured by the light of Vaishvanar, the manifester of ambrosial (rain); all the regions are overspread (by the vapour) on his brow, and the seven gliding (streams) spring from thence like branches.

(*Rig Ved*. M-6, S-7, R-6)

5. He (Som), like the sun is the supervisor (of all acts); he hastens to the lakes, he unites with the seven down-descending rivers from heaven.

(*Rig Ved*. M-9, S-54, R-2)

6. The seven sister mothers approach the newborn, victorious, sagacious infant, Som, abiding amidst the waters, supporter of water, divine the contemplator of men to make him the ruler of the whole world.

(*Rig Ved*. M-9, S-56, R-36)

7. May Indra be the remover of thirst and hunger, for he, Maghvat, is lord over precious riches; these seven rivers of the powerful showerer (Indra), flowing down a declivity, augment food.

(*Rig Ved*. M-10, S-43, R-3)

The *Veds* thus confirm the information derived from the *Avesta* that the river of Arjika breaks into seven distributaries. Arjika is, therefore, a delta and the seven Karshvares that have been mentioned in the *Avesta* are the islands in this delta. In the *Rig Ved*, there is a reference similar to this, but instead of seven Karshvares, it speaks of three times seven grasslands. It appears that these seven distributaries of Ardvi Sura Anahita had further channels inter-connecting each other, as is the general pattern of distributaries in deltas. The *Veds* mention the further break-up of the islands by these streams cutting across. There seems to be a reference to these inter-connecting channels also, as the *Veds* mention three-times seven streams.

1. By him the thrower, unaided, were pierced asunder the thrice seven table-lands of the mountains heaped together; neither god nor mortal could do what he, the showerer, in his full-grown strength has done.

    (*Rig Ved*. M-8, S-96, R-2)

2. We invoke for protection the thrice seven flowing rivers, great waters, the trees, the mountains, Agni, Krishanu, the archer and Tishya, to the assembly; (we invoke) Rudra, worthy of the praise of the Rudras, for the good of the praisers.

    (*Rig Ved*. M-10, S-64, R-8)

Based on the information provided by the *Veds* and the *Avesta*, if the geographical features of Arjika or Airyana Vaego are listed, the following would emerge.

1. It is an extremely cold place, with ten months of winter and two months of summer wherein winters are very severe.
2. There is a huge waterbody, big enough to be called a sea. The *Avesta* has mentioned its waters to be saline, while the *Veds* are silent on this issue.
3. There is a mountain nearby, which most likely is to the south of the lake.
4. A major river flows down from this mountain with all the force of a hill river. The distance between the mountain and the lake is not much as the river maintains its force when it falls into the lake and causes turbulence.

5. Within the short distance between the mountain and the lake, the river breaks down into distributaries. These have been said to be seven at that time. This number need not be sacrosanct, as several thousand years have elapsed, but the behaviour has to remain the same, the river does not terminate as an estuary, but forms a diffused delta.

Based on these geographical features, Arjika has to be located. These Aryans were on the west of the Caspian Sea before this and have emerged on its east later. Arjika has been stated to be a very cold place, which means that they have circumvented the Caspian Sea from its north. As the general drift of the migration has been from north to south, evidently the Aryans were moving away from the cold. For this reason, they could not have moved back to the north from the edge of the Caspian Sea. Thus, the latitude at the northern end of the Caspian Sea can be fixed as the northern limit of the search. The Caspian Sea provides the western limit. Within this area, if the first element of the geographical features, that the place is extremely cold, is introduced, it will need the search to remain close to the northern limit so fixed. This creates a thin band on the map along the latitude of the northern end of the Caspian Sea, and right there, within this band a perfect match is found for all the other geographical features listed. Lake Balkash, with the Tian Shan Mountains to its south, having the Ili river flowing down to form a very diffused delta before falling into the lake, all in southeastern Kazakastan of present times. This is Arjika. This is Airyana Vaego.

If the individual features are examined, the first is Lake Balkash. It has an area of 16,400 square kilometres, with a length of about 600 kilometres and a width ranging from 9 to 19 kilometres, a lake large enough to be called a sea, if someone chooses to do so. The water is sweet where the Ili river meets and is saline elsewhere. The name Balkash seems to have its origins from Vouru Kasha. It had changed to something very close in the Pahlavi language, which is visible in this passage.

The Hom, which is the preparer of the dead, is grown in the sea Varkash, in that which is the deepest place, and

99,999 guardian spirits of the righteous are appointed as its protection.

(Dina-i Mainog-i Khirad. Chapter LXII)

From Varkash in Pahlavi to Balkash is a very short distance. The syllable 'v' changing to 'b' can be ignored as this change is extremely common in the languages originating from Sanskrit. The real change is in the sound 'r' becoming 'l', which is also seen at some places in these languages. This is, however, not to suggest that the usage of Varkash became Balkash over a period of time. It seems to have emerged from Vouru Kasha amongst different people, independently. The only thing left to give the final confirmation that Lake Balkash is Vouru Kasha, would be the existence of the Som plant there. Both scriptures have stated that it grows on the banks of this lake. The above passage from the Dina-i Mainog-i Khirad shows that it was not only in India that the Aryans did not have Som and had substituted it with other things as it was an integral part of their rituals, but even in Iran and elsewhere in Central Asia they did not have Som once they left Arjika, though the Aryans in Iran had remained in contact with the homeland that they had acquired after migrating from the delta of Ili river. Som appears to be a plant that grows only in Arjika, because if it had been found in any of the places where these Aryans lived after this, the Aryans of Iran would have known of it and would have had access to it. Som disappearing from them is, therefore, not because the plant became extinct for some natural reasons, but because it grows only in the limited area of Lake Balkash and along the Ili river and not anywhere else, and our Aryans migrated out of this place losing all contact with it and forgot its whereabouts. It is possible that this plant still grows there and could be found even now. A reference from the *Avesta* which gives some idea about this plant is here.

I praise the cloud that waters thee, and which make thee grow on the summits of the mountains; and I praise the lofty mountains where the Hom branches spread. Swift and wise hath the well-skilled Deity created thee on high Haraiti did He, the well-skilled, plant thee. There, Hom, on the ranges dost thou grow of many kinds. Now thou growest of milky whiteness, and now thou growest golden. With manifold retainers dost thou Hom, endow the man who drinks thee mixed with milk.

(Yasna X)

Some passages from the *Veds* on the subject are given here.

1. The season is the parent (of the Som plant) which, as soon as born of her, enters into the waters in which it grows; thence it is fit for expression, as concentrating (the essence of the) water, and the juice of the Som is especially to be praised.

(*Rig Ved.* M-2, S-13, R-1)

2. When the yellow Som plant milks forth (their juice) as cows from their udders, when the devout (priests) repeat the words of praise, then O Ashwins preserve us.

(*Rig Ved.* M-8, S-9, R-19)

3. The large rattling dice exhilarate me as torrents born on a precipice flowing in a desert, the exciting dice animate me as the taste of the Som of Maujvat.

(*Rig Ved.* M-10, S-34, R-1)

4. Rishi Kashyap, raising your voice with the praise of the hymn-maker, adore the royal Som, who is born the lord of creeping plants; flow, Indu for Indra.

(*Rig Ved.* M-10, S-114, R-2)

These passages show that Som was a seasonal, semi-aquatic plant, possibly a creeper, which grew on the banks of rivers and Lake Balkash and its stems spread into the water. The *Veds* have given its colour to be yellow or golden while the *Avesta* has given two colours, milky white and golden. The process of extraction of its juice, as emerges from the *Veds*, was that its branches were placed on a stone slab and pounded with a mortar. After pounding, a little water was sprinkled and it was twisted to squeeze out the juice, which was filtered through fleece and kept in a wooden vat overnight to be drunk neat in the morning, mixed with milk in the afternoon and with curd in the evening. As its stems survived pounding by a stone mortar to be twisted, they have to be having sufficiently strong fibres. It looks like a seasonal, semi-aquatic reed which grew in plenty in the delta of the Ili river, Lake Balkash and upstream of the river. The best Som is reported to be of Mount Maujvat, which could be somewhere along the course of this river. The recipe of the cocktail may or may not be correct. The *Veds* have mentioned mixing it with milk or curd while the *Avesta* has mentioned only milk. This may be of a time, when Som was not available and had been substituted in rituals by milk and curd in which Som was imagined. There would, however, be no harm in trying the recipe if the plant is found.

The next geographical feature is the Tian Shan mountain. It is a major mountain range, the highest these Aryans would have come across so far and the highest they encountered till they reached the Himalayas. The *Avesta* as well as the *Veds* have mentioned it to be close to the Sharyanavat or Sea Vouru Kasha. Its distance from lake Balkash matches these descriptions. The Ili is a major river. 70 per cent of the inflow of water into lake Balkash is from it. It descends from the mountains and travels a very short distance in the plains, before terminating into the lake after breaking down into several distributaries and forming a diffused delta. It is a perfect match for the description of the Ardvi Sura Anahita, with its seven distributaries taking water to the seven Karshvares.

Based on the information provided by the scriptures, there appears no reason to be unsure that the delta of the Ili river is the place that was so important to the Devs and Asurs where they shed so much blood and started a chain of events that had far reaching effects on history. Their stay here was significant in many ways. First of all, the seeds for the emergence of the two oldest Aryan religions, the Vedic and the Zoroastrian were sown here. The common Aryan religion practised so far, gradually became hazy, with both sides developing their own practices, though much of it remained at the base. The compilation of the *Veds* starts from this period though it would be incorrect to say that the tradition of composing hymns that form the text of the *Veds* started from this point of time. The Aryans had an old tradition of singing hymns. A Richa from the *Rig Ved*, that has been quoted while talking of the Ribhus, has given the sequence in which different rituals emerged, leading finally to the sacrifice. This stated that first there was singing of hymns, then fire and then oblations. It shows that in the initial stages singing of hymns was the only religious practice of these Aryans. The composition of hymns thus started very early though they were not retained but were sung as long as they survived and were either lost or modified. The tradition of compiling and retaining the old texts in the exact manner in which it was composed started from this period. New compositions were added without disturbing what was already there. This was all in an oral tradition as there was no writing and a lot of stress was given on maintaining the exact pronunciation with the voice rising and falling at the same point in the same manner. It can be said without an iota of doubt that the way they are recited or sung today in India, is exactly the same in which Kavya Ushana recited them all these millenniums ago. There is evidence in the *Veds* to show that Kavya Ushana started the process of compilation of the hymns which, in due course, became the *Veds*. These are given here.

1. The Rishi, the sage, the foremost of men, the far shining, intelligent Ushana, he verily by his poetic gift discovered the secret milk of those cows which were hidden and concealed.

    (*Rig Ved.* M-9, S-87, R-3)

2. Reciting sacred praise like Ushana the praiser (Vrishgan) proclaims the births of the gods, purifying (from sin), he approaches the filter making a noise (as) a wild boar (makes a noise) with its foot.

    (*Rig Ved.* M-9, S-97, R-7)

3. The god declares the deity's generation, like Ushana proclaiming lofty wisdom. With brilliant kin, far-reaching, sanctifying, the wild boar, singing with the steps, advances.

    (*Saam Ved.* Part I, Book VI, Chapter I)

4. Atharvan had very first extended all the ways and manners of performing the offering and then Lord Sun had appeared for sustaining the resolution. Thereafter, Ushana (the ever-brilliant rays) had made all the cows (the rays or speech) able to come out

from the cave of the mountain. All of us worship the immortal as also the regulator of this whole universe, Lord Indra.

(*Atharv Ved*. Kand 20, Sukt-19, R-5)

The compilation of the *Veds* thus starts from the banks of lake Balkash. The farthest geographical feature from there, which is identifiable in the *Veds*, is the Saryu river, which flows between Lucknow and Varanasi. A major impact of the Devs starting the process of compiling the *Veds* and maintaining the manner of their recitation was on their language. The language stood frozen in time. This is visible by a comparison of the language of the *Veds* and the *Avesta*. As the Asurs did not do this their language changed over time and the language looks like a corrupted form of the Vedic language. As the language of the Devs had the *Veds* at its centre, they continued to retain the same clarity, though very soon this must have remained the language of only the educated, while the general usage could have changed, as is seen with the emergence of Prakrit language later.

While at Arjika, a number of new gods were added to the divinities of the Devs with Indra as the foremost. He came to be called the king of Devs and became more important than all others, including those that were already there. Tvasta or Dyau got relegated to a position where he was treated as the father of all gods, with very little importance. Vishnu and Brahaspati or Brahmanaspati also emerge from here. Vishnu of the *Veds* is not the same as Vishnu of the *Purans*, where he is projected as the Supreme God, with several incarnations. In the *Veds*, he is just one of the gods subordinate to Indra and has received less attention than even Brahaspati. None of his incarnations find mention anywhere except his measuring the earth with three steps, which in the *Purans* is one of them as a dwarf. This imagination is found in the Brahmans also, though it is unlikely for Vishnu to be a dwarf not only because no such thing is mentioned in the *Veds* but also because he fought the war against Vritra alongside Indra. This may have been added to make the measuring of the earth look dramatic.

Three goddesses, too, emerge from this period, Ila, Mahi and Saraswati. At places Mahi has been called Bharati. Their role in the happenings at Arjika, is not stated anywhere. They have, however, been projected as a group, which shows that there is something common about them. The reasons for their deification emerge from some of these passages of the *Veds*.

1. May the three undecaying goddesses, givers of delight, Ila, Saraswati and Mahi, sit down upon the sacred grass.

   (*Rig Ved.* M-1, S-13, R-9)

2. The gods formerly made you, Agni, the living general of the mortal Nahush; they made Ila, the instructress of Manu, when the son of my father was born.

   (*Rig Ved.* M-1, S-31, R-11)

3. May the purifying, amiable, graceful Saraswati, the bride of the hero, favour our pious rite. May she, together with the wives of the gods, well pleased, bestow upon him who praises her a habitation free from defects and impenetrable and (grant him) felicity.

   (*Rig Ved.* M-6, S-49, R-7)

4. Both the Ashwins defended (you), Indra, like two fathers (defending) a son with glorious exploits, when (triumphing) through the deeds of valour, you drank the grateful libation, Saraswati approached you, O Maghvat.

   (*Rig Ved.* M-10, S-131, R-5)

5. I, from my father have obtained knowledge of eternal law; I was born like unto the sun.

   (*Saam Ved.* Part II, Book VII, Chapter I)

6. Let the priest offer sacrifice to the three goddesses and balm. Let the three triple active ones, let Ila and Saraswati and Bharati the mighty dames, consorts of Indra, who receive our sacrificial offerings, enjoy the butter, etc.

   (*Yajur Ved.* Adhyay-28, Yajush-8)

The first and the sixth passages mention the three goddesses as a group. The third and the fourth Richas give a hint that Saraswati was the wife of Indra. The sixth passage states that all three were wives of Indra. Evidently, they were the wives of Manu. The second Richa calls Ila the instructress of Manu. The text can also be translated to mean as Ila being the instructress of the teachings of Manu, which seems to have been the intention of the Richa. Being a wife of Manu, Ila seems to have been well versed in the rituals of the sacrifice and was an instructress of the same for the later generation. This emerges from several passages of the *Veds*, where it is stated while describing a sacrifice, that the sacrificer lit the fire on the footsteps of Ila. The commentators have explained the altar to be the footsteps or the footprints of Ila, but it seems to mean in the manner in which Ila had instructed. Manu has not claimed originality in any of the things that were propounded by him. He has stated that it was the teachings of his father, Bhrigu. This emerges from the fifth Richa also. However, as for all practical purposes, the teachings were coming from Manu, Ila has been called an instructress of the teachings of Manu and not Bhrigu. Being the wives of Manu, these three goddesses would have been the mothers of Ushana. Their deification would have begun with Ushana composing some verses in veneration of his mothers.

The *Avesta* seems to have noticed the deification of these goddesses. The passage showing this is mentioned here.

I drive away Ishire; I drive away Aghuire, I drive away Aghra,
I drive away Ughra, I drive away Sarana, I drive away Sarasti,
I drive away the rottenness which Angra Mainyu has created
by his witchcraft.

(Vendidad. Fargard XXI)

In this passage, Sarasti is too close to Saraswati to be missed. In another similar prayer, she has been called Sarastya. The deification of these persons by the Devs and certain changes that came about after they left Arjika, has caused several difficulties in the understanding of the *Veds*. The Devs, after leaving Arjika, ceased to call themselves Devs. Instead, they called themselves the descendants of Manu. The words used for this are Manav and Manushya, both have meant humans later. Calling their ancestors Devs while deifying some, and calling themselves Manavs later, created a situation wherein the story of men living in Arjika gave the impression that it was the story of gods and not humans. As the Asurs were fighting these gods, they got projected as supernatural creatures representing evil. To add to the confusion is their style, wherein even later Asurs were reported killed by thanking Indra on behalf of the person responsible adding to the idea of the story being of gods and demons. The term Dev, in due course, came to mean god and even divinities that were there before the Aryans reached Arjika, were later called Dev only. It is not clear, what they called them before this, but it is likely that the term used was Asur, which means the Lord. This can be said not only because the Asurs continued to do so right up to Ahur Mazda, where Asur has become Ahur, but also because at some places in the *Veds*, Tvasta, Varun and Indra have been addressed as Asurs. Heaven is the abode of gods. As some of the Vedic gods lived in Arjika, this place got identified with heaven. There are several passages in the *Veds* where the distinction between heaven and Arjika appears hazy. This change in the perception of the Manavs about themselves while at Arjika and later, created mythology out of the story of man leading to interpretations that are humanly impossible.

Glimpses of the level of development reached by the Aryans while at Arjika can be seen in these scriptures. Agriculture and animal husbandry were their primary occupations with irrigation being used for cultivation. This shows that in agricultural practices they had reached a stage at which agriculture remained till just a few decades ago when chemical fertilizers, pesticides and machines came to be introduced. In Arjika, they were practising settled cultivation, using manure to fertilize the soil and flow of water by channels to irrigate their fields. The climate of the place would have enabled only one crop, as winter was very long and severe. This passage from the *Avesta* gives an idea of their agricultural implements.

He shall piously give to the godly men a set of all the implements of which the husbandmen make use, as an atonement, namely, a plough with share and yoke, an ox whip, a mortar of stone, a hand-mill for grinding corn, a spade for digging and tilling.

(Vendidad. Fargard XIV)

Though of a little later period, the agricultural implements mentioned in this Fargard would have been in use in Arjika. Barley seems to have been their main crop at this stage. The *Veds* refer to barley and barley cakes all through. Though they do not give an impression that this was the only crop that they grew, the *Avesta* shows that after leaving Arjika, some new crops came to be known to these Aryans, yet the Devs, perhaps driven by orthodoxy that the gods cultivated only barley, stuck to only barley for a long time, while the Asurs were progressive enough to adopt new ones. The passage stating so is here.

> O Maker of the material world, thou Holy One! What is the food that fills the law of Mazda? Ahur Mazda answered, 'It is sowing corn again and again, O Spitma Zarathustra! He who sows corn, sows holiness; he makes the law of Mazda grow higher and higher. When barley is coming forth, the Daevas start up; when the corn is growing rank, then faint the Daevas' hearts, when corn is being ground, the Daevas groan, when wheat is coming forth, the Daevas are destroyed. In that house they can no longer stay, from that house they are beaten away, wherein wheat is thus coming forth.'
>
> (Vendidad. Fargard III)

The *Veds* show the importance of barley over other crops at many places, but in the Richa below they have called themselves barley-eaters, confirming what the *Avesta* has stated about them.

> When we, the grass-eaters of men (are) together, I (am) amongst the barley-eaters in the wide field; here he who is yoked would like one to unloose him, and the assailant would yoke him who is unyoked.
>
> (*Rig Ved*. M-10, S-27, R-9)

Their level of prosperity can be seen from their religious practices too. Till then the oblations offered were just a token offering. It involved nothing additional. The Devs had started a practice wherein the offering was consigned to fire. This meant an additional cost. They had reached a level of well-being wherein they were in a position to spare this. The size of the sacrifice or 'yagya' too had become bigger. Though the scriptures speak of thousands of animals being sacrificed in a single 'yagya' even if these are exaggerations, the number would have been large. Their prosperity is also seen from the fact that they could afford the luxury of fighting a long-drawn war over ideas. The dispute between the two groups was not over land, water or any material necessity of life. Evidently, they had crossed the stage of struggle for survival. It is only in a state of prosperity, wherein the necessities of life have not remained an issue any longer that people can fight and kill over ideas and differences of opinions. Whether the offerings to the gods were to be just raised as a token and thereafter eaten by the faithful or to be consigned to the flames was reason enough for them to leave every other occupation and fight. In this background, instead of just making implements and tools for agriculture and other necessities of life, they started making weapons of war. The first was the Vajra of Indra or the battleaxe, but soon this led to an arms race and a lot many weapons emerged, which can be seen from these passages of the *Avesta*, which are again of a slightly later period, but show what it led to.

1.   He shall piously give to godly men a set of all the war implements of which the warriors make use, as an atonement, the first being a javelin, the second a knife, the third a club, the fourth a bow, the fifth a quiver with shoulder-belt and thirty brass-headed arrows, the sixth a sling with arm-string and with thirty sling stones, the seventh a cuirass, the eighth a hauberk, the ninth a tunic, the tenth a helmet, the eleventh a girdle, the twelfth a pair of greaves.

                                          (Vendidad. Fargard XIV)

2.   That man shall not be wounded by the weapons of the foe who rushes Aeshma-like and is Drug-minded; not the knife, not the cross-bow, not the arrow, not the sword, not the club, not the sling-stone shall reach and wound him.

                                          (Ormazd Yast I)

3.   On a side of the chariot of Mithra, the lord of wide pastures, stand a thousand bows well-made, with a string of cow gut; they fall through upon the skulls of the Daevas. On a side of the chariot

of Mithra, the lord of wide pastures, stand a thousand vulture-feathered arrows, with a golden mouth; they fall through the heavenly space upon the skulls of the Daevas. On a side of the chariot of Mithra, the lord of wide pastures, stand a thousand spears; they fall through the heavenly space upon the skulls of the Daevas. On a side of the chariot of Mithra, the lord of the wide pastures, stand a thousand steel-hammers; they fall through the heavenly space upon the skulls of the Daevas. On a side of the chariot of Mithra, the lord of the wide pastures, stand a thousand swords; they fall through the heavenly space upon the skulls of the Daevas. On a side of the chariot of Mithra, the lord of the wide pastures, stand a thousand maces of iron; they fall through the heavenly space upon the skulls of the Daevas.

(Mihir Yast XXXI)

6
Simmerings in the New Homeland

S HAMBAR RULED FOR FORTY YEARS. Yam would have ruled for about the same period. Thus, the Devs were uprooted from Arjika about seventy to eighty years before the Asurs. They would have been comfortably settled in their new homeland by the time the Asurs met the same fate. The accounts of the *Veds* show the Devs being happy on the defeat of the Asurs at the hands of Divodas and Sudas and at their being forced to leave Arjika. This was, however, a tragedy. Had the Asurs continued in Arjika, the two sides would have been separated by a long distance and would have lost contact with each other. In such a situation, both sides would have remembered their wars and victories in mythologies, but would have lost the identity of the other side. The Dev Asur Sangram would have been over. Both would have become two different people and would have been strangers to each other with no hostile past. It seems that destiny had decided against their parting ways and for following each other. The Asurs, on being uprooted from Arjika, reached the same place where the Devs were and the war continued.

The events in this new homeland are not very clear. Both sides have mentioned their victories prominently without giving details because of which there are difficulties in matching them in the two scriptures. The chain of these events also does not emerge from what has been recorded. They all appear to be isolated instances of violence with no link with each other. The absence of a detailed account of war, as was done earlier, shows that these are not records of warfare but only of violence. It emerges from these scriptures that the two sides were living together at the new location. In this situation, the fights mentioned, would not have been regular wars. At Arjika, the fights were of the nature of a war as the two sides, while fighting, were not sharing the same habitations. There, one side approached with an army and fought, giving it the ingredients of a war. At the new location, both sides continued to share the same habitation throughout. There was no approach of an army, no attack and no dispossession of the defeated side. Being depicted in the same style as the earlier fights, they appear to be wars, but in reality they would have been cases of violence or street fights between two groups. The references which show that the two sides were sharing the same habitation are here.

1. O Maker of the material world, thou Holy One! If there be a number of men resting in the same place, on adjoining carpets, be there two men or fifty; and of those one happens to die; how many of them does the Drug Nasu envelop with infection and uncleanness? Ahur Mazda answered, 'If the dead one be a priest, the Drug Nasu rushes forth, O Spitama Zarathustra, she falls on the eleventh and defiles the ten...' O Maker of the material world, thou Holy One! If the dead one be a wicked, two-footed ruffian, an ungodly Ashemaogha, how many of the creatures of the good spirit does he directly defile, how many does he indirectly defile in dying? Ahur Mazda answered, 'No more than a frog does. Whilst alive, indeed, O Spitama Zarathustra! that ungodly Ashemaogha defiles the creatures of the good spirit. Whilst alive he smites the water, he blows out the fire, he carries off the cow, he smites the faithful man with a deadly blow; not so will he do when dead. Whilst alive, indeed O Spitama Zarathustra! That ungodly Ashemaogha, never ceases depriving the faithful man of his food, of his clothing, of his house, of his bed, of his vessels; not so will he do when dead.'

    (Vendidad. Fargard V)

2. The ruffian who lies unto Mithra brings death unto the whole country. Break not the contract, O Spitama! neither the one that thou hadst entered into one of the unfaithful, nor the one that

thou hadst entered into with one of the faithful. For Mithra stands for both the faithful and the unfaithful.

(Mihir Yast I)

3. It is for a decision as to religions, man and man, each individually for himself. Before the great effort of the cause, awake ye (all) to our teaching! Thus are the primeval spirits who as a pair (combining their opposite strivings) famed (of old). (They are) a better thing and a worse. And between these two let the wisely acting choose a right. (Choose ye) not (as) the evil-doers.

(Yasna XXX)

4. And if by this means the indubitable truths are not seen, then as better (than these words) I will come to you with that power and in that way according to which Ahur Mazda appoints His ruler, that ruler over both the two (struggling) bands, in order that we may live according to Righteousness. And that keenness, that deciding satisfaction, which Thou hast given by (Thy) Spirit, and (Thy) Fire, and by Thy Righteousness (itself) to the two battling (sides), do Thou declare unto us, O Ahur!

(Yasna XXXI)

5. (May that heroic settler grant him this gift) he who may make the (last imperilled) form to flourish in the vigour of Thy blest prosperity, the track which lies nearest (to the fields) which our foeman holds as his.

(Yasna L)

6. O Maker of the material world! If a worshipper of Mazda want to practise the art of healing, on whom shall he first prove his skill ? On the worshippers of Mazda or on the worshippers of the Daevas? Ahur Mazda answered, 'On worshippers of the Daevas. If he treat with the knife a worshipper of the Daevas and he die; if he treat with the knife a second worshipper of the Daevas and he die; if he treat with the knife for the third time a worshipper of the Daevas and he die, he is unfit to practise the art of healing. Let him, therefore, never treat with the knife any worshipper of Mazda. If he treat with the knife a worshipper of the Daevas and he recover; if he treat with the knife a second worshipper of

the Daevas and he recover; if for the third time he treat with the knife a worshipper of the Daevas and he recover; then he is fit to practise the art of healing. He may henceforth at his will treat with the knife worshippers of Mazda.'

(Vendidad. Fargard VII)

All these passages give an impression that both sides were living together despite their differences and bickerings. The first passage has a situation of people resting together and one dying, perhaps in a 'sarai' or inn. Amongst the list of persons, who this dying man could be, is a Dev worshipper, an ungodly Ashemaogha, whose death causes no defilement. He causes defilement while alive. The things he is reported to be doing while alive give the impression of a hostile neighbour and not an enemy coming with an army. He smites the water, blows out the fire, steals the cow, kills the faithful man and deprives him of his food, clothing, house, bed and vessels. The second passage shows that the two sides had a normal functional relationship entering into contracts, at times, with the other side. This enjoins that a contract must be honoured whether it is with the faithful or the unfaithful. The third passage is an address by Zoroaster to the people asking them to make an individual choice between the two religions before them. The fourth passage has both struggling bands and the two battling sides together. It speaks of the same keenness and the same deciding satisfaction that has been given by God to both sides and of Ahur Mazda appointing a ruler, who would rule over both rivals. The fifth passage mentions agricultural lands of the two sides being adjoining each other. The sixth passage shows the inter-dependency of the two sides. They could even risk the dangerous knife of a surgeon of the other faith, when it became necessary. Though this advice to the surgeon to first test his skills on the Dev worshippers, would have been in humour, it shows a normal social relationship between the two sides at the individual level, despite all the tension that may have been there at the collective level and amongst theologians.

In the *Veds* too, the description of disturbances caused by Asurs at this stage show that rivals were very close. They are not the outcome of wars where the defeated side loses land or sovereignty. They are disturbances caused by people in the neighbourhood to prevent them from performing their rites. A few Richas are given here.

1. Imploring them for ample wealth, and (having recourse to him) for protection, we glorify them with this praise; like the five chief priests whom Trita detained for (performing) the sacrifice, and to protect it with their weapons.

   (*Rig Ved.* M-2, S-34, R-14)

2. Indra, the invoked of many, thirty hundred mailed warriors (were collected) together on the Yavyavati, to acquire glory, but the Vrichivats advancing hostilely, and breaking the sacrificial vessels, went to (their own) annihilation.

   (*Rig Ved.* M-6, S-27, R-6)

The first Richa speaks of five chief priests having been detained by Trita for performing the sacrifice. The next Richa describes a sacrifice that seems to have been disturbed while it was being performed. The various vessels and things being used in rituals have been broken or scattered. Such things do not happen in wars, where both sides are on the battlefield. They happen in normal times, with people performing sacrifices and hostile persons of the neighbourhood causing disturbances. This situation makes the wars between the two sides different in this homeland. The Dev Asur Sangram, which had regular battles in Arjika, was a low-key affair here with cases of individual violence or rioting between two groups living together.

Though it is difficult to give a sequence of the wars that have been mentioned in the two scriptures, it appears that those mentioned in the *Avesta* in which the Asurs have won, are of the earlier period. This can be said because while living in this homeland, after a stage, the Manavs had achieved complete ascendency as by the time Zoroaster emerged, the Asurs were in complete disarray. The Asur successes could have been only before the Manavs established their ascendency.

The most significant person mentioned by the *Avesta* for this period is Keresaspa. He finds mention at several places. Some references are given here.

1. To her did Keresaspa, offer up a sacrifice behind Vairi Pisanah. He begged of her a boon saying, 'Grant me this, O good, most beneficent Ardvi Sura Anahita! That I may overcome the golden-heeled Gandarewa though all the shores of the Sea Vouru Kasha are boiling over; and that I may run up to the stronghold of the fiend on the wide earth whose end lies afar.'

(Aban Yast X)

2. To him did the manly-hearted Keresaspa offer up a sacrifice by the Gudha, a channel of the Rangha. He begged him of a boon, saying, 'Grant me this, O Vayu! that I may succeed in avenging my brother Urvakhshaya, that I may smite Hitaspa. The Gandarewa who lives beneath the waters is the son of Ahur in the deep, he is the only master of the deep.'

(Ram Yast VII)

3. The third time when the Glory departed from Yim the son of Vivanghant, in the shape of a Varaghna bird. Then the manly-hearted Keresaspa seized that Glory. Who killed the snake Srvara, the horse-devouring, men-devouring, yellow, poisonous snake, over which yellow poison flowed a thumb's breadth thick? Upon him Keresaspa was cooking his food in a brass vessel, the fiend felt the heat; he rushed from under the brass vessel and upset the boiling water; the manly hearted Keresaspa fell back affrighted. Who killed the golden-heeled Ganderewa, that was rushing with open jaws, eager to destroy the living world? Who killed the brood of Pathona, all the nine, and the brood of Nivika, and the brood of the Dastayana? Who killed the golden-crowned Hitaspa, and Vareshava, the son of Dana, and Pitaona, attended by many Parikas? Who killed the Azero-Shamana. Who killed Snavidhaka. Thus did he exclaim to all around, 'I am an infant still; if I grow of age, I shall bring down the Good Spirit from the Garonmana; I shall make the Evil Spirit rush up from the dreary Hell. They will carry my chariot, unless the manly hearted Keresaspa kill me.' The manly-hearted Keresaspa killed him.

(Zamyad Yast VII)

4. Thereupon gave Hom answer; Thrita (the most helpful of the
   Saams) was the third man who prepared me for the corporeal
   world. This gain did he acquire, that to him two sons were born,
   Urvakhshaya and Keresaspa, the one a judge, the other a youth
   of great ascendant. He who smote the horny dragon, swallowing
   men, and swallowing horses, poisonous and green of colour, over
   which, as thick as thumbs are, greenish poison flowed aside, on
   whose back once Keresaspa cooked his meat in an iron caldron
   at the noonday meal; and the deadly, scorched, up-started and
   springing off, dashed out the water as it boiled.

   (Yasna IX)

5. And the advantage from Sahm was (this) that the serpent Srovar
   and the wolf Kapud, which they also call Pehino, the watery
   demon Gandarep, the bird Kamak, and the deluding demon, were
   slain by him.

   (Dina-i Mainog-i Khirad. Chapter XXVII)

6. At another time it came to Keresaspo the Saman, owing to the
   share of warriorship which is the second avocation of the religion
   and through it the serpent Srobovar, which was swallowing horses
   and swallowing men, the golden-heeled Gandarepo, and much
   other production of adversity were destroyed by him.

   (Dinkard. Book VII. Chapter I)

The fourth passage says that Keresaspa was the son of Thrita, the Saman.
Saman was a term used for persons who sang the Saams or lyrics during
the sacrifice. These Saams have been later collected in the *Saam Ved*.
The Asurs, too, having Samans shows that this tradition was older than
the time when the two sides broke up. Thrita is the same as Trita of
the *Veds*. He was the common ancestor of both Manu and Yam. The
mention of Thrita as the father of Keresaspa is a reference to the same
ancestor, as all persons of the clan used the name. A Richa of the *Rig Ved*
quoted earlier, mentions Trita, who detained five chief priests for having
performed a sacrifice. This is a reference to Keresaspa. The things that he
is reported to have done in these passages are specific. He killed Srvar,
who has been called Srovar and Srobovar in Pahlavi, the horse-devouring
and man-devouring serpent. He killed Hitaspa to avenge the killing of

his brother Urvakhshaya. He killed the golden-heeled Gandarewa. He killed the brood of nine Pathonas, the brood of Nivika and the brood of Dastayana. He killed Vareshava, the son of Dana and Pitaona, attended by many Parikas. He killed Azero-shaman and Snavidhaka.

Apart from giving information about the people killed by Keresaspa, the second passage gives a hint about the place where these events took place. It states that Keresaspa performed the sacrifice by the Gudha, a channel of Rangha, made by Mazda. Apparently, Rangha is a river and Gudha, one of its distributaries. The place is again a delta.

Keresaspa can be located in the *Veds*, because according to the accounts of the *Avesta*, he is the only Asur before Zoroaster, who caused large-scale disturbances and killed many Manavs. In the *Veds*, he seems to be Kuyav, which seems to have been coined to make the reference derogatory, as it means bad barley. The references in the *Veds* about him are mentioned here.

1. The Asur, knowing the wealth of others, carries it off for himself; present in the water, he carries off, of himself, the foam. The two wives of Kuyav bathe with the water; may they be drowned in the depths of the Sipha river.

2. The abiding-place of the vagrant (Kuyav) was concealed (in the midst) of the water; the hero increases with the waters formerly (carried off) and is renowned (throughout the world); the Anjasi, Kulisi and Virpatni rivers, pleasing him with their substance, sustain him with their waters.

3. Since the track that leads to the dwelling of the Dasyu has been seen by us, as a cow knows the way to her stall, therefore do you, Maghvan (defend us) from his repeated violence; do not you cast away as a libertine throws away wealth.

                                              (*Rig Ved*. M-1, S-104, R-3 to 5)

4. The sage praises you, Indra, for the grant of desirable, since you have made the earth the bed of the Asur, Maghvan has made the three (regions) marvellous by his gifts, and has destroyed for Duryoni, the Asur Kuyavac in combat.

                                              (*Rig Ved*. M-1, S-174, R-7)

5. You have provided a passage for the easy crossing of the flowing waters for Turviti and Vayya; rendering (yourself) renowned, you have uplifted the blind and lame Paravrij from the lowliness (of affliction); you are he who is to be praised.

(*Rig Ved.* M-2, S-13, R-12)

6. The lord of acts, the wise Indra, has borne across Turvash and Yadu, when denied inauguration.

(*Rig Ved.* M-4, S-30, R-17)

7. You, Indra, who make (your enemies) tremble, have caused the waters, detained by Dhuni, to flow like rushing rivers; so, hero, when, having crossed the ocean, you have reached the shore, you have brought over in safety, Turvash and Yadu.

(*Rig Ved.* M-6, S-20, R-12)

8. May that youthful Indra, who by good guidance brought Turvash and Yadu from afar (be) our friend.

(*Rig Ved.* M-6, S-45, R-1)

9. Well knowing those (sacrificial) deeds of Turvash and Yadu, he overcame Anhavayya in battle.

(*Rig Ved.* M-8, S-45, R-27)

10. May all your paths beneath the sky whereby you speed Vyasava on; yea, let all spaces hear our voice.

(*Saam Ved.* Part I, Book II, Chapter II)

These passages referring to Keresaspa, show the Manavs to be at the receiving end, but finally Keresaspa seems to have been killed. They also give an idea of the geographical features. The first Richa names the river as Sipha, in which they have wished the two wives of Kuyav, who bathe there, to drown. Since the wives of Kuyav used to bathe in the river the place is warmer than the Ili. Sipha would be the same as Rangha of the *Avesta*. The next Richa has three more rivers—Anjasi, Kulisi and Virpatni. They seem to be distributaries of the Sipha. The fights here, at least on some occasions, seem to have been over water. As both sides were living together, they would have had adjacent farms. They seem to have had water channels from the river to their fields in the same way as they had in Arjika. Such a system requires a lot of cooperation, because the channels are along the gradient of land, passing through different fields. If someone along the way blocks or diverts it to another direction, the fields down the line would not get water. In Arjika, Val had done it by way of an order of the sovereign authority. Here the Asurs and the Manavs appear to be doing it to create problems for each other. The second Richa speaks of the waters, which were formerly carried off have now been increased. The seventh Richa repeats the same.

Keresaspa appears to have been called by more than one name. He has been addressed as Kuyav, Kuyavac and Anhavayya. His terror is evident. People had fled from the place to escape, leaving the Rishis to curse him with a wish that his two wives drown. The third Richa speaks of his repeated violence. Several names of people who fled are mentioned. As a part of the style of writing, the names of those killed do not find place. The fifth Richa says that Turviti and Vayya have fled after crossing the flowing waters of the river. The sixth Richa speaks of the fleeing of Turvash and Yadu, while the seventh informs that they returned safely, perhaps after Kuyav was killed. This is repeated in the eighth Richa. The tenth passage speaks of Vyasava speeding away. All these events show that Keresaspa had his sway in his time and the Manavs were unable to cope with him, justifying all the importance he has received in the *Avesta*. This was, however, not a situation of a king with an army, whose authority does not get affected with age. It was a situation of a strong individual dominating neighbours. Age had to catch up and it appears Keresaspa was killed in the end. The fourth Richa speaks of Indra killing Kuyavac in combat for Duryoni and the ninth says that he overcame Anhavayya in combat for the sacrificial deeds of Turvash and Yadu. The latter two had fled earlier and have been said to have been brought back safely in the other Richas. It seems that Keresaspa was killed by Duryoni.

In the *Avesta* and the later Pahlavi texts, names of several persons have been mentioned who were killed by Keresaspa. These cannot be identified in the *Veds*, except the Gandarewa, who has been called the golden-heeled. Gandharv, in Indian mythology, are demi-gods like the Yaksh were in Arjika. However, unlike the Yaksh, who are associated with strength and power, the Gandharvs are linked to music and dance. This seems to be another Aryan tribe that the Manavs encountered in the new homeland. In mythology, they are friends of the Devs and are often depicted as providing entertainment by singing and dancing. Evidently, they had been converted by the Manavs to their religion and in the conflict with the Asurs were on their side. The Gandharvs seem to have been a tribe of exceptionally beautiful people, as they are the only ones whose women have been mentioned separately with a distinct name. They have been called Apsara, a term, in later Sanskrit synonymous with beauty par excellence. The fact that Apsaras were Gandharv women is brought out from the following references.

1. Wandering in the track of the Apsaras and the Gandharvs, and the wild beasts, the radiant (sun), cognizant of all that is knowable (is my) sweet and most delightful friend.

    (*Rig Ved*. M-10, S-136, R-6)

2. They that are noisy, dusky, dice-loving, mind-confusing to those Apsaras, who are the wives of Gandharvs, have I paid homage.

    (*Atharv Ved*. Kand 2, Sukt-3, Richa-5)

3. Homage to the Gandharv's mind, and homage to his terrible eye we pay; O Vishwavasu, homage to you with worship, to your wives the Apsaras.

    (*Atharv Ved*. Kand-14, Sukt-2, Richa-35)

It appears that the Gandharvs and Apsaras, apart from being an Aryan tribe of exceptional beauty, were people with a zest for life. They had a lot of music, dancing and gambling in their lives. The Rishis coming from the frosty banks of Ili, where religion was so important that a small disagreement led to bloodshed, were floored by these beautiful, bohemian people and were always keen to be a part of their fun and frolic. This is what we find them praying for.

1. The wise taste, through their pious acts, the ghee-resembling waters of these two (abiding) in the permanent region of the Gandharvs.

    (*Rig Ved*. M-1, S-22, R-14)

2.   The cloudy one, gleamer, starry one—you that accompany the Gandharv Vishwavasu, to you there, O divine ones, homage do I pay.

(*Atharv Ved*. Kand 2, Sukta-3, Richa-4)

3.   He who made these riches for our playing, who the taking and leaving of the dice—that god, enjoying this libation of ours—may we revel in a joint revelling with the Gandharvs.

(*Atharv Ved*. Kand 7, Sukta-114, Richa-5)

After a lapse of time some Gandharvs seem to have adopted the Asur religion. This is reflected from the following Richas.

1.   By you do we expel the Apsaras, the Gandharvas; O goat-horned one, drive the demon; make all disappear by (your) smell.

2.   Let the Apsaras go to the stream, to the loud down-blowing of the waters: Guggulu, Pila, Naladi, Aukshagandhi, Pramadani: so go away, you Apsaras; you have been recognized.

3.   Where (are) the ashvaths, the nyagrodhs, great trees with crests, thither go away, you Apsaras, you have been recognised.

4.   Where (are) your swings, green and whitesh, where cymbals (and) lutes sound together—thither go away, you Apsaras, you have been recognised.

5.   Hither has come this mighty one (viryavant) of the herbs, of the plants; let the goat-horned arataki, the sharp-horned, push out.

6.   Of the hither-dancing, crested Gandharv, Apsara-lord, I split the testicles, I bind fast the member.

7.   Terrible are Indra's missiles, a hundred spears of iron; with them let him push out the oblation-eating, avaka-eating Gandharvs.

(*Atharv Ved*. Kand–4, Sukta–37, Richas 2 to 8)

The seventh Richa discloses the reason for this animosity being expressed against the Gandharvs and the Apsaras. They had begun to eat the oblation, an indication of their conversion.

So much for the Gandharvs in general, the individual who is reported killed by Keresaspa, appears to be Vishwavasu in the *Veds*. The passages relating to him are given here.

1. Beholding Som, the Gandharv Vishwavasu, the waters have come forth by means of the sacrifice; Indra impelling them knew of this (their approach) and looked round the rims of the sun.

2. May the celestial Gandharv Vishwavasu the measurer of the water, declare to us that which is the truth, and that which we do not know; accepting our praises (Vishwavasu), protect our sacrifices.

3. (Indra) discovered the cloud in the region of the rivers, he set open the portals of (the waters) whose dwelling is in the clouds; Indra (in the form of) the Gandharv (Vishwavasu), proclaimed the ambrosial (waters), he knew the strength of the serpents.

                                             (*Rig Ved.* M-10, S-139, R-4 to 6)

4. For safety of this all, let the Gandharv Vishwavasu lay you round as a protection. You are the sacrificer's guard, you, Agni, lauded and worshipped to receive laudation. Indra's right arm are you.

                                             (*Yajur Ved.* Adhyay-2, Yajush-3)

These passages show that the dispute was over water as they all speak of water coming forth, water being measured and portals of water being set open. The third Richa states that the Gandharv Vishwavasu came forward to assist the Manavs by saying that Indra in the form of the Gandharv did so and he knew the strength of the Ahis, the serpents, a term used for the Asurs. The second Richa seeks the protection of Vishwavasu for the sacrifices, as does the fourth passage. Apparently, Gandharv Vishwavasu resisted Keresaspa for sometime, but was finally killed, as reported in the *Avesta*.

In the *Veds*, names of several Asurs have been mentioned who seem to have been killed during this period after the Asurs ceased to be a force with Keresaspa dead. It appears that the rise of the Manavs and their dominance was either because of people getting converted to their religion or the departure of a sizeable Asur population. Once the Manavs became dominant, the Asurs had limited choices. The *Veds* reflect a long period of Manav dominance in which the Asurs seem to have been killed at random. There does not seem to have been any major combat as the events are not reported with their details. Just the names have been mentioned. From the side of the Manavs, the name of Dabhiti is mentioned quite often. He seems to have been a strong personality of his time, who appears to have killed quite a few Asurs. Some passages relating to him are mentioned here.

1. Encountering the (Asurs) carrying off Dabhiti, he burnt all their weapons in a kindled fire, and enriched (the prince) with their cattle, their horses and their chariots, in the exhilaration of the Som, Indra has done these (deeds).

2. By his great power he turned the Sindhu towards the north; with his thunderbolt he ground to pieces the wagon of the dawn, scattering the tardy enemy with his swift forces; in the exhilaration of the Som, Indra has done these (deeds).

   (*Rig Ved.* M-2, S-15, R-4 and 6)

3. You have slain the Dasyu Chumuri and Dhuni, having cast them into sleep; you have protected Dabhiti, whilst his chamberlain gained in that (contest) for the gold (of the Asurs); in the exhilaration of the Som, Indra has done these (deeds).

   (*Rig Ved.* M-2, S-15, R-9)

4. May the praises of Gauriviti exalt you; you have humbled Pipru for the son of Vidhathin; Rjisvan preparing dressed viands has through your friendship brought you (to his presence) and you have drunk of his libation.

   (*Rig Ved.* M-5, S-29, R-11)

5. Rjisva, the son of Ushija, with Indra's praises shattered the cow pen of Pipru with the thunderbolt, when having expressed (the Som) the venerable sage recited his praises (Indra) proceeding against the cities (of the enemy) triumphed with his body.

   (*Rig Ved.* M-10, S-99, R-11)

These Richas use the name Rjisvan also for Dabhiti. He has been called the son of Vidhathin in the fourth Richa and of Ushij in the fifth. Ushij appears to be the name of a forefather. He is reported to have killed Pipru, Chumuri and Dhuni. The first Richa shows that, to start with, the Manavs were weak and the Asurs had an upper hand as Dabhiti is reported to have been carried away by them and somehow managed to survive. The Richas after this have Dabhiti winning. The second gives an idea of the river flowing in this homeland. It is flowing south to north though named Sindhu. Apart from the exploits of Dabhiti, the names of several Asurs that appear to have been killed emerge from the texts. The most prominent amongst them is Arbud. The passages about him are here.

1. You have defended Kutsa in fatal fights with Shushna, you have destroyed Shambar in defence of Atithigva; you have trodden with your foot upon the great Arbud; from remote times were you born for the destruction of oppressors.

    (*Rig Ved*. M-1, S-51, R-6)

2. Pierce the water holding the domain of the great Arbud; achieve, Indra, this manly exploit.

    (*Rig Ved*. M-8, S-32, R-3)

3. The brilliant Indra slew Vritra, Aurnavabh, Ahishuv; he killed Arbud with snow.

    (*Rig Ved*. M-8, S-33, R-26)

The third Richa is significant, as it states that Arbud was killed by snow. This is a direct evidence from the *Veds* to establish that these fights were not in the warm plains of Sapt Sindhu, but in much colder regions. Apparently, Arbud fled the place, like so many Manavs had done when Keresaspa was there. He seems to have been unlucky to succumb to the ruthless Central Asian winter. He could have been the Kavi of the Asurs. The *Aitarey Brahman* and the Shat Path Brahman, have references to him, which give an interesting insight of the situation. They are given here.

1. The gods held a sacrificial session in Sarvacharu. They did not succeed in destroying the consequences of guilt. Arbud, the son of Kadru, the serpent Rishi, the framer of mantras, said to them, 'You have overlooked one ceremony. I will perform it for you, then you will destroy the consequences of guilt.' They said, 'Well, let it be done.' At every midday libation he then came forth, and repeated spells over the Som squeezing stones. Thence, they repeat spells at every midday libation over the Som squeezing stones,

in imitation of him. The way in which the serpent Rishi used to go when coming from (his abode) is now known by the name Arbudoda Sarpani.

(*Aitarey Brahman*. Book VI, Chapter I)

2. 'Adhvaryu,' he (the Hotri) says. 'Havai Hotar,' replies the Adhrvaryu. 'King Arbud Kedraveya,' he says, 'his people are the snakes, and they are staying here,' both snakes and snake-charmers have come thither; it is these he instructs, 'the Sarpavidya (science of snakes) is the Ved; this it is.'

(Shat Path Brahman. Kand XIII, Adhyay-4, Brahman 3)

The passage from the Shat Path Brahman calls Arbud a king and his people, the snakes, a term used in the *Veds* for Asurs. His teachings have been called Sarpavidya or the science of snakes. It seems that over time, understanding of the terms had changed. Arbud was evidently an Asur, but a wise and pious man. His teachings seem to have been adopted by the Manavs on certain issues and appear to have got merged in the *Veds* and the Brahman literature. Since it came from an Asur, it was called Sarpavidya or the knowledge that came from the snake. This meaning appears to have been lost and it was thought to be a science of snakes. It is, however, beyond doubt that whatever had been prescribed by Arbud became a part of the rituals of the Manavs. The first passage confirms this. It also talks of destroying the consequences of guilt. Apparently, despite whatever emerges from the scriptures with both sides revelling at the killings of the other, when it was all happening, there appears to have been a sense of guilt and remorse. They could see that it was fratricide and so was extremely unfortunate. Even, if they were unable to stop it, they do not seem to have had the feeling of glee which gets reflected from the texts of later times, once these killings turned into mythology and the opponents became snakes and demons. It also shows that they had respect for the learned of the other side as Arbud has been called a Rishi, though a serpent Rishi and the Manavs have taken his help in correcting their sacrificial rituals. This speaks volumes about the mutual relationship of the two sides and should not be missed in the din of Indra's chariot and thunderbolt.

The Zoroastrian scriptures have similar features. There is a passage where Ahur Mazda shows Zoroaster the soul of Keresaspa being put through the tortures of hell. At places it gives the reason for it, as his killing of the people, though finally it states that he met this fate because he had offended Fire. Evidently, when initially such a story emerged, it was a time when people thought that what he had done was sinful. Over time, the legend ripened to be a story of a hero killing demons, snakes and other evil creatures. His suffering the tortures of hell then needed a new explanation for which Fire had to be brought in. This is in the following passage.

> The fourteenth fargard, Ad-fravakhshya, is about Auharmazd's showing to Zartust the terrible condition of the soul of Keresasp; the dismay of Zartust owing to that terrible condition; the sorrowful speaking of Keresasp as regard the slaying of multitudes, whereby abstentions from sin occurred; and the recognition of him by the creator, Auharmazd, as smiting his fire…
>
> The petition of Zartust to the fire to have compassion upon what was owing to Keresasp's sin; the compliance of the fire with the petition, and the departure of the soul of Keresasp to the ever-stationary existence.
>
> (Dinkard. Book IX. Chapter XV)

There are several passages in the *Veds* giving names of Asurs who appear to have been of this period. They do not say much about what happened except that they were killed. A few references are given here.

1. To him has that praise been offered which he, sole (victor over his foes), and lord of manifold wealth, prefers (to receive) from those (who praise him), Indra has defended the pious sacrificer Etash when contending with Surya, the son of Svashwa.

    (*Rig Ved*. M-1, S-61, R-15)

2. You, who are (famed for) many exploits, put on today an unclouded countenance (as prepared) to slay Sahavasu, son of Narmar, with the sharpened (edge of the thunderbolt), in defence of the (sacrificial) food, and for the destruction of the Dasyu; you

are he who is to be praised.

(*Rig Ved.* M-2, S-13, R-8)

3. Sufficient was he for (the protection of) this (world), which he its defender, fabricated with his two arms for the sake of all mankind, over whom he was supreme by his wisdom, whereby (also) he the loud-shouting, having struck Krivi with the thunderbolt, has consigned him to (eternal) slumber on the earth.

(*Rig Ved.* M-2, S-17, R-6)

4. You have slain the five hundreds and thousands (of the followers) of the slave Varchin (surrounding) him like the fellies (round the spokes of the wheel).

(*Rig Ved.* M-4, S-30, R-15)

5. Indra, the granter of wished-for felicity, compelled the many-fraudulent Etasha and Dasoni, Tutuji, Tugra and Ibha always to come submissively to Dyotana, as a son (comes before a father).

(*Rig Ved.* M-6, S-21, R-8)

6. You have brought to Vrishabh a great war-chariot, you have protected him warring for ten days, you have slain Tugra along with Vetasu, and you have exalted Tuji glorifying you.

(*Rig Ved.* M-6, S-26, R-4)

7. Favouring Abhayavartin, the son of Chayaman, Indra destroyed the race of Varshik, killing the descendants of Vrichivat (who were stationed) on the Hariyupiya, on the eastern part, whilst the western was scattered through fear.

(*Rig Ved.* M-6, S-27, R-5)

8. His bright prancing horses, delighted with choice fodder, proceed between (heaven and earth), gave up Turvash to Srinjay, subjecting the Vrichivats to the descendants of Devavat.

(*Rig Ved.* M-6, S-27, R-7)

9. The fierce (deity) who, liberating the waters, has slain Sribind, Anarshani, Pipru and the Dasyu Ahisuva.

(*Rig Ved.* M-8, S-32, R-2)

10. May we once more know you as such, O gracious hero, as when you did aid Etash in the decisive battle, or Vash against Dashvraj.

(*Rig Ved.* M-8, S-50, R-9)

11. They that ruled a thousand (years) and were ten hundreds, those Vaitahavyas, having devoured the cow of the Brahman, perished.

12. The cow herself, being slain, pulled down those Vaitahavyas, who cooked the last female goat of Kesarprabandh.

(Atharv Ved. Kand 5, Sukt-19, Richa-10 and 11)

The geographical features of this homeland are mentioned while describing the events. The *Avesta* mentions the Rangha river with one of its channels while speaking of the exploits of Keresaspa. The *Veds* talk of the Sipha river. They also mention three more rivers. The direction of the flow of the river is also indicated south to north. Apart from these references, which are in connection with certain events, this Richa of the *Rig Ved* confirms that the place has four rivers.

> The deeds of that graceful Indra are most admirable; his exploits are most glorious, in that he has replenished the four rivers of sweet water, spread over the surface of the earth.
>
> (Rig Ved. M-1, S-62, R-6)

There is an indication in the *Avesta* also that this place had four rivers. It is given here.

> Whose long arms encompass what he seizes in the easternmost river and what he beats with the westernmost river, what is by the Sanaka by the Rangha and what is by the boundary of the earth.
>
> (Mihir Yast XXVII)

These people were again in the delta of a river. The great waters mentioned in connection with the golden-heeled Gandarewa refer to the sea. The geographical features here are similar to those of Arjika, except that the mountain is missing as in all descriptions there is no mention of a mountain or the rivers flowing swiftly or causing turbulence in the sea. There is an indication in the *Veds* that this location does not have mountains. The Richa is given below.

> Destroyer of foes, praised by the Angiras Rishis, you have scattered the darkness with the dawn, and with the rays of

the sun; you have made straight the elevations of the earth;
you have strengthened the foundations of the ethereal region.

(Rig Ved. M-1, S-62, R-5)

With this one difference in the geographical features this homeland
has to be located in the map. It is not difficult because before this they
were near lake Balkash, and after this, a group from them emerges
in the capital of Persia. This homeland has to be on the way. It is the
Amu Dariya river flowing into the Aral Sea forming a delta, which is
not as diffused as the delta of the Ili. This homeland falls in Uzbekistan
in modern times. Unfortunately, the Amu Dariya does not flow any
longer as its entire water has been diverted for irrigation projects.
Even the Aral Sea is no longer the same and has shrunk to a quarter
of what it used to be.

The region of the Amu Dariya being their homeland at this stage
is confirmed by the *Avesta* where Ahur Mazda tells Zoroaster about the
various lands and countries that he has created. In this, after naming
Airyana Vaego as the first of the good lands and countries created by
him, the next is in this passage.

The second of the good lands and countries which I, Ahur
Mazda created, was the plains in Sughdha. Thereupon came
Angra Mainyu, who is all death, and he counter-created by
his witchcraft the fly Skaitya, which brings death to the cattle.

(Vendidad. Fargard I)

Sughdha is this very region. The *Avesta* naming it next after Airyana
Vaego points to it being the homeland after Arjika.

7

Other Possible Migrations

T HE STORY THAT WE HAVE, emerges from the *Veds* and the
Zoroastrian scriptures. It is limited to people who remained
linked to these two religious identities. In the upheaval that began
at Arjika and continued in Sugadha, it is likely that some groups of
this tribe moved away in directions different from where these two
were and lost contact with them, developing a different identity for
themselves. This seems to be possible more in the case of the Asurs,
as Zoroaster, when he appeared on the scene, found very few of them.
His conversions were more amongst the Persians, who were a different
Aryan group. Writings of Greek writers show that the Kimmerians
were one such group. Also called Cimmerians, these people have been
noticed by several ancient sources, including the *Bible* and Homer. The
information of interest that emerges from some of them is mentioned
here.

1. The Scythians in truth, had ruled Upper Asia for eight and twenty
    years; for they invaded Asia in pursuit of the Kimmerians and they
    had disposed the Medes from their rule over Asia, who had rule
    over Asia before the Scythians came.

    (Herodotus. *The Histories*. Book 4. Para 1)

2. This whole land which has been described is so exceedingly severe
    in climate, that for eight months of the year there is frost so hard
    as to be intolerable; and the sea is frozen and the whole of the
    Kimmerian Bosphorus, so that the Scythians make expeditions
    and drive their wagons over into the country of the Sindians.

    (Herodotus. *The Histories*. Book 4. Para 28)

These references indicate the place where the Kimmerians initially dwelt, before they were driven out by the Scythians. They are reported to be in the northern part of Central Asia, a region which had a very severe winter. A large water body is also reported, which has been called the Kimmerian Bosphorus. The winter is so severe that this water body freezes to enable people to take wagons over it. They have been reported to have been driven out by the Scythians from this homeland. In reading Herodotus and other Greek writers an impression emerges that the term Scythian was used for any race coming from the north, to which the Greeks had not given an independent name. In describing the military campaigns of Darius, Herodotus states that he proceeded to the east of the River Oxus to fight the Scythians. Again while dealing with similar campaigns of his son Xerxes, he places the Scythians to the north of the river Danube in Europe. At times they are stated to be on the shores of the Arabian Sea while some references place them on the south of the Black Sea. Some Scythians are referred to as nomads, while some are reported to be practicing agriculture and some have been called Royal Scythians. A single race cannot be spread over such a vast area and be at such varied levels of development to be nomadic and settled at the same time.

The following passage gives an account of the Kimmerians being dislodged by the Scythians from their homeland and their movement thereafter.

There is however also another story, and to this I am most inclined myself. It is to the effect that the Nomad Scythians dwelling in Asia, being hard pressed in war by the Messagetai, left their abode and crossing the river Araxes came towards the Kimmerian land (for the land which is now occupied by the Scythians is said to have been in former times the land of the Kimmerians); and the Kimmerians, when the Scythians were coming against them, took counsel together, seeing that a great host was coming to fight against them; and it proved that their opinions were divided, both opinions being vehemently maintained, but the better being that of their kings: for the opinion of the people was that it was necessary to depart and that they ought not to run the risk of fighting against so many, but that of the kings was to fight for their land: and as neither the people were willing to agree to the counsel of the kings nor the kings to that of the people, the people planned to depart without fighting, while the kings resolved to die and to be laid in their own land, and not to flee. Having resolved upon this, they parted into two bodies, and making their numbers equal they fought with one another: and when these had all been killed by one another's hands, then the people of the Kimmerians buried them by the bank of the river Tyras, and having buried them, then they made their way out of the land.

And there are at present time in the land of Scythia Kimmerian walls, and a Kimmerian ferry; and there is also a region which is called Kimmeria, and the so-called Kimmerian Bosphorus. It is known, moreover, that the Kimmerians in their flight to Asia from the Scythians, also made a settlement on the peninsula on which now stands the Hellenic city of Sinope; and it is known too that the Scythians pursued them and invaded the land of Media, having missed their way; for while the Kimmerians kept ever along by the sea in their flight, the Scythians pursued them keeping Caucasus on their right hand, until at last they invaded Media.

Aristeas, however, said that he came to the land of Issedonians being possessed by Phoebus, and that beyond the Issedonians dwelt Arimaspians, and beyond them the Hyperboreans extending as far as the sea: and all these except the Hyperboreans beginning with the Arimaspians, were continually making war on their neighbours, and the Issedonians were gradually driven out of their country by the Arimaspians and the Scythians by the Issedonians, and so the Kimmerians, who dwelt on the Southern Sea, being pressed by the Scythians left their land. Thus, neither does he agree in regard to this land with the report of the Scythians.

(Herodotus. *The Histories*. Book 4. Paras 11 to 13)

This passage gives another geographical feature of the homeland of the Kimmerians. There is a river flowing which has been named Tyras. The presence of a large water body called the Kimmerian Bosphorus has also been confirmed. The manner in which these people are reported to have been uprooted is of interest. It states, that in the face of an impending invasion, the kings decided to fight, while the common people decided to leave. The kings, therefore, divided themselves in two equal groups and fought each other till death to be given a burial near the river Tyras by the common people, before leaving. The manner in which the kings got killed is unusual. Throughout history whichever side has decided to die fighting, has died fighting the enemy. There has been no instance wherein it divided itself into two groups and fought each other till all were killed. The forefathers of the Kimmerians could not have done this, either. It appears that these people remembered certain facts of their past but forgot their details because of which distortions crept into their folklore which got passed over to Herodotus. It seems that they remembered that they had fought one or more fratricidal wars and that they were driven out of their homeland by a neighbouring tribe. The causes of the fratricidal wars and they being wars different from the one by which they got dislodged from their homeland, seem to be the facts that were forgotten. In a situation wherein the causes of the fratricidal wars had to be explained, their folklore linked them to the only other remembered fact, of being driven out and wove a story that has come down to us. These affairs seem to be referring to the incidents of Arjika. The fratricidal war of their past, that has been remembered by the Kimmerians, appears to be the Dev Asur Sangram, beginning with the war between Manu and Ardh Shipra, and continuing thereafter. They being dislodged by the Scythians, seems to be a reference to the wars against Shambar that were fought by Divodas and Sudas. As they have remembered that it was not their kinsmen but people from elsewhere who dislodged them, the Kimmerians appear to be the Asurs of the *Veds*. The passage also shows that these people migrated along the Caspian Sea to the south and then west.

The Kimmerians being Asurs is indicated also by the interest the Persians evinced in the attack on them by the Scythians. Their interest emerges from the following passage.

> For all the armies of which we have knowledge this proved to be by far the greatest; so that neither that led by Dareios against the Scythians appears anything as compared with it, nor the Scythian host, when the Scythians pursuing the Kimmerians made invasion of the Median land, for which invasion afterwards Dareios attempted to take vengeance, nor that led by the Atreus to Ilion.
>
> (Herodotus. *The Histories*. Book 7. Para 20)

Herodotus is describing the army of Xerxes wherein he has stated, that it was greater than that of Darius against the Scythians, of the Scythians against the Kimmerians and of the Greeks against Troy. This shows that the Scythian attack on the Kimmerians had become a part of the mythology with the Persians because of which the size of the Scythian army had acquired mythological proportions. Of the times the attack has been spoken of, the Scythians could not have had the capacity to assemble an army of a size to be considered to be comparable with that of Xerxes. It has also been stated that Darius attempted to take vengeance for this invasion. Darius having reasons to consider it necessary to take vengeance on the Scythians for their attack on the Kimmerians, too is indicative of their Asur identity as the Persians were Zoroastrians.

The Kimmerians, in their migration appear to have reached the western most parts of Asia and were noticed near the Strait of Bosphorus. At a stage they seem to have had their rule over the area, as well as a flourishing city. This emerges from the following passage.

1. And I am not able to understand for what reason it is that to the Earth, which is one, three different names are given derived from women, and why there were set boundaries to divide it, the river Nile of Egypt and the Phasis of Colchis (or as some say the Maiotian river Tanais and the Kimmerian ferry).

> (Herodotus. *The Histories*. Book 4. Para 45)

2. After the Tauric land immediately come Scythians again, occupying the parts above Tauroi and the coasts of the Eastern Sea, that is to say parts of the West of the Kimmerian Bosphorus and of the Maiotian Lake, as far as the river Tanais, which runs into the corner of this lake.

(Herodotus. *The Histories*. Book 4. Para 100)

3. Homer, then, knows and clearly describes the remote ends of the inhabited earth; and he is just as familiar with the region of the Mediterranean Sea. For if you begin at the Pillars of Heracles, you will find that the Mediterranean Sea is bound by Libya, Egypt and Phoenicia, and further on Cyprus; then by the territory of the Solymi, by Lycia and by Caria, and next by the seaboard between Mycale and the Troad; and all these lands are mentioned by Homer, as well as those farther on; more than that, he knows the Kimmerian Bosphorus, because he knows the Kimmerians—for surely, if he knows the name of the Kimmerians, he is not ignorant of the people themselves—the Kimmerians who, in Homer's own time or shortly before his time, overran the whole country from the Bosphorus to Ionia. At least he intimates that the very climate of their country is gloomy, and the Kimmerians, as he says, are 'shrouded in mist and cloud, and never does the shining sun look upon them, but deadly night is spread over them'.

(Strabo. Geographica. Book I. Chapter 1. Para 10)

4. Kimmericum was in earlier times a city situated on the peninsula, and it closed the isthmus by means of a trench and a mound. The Kimmerians once possessed great power in the Bosphorus and this is why it is named Kimmerian Bosphorus. These are the people who overran the country of those who lived in the interior on the right side of the Pontus as far as Ionia.

(Strabo. Geographica. Book XI. Chapter 2. Para 5)

These passages from Herodotus and Strabo show that the Kimmerians were close to the Strait of Bosphorus. They also ruled over the area and had a flourishing city with the name Kimmericum. In the second passage Herodotus has named Kimmerian Bosphorus with reference to the location where the Bosphorus is presently known. In the first passage he has called it the Kimmerian Ferry and has mentioned it as the dividing line between Europe and Asia. However, in the earlier references Kimmerian Bosphorus has been mentioned by him at a location in Upper Asia where winters are very severe and it freezes. This gives an impression that the name Bosphorus was with the Kimmerians for a water body in their homeland and they gave it to the next water body too in their new place of settlement. The word could have Vouru Kasha for its origin. The passages from Strabo give further details about them at this location on the western edge of Asia.

After this long journey in Asia, the Kimmerians were finally pushed over to Europe. This movement is brought out from the following passages.

1. Now when Ardys had been king, Sadyattes his son succeeded and after him Alyattes. This last made war against Kyaxares the descendant of Deiokes and against the Medes, and he drove the Kimmerians forth out of Asia.

    (Herodotus. *The Histories*. Book 1. Para 16)

2. Others, however, say that the Kimmerians who were first known to the ancient Greeks were not a large part of the entire people, but merely a body of exiles or a faction which was driven away by the Scythians and passed from the Maeotic Lake into Asia under the lead of Lygdamis; whereas the largest and most warlike part of the people dwelt at the confines of the earth along the outer sea, occupying a land that is shaded and wholly sunless by reason of the height and thickness of the trees; and as regards the heavens, they are under that portion of them where the Pole gets a great elevation by reason of the declination of the parallels, and appears to have a position not far removed from the spectator's zenith, and a day and night divide the year into two parts. From these regions, then, these Barbarians sallied forth against Italy, being called at first Kimmerians, and then not inappropriately, Cimbri.

    (Plutarch. Life of Marius)

In the first passage, Herodotus tells about the Kimmerians being driven out of Asia. The second is from Plutarch who lived between AD 46 and

120. This is very significant, as apart from locating the Kimmerians in Italy, it gives information about something that the Kimmerians would have remembered of their past and would have passed it on to others. It states that they came from a place where the Pole gets a great elevation and appears to have a position not far removed from the spectator's zenith and a day and night divide the year into two parts. It is evident that this is a reference to the Arctic Circle. The Kimmerians had remembered this ancient homeland, and this statement from them confirms the information emerging from the *Veds* and the Avesta that the journey of this Aryan group began from the Arctic Circle. Homer too seems to have been aware of this though he has mentioned only a long night, and not also a long day. This could have been, because that suited his story as he had taken Odysseus for a visit to Hades. This is what we have him say.

> We had attained Earth's verge and its girdling river of Ocean, where are the cloud-wrapped and misty confines of the Kimmerian men. For them no flashing Sun-God shines down a living light, not in the morning when he climbs through the starry sky, nor yet at day's end when he rolls down from heaven behind the land. Instead an endless deathful night is spread over its melancholy people.
>
> (*Odyssey*. Book 11)

The *Bible* has the name Gomer for the Kimmerians. There is a mention of Asshur also along with them. The relevant extracts are here.

1. Now these are the generations of the sons of Noah; Shem, Ham and Japeth: and unto them were sons born after the floods. The sons of Japeth; Gomer, and Magog, and Madai, and Javan, and Tubal, and Mesheeh, and Tiras. And the sons Gomer; Ashkenaz, and Riphath, and Togarmah.

    (*Bible*. Genesis. Chapter 10. Paras 1 to 3)

2. Out of that land went forth Asshur, and builded Ninevah, and the city Rehoboth, and Calah.

    (*Bible*. Genesis. Chapter 10. Para 11)

3. The children of Shem; Elam, and Asshur, and Arphaxad, and
    Lud, and Aram.

                              (*Bible*. Genesis. Chapter 10. Para 22)

The mention of Asshur as different from Gomer is significant. The
available information shows that neither the Kimmerians nor, later
the Zoroastrians, called themselves Asshurs. It is only the Vedic
people who called them so. The people who called themselves
Asshur were the Assyrians. The first city that they built was named
Assur, the area where they dwelt was called Asuristan, the God
they worshipped was Ashur and several of their kings had the word
pre-fixed to their name like Ashur Bel Kala, Ashur Rabi, Ashur
Nasirpal, Ashur Dan, Ashur Haddon, Ashur Banipal and Ashur
Ilani etc. The *Bible* too is referring to these people only as there is
a mention of Ninevah which was their capital. In what way, if any,
were these Ashurs related to the Asurs of the *Veds* cannot be said
with the available information.

   If a match for the name Kimmerian is looked for on the Indian
side, we have the Kinnars. These are demi-gods in Indian mythology,
along with Yakshs and Gandharvs, and have the image of being the
minstrels of the Devs. The word Kinnar has been formed by joining
two words, 'kim' and 'nar'. 'Kim' means 'what', while 'nar' means
'man'. In later Sanskrit, it has been explained to mean 'what a man'
and has been used for eunuchs. This does not appear to have been
the earlier meaning as the word has its origin in the *Veds* where
'Kimidin' has been used for certain people. Yask, the Vedic scholar
of the seventh century BC has, in his work 'the Nirukt', explained
this to mean people who went around saying, 'Kim Idaaneem' which
means 'what now', or 'Kim Idam' which means 'what is this'. Sayan
has agreed with this statement. This only goes to show that even as
early as the seventh century BC the meaning of this word had been
lost. The passages that mention Kimidins are here.

1. Indra and Som, fall upon the Rakshas and the performer of
    unprofitable rites, so that, consume (by your wrath), he may perish
    like the offering cast into the fire; retain implacable hatred to the

hater of the Brahmans, the cannibals, the hideous, the Kimidin.

(*Rig Ved*. M-7, S-104, R-2)

2. Let not the Rakshas do us harm, let the dawn drive away the pair of Kimidins, may the earth protect us from terrestrial, the sky protect us from celestial wickedness.

(*Rig Ved*. M-7, S-104, R-23)

3. Let the Yatudhan cry out, let the devouring Kimidins; then do you, O Agni together with Indra, welcome this our oblation.

(*Atharv Ved*. Kand-1, Sukt-7, Richa-3)

4. Hither had come forth god Agni, demon slayer, disease expeller, burning away deceivers, Yatudhans, Kimidins.

5. Burn against the Yatudhans, against the Kimidins, O god; burn up the sorceress that meet you, O black-tracked one.

(*Atharv Ved*. Kand-1, Sukt-28, Richas 1 and 2)

6. I have seized out his shelter the Yatudhan, the Kimidin; with it do I see everyone, both Shudra and Aryan.

(*Atharv Ved*. Kand-4, Sukt-20, Richa-8)

7. Bless us in fights, O formidable ones; visit with (your) vajra whoever is a Kimidin; I praise Bhav and Sharv; as a suppliant I call loudly on (them); do you free us from distress.

(*Atharv Ved*. Kand-4, Sukt-28, Richa-7)

8. O Indra and Som, against the evil-plotter, the evil heat let boil all up like a fiery pot; assign unavoidable hate to the Brahman-hating, flesh-eating Kimidin of terrible aspect.

(*Atharv Ved*. Kand-8, Sukt-4, Richa-2)

9. What Gandharvs, Apsaras (there are), and what Aryas, Kimidins, the Pishachs, all Rakshas—them do you keep away from us, O earth.

(*Atharv Ved*. Kand-12, Sukt-1, Richa-50)

These Richas give a picture that Kimidin is a term used in the *Veds* for the Asurs. It seems that the term got coined while the Devs were reviling them for their language, which had not remained chaste as was that of the Devs. It appears that these people used to say 'Kimidin' either for 'Kim Idaaneem' or for 'Kim Idam', the terms mentioned by Yask. Language was a major issue on which the Devs reviled the Asurs. At several places in the *Veds* they have been called babblers and people with a discordant tongue, etc. Kinnar should therefore not be understood to mean 'what a man' but as 'the Kim people'. The name seems to have got affixed to them, who would have had something similar in their language which got Hellenized as Kimmerian. It appears that they were there in the delta of the Amu Dariya as they have been named along with the Gandharvs and Apsaras in the ninth Richa. They must have migrated away after the Devs gained ascendency in the area and were creating problems for their rivals. This, however, would have been before the advent of Zoroaster as he did not have any influence on them.

8

In The Persian Capital

THE BASIN OF THE AMU Dariya remained the homeland of these Aryans for very long. Neither side was uprooted and migrations from here were normal migrations motivated by considerations of better prospects or growth of population. They were not forced out, as was the case on the earlier occasion. The Aryans, who came to India and brought the *Veds* with them, emerge in the Persian capital after this and have been noticed in history. They have been called the Magis and Medes. In the Persian capital, they came across another Aryan tribe which in history has been called the Persians. They spoke Pahlavi, a language different from the language of the Magis, and which became Persian later. Despite this difference they had the Magis as their priests. This is significant, as religion is something intimate to a society in which it trusts only its own people. The Persians adopting the Magis as their priests shows that they considered them more suitable than their own people, so far as religion was considered. Apparently, they had been converted to the religion of the Devs, who had taken up missionary activities from very early times and, therefore, trusted the Magis as their priests more than their own people. Herodotus provides some very useful information about the relationship of the Magis and Medes with this Aryan tribe. A quote from him is mentioned here.

The Medes served in the expedition equipped in precisely the same manner; for this equipment is in fact Median and not Persian: and the Medes acknowledged as their commander Tigranes an Achaimenid. These in ancient times used to be generally called Arians; but when Medea the Colchian came from Athens to these Arians, they also changed their names. Thus, the Medes themselves report about themselves.

(Herodotus. *The Histories*. Book 7. Para 62)

The army of Xerxes is being discussed, wherein the Medes had a contingent. It has been stated that the Medes were called Aryans in earlier times. This is an important piece of information as it links the Medes to the Aryan tribe coming from Arjika, because although there were several Aryan groups in Europe and Central Asia, none except the tribe coming from Arjika and with its influence the Persians, has used this name for itself. It has also been mentioned that they changed their name to Mede when Medea came to them from Athens. It would emerge ahead that while fleeing from Persia the followers of the Vedic religion went to Greece also, just as they came to India. Medea was evidently of the same tribe and is reported to have come from Athens. This statement would add to the evidence that the group of Aryans which came to India to be called the Indo-Aryans had branched off to go to Greece also. The relationship of the Magis, Medes and Persians emerges from the following passages.

1. Replying to this the Magians said: 'To us also, O king, it is of great consequence that thy rule should stand firm; for in the other case it is transferred to strangers, coming round to this boy who is a Persian, and we being Medes are made slaves and become of no account in the eyes of the Persians, seeing that we are of a different race; but while thou art established as our king, who are one of our own nation, we both have our share of rule and receive great honours from thee.'

    (Herodotus. *The Histories*. Book 1. Para 120)

2. Then said Gobryas: 'Friends, at what time will there be a fairer opportunity for us either to recover our rule, or, if we are not able to get it again, to die? Seeing that we being Persians on the one hand lie under the rule of a Mede, a Magian and that too, a man whose ears have been cut off...'

    (Herodotus. *The Histories*. Book 3. Para 73)

The Persians have also been called Medes at some places by Herodotus and other authors, but these passages show that the Magis and Medes were one people while the Persians were a different Aryan tribe.

Persia, at that time, was ruled by a dynasty which used the word Kavi for king in the tradition of Val, Manu and Yam. The word Kavi became Kai in Pahlavi because of which it has been called the Kayan dynasty. A few names are mentioned in the *Veds* too, but the *Avesta* provides a better account of the kings of this dynasty. This passage gives the names of the kings up to Husravah who has become Khusro in Pahlavi.

> That clave unto Kavi Kavata, and unto Kavi Aipivohu, and unto Kavi Usadha and unto Kavi Arshan, and unto Kavi Pisina, and unto Kavi Byarshan and unto Kavi Syavarshan. That clave unto Kavi Husravah, for the victory made by Ahur, for the extermination of the enemies at one stroke. So that King Husravah (had the lead) all along the long race, and he could not pass through the forest, he, the murderer, who was fiercely striving against him on horseback; the lord Kavi Husravah prevailed over all; he put in bonds Frangrasyan and Keresavazda, to avenge the murder of his father Syavarshana, a man, and of Aghraeratha, a semi-man.
>
> (Zamyad Yast XII)

The accounts elsewhere show that Husravah was succeeded by Loharasp, who was succeeded by Vistasp. It was Vistasp, who was converted to Zoroastrianism, the name acquired by the religion of the Asurs from his time onwards. The accounts of the *Avesta* show that the kings of this dynasty until the conversion followed the religion of the Dev worshippers, a term used for the Vedic religion at the time. Turan was an adjoining kingdom which, too, followed the same religion. Some references which show that the Vedic religion was being followed by the kings of this dynasty are given here.

1. To her did the great, most wise Kavi Usa offer up a sacrifice from Mount Erezifa. He begged of her a boon saying, 'Grant me this,

O good, most beneficent Ardvi Sura Anahita! That I may become the sovereign lord of all countries of the Daevas and men.'

(Aban Yast XII)

2. About the exercise of sovereignty by Kai Us, over the earth of seven regions; the construction of his seven dwellings in the midst of Alburz, the restraining of the many Mazonik demons, and confining them to their own duty. Afterwards, the consultation of the demons about the death of Kai Us, and the coming of Aeshm to Kai Us, therefore making him wretched in his mind about the great sovereignty which was possessed by him over the seven lands, and causing him to long for the sovereignty of the heavenly region of the archangels. And, owing to the seductiveness of Aeshm, and the other demons, Kai Us was even engaged in opposing and molesting the sacred beings. Also his not returning across Alburz, but rushing upwards with many demons and wicked people, unto the outer edge of darkness. The previous separation of Kai Us from the troops and his not turning from that ill-advisedness even on renewed strife aloft with the supreme sacred beings. Afterwards, the Creator's calling back the glory of the Kayans to himself, the falling of the troops of Kai Us to the earth from that height, and the flying of Kai Us to the wide-formed ocean.

(Dinkard. Book IX, Chapter XXII)

The second passage above shows that Kai Us, who is Kavi Usadha in the *Avesta* language, was a Dev worshipper. The demons in the translations would be Devs in the original text. This Kayan dynasty had Vedic priests and was following their religion. It is noteworthy here that it has been mentioned that Kai Us longed for the sovereignty of the heavenly region of the archangels. As the Dinkard is speaking of the religious practices of a rival religion, the presentation is understandably twisted. As would emerge ahead, the Vedic religion had two streams, the spiritual and the ritualistic. On the spiritual side, an effort was made to realize the self, in which the person ceased to identify himself with his physical existence and realized that he and God were the same. The concept of realization of this oneness of the individual with God has been expressed by the Dinkard, but twisted to mean that Kai Us wanted to become God in the conventional sense of the term. Husravah too has been mentioned prominently in the text. He seems to have united all the areas in Persia into one kingdom and fought a war with Turan to avenge the killing of his father. The incident of the killing of his father has not been mentioned anywhere except in connection with the revenge taken by Husravah. It seems a war was fought between Iran and Turan before Husravah, in which the king of Iran was defeated and killed, to avenge which Husravah fought the war that has been mentioned. The passages relating to Husravah are given here.

1.   To her did the gallant Husravah, he who united the Aryan nations into one kingdom, offer up a sacrifice; 'Grant me this boon, O Drvaspa! That I may kill the Turanian murderer, Franghrasyan, to avenge the murder of my father Syavarshana and of Aghraeratha, a semi-man.'

(Gos Yast V)

2.   To him did Aurvasara, the lord of the country offer up a sacrifice. He begged of him a boon saying, 'Grant me this, O Vayu! that the gallant Husravah, he who unites the Aryan nations into one kingdom, may not smite us, that I may flee from King Husravah.'

(Ram Yast VIII)

3.   Abstain far from the service of idols and demon-worship. Because it is declared that, 'If Kai Khusroi, should not have extirpated the idol-temples which were on lake Kekast, then in these three millenniums of Hushedar, Hushedar-mah and Soshans—of whom one of them comes separately at the end of each millennium—the adversary would have become so much more violent, that it would not have been possible to produce the resurrection and future existence.'

(Dina-i Mainog-i Khirad. Chapter II)

4.   And the advantage from Kai Khusroi was this, such as the slaying of Frasiyak, the extirpation of the idol-temples which were on Kekast lake and the management of Kangdez.

(Dina-i Mainog-i Khirad. Chapter XXVII)

From these the first thing that emerges is that Husravah united the Aryan nations into one kingdom. Apparently, there were several small sovereign states that were defeated by him to form a bigger unit. This consolidation of political power led to the rise of Persia as an empire. Turan remained an independent rival state, with which Husravah fought a war to avenge the killing of his father Syavarshana. Another thing that emerges is that he destroyed the idol-temples on lake Kaekasta. This lake seems to be the Caspian Sea as it is described as the deep lake of salt waters. Though the impression these scriptures are trying to give is that these idol-temples were of the Dev worshippers but this does not seem possible because firstly, Husravah, himself was a Dev worshipper and secondly, the Dev worshippers in Central Asia and the followers of the Vedic religion in India did not worship idols and did not have temples for them. Yagya or sacrifice was at the centre of their religious practices, in which a fire was kindled on an altar and sacrificial items consigned to it with mantras or hymns accompanying them. From the details available, it is not clear who these people were who had idol-temples on the bank of the Kaekasta lake. Husravah, despite being a Dev worshipper has been eulogized in the *Avesta* because his grandson, Vistasp, was converted to Zoroastrianism and played an important role in its spread. Much of these works were written in the times of Vistasp and his successors.

Husravah of the *Avesta* is Sushravas of the *Veds*, where we find confirmation of some of the deeds ascribed to him in the *Avesta*. The king of Turan, who is named Franghrasyan in the *Avesta*, seems to be Turvayan in the *Veds*. Tur seems to be a prefix to the name, indicating the Aryan tribe of the person which was different, though closely linked to the Dev worshipping Magis. Similar names have appeared earlier as Turvash and Turviti. The Richas in the *Veds* mentioning Sushravas are here.

1. You, renowned Indra, overthrown by your not to be overtaken chariot-wheel, the twenty kings of men, who had come against Sushravas unaided, and their sixty thousand and ninety-nine followers.

2. You, Indra, have preserved Sushravas by your succour, Turvayan by your assistance; you have made Kutsa, Atithigva and Ayu subject to the mighty though youthful Sushravas.

    (*Rig Ved.* M-1, S-53, R-9 and 10)

3. That exploit is celebrated in the present day (which you have) achieved for Kutsa, for Ayu, for Atithigva. To him you have given thousands, and you have quickly elevated Turvayan over the earth by your power.

    (*Rig Ved.* M-6, S-18, R-13)

4. O Lord Indra! You have beheaded twenty kings and their sixty thousand ninety-nine soldiers by the wheel of your chariot, who stood for war against the single king, Sushravas. Thus, you are most popular for the excellent war craft known to you.

5. O Lord Indra! You had protected Sushravas by means of protective measures and Turvayan by means of maintenance and you have enslaved the kings namely Kutsa, Atithigva and Ayu for this great young king.

    (*Atharv Ved.* Kand 20, Sukt-21, Richa-9 and 10)

These Richas confirm the statement of the *Avesta* that Husravah united the Aryan nations into one kingdom. Amongst the kings defeated, mention is of Kutsa, Atithigva and Ayu. Kutsa was the name of Ushana's son and Atithigva was one of the names of Divodas, who had defeated Shambar. Apparently, these kings were Dev worshippers and had kept names of their legendary heroes of the Arjika days. Turvayan has been mentioned as a king. Indra has elevated him over the earth by his power. Sushravas defeating and killing Turvayan has not been mentioned in the usual style of the scriptures. Evidently, he was a Dev worshipper and was linked to the Rishis of the *Veds* more closely than Sushravas who was their patron. As would emerge ahead, the Turs and the Dev worshipping Magis appear to have developed a common religious and political identity, though maintaining a separate racial status, which would have become something like a clan difference within a group. It appears that because of this ethnic and political affinity, the Rishis of the *Veds* found it difficult to eulogize their patron Sushravas for his victory over Turan, though it must have been as significant, if not more, than his victories over the minor kings whom he defeated while consolidating the Persian kingdom.

Firdausi has devoted a long portion of his work to this war between Iran and Turan. He has brought in the legendary figure of Rustam, who is shown as a ruler of Kabulistan and Zabulistan who accepted the suzerainty of Iran. In the *Shahnama* he lives on while several generations of the Kayan kings come and go. He is called over by the king of Iran, Khusro, to fight Afrasib, the king of Turan. In his style, Firdausi describes a number of supernatural feats of Rustam who is shown to have defeated Afrasib several times, but each time he escapes. Unfortunately, the *Avesta* or any other Zoroastrian scripture have no mention of Rustam or any personality who would match his character as projected by Firdausi. The king of Iran has also been shown as Manuchehr in the *Shahnama* at the initial stages of Rustam's career. On the other hand, Keresaspa finds no mention in the *Shahnama*. It appears that in the Iranian folklore, the legends of Keresaspa got mixed up with the Iran–Turan war and this is what has been stated by Firdausi in the legend of Rustam. Such a hint comes from the fact that the name of Rustam's grandfather has been stated to be Sam, which is what would have become of Saman, the name given in the *Avesta* of Keresaspa's father. One incident mentioned about Keresaspa in the Zoroastrian scriptures of his cooking food mistakenly over the sleeping Ganderewa, finds an echo in Rustam's deeds in the *Shahnama*, though the Ganderewa has been replaced by a dragon.

During the reign of Vistasp who was the grandson of Husravah, Zoroaster emerged. Many observers have held a view that Zoroaster founded a new religion, which was a revolt against the established Aryan religion as is found in the *Veds*. This new religion had a form of dualism in which, along with the Supreme Being, the God, there was an eternal Evil Being, similar to the devil of the *Bible*. It was also monotheistic in revolt against the polytheistic Vedic religion. The history of the Magis shows that it was not Zoroaster who made a departure from the earlier established religion of these Aryans, but the Devs in Arjika led by the seven Angiras Rishis who did so. The Asurs were all along fighting against this, as they considered it to be heretical and wanted the earlier religious practices to continue. Zoroaster's role was a continuation of this effort. Establishing a new religion was not his intention and at no stage did he do anything which can even remotely be said to be in this direction. He had before him the objective of having the religion propounded by the Devs to be declared false and the acceptance of the religion as it prevailed before those changes had been brought in and throughout his efforts were in this direction.

Apart from what emerges from the common history of the two groups, there are several references in the *Avesta* and other Zoroastrian books which state that it was a long continuing religion and not something new that was propounded. Some of them are given here.

1. These doctrines (therefore) we are earnestly declaring to you as we recite them forth from memory, words (till now) unheard (with faith) by those who by means of the doctrinal vows of the harmful lie are delivering the settlements of Righteousness to death, but words which are of the best unto those who are heartily devoted to Ahur.

   (Yasna XXXI)

2. And this doctrine was the first of rules to regulate our actions. Yet the opposer speaks beside Thee. For when first, O Ahur Mazda! Thou didst reveal the religious laws; and when Thou gavest (us) the understanding from Thine own mind, and didst moreover deliver to us (nearer) injunctions whereby (as by a rule) the wisher may place his choices. (There strife at once arose, and still is raging). There (beside Thy prophet) the truthful or liar, the enlightened or unenlightened, lifts his voice (to utter his faith). (But without hindrance from this striving, our) Piety steadily questions the two spirits (not here on earth) but (there in the spirit-world) where (they dwell as) in their home.

   (Yasna XXXI)

3. And to the Mathra Spenta, the holy, the effective, the law against the Daevas, the Zarathustrian statute, and to the long descent of the good Mazdayasnian religion.

   (Yasna IV)

4. And we worship the Praises of the Yasna which were the production of the ancient world, those which are (now) recollected and put in use, those which are now learned and taught, those remembered and recited.

(Yasna LV)

5. And we worship the entire bounteous Mathra, even the entire system of the faith set up against the Daevas; and we worship its complete and long descent.

(Yasna LXXI)

These passages state without ambiguity that the doctrines were very old and had been given up by the opposite side. The *Avesta* was striving to re-establish them. On the issue of Zoroaster propounding a dualism similar to the *Bible*, the nature of Angra Mainyu needs to be examined to see whether he has the necessary attributes to be the devil of the *Bible*. It is true that in the scriptures, Angra Mainyu has been painted as absolutely evil and is responsible for the creation of evil in the world, but he is not an eternal entity. At the end of the struggle, between good and bad, Angra Mainyu and all his evil creations would be destroyed and only the good will survive. To start with, he was not an integral part of the religion but represents an external threat, starting as a heresy and gradually developing into a rival faith. As it represented a rival religion, everything bad was associated with it, making him the symbol of evil. It is because of this repeated association with everything bad that Angra Mainyu, in course of time, assumed an image which is close to that of the devil in the *Bible*. To this extent even the *Veds* have Asurs, who have been pictured as wicked and constantly at war with the good. Dualism has not been attributed to the *Veds* despite this, perhaps because the Asurs remain in a large number and no one individual has been singled out to be above the rest. In the *Avesta*, all the Daevas have been termed evil, but Angra Mainyu is termed as the Daeva of the Daevas, their leader. The difference between what is projected in the *Veds* and what is there in the *Avesta* is thus only of the *Veds* holding all Asurs to be equally evil while the *Avesta* holds Angra Mainyu to be leading all the evil beings. This is because of historical reasons. Manu can be singled out by the Zoroastrians as the worst of the culprits because he was responsible for destroying the established order, wherein the Kavi was dethroned, the crown prince killed and the Asurs driven out of Arjika with their belongings seized by the Devs. The Devs, on the other hand, had no one to single out. If someone came close, it would have been Yim, the good shepherd, who defeated the successors of Manu and not only took back Arjika from the Devs, but uprooted and drove them out of the region. He, however, had his fortune, as instead of being vilified he got deified as Yam, the god of death. However, this difference of singular and plural between the *Veds* and the *Avesta* does not change the nature of the two entities. Angra Mainyu remains closer to the Asurs of the *Veds* rather than to the devil of the *Bible* because they are the counterparts of each other in the two religions both representing evil and constantly at war with the other. Both destined to be finally destroyed, because in the struggle between good and bad, the good has to finally win. Moreover, the devil in the *Bible* is not credited to have created anything. He only seduces people to be evil. Angra Mainyu is said to have created everything evil.

In the divinities of Zoroastrianism, Zoroaster seems to be advocating what had been laid down by the Ribhus. This is again just a rejection of the changes that got introduced in the religion by the Devs. The Ribhus had split one ladle into four. They had created four gods in place of one, Agni, Varun, Pushan and Mitra. The earlier god Tvasta, had been raised to the status of the father of the gods with the more frequently used name Dyau, having a wife who is named Prithvi or Earth at most places and Aditi at some. She is the mother of all gods. Ahur Mazda with Armaiti Spenta as his wife appears to be Dyau with Prithvi of the *Veds*. The passages from the *Avesta* that state this are given here.

1. Thy father is Ahur Mazda, the greatest of all gods, the best of all gods; thy mother is Armaiti Spenta; thy brothers are Sraosha, a god of Asha and Rashnu, tall and strong, and Mithra, the lord of wide pastures; thy sister is the law of the worshippers of Mazda.

(Ashi Yast II)

2. Then Yim stepped forward, towards the luminous space, southwards to meet the sun, and he pressed the earth with the golden ring and bored it with the poniard, speaking thus, 'O Spenta Armaiti, kindly open asunder and stretch thyself afar, to bear flocks and herds and men.' And Yim made the earth grow larger by one-third than it was before.

(Vendidad. Fargard II)

These passages show that Armaiti Spenta is not only the mother of all gods and goddess, except Ahur Mazda, who is their father, but is also identified as the earth. It makes father Ahur Mazda and mother Armaiti Spenta the exact counterparts in the *Avesta* of father Dyau and mother Prithvi of the *Veds*. With Ahur Mazda as the father, Zoroastrian pantheism has a large number of divinities, his sons Sraoshas, Atar or Fire, Mithra and others and his daughters, the seven Amesha Spentas. Then there are the Fravashis or the guiding spirits of all people—dead, alive and yet to be born. Despite so many divinities, Zoroastrianism gives the impression of monotheism, while the *Veds* of polytheism, because Zoroaster gave prime importance to Ahur Mazda, the father, and made all other divinities to be His creation and representing His attributes, while the *Veds* have projected Dyau as a retired father and his children, the Devs have acquired the central position, with Indra as their leader. As Zoroaster retained Ahur Mazda in the primary position and has kept the other divinities to be subordinate to Him, it appears that this was what the Ribhus had ordained while splitting one ladle into four. It seems that the Magis all along had Dyau, with whatever name, as the one Supreme God and all the gods that were created were deemed to be His form and an expression of His attributes only. The historical accidents that took place at Arjika caused certain things that have made the *Veds* give an impression of polytheism because the new gods created at that stage were the deification of their immediate forefathers, who were more closely related and so more frequently remembered, apart from the fact that one of them, Indra, was a god of war and so, was more frequently needed. It seems that the enhanced importance given to the new gods was accidental and not intended, as the *Veds* continue to speak of one Supreme Being and all gods being His expression only.

The Hindus have always believed that the *Veds* represent an absolutely undiluted monotheism. The scholars from other cultures have found it difficult to accept this in view of so many gods and goddesses being named and prayed to repeatedly in the *Veds*. Here, they have ignored a very important Indian tradition which tells us that the *Veds* have two distinct lines of followers and their beliefs. One is the ritualistic side with the Brahman literature being the commentaries on the *Veds* from this angle, which were further developed in the *Kalp Sutra* of Jamini. The other is the spiritual and philosophic tradition, which has the *Upanishads* as the works that have expounded the cryptic expressions of the *Veds* on philosophic lines, which find further expression in the *Gita* and at the Sutra level in the *Brahm Sutra* of Badrayan Vyas. While there is no reservation from any quarter to the *Upanishads* and the *Gita* representing an absolute monotheism, the *Veds* remain an area of contention. But the *Veds* have any number of passages to show that the polytheism expressed is only apparent. It has no real substance. The Real is only One. Some of these are mentioned here.

1. They have styled him Indra, Mitra, Varun, Agni and he is the celestial, well-winged Garutmat, for the learned priests call one by many names as they speak of Agni, Yam, Matrishvan.

   (*Rig Ved.* M-1, S-164, R-46)

2. I am Indra, I am Varun, I am those two in greatness; (I am) the vast, the profound, beautiful heaven and earth; intelligent, I give like Tvasta animation to all being; I uphold earth and heaven.

3. I have distributed the moisture-shedding waters; I have upheld the sky as the abode of the water; I have become the preserver of the water, the son of Aditi, illustrating the threefold elementary space.

   (*Rig Ved.* M-4, S-4, R-3 and 4)

4. He is Hansa (the sun), dwelling in light; Vayu (the wind), dwelling in the firmament; the invoker of the gods (Agni), dwelling on the altar; the guest (of the worshipper), dwelling in the house; (as the culinary fire) the dweller among men, (as consciousness), the

dweller in the most excellent (orb of the sun), the dweller in truth, the dweller in the sky (the air) born in the waters, in the rays of light, in the verity (of manifestation) in the (eastern) mountain, the truth (itself).

(*Rig Ved.* M-4, S-40, R-5)

5. You, Agni, are born Varun, you are Mitra, when kindled; in you, son of strength, are all the gods; you are Indra, a son of strength to the mortal who presents (oblations).

6. You are Aryaman in relation to maidens; you bear, enjoy sacrificial food, a mysterious name, they anoint you like a welcome friend with milk and butter, when you make husband and wife of one mind.

7. For your glory the Maruts sweep (the firmament), with your birth, Rudra is beautiful and wonderful; the middle step of Vishnu has been placed, so you cherish the mysterious name of the waters.

(*Rig Ved.* M-5, S-3, R-1 to 3)

8. Surya spreads his vast and numerous rays over all the crowds of men, shining bright by day, he is beheld the same, the creator, the created; he is glorified by his worshippers.

(*Rig Ved.* M-7, S-62, R-1)

9. Indra is Brahma, Indra is the Rishi, Indra is the much-invoked of many, mighty with mighty deeds.

(*Rig Ved.* M-8, S-16, R-7)

10. Agni is one, though kindled in various ways; one is the sun, pre-eminent over all; one dawn illumines this all; one is that which has become this all.

(*Rig Ved.* M-8, S-58, R-2)

11. He who is our preserver, our parents, the Creator (of all), who knows our abodes (and knows) all beings, who is the name-giver of the gods, he is one; other beings come to him to inquire.

(*Rig Ved.* M-10, S-82, R-3)

12. The wise seers through their praise make into many forms the bird which is one; holding the metres at the sacrifice, they measure twelve bowls of Som.

(*Rig Ved.* M-10, S-114, R-5)

13. (To him) who is the giver of soul, the giver of strength, whose commands all, even the gods obey, whose shadow is immortality, whose (shadow) is death, let us offer worship with an oblation to the divine Ka.

14. He who by his might beheld the waters all around containing the creative power and giving birth to sacrifice, he who among the gods was the one supreme God, let us offer worship with an oblation to the divine Ka.

(*Rig Ved.* M-10, S-121, R-2 and 8)

15. The Creator of creators, he who is the protector of the universe, (him I praise), the divine defender, the destroyer of enemies; may the two Ashwins, Brahaspati, and the gods, protect this sacrifice, and save the sacrifice from disappointments.

(*Rig Ved.* M-10, S-128, R-7)

16. The glow that is contained in the core of the star, that glow that is released by the rays, the glow that the truth-seeker scholar is endowed with, should form me.

(*Saam Ved.* Part I, Book VII, Chapter V)

17. Motionless, one, swifter than mind; the Devs failed to overtake it speeding before them. It standing still, outstrips the others running. Herein does Matrishvan establish action.

18. It moves, it is motionless. It is far distant, it is near. It is within this all, it surrounds this all externally.

(*Yajur Ved.* Adhyay-40, Yajush-4 and 5)

These are just a few of the passages which show that the polytheism of the *Veds* is not real. There are many more. The first Richa says that they have styled him, Indra, Mitra, Varun and Agni as the learned call one by many names. This is the true spirit of the *Veds*. Name makes no difference, the Supreme Being remains one. This spirit permeates the Hindu psyche till now. Despite having an Isht Dev or a chosen God, a Hindu continues to respect God by whatever name he may be called. He does not have a concept of one true God that is his own and other false gods that are of others. God remains God for him, irrespective of the name being used, even if it is used by people of a different religion. This spirit is inherited from the *Veds*, which has survived all these centuries, despite so many changes in religious practices that it may be difficult to link them to what the *Veds* had prescribed.

Scholars who do not accept the link between the *Veds* and the *Upanishads* have ignored another very important Indian tradition. The *Veds* were taught in ashrams and used to take about twenty years to learn. Tradition tells us that at the end of the study, the guru or the teacher, used to select the students whom he considered fit to be imparted with the secret knowledge of the *Veds*. The other students were sent away, while these selected were taken to a remote place in the forest, to ensure that there was nobody else around, where the guru used to impart the secret knowledge of the *Veds*. It is obvious that the *Veds* have been written in a coded language, so far as real philosophy and religion is concerned. The guru used to give the key of this code to his selected students deep in the forest, with the application of which the *Veds* gave a totally different meaning and meant what the *Upanishads* have stated. In this short outing to the deep forest, there could have been nothing more that the guru could have done for something which required twenty years to master. At some stage, the *Upanishads* were written. With these coming in, it was no longer necessary to understand the secret knowledge of the *Veds* by the application of the key to the code, as it could be accessed from the *Upanishads* directly without any difficulty. In such a situation, the key to the code became redundant and was not passed on to the next generation of students and has been lost. It is due to the absence of the key that we are unable to decipher the coded statements because of which we are unable to understand the *Veds* in the way they were expected to be understood to mean what the *Upanishads* are saying, and we are unable to see the link between the *Veds* and the *Upanishads* and refuse to accept the Indian tradition that the *Upanishads* represent the secret knowledge of the *Veds*. The *Veds* have indicated that a coded language has been used and that there is something more than what meets the eye. The passages are stated here.

1.   Man glorifying (Vishnu), tracks two steps of that heaven-

beholding (deity), but he apprehends not the third; nor can the soaring-winged birds (pursue it).

(*Rig Ved.* M-1, S-155, R-5)

2. Immature (in understanding) undiscerning in mind, I inquire of those things which are hidden (even) from the gods; (what are) the seven threads which the sages have spread to envelop the sun, in whom all abide?

3. Ignorant, I inquire of the sages who know (the truth), not as one knowing (do I inquire), for the sake of gaining knowledge; what is that one alone, who has upheld these six spheres in the form of the unborn?

4. Let him who knows this (truth) declare it; the mysterious condition of the beautiful ever-moving; the rays shed (their) milk from his (exalted) head investing his form with radiance; they have drunk up the water by the paths (by which they were poured forth).

(*Rig Ved.* M-1, S-164, R-5 to 7)

5. In the tree into which the smooth-gliding (rays) feeders on the sweet (produce), enter, and again bring forth (light) over all; they have called the fruit sweet, but he partakes not of it who knows not the protector (of the universe).

(*Rig Ved.* M-1, S-164, R-22)

6. The immortal cognate with the mortal, affected by (desire of) enjoyment, goes to the lower or the upper (sphere); but (men beholding them) associated, going everywhere (in this world together); going everywhere (in other worlds together); have comprehended the one, but have not comprehended the other.

(*Rig Ved.* M-1, S-164, R- 38)

7. The three, with beautiful tresses, look down in their several seasons upon the earth; one of them, when the year has ended, shears (the ground); one by his acts overlooks the universe; the course of one is visible, though not his form.

8. Four are the definite grades of speech, those Brahmans who are wise know them; three deposited in secret, indicate no meaning; men speak the fourth grade of speech.

(*Rig Ved.* M-1, S-164, R-44 and 45)

9. What is the value of this to us? What is its advantage? Inform us, Jatved, for you know; (tell us) what is the best (course) for us on this secret path, so that we may follow unreproached the direct road.

                                                     (*Rig Ved*. M-4, S-5, R-12)

10. The sweet water swells up from the firmament; by the ray (man) obtains immortality; that which is the secret name of clarified butter is the tongue of the gods, the navel of ambrosia.

                                                     (*Rig Ved*. M-4, S-58, R-1)

11. He who is the sustainer of the worlds, who knows the hidden and secret names of the rays, he is the sage who cherishes the acts of sages, as the heaven cherishes numerous forms. May all our enemies perish.

                                                     (*Rig Ved*. M-8, S-41, R-5)

12. The green-tinted Som being let loose propels the voice that indicates the path of truth as the boatman (propels his) boat; the bright Som reveals to his worshipper on the sacred grass the secret names of the gods.

                                                     (*Rig Ved*. M-9, S-95, R-2)

13. One (man) indeed seeing Speech has not seen her; another (man) hearing her has not heard her, but to another she delivers her person as a loving wife well-attired presents herself to her husband.

14. They call one man firmly established in the friendship (of Speech), they do not exclude him from (the society of) the powerful (in knowledge), another wanders with an illusion that it is barren, bearing Speech that is without fruit, without flower.

                                                     (*Rig Ved*. M-10, S-71, R-4 and 5)

15. He who has drunk thinks that the herb which men crush is the Som; (but) that which the Brahman knows to be Som, of that no one partakes.

                                                     (*Rig Ved*. M-10, S-85, R-3)

16. Surya, the Brahmans know your two chariot wheels in their season; the single wheel that is concealed, the sages know it also.

                                                     (*Rig Ved*. M-10, S-85, R-16)

All these Richas refer to something hidden, to something which does not meet the eye, but the fifteenth leaves no scope of doubt that there is a hidden meaning to the terms used. The description is in a coded form, the key to which was known to the Brahman. Even if some of the events, and the manner in which the *Veds* have described them, are examined, they give the same indication that a coded language has been used and there is a meaning to it more than what meets the eye. The killing of Vritra has been mentioned on several occasions. If this story is examined, it will be seen that Vritra has to be killed because by doing so water, light and cows are released. To kill him, the first thing required is yagya or sacrifice, in which Agni comes first. Agni is accompanied by Mitra and Varun. Vishnu is needed as he covers the entire universe with his three steps. Brahaspati guides the way and is the constant partner. Finally, it is Indra who breaks the stone enclosure of Val to release the cows and kills Vritra. He is constantly accompanied by the Maruts. His powers are increased when he drinks Som, which is obtained by crushing between two stones. It appears to be an algebraic equation. It may be possible to decipher this code and find the key, especially because the *Upanishads* and Sutras tell us their meaning. There are, however, difficulties. Firstly, the *Veds* have not remained in the hands of only those who were communicating the mystical ideas. They have also been handled by Rishis whose area was limited to the ritualistic side. They would not have been acquainted with the code and the key. As a result, while giving a description of a particular deity, at places, care has not been taken to ensure that the qualities are applicable to both meanings. Due to this, in an attempt to break the code, if a particular deity is assumed to be something, the description matches for very long and then suddenly a quality is mentioned which contradicts it. Secondly, a very large number of ideas have been expressed making it confusing to match the right passages with the right ideas before looking at the code. To top it all, the text is jumbled up. It follows no particular sequence and is arranged neither according to the date of composition nor by the theme. As a result, part of an idea may be at one place and the rest some two thousand Richas later, somewhere totally out of context.

Whether we are able to break the code or not, it would be unfair not to admit its existence and that the *Veds* have expressed ideas in a manner that they could be understood correctly only with the application of the key to this code. Without that they appear ritualistic with a large number of gods and goddesses. The monotheism of the *Upanishads* has to be taken to be the monotheism of the *Veds*, despite Indra, Varun, Mitra, Agni, Vishnu and any number of entities to whom hymns have been addressed. This is what Zoroaster too was propounding when he had Ahur Mazda occupying the central position with a large number of divinities around him, who are all his creation and represent his attributes.

The monotheism of the *Veds* and the *Upanishads* is, however, different from what monotheism is conventionally understood. In the usual sense, monotheism differs from polytheism only to the extent that it believes in one God instead of many. With this, the difference becomes cosmetic and is not material. The nature of God, so far as it concerns the worshipper, remains the same. The relationship between the worshipper and God too remains the same and the objectives to be achieved by worship also remain the same. This is because a common worshipper does not approach religion in search of God. He approaches religion in search of worldly things through God. This being the objective, God is a benefactor for him. It may be wealth, success, protection from danger, relief from disease, the worshipper approaches God, because he believes that He can give it to him. The nature of God that is material to him is this only. God is not relevant, only the benefactor is. This benefactor could be one or there could be many, makes no difference to him, as his only concern is to get what he wants. The relationship between God and the worshipper is thus that of a benefactor and a seeker. In this, as he has conceptualized God in his own image, the ultimate authority, who has the powers to give the most of the things, is the king. So he has imagined God to be the king and the objective to be achieved by worship is to please this king. In this nature of God, which is the only aspect material to the worshipper, monotheism and polytheism have no substantial difference and neither can be said to be more logical.

There is, however, another aspect of the nature of God which has only cosmetic relevance. This is where His powers and qualities are described. He is described as omnipotent, omnipresent, omniconscious, the Creator, the Preserver, the Destroyer etc. It is in this aspect of God's nature that monotheism appears more logical than polytheism, because of which it is considered to be the belief of a superior intellect. This is so because the powers of one omnipotent entity would be restricted by the powers of the other omnipotent entity in a polytheistic paradigm. Similarly, the presence of one omnipresent entity would be restricted by the presence of the other omnipresent entity. In effect, the jurisdictions of one king and his kingdom would be limited by the jurisdictions of the other kings and their kingdoms. The situation would look more human than divine with a large number of kings with their areas of influence. To make it favourably disposed to the worshipper, all the kings would have to be allied to each other and to maintain order amongst them one would have to be their king, the king of the gods. Though man created God in his own image, he does not want to believe it to be so. Polytheistic situations appear more human than divine, while monotheism presents one king with the entire universe as His kingdom, something which is not to be seen on the human plane. But this difference is not material to the worshipper, because he was not in search of God. He was in search of only a benefactor. From this benefactor too, he does not seek things that would need his omnipotent powers, like the creation of another universe or a shift in the position of the sun or change in the nature of life and so on. He looks for petty things, a little wealth, a little success, protection from a petty danger and so on. As his interests are limited to his desires being fulfilled, it remains only of cosmetic value, whether the king was of the entire universe or had other kings to share the space with their kingdoms.

Monotheism of the *Veds* and the *Upanishads* differs from this in all three aspects, the nature of God, the relationship of God and the worshipper and the objective to be achieved by the worshipper through worship. In the *Veds* and the *Upanishads*, in describing the nature of God, some adjectives like Creator, Preserver etc. have been used, but His ultimate description is by the term 'Neti'. This Sanskrit word is made by joining two words 'Na' and 'Iti'. 'Na' is a negative while 'Iti' is used for signifying the conclusion of something. To say 'that is all'. 'Neti' thus means 'that is not all'. The *Upanishads* propound a view that God is not a matter of discussion. He is not something that can be proved by logic and arguments, but has to be realized. By the term realization is meant direct perception or direct experience which is different from knowledge. This has been explained by Adiguru Shankaracharya in his commentary on the *Brahm Sutra* with the oft-quoted example of the snake and the rope. He has said that, if someone sees a rope in the dark and perceives it to be a snake, the rope is not a rope but a snake for him as it would create all reactions that a snake would have created. He would scream, run away, look for a stick to kill it. If someone stops him and tells that it is not a snake but a rope, this is the stage of knowledge. He stops running but his fear does not go. His fear goes when he looks more carefully and is himself able to see that it is not a snake but a rope. This is the stage of realization. The mystical side of the *Veds* and the *Upanishads* are records of people who had realized God. They have no argument to offer, no logic to present, but make a simple invitation, that if you want to see Him see for yourself. All that we can do is to tell the way. Having realized God, having had a direct experience with Him, their description of Him is 'Neti'. They have said that the closest description of God could only be silence, because whatever would be said would only be farther from the truth. 'Neti' is an expression of this silence. This point has also been explained by the Adiguru in the same work. He has said that when two people talk, the medium of their expression is language, which has to be understood by both sides. In language, everything has a name with a corresponding form. Both sides talking have to know the name as well as the form of the thing, so that when one person names something the image of the form of that thing emerges in the mind of the other and he understands what is being spoken of. If the name of the thing seen by someone is not known to him, he describes it by giving the attributes of it as he had seen or compares it with something similar to enable the other person to understand. In describing God the language fails. What has been seen by the person has no name in the language. The attributes that have been seen are beyond whatever is known and there is nothing which comes anywhere close with which it could be compared to. It transcends everything. If the person tries to explain or describe what he has seen, he may only be babbling something and people may consider him to be insane. Adiguru Shankaracharya has explained this with an example. He has said that there was a place far from the sea where nobody had ever seen the sea. One person from a village went on a journey and returned after seeing the sea. In trying to describe it, he told the people that it was a massive water body. Someone asked whether it was ten times the size of the village pond. The man was surprised and said that it was not comparable in size. The next asked whether it was a hundred times the size of the lake that was on the outskirts of the village and the man had the same response. The villagers thought that he was mad as they felt that there could be nothing as big in size as a hundred times the size of the lake on the outskirts of the village, which in itself was a very big lake, the biggest water body they had ever seen. The position of the person who has realized God is the same. There is nothing in the language of man which can correctly come even close to describing Him. The Rishis have, therefore, simply said 'Neti'. Passages from the *Veds* which say so are given here.

1. Whose greatness my colleagues loudly extol; who has manifested His real form to the priests; who is recognized at oblations by His variegated radiance, and who though frequently growing old, again and again becomes young.

    (*Rig Ved.* M-2, S-4, R-5)

2. He who directs towards the worshipper his well-yoked prancing steeds, he (Indra), the swift bearer of blessings (produces) rain, he, who being comparable only to himself, is delivered (from all his enemies).

    (*Rig Ved.* M-8, S-69, R-13)

3. Indra, were there a hundred heavens to compare with you, or were there a hundred earths, O thunderer, not even a thousand suns would reveal you; yea, no created thing would fill you, nor heaven and earth.

    (*Rig Ved.* M-8, S-70, R-5)

4. I make this sacrificial hymn, reaching to the eight points (of the sky) and rising to the ninth (the sun in the zenith), though it is less than (the dimensions of Indra).

(*Rig Ved.* M-8, S-76, R-12)

5. It, in fact, is greater than its greatness. It is the master of both the created as well as non-created worlds.

(*Saam Ved.* Part I, Book VII, Chapter IV)

Greater than its greatness, the expression sums it all. Once this is what has been understood for God, the objective for the worshipper, is not to please God to seek something. It is to realize Him, to see Him, to have a direct experience of Him. Three paths have been mentioned for this, the path of Gyan or Knowledge, with Yog as one of its methods, the path of Karm or Action and the path of Bhakti or Devotion. All three are equally good and it is left to the person to choose depending on his inclinations and aptitude. As a 'worshipper' moves on his way towards the realization of God, he realizes his own true self. As he realizes his own self, what he sees is that this self is the Creator, the Preserver and the Destroyer. He finds that he and He are the same. He either declares 'Aham Brahm Asmi' meaning, I am Brahma, or says 'Tat Twam Asi' meaning, Thou are that. Both mean the same because if he is Brahma, everything is he and if Thou are that, everything, including him, is Thee. The relationship between the two is neither of a seeker and a benefactor nor of a king and his subject, but of oneness. There is no difference between the two. They are one and the same and are in everyone and everything around. Some passages that speak of this are given here.

1. Comprehending hidden (mysteries) here on earth, they have, through their power, made manifest (the things of) heaven and earth; they have set limits to them by their elements; they connected them, both mutually united, widespread and vast, and fixed the intermediate (firmament) to sustain them.

(*Rig Ved.* M-3, S-38, R-3)

2. Mine ears are turned (to hear him), mine eyes (to behold him); this light that is placed in the heart; my mind, the receptacle of

distant (objects), hastens (towards him), what shall I declare to him; how shall I comprehend him?

(*Rig Ved*. M-6, S-9, R-6)

3. The man who in his self beholds all creatures and all things that be. And in all being sees his self, thence doubts no longer, ponders not.

4. When, in the man who clearly knows, the self has become all things that are, what bewilderment, what grief is there in him who sees the One alone?

5. He has attained unto the bright, bodiless, woundless, sinewless, the Pure, which evil has not pierced. Far-sighted, wise, encompassing, he self-existent has prescribed aims, as propriety demands, unto the everlasting years.

(*Yajur Ved*. Adhyay-40, Yajush-6 to 8)

Though nothing in the Zoroastrian scriptures has been found, that can be treated to be the counterparts of the *Upanishads*, some references in the *Avesta* show that the Asurs had a similar tradition. They are mentioned here.

1. 'There is many a one, O holy Zarathustra!' said Ahur Mazda, 'who were a Paitidana; when such a man says, "I am an Athravan" he lies; do not call him an Athravan, O holy Zarathustra!' thus said Ahur Mazda. 'Him thou shalt call an Athravan, O holy Zarathustra! Who throughout the night sits up and demands of the holy Wisdom, which makes man free from anxiety, with dilated heart, and cheerful at the head of the Kinvat bridge, and which makes him reach that world, that holy world, that excellent world, the world of paradise.'

(Vendidad. Fargard XVIII)

2. 'And whosoever of you, O men,' said Ahur Mazda, 'O holy Zarathustra! whosoever shall long for the illumination of knowledge, he has the gifts of an Athravan; whosoever shall long for fullness of knowledge, he has the gifts of an Athravan.'

(Zamyad Yast VIII)

3. And therefore, O Great Creator, I approach You to grant me

(as a bountiful gift) for both the worlds, the corporeal and (for that) of the mind, those attainments which are to be derived from the (Divine) Righteousness, and by means of which (that personified Righteousness within us) may introduce those who are its recipients into beatitude and glory.

(Yasna XXVIII)

These passages show that similar to the Vedic traditions, the Zoroastrians too, had two parallel streams running. On one side was ritualistic and on the other, the spiritual and the mystic. As per tradition, the mystic side was required to be kept absolutely secret. It was to be passed down from the teacher to only his tested and deserving students. The Asurs seem to have maintained this tradition and somewhere along the way lost it, just as it got lost on the Vedic side also, but fortunately, only after something had been written about it. Because of the loss of the mystic tradition, Zoroastrianism was left only with the ritualistic side, with only traces which show the existence of the Upanishadic traditions amongst them at a stage in the past.

The existence of the Upanishadic traditions amongst the Asurs establishes that this tradition was older than the time when the two sides split. The *Rig Ved* has references which confirm this. They are stated here.

1. Those ancient sages, our ancestors, observant of truth, rejoicing together with the gods, discovered the hidden light, and, reciters of sincere prayers, they generated the dawn.
2. When the common herd then, associating, they concurred, not mutually contended; they obstructed not the sacrifices of the gods, but, unoffending they proceeded with the light (that had been discovered).

(*Rig Ved*. M-7, S-76, R-4 and 5)

The Upanishadic tradition, though not the *Upanishads* themselves, is thus older than the time from when the compilation of the *Veds* began. It could be as old as the time of the Ribhus. The evolutionists may object to this, as they believe that man has evolved over time and such profound thoughts, as are found in the *Upanishads*, could not have been the product of the human brain in such antiquity. But this is not an achievement of the human brain. It is not based on logic or logical deductions, but on direct perception. It is what has been known by something beyond the brain. The brain, to an extent, is an obstruction in this journey. Three Sutras from the *Yog Sutra* which define Yog are very important in this regard. They are stated here.

1. Yogah Chittvritti Nirodhah.
2. Tada Drashtu Swarupe Awasthanam.
3. Vritti Sarupyam Itaratra.

(Sutra 2 to 4)

Chitt can be loosely translated as the mind. Chittvritti would be the normal functioning of the mind which would include thinking, imagining, etc. The first Sutra defines Yog as the process that stops the normal functioning of the mind. The second says that then the seer can abide in its essence. The third that, otherwise there is identification with the nature of thought. This shows that as long as the mind is active, it is thinking about something or imagining something, the seer remains identified with those thoughts. Once the normal functioning of the brain has been rested, the seer reaches the real essence and abides therein. The entire effort in Yog is, therefore, only to stop the normal functioning of the mind. Yog is a later development as it is not found amongst the Zoroastrians, which shows that it developed after the two sides had got separated. It seems that though Yog had not been developed till then, either some of the people had found some way to still the mind or it just happened naturally to someone and then all the rest interested in it tried different methods to achieve the same results, because of which different paths were found which find expression later in the *Upanishads* and the *Gita*.

Yog seems to have been developed fully by the Manavs after their departure from Arjika but before they left Persia for India. It has been mentioned in the *Veds*, which shows that it is certainly a practice as old as the Vedic period. Some passages from the *Veds* which speak of Yog are given here.

1. Men verily call upon him in battle; the devout inflictors of austerity upon their persons constitute him their Preserver; when both approach together the bountiful Indra, men (succeed) in (obtaining) the gifts of sons and grandsons.

    (*Rig Ved.* M-4, S-24, R-3)

2. Just as water vapours are carried higher in the form of clouds and are condensed in the presence of cold air existing in the sky, similarly one can reach the height of spiritual progress and can get strengthened by restraining the breath though Yogic exercise.

3. One can get the higher goals of spirituality, by committing oneself to Yogic exercises.

4. Whenever one gets accomplished in the observance of Yog, he is endowed with both the powers, physical and intellectual, like the two hooves of a cow.

5. When one gets perfection in Yog, he can recognize everything, just as truth is recognized with the eyes.

    (*Yajur Ved.* Adhyay-23, Yajush-26 to 29)

These references, especially of the *Yajur Ved*, speak of the final stages of Yog. They do establish that Yog had received its final shape during the Vedic period, but it cannot be said whether these parts of the *Veds* were composed in India or before. There are, however, other evidences to show that Yog had been there with the Aryans while they were in Central Asia. One is the existence of Sufism in that region. The near identical spiritual practices of the Sufis and the Yogis point to their common origin. Sufism, today, is a part of the Islamic heritage. This is because whatever is known about the Sufis is of the period when Islam was the religion of the people of the region. Sufism is, however, a much older tradition. This is brought out in the *Shahnama* where Firdausi tells us that Alexander, after his conquest of Persia gave directions to all the provinces to protect the Sufis in the exercise of their religion. This statement of Firdausi not only shows that Sufis were there in Persia in the fourth century BC, but that they belonged to a religion which was different from the predominant religion of the country and that they needed protection. Persia at that time was Zoroastrian and the only other religion that could have been there at that time was the religion of the Dev worshippers. These Sufis were Yogis in the time of Alexander and had survived all the persecution that was faced by the Dev worshippers. Yog is neutral to religion, because it has no rituals and no dogmas. It may have as its adepts, people of any religion. It does not ask anyone to believe in something or to go by blind faith. Like experiments in the field of any of the sciences, it presents the experiences of earlier Yogis and leaves it to the adept to check it like an experiment of physics or chemistry to see whether the results are the same. People of Central Asia, as well as those following its practices, becoming Muslims would not have had any effect on it so long as there were people going in for it with all sincerity.

Sufism not being limited to Islam in the earlier centuries emerges also from the works of Jalaluddin Mohammed Rumi, the most celebrated Sufi of the Classical Period. His best known work is the *Masnavi*. In his other work, the *Diwan-e Shams-e Tabriz* he has mentioned a Buddhist Sufi with the name Ibrahim Balkhi. The name Balkhi indicates that he was from Balkh, the town in Afghanistan that was the home of Rumi's family from where his father fled in the wake of a Mongol invasion. Rumi lived between AD 1207 and 1273. A mention from him of a Buddhist Sufi shows that at least up to the thirteenth century AD Sufism transcended religion and was not limited to Islam. Before the period when Persia and the neighbouring countries were converted to Islam, the Yogis have been noticed by the *Avesta*. Here are some passages which show this.

1. Then let (the priest) teach people this holy saying, 'No one who does not eat has strength to do works of holiness, strength to do works of husbandry, strength to beget children. By eating every material a creature lives, by not eating it dies away.'
   (Vendidad. Fargard III)

2. Verily I say it unto thee, O Spitama Zarathustra, the man who has a wife is far above him who begets no sons; he who keeps a house is far above him who has none; he who has children is far above the childless man; he who has riches is far above him who

has none. And of the two men, he who fills himself with meat is filled with the good spirit much more than he who does not do so; the latter is all but dead; the former is above him. It is this man that can strive against the onset of Asto-Vidhotu; it is this man that can strive against the ungodly Ashemaogha who does not eat.

(Vendidad. Fargard IV)

3. Therefore, when the Daevas and the worshippers of the Daevas bow their backs, bend their waists, and arrange all their limbs, they think they will smite and smite not, they think they will kill and kill not; and then the Daevas and the worshippers of the Daevas have their minds confounded and their eyes made giddy.

(Bahram Yast XVII)

4. With us the keeping of a fast is this, that we keep a fast from committing sins with our eyes and tongue and ears and hands and feet. Some people are striving about it, so that they may not eat anything all day and they practise abstinence from eating anything. That which in other religions, is fasting owing to not eating is, in our religion, fasting owing to not committing sins.

(Sad Dar LXXXIII)

Being practices of the rival religion, the *Avesta* and the subsequent works have noticed only the external features of the Yogis, who have been called Daeva worshippers and Ashemaogha. They have observed that they eat a little and are often fasting and have renounced the world with no homes, wealth or families. They practise something in which they bow their back, bend their waists and arrange their limbs. The outright rejection of all these practices is an indication that Yog began amongst the Devs and later Manavs only after the Asurs had parted. This was considered to be unadvisable perhaps because the rivals were doing so. It appears that the two sides had a debate on the issue of fasting. The response of the Manavs to the objections brought forward by the Asurs on this point seems to be in this Richa.

The gods have not assigned hunger as (the cause of) death,
for deaths approach the man who has eaten; the riches of one

who gives do not diminish, he who gives not finds no consoler.
(*Rig Ved.* M-10, S-117, R-1)

Firdausi has given an elaborate description of Khusro renouncing the world. This Khusro is the same as the Sushravas of the *Veds* and Husravah of the *Avesta*. Being the grandfather of Vistasp, who got converted to Zoroastrianism, he was a Dev worshipper. The description is very long. With some portions omitted, it is given here.

The rich soul of the king grew full of thought.
He said, 'All of the peopled world around,
All this from enemies have I made free.
Yet though from God all my desires I gained,
My heart from vengeance have I not restrained.
Now have I taken vengeance for my sire,
Have killed him who to execute was right.
He who the prosperous sends the earth to bless,

My soul may to the righteous place convey,
For this Kais' throne and crown must pass away.
The secret of the world I have seen and known.
He washed his head before he went to pray,
With reason's light he sought of God the way.
He said, 'O thou who are higher than the soul,
Preserve and wisdom into me instil,
And give me fitting thoughts of good and ill.
Ward off the power of the Div from me,
So that destroyed my own soul may not be.
My soul to that abode of bliss convey,
And guard me in the same special way.'
Day and night, a whole week he was standing there.
Seven days elapsed and Khusru grew so weak.
Upon the eighth he left the place of prayer,
In haste towards the king's throne to repair.
And all the Pehlavans of Persia's host,
At the king's doings were perplexed the most.
His earnest supplication thus to pour,

He stood five weeks the Most High God before.
He did not sleep the dark night through from pain.
He slept himself but not his spirit clear,

Which in this world was ever to wisdom near.
It seemed to him that in a vision clear,
A heavenly messenger spoke in his ear.
'Thou, king, beneath propitious star wast born.
Since thou hast now gained all of thy desire,
If thou couldst, hastening from this world retire,
To God's pure neighbourhood, to find thy way,
Here in this darkness do thou not delay.
To others leave this fleeting world below.
Choose then as one who is fitted for the throne.
Yet do not rest when thou the world hast shared,
For destiny that meets thee be prepared.
Virtue like this in Lehrasp do thou know,
The kingship, throne, and belt on him bestow.
As thou from God has sought for such a grace,
Arise! As an immortal take thy place.'
And when he woke up from this painful dream
And then he said, 'If I in haste depart,
God will have given the wishes of my heart.'
He came and sat upon the throne as king,
The king then bade Lehrasp himself begone,
And said to him as well, 'My days are done.
Go, on the royal throne to sit proceed.'

Lehrasp in haste then from his charger leapt,
And kissed the ground and loud in sorrow wept.
And Khusru said to him, 'Now take thy leave,
Be warp with woof when justice thou would weave.'
There went with him the chiefs of Iran then,
Wise nobles too, and all the valiant men.
From plain they moved up to the crested hill.
Wailing and mourning what the king had done.

'How was it, king,' cried everyone that came,
'Thy bright heart full of scars and smoke became?
Or this thy crown if thou dost now despise,
Tell it to us, but Iran do not leave,
New king to an old country do not give.'
At this event bewildered grew the Kai,
And from the crowd he bade the Mobeds hie.
He said to them, 'As now here all is well,
On what is good with sorrow do not dwell.

We shall together come, and soon, once more,
At my departure, therefore, be not sore.'
And to the chieftains all he said in turn,
'Kingless ye from this hill must now return.'
Three of those heroes, then, of haughty look,
Would not turn back or there the monarch leave.
With him for one whole day and night they went.
Then to the margraves the monarch did say,
'Tonight we go no further on our way.
For after this, me no one will behold.
When the bright sun shall raise his standard grand
For me of parting will have come the day.
And would my soul now from this road depart,
I would at once tear out my darkened heart.'
Of the dark night a portion had been spent,
Before his God the famous monarch bent,

And from the Zandavasht in secret read.
The words on those famed wise men sadly fell,
'I now for ever bid you all farewell.
Tomorrow in this sand do not remain,
And towards Iran the way ye may not find.'
Up from the hill the sun his head thus brought,
The nobles' eyes in vain their monarch sought.
Of Khusru they then found no single track.
As if of sense deprived then turned they back.

In this narration some distortions are there, which do come in folklores. Khusru has been shown reading the *Zandavasht*, though he was the grandfather of Vistasp, in whose time Zoroaster preached his religion and the compilation of the *Avesta* started. He has also been shown praying to ward off the power of the Div from him, though he was a Dev worshipper and it was only later that his successors and the people of Iran were converted to Zoroastrianism. Ignoring these distortions, if the narrative is seen, it would match any number of instances of ancient India, where highly successful people, whether kings or otherwise, reached a stage when they felt something missing in their understanding of the puzzle of life and renounced everything to go away from home and family in search of the reality. The folklore was amongst people where this tradition had been lost and they could not understand, why Khusru did so, because of which all Mobeds and chieftains have been shown to be in a state of bewilderment. In his time, the people would have understood what Khusru was doing as it was nothing new to the Vedic traditions. Earlier to Khusru, Kai Us has been reported by the Dinkard to have done the same as has already come up.

The Upanishadic traditions being of very remote origin and certainly older than the *Veds*, explain two things—one, the total unconcern of the Rishis on how many gods were being created and worshipped by the people, and two, the necessity of using a coded language in the composition of the hymns of the *Veds*, in which the meaning from the mystic sense could be understood only on the application of a key without which they would appear to be simple prayers in praise of the gods. They had before them the task of addressing, through the same text, two distinct audiences with mutually divergent requirements. One audience was of common worshippers who, they could see, had not come in search of God. They were worldly people with worldly desires which they felt could be fulfilled if they were able to please God. As they were looking for a benefactor and not God, it did not matter who He was and whether He was one or many. Though they had much greater things to offer, there was no way that they could have succeeded in convincing these people to take them. The situation is that of a child who wants a doll. She cannot be convinced to take a diamond necklace in its place by telling her its worth. The child needs a doll and will be happy only if she gets it. The diamond necklace would have to wait till she matures to know its worth. The requirements of these people could not have been ignored. They constituted almost the entire society. If they had started agriculture, which was something new and needed to get the confidence that a specialized divinity was there to help them in each of its basic ingredients, so be it. One single Tvasta gets the company of three more. Some poets enamoured by the beauty of the rising sun, bring out some verses and the Ashwins are created. It would not have mattered to people at that level of spiritual maturity. They would have viewed it with a certain degree of amusement.

For the second audience, all secrets would have been disclosed. The key of the code would have been passed on to them to enable them to know what the texts meant. They would get to know that the issue is not relevant. Whether God is one or many had to be seen by them themselves. The journey had to be covered by them. The scriptures told the way and the experiences of people who had trodden before. The guru is there to guide in understanding what had been laid down, but beyond that the voyager is alone with his endeavour. In this search, he does not have to look for God. He does not have to look for anything which is away. He has to journey inward and look for his own true self, because what is within is beyond. The two are one and the same. Once he is able to see his own true self, he sees God. This self of his is hidden by illusion which prevents him from seeing his true form and enables him to see only his individual person. This illusion has to be pierced. Vritra has to be killed so that cows can be released, water can be released, light can be released. The identity of the self and God has been explained by the Adiguru by two beautiful examples. One is of a pitcher, which encloses a certain space within it. In this situation, whether the space within and the space outside are the same or different from each other? At all times they are the same and yet different, because the space within has a certain defined character which can be used in a certain manner. Yet it is a part of the space outside, that has only been enclosed. Once the pitcher breaks and the enclosure is no longer there, the space within has no longer a separate identity. It is a part of the general space as it always was with an illusion in between that it was different. The second example is of the sea and the waves in it. Whether the sea and the waves are different or both are the same. The waves would have to be called the same as the sea, yet different from it. As they rise they assume an individual identity and as soon as they fall this identity is lost and they are the sea again. The task before the mystic adept was only to realize this and know his true identity. It is not the body but something beyond which is his real self. A single god or a multiplicity of gods had no meaning for him, because he could see that not only Mitra, Varun, Agni, Pushan etc. were the same, but even Manu, Val, Ardhshipra, Shushna, Kutsa, Yam, Dadhich and Shambar were also same.

So far as hiding the true meaning is concerned, the reasons are obvious. The common worshipper could not have been possibly allowed to know that all these gods were there just to give him confidence in his endeavours and solace in his failures. Had he known that there was no benefactor, no saviour, no protector other than he himself, he would have lost half the battle before it was fought. His requirement was to hold a hand. His requirement was to feel that he has now been able to appease the god so there would be no difficulty in acquiring wealth for which he was already making an effort, there would be no difficulty in defeating an enemy for which he was already fighting a war and there was no need to fear from a danger for which he had already taken care to see that he had been protected. In case this did not happen, his requirement was to have solace that there would be another time. Last time there was something missing which did not appease the god, but he can try again because the god is merciful and is always there to be with his worshippers. This faith could not have been broken while addressing the audience that wanted the mystic teachings. The *Veds* had to be composed in a manner, that on the face of it, they appear to be addressed to the vast majority of people who were looking only for the rituals that could appease the gods to fulfil their desires. There was no other way as the text was common. The other audience was very small and what had to be told to it could be done in a way that was limited to a few people. They found a way to communicate their message by applying a simple code, the key to which could be passed over from the teacher to the selected disciples in a short time when the two went away from the ashram to a secluded place. It is a testimony to their brilliance that they succeeded so completely in their effort, that not only people from both segments received what they were looking for, but once the key was lost, people now find it difficult to believe that these books contain anything but prayers of a ritualistic religion, in which all possible forces of nature were believed to be gods and were worshipped by a group of ignorant or semi-ignorant people.

9
Zoroaster and Persia

T HE DEV WORSHIPPERS, WHO CALLED themselves Manavs, were in complete ascendency in Central Asia when Zoroaster emerged on the scene. Iran and Turan were then two important kingdoms. The ruling class, as well as the majority of the population of both kingdoms and other parts of Central Asia were followers of their religion. The Asurs had been reduced to a very small number and were in disarray. This emerges from the *Avesta*. Some such passages are mentioned here.

1. (We worship) the tall-formed Strength; Verethraghna, made by Ahur; the crushing ascendant, and Spenta Armaiti. And with help of Spenta Armaiti, break ye asunder their malice, turn their minds astray, bind their hands, make their knees quake against one another, bind their tongues. When, O Mazda! Shall the faithful smite the wicked? When shall the faithful smite the Drug?

    (Ormazd Yast I)

2. The cows driven astray invoke him for help, longing for the stables. 'When will that bull, Mithra, the lord of wide pastures, bring us back and make us reach the stables? When will he turn us back to the right way from the den of the Drug where we were driven?'

    (Mihir Yast XXII)

3. Unto you (O Ahur and Asha), the soul of the kine (our sacred herds and folks) cried aloud, 'For whom did ye create me, and by whom did ye fashion me? On me comes the assault of wrath and of violent power, the blow of desolation, audacious insolence and (thievish) might.' Upon this the creator of the kine (the holy herd) asked Righteousness, 'How was thy guardian for the kine

(appointed) by thee when, as having power (over all her fate) ye made her? Whom did ye select as her master who might hurl back the fury of the wicked?'

(Yasna XXIX)

4. The Great Creator (is himself) most mindful of the uttered indications which have been fulfilled beforehand hitherto in the deeds of Daeva gods and Daeva worshippers. He, Ahur is the discerning arbiter, so shall it be to us as He shall will. Therefore it is that we both, my soul (Zarathustra's soul) and (the soul) of the mother kine (one) making our supplications for the two worlds to Ahur, and with hands stretched out in entreaty, when we pray to the Great Creator with questions in our doubt and He will answer. Not for the righteous liver, nor for the thrifty tiller of the earth shall there be destruction together with the wicked.

(Yasna XXIX)

5. What is then your kingdom, O Mazda? Where are Thine offerers, O Mazda, who are the enlightened of the Good Mind producing the doctrines with wide mental light as inherited treasures, Thy word in misfortune and in woe? I know none other than You. Through these our deeds (of sacrifice and zeal) they are terrified among whom there was (once) destruction and for many (at the time) when the oppressor of Thy holy vows was as the stronger oppressing the weaker.

(Yasna XXXIV)

6. This I ask thee, O Ahur! Tell me aright, how shall I banish this Demon of the Lie from us hence who are filled with rebellion? The friends of Righteousness (as it lives in Thy saints) gain no light (from their teachings), nor have they loved the questions which Thy good mind asks in the soul. This I ask Thee, O Ahur! Tell me aright, how shall I deliver that Demon of the Lie into the two hands of Thine Order (as he lives in our hosts) to cast him down to death through Thy Mathras of doctrine, to keep those deceitful and harsh oppressors from reaching their fell aims? This I ask Thee, O Ahur! Tell me aright. If through Thy Righteousness (within our souls) Thou hast the power over this for my protection, when the

two hosts shall meet in hate (as they strive) for those vows which Thou dost desire to maintain, how, O Mazda! And to which of both wilt Thou give the day?

(Yasna XLIV)

7.   To what land to turn, aye whither turning shall I go? On the part of a kinsman, or allied peer, none to conciliate, give to me (to help my cause), nor yet (still less) the evil tyrants of the province. How then shall I establish well the faith and thus conciliate Thy grace, O Lord? This know I, Mazda! Wherefore I am thus unable to attain my wish, and why my flocks are so reduced in number, and why my following is likewise scant. To whom for help does he (their chief) approach, Thee, for mine exhorter and commander, Living Lord! I choose. (But before these helpers come to me) all rests as yet in gloom. The evil man is holding back those who are the bearers of the Righteous Order from progress with the kine (from progress with the sacred cause) within the region, or the province, he, the evil governor, endowed with evil might, consuming life with evil deeds. Wherefore, whoever hurls him from his power, O Mazda! Or from life, stores for the kine in sacred wisdom shall he make.

8.   (And they and I have every need for help for now) the Karpan and the Kavi will join in governments to slay the life of man with evil deeds, they whom their own souls and their own conscience will becry.

(Yasna XLVI)

9.   When Mazda! Shall the men of mind's perfection come? And when shall they drive from hence, the soil of this (polluted) drunken joy, whereby the Karpans would crush us, and by whose inspiration the tyrants of the provinces (hold on) their evil rule? Yea when shall our perfected Piety appear? When shall she come, as having the amenities of home for us, and provide with pastures? Who shall give us peace from the cruel (men) of evil life and faith?

(Yasna XLIX)

10. (But this Thy bounteous spirit doth not alone bestow rewards and blessings on the good). The wicked are harmed, and from (the motives which move) that bounteous spirit, O Mazda! But

not thus the saints. (And yet the ruler's pride would ever slight the righteous) the feeble man alone stands free to give in kindly oblation to Thy saint, but having wealth and ruling power, the evil (man) is (at the service) of the wicked, and for much.

(Yasna XLVII)

These passages confirm that not only the ruling class but even the population was mainly of Dev worshippers in the region. In the seventh passage Zoroaster narrates the situation. He has stated that his flocks are reduced in number and his following is scant. All the other passages have references that confirm this. The ruling power is with the Dev worshippers who have been using it to establish themselves as firmly as possible. The Asurs are few in number and seem to be suffering at their hands. The *Veds* confirm this position. There are a number of passages which show a long period in which the Manavs were in total dominance with no challenge, whatsoever, to their position, from the Asurs. A few are mentioned here.

1. Indra has slain the Dasyus, Som, in battle, Agni has consumed them before the noon, he (Indra) has destroyed the whole of the many thousands, as (robbers are destroyers of those) going upon (their own) business, in a difficult and dangerous (place).
2. Indra, you have made these Dasyus devoid of all, you have made the Dasyus abject; may you (Som and Indra) repel and destroy enemies; accept our homage for their destruction.

(*Rig Ved.* M-4, S-28, R-3 and 4)

Zoroaster started his efforts to dislodge the Manavs and their religion and to establish the earlier form of worship. What he did has been stated in the *Avesta* in this passage.

We worship the Fravashi of the holy Zarathustra. Who first thought what is good; who first knew and first taught; who first possessed and first took possession of the Bull, of Holiness, of the Word, the obedience to the Word and dominion and all the good things made by Mazda; Who was the first Priest, the first Warrior, the first Plougher of the ground; who took the turning of the wheel from the hands of the Daeva, who first pronounced the praise of Asha, thus bringing the Daevas to naught, and confessed himself a worshipper of Mazda, a follower of Zarathustra, one who hates the Daevas and obeys the laws of Ahur. Who first said the word that destroys the Daevas, the law of Ahur; who first proclaimed the word that destroys the Daevas, the law of Ahur; who first declared all the creation of the Daevas unworthy of sacrifice and prayer; the first bearer of the law amongst the nations; In whom was heard the whole Mathra, the word of holiness; the praiser of Asha; who had a revelation of the law, that most excellent of all beings.

(Farvardin Yast XXIV)

This passage shows what Zoroastrians, a few centuries after Zoroaster, thought of his contribution. The most important from the historical perspective, is that he took the turning of the wheel from the hands of the Daevas. The second is that he proclaimed the law of Ahur. And the third is that he heard the whole Mathra. The first is the political side, that the ruling class was converted to Zoroastrianism with which the sovereign power of the state was used for the furtherance of the interests of its believers and to suppress the Dev worshippers. The second and third are significant as with this Zoroaster gave a new face to an old religion because of which it acquired its name from him. Evidently, Zoroaster had understood the reasons for the success of the religion of the Manavs. They had a tradition of composing and singing hymns from the past. These were, however, not compiled. The Devs started the practice of compiling them from the time of Ushana, which was shortly after the two sides had split. By Zoroaster's time, this would have been a reasonably big text. Once a text had developed, all moral laws and ritualistic practices found place in it. The Manavs, therefore, had a scripture which had the stamp of antiquity. People in matters of religion, have respect for the old. Something of antiquity attracts more people to believe in it. The Asurs had not done any such thing. They had hymns with much the same contents and folklore as the Manavs, but these were not compiled. They were composed, sung and lost to be replaced by new ones, perhaps at times with the same content. This made the Asurs have a religion without scriptures. Being without a scripture, they did not have anything which clearly laid down the moral and social laws or the religious rituals except traditions. Zoroaster changed this trend and the Asurs also started the practice of compiling hymns that were already there and adding new ones to them. With this the process of the compilation of the *Avesta* started. Once a scripture was there it contained all that a religion lays down. The social and moral laws now had the scriptures and were declared to be the law of Ahur. The rituals, too, that had not been codified, were given a final shape and laid down in them. Here the priests seem to have gone with great zeal, as the rituals appear to be very elaborate, far more than even the Vedic rituals. Mathra is what has become in the language of Mantra of Sanskrit. The sacrifice and all other rituals were accompanied by them, which were essentially hymns addressed to certain divinities. The passage says that Zoroaster heard the whole of it. The hymns that were sung to accompany the sacrifices had in them all the information of the past that had survived. The Asurs, as they were late in starting the process of retaining them, had lost much of it or had very scanty or distorted information left with them about their past. This is evident after comparing the information emerging from the *Veds* and the *Avesta* about remote times. The *Veds* have retained very vital information about the Ribhus and what they did. The *Avesta* only remembers Haoshyangha and the thirty-three divinities but nothing about what they did. Even in remembering the places which were their homelands earlier, the *Avesta* has memory of only Airyana Vaego, while the *Veds* have references to the western shore of the Caspian Sea and the Arctic Circle before that.

This passage should not cause confusion where it has been stated that Zoroaster was the first to confess to be a worshipper of Mazda and a follower of Zarathustra. Zoroaster has been said to be a follower of Zoroaster. This is a part of a pledge laid down in the *Avesta*, which precedes prayers. It is there at a large number of places and has been mentioned in this passage without modification to mean that he was the first to take this pledge. As it included an affirmation from the worshipper that he is a follower of Zarathustra, it has come in unchanged, though it was speaking of Zoroaster himself. Though at many places this confession is in an abridged form, its bigger version is almost a prayer in itself, which briefly, is given here.

I drive the Daevas hence. I confess as a Mazda worshipper of the order of Zarathustra, estranged from the Daevas, devoted to the lore of the Lord; and of Ahur Mazda, I attribute all things good to the holy One; whose is the kine, whose is Asha whose are the stars. And I choose Piety, mine may she be. And therefore I loudly deprecate all violence against the (sacred) kine and the wasting of Mazdayasnian villages. Away from thoughts the wandering at will (away the thought of) free nomadic pitching of the tent, for I wish to remove all wandering from their kine. Never may I stand as a source of wasting, never as a source of withering to the Mazdayasnian village. Away do I abjure the headship of the Daevas, evil as they are, bereft of good, and void of virtue, deceitful in their wickedness, of (all) beings those most like the Demon of the Lie. Off, off, do I abjure the Daevas and all possessed by them; away do I abjure their shelter and their headship and the iniquitous of every kind who act as Rakhshas act. Thus and so in very deed might Ahur Mazda have indicated to Zarathustra in every question which Zarathustra asked. Thus and so might Zarathustra have abjured the shelter and the headship of the Daevas. And so I myself, as a worshipper of Mazda, and of the Zarathustra's order, would so abjure the Daevas and their shelter, as he who was the holy Zarathustra abjured them. To that religious sanctity do I belong, to that sanctity to which the kine of the blessed gift, to that sanctity to which Ahur Mazda who made both kine and holy men. Of that creed which Zarathustra held, which Kavi Vistasp and those two Frashaostra and Gamasp; of that creed and of that lore am I. A Mazda worshipper I am, of Zarathustra's order, so do I confess, as a praiser and confessor. Yea I praise at once the faith of Mazda, the faith that wields the felling halbert, the faith of kindred marriage, Ahur's Faith, the Zarathustrian creed.

(Yasna XII)

Zarathustra declaring the law of Ahur and hearing the whole Mathra are matters of religion. His taking away the turning of the wheel from the hands of the Daevas involved politics which had far-reaching consequences. How he went about it emerges with a reasonable amount of clarity from the *Avesta* and later texts of Zoroastrianism. Being a man of religion, he began with attempts to convert people by preaching. These attempts seem to have been amongst the Magis and in all likelihood in the Magi homeland along the Amu Dariya. He made appeals to people to individually examine what the two sides were saying and decide for themselves which of the two was the true religion of their forefathers. Some passages in the *Avesta* have these exhortations, which are given here.

1. And now I proclaim, O ye who are drawing near and seeking to be taught those versions which appertain to Him, the praises which are for Ahur and the sacrifices, and likewise the benignant meditations. Hear ye then with your ears. It is for a decision as to religions, man and man, each individually for himself. Thus are the primeval spirits who as a pair (combining their opposite strivings) and (yet each) independent in his action, have been famed (of old). (They are) a better thing and a worse. And between these two let the wisely acting choose aright. (Choose ye) not (as) the evil-doers. And between these two spirits the Daevas and the Daeva worshippers can make no righteous choice. As they are questioning and debating in their council, the (personified) Worst Mind approached them that he might be chosen. And thereupon they rushed together unto Angra Mainyu that they might pollute the lives of mortals.

(Yasna XXX)

2. And which of the (religions) is the greater (and the more prevailing?) Is it that which the righteous believes, or the wicked?

(And you, ye assembled throngs) let not a man of you lend a hearing to Mathra or to command of that sinner (ignorant as he is) for home, village, region and province he would deliver to ruin and death. But (fly ye to arms without hearing) and hew ye them all with the halberd.

(Yasna XXXI)

Zoroaster's efforts to propagate his religion amongst the people would have evoked a response from the other side on the same lines. This seems to have led to debates between Zoroaster and the Rishis from the religion of the Dev worshippers. Ancient India had a tradition of Shashtrartha or a debate on the meaning of the scriptures, in which scholars having different points of view debated in the presence of an audience, which often included the king. The audience used to judge. It appears that the Aryans in ancient Persia had a similar tradition, because the *Avesta* mentions Zoroaster's repeated efforts to defeat a rival, though without success. The passage on this is stated here.

Bendva has ever fought with me (yea since he first appeared at hand to threaten, and alas to his advantage in the strife). He is the most powerful (in brutal might) and (in his predominance) would crush my strength as I seek to win back the disaffected (in my host) through Righteous (zeal) O Mazda, come then with gifts of good to meet my sorrow. Through (Thine inspiring) Good Mind obtain (for me) that (Bendva's) death. (Aye he is indeed the greatest) for that Bendva's evil judge doth cause me to hesitate and ponder (in my earnest course of propagation and reform) a deceiver as he is (estranged) from the Righteous Order. The bountiful and perfect Piety he has not maintained, nor questions with Thy Good Mind hath he asked to gain him light, O Lord. But (all is not yet lost) for this religious choice (our holy creed for which our last lost battle has been fought) O Mazda! (But) for (that evil) Judge, the Demon of the Lie (is set) to deal (for him) his wounds. Therefore, do I pray for the sheltering leadership of Thy good mind (within our folks and our commanders). And all the allies of the wicked I abjure. They who with evil scheme and will, shall cherish and help on the Wrath of Rapine and with her Rama and (not by silent favour but) with their very tongues, whose will and wish (run) not with good but evil deeds. These settle and support the Daevas (in their power, not the Lord). It is the wicked's faith and insight so to do. Their faith is perverted.

(Yasna XLIX)

The translators have taken these references of fight to mean war, because of which they have added 'brutal strength', 'commanders' and suchlike terms in an attempt to clarify the portions that needed some additions. The passage is about Zoroaster repeatedly losing to Bendva in a debate and not war. It mentions a judge between the two sides, who has been termed evil. He caused Zoroaster to hesitate and ponder, perhaps by asking questions in the midst of the debate. It also mentions that Bendva was doing all this by his tongue. Bendva has been mentioned as the most powerful person. He seems to be Rishi Vamdev. This appears not only because the name is close, but also because some Richas of the *Rig Ved* ascribed to Rishi Vamdev Gautam hint at such encounters. These are given here.

1. Invoker (of the gods) young (of the deities), possessed of excellent wisdom, through the alliance (with you produced) by the holy text, which came to me from my father Gotam, I demolish the powerful (Asur); do you who are the humbler (of foes), be cognizant of our praises.

    (*Rig Ved*. M-4, S-4, R-11)

2. Vamdev speaks, 'Let me come forth by this path, for it is difficult (of issue); let me come forth obliquely from the side; many acts unperformed by others are to be accomplished by me; let me contend (in war) with one (enemy), in controversy with one opponent.'

    (*Rig Ved*. M-4, S-18, R-2)

There is another passage in the *Avesta* which confirms that it was not a war but a debate, or several of them, that had taken place with Rishi Vamdev. In this he has been mentioned by his family name of Gautam as it has become in the *Avesta* language.

> Through their glory a man is born who is chief in assemblies, who listens well to the (holy) words and who returns a victor from discussions with Gaotema, the heretic.
>
> (Farvardin Yast I)

Apparently, Zoroaster did not get much success in trying to convert people by preaching and debating with opponents. He was at a disadvantage as Dev worshippers were in dominance for several centuries and majority of the population consisted of them. They had also a sacred text to quote from. Zoroaster would have been alone in his endeavours and without the help of a text. It would have required a lot of perseverance on his part to struggle for his cause despite all setbacks. At times, he does sound despondent in his uttering. At one stage he is reported to be complaining that after preaching for ten years he has been able to convert only one person. This is mentioned here.

> On the completion of revelation, that is, at the end of ten years, Medyomah, son of Arastai became faithful to Zartust. Afterwards, on having obtained his requests, he came back to the conference of Auharmazd, and he spoke thus: 'In ten years only one man has been attracted to me.'
>
> (Zad Sparam. Chapter XXIII)

After a stage, he seems to have decided to seek sovereign support. He felt that the Dev worshippers could be dislodged and his religion propagated only if it was done as a state policy. There are several passages in the *Avesta* which show this. Some are here.

1. This man is found for me here who alone has come to our enunciations, Zarathustra Spitama. Our mighty and completed acts of grace he desires to enounce for us, for (Me), the Great Creator and for Righteousness. Upon this the soul of the kine lamented, 'Woe is unto me since I have obtained for myself in my

wounding a lord who is powerless to effect (his) wish, the mere voice of a feeble and pusillanimous man, whereas I desire one who is lord over his will and able as one of royal state to bring what he desires to effect.'

Zarathustra speaks, 'Do ye, O Ahur, grant gladness unto these and the sovereign kingdom such as is established by which one bestows upon them the peaceful amenities of home. And when shall the sovereign power come hastening to me (to give me strength for my task and mission), For without this I cannot advance or undertake my toil.'

(Yasna XXIX)

2. And when the Divine Righteousness shall be inclined to my appeals, I will pray for that mighty kingdom by whose force we may smite the Lie-demon.

(Yasna XXXI)

3. What is the (potent) prayer to bring on Thy holy reign? How shall I seek the open helpers for (the spread and maintenance of) Thy (great) Order?

(Yasna XLVIII)

4. The good government is to be chosen (among all wished for things) as that lot which most of all brings on (our happiness). Actions that oppress us it opposes. Therefore, O Great Creator! Let me produce and help bring on (that sovereign power) which is the best for us at every present hour. And first I will ask for these two blessings of Your own, grant me this your sovereign rule over our desired wealth.

(Yasna LI)

These passages are explicit. Zoroaster has tried, but has not achieved much in bringing people to his faith by persuasion and preaching. The only option left is to somehow convert the king to establish the religion and convert the people under the authority of the sovereign rule. In the first passage, the soul of the kine is lamenting on being told that for her protection Zarathustra is being sent. She says that he is powerless to effect his wish, which is just a voice of a feeble man. She desires one who is the lord of his will, like a royal state that is able to bring into effect what he desires. Thereafter, in the same passage, Zoroaster is praying to the Creator to bring the assistance of the sovereign power to him. The third passage has similar sentiments. Here Zoroaster is seeking to know from Ahur, which is the prayer that is potent enough to bring the holy reign with which he could get open helpers for the spread of the holy order.

Religion has to be spread as a part of the state policy. With this objective in mind, Zoroaster had two major kingdoms before him, Turan and Iran. There would have been some minor independent states too, but their siding with Zoroaster would not have had much of an impact, because apparently, the Magis were his first concern, as they were his own people. The Magis were more or less in areas which were under the dominance of these two kingdoms. Apart from that, if the religion had to be spread with the support of state power, it would have been effective only if the state was powerful. It would have been possible for it to impose its will on the weaker kingdoms in the neighbourhood, as did happen with the conversion of Iran. In the given situation, the task before Zoroaster was clearly laid down. He had to try and convert the kings of Turan and Iran. How he went about it has been described in the Zoroastrian scriptures. The relevant passage is here.

> It is declared that upon those words, innumerable Kigs and Karaps have rushed upon Zaratust and strove for his death, just like this which revelation states, 'It is then a number have run away who have sat in the vicinity of Tur's progeny. This Tur was Aurvaita-dang, the scanty giver and the multitude told him they would seize the great one from him who is little. But the progeny of Aurvaita-dang the Tur, spoke thus, "Should we for that speech destroy him, who mingles together those propitious words, where we are thus without doubt as to one thing therein such as next of kin marriage. Thou shalt not destroy that man."' The nobles of Aurvaita-dang the Tur were angry and clamorous for Zaratust's death, but he invited

the Kigs and Karaps to the religion of Auharmazd, just as this passage states that Zaratust also spoke thus, 'Worldly righteousness, O Aurvaita-dang thou Tur, is the whole of the worship of the Daeva and the termination of the Mazda worship of Zaratust.' And Aurvaita- dang the Tur spoke thus, 'O Zaratust thou shalt not attract me to this evil in which thou really art.'

One prodigy of the demons is specified who was the enemy, a Karap Vaedvoist by name. And Auharmazd spoke thus, 'I so befriend that man O Zaratust, whom thou shall invite. Do thou therefore proceed, O Zaratust, and thou shalt demand from him for me a hundred youths of vigour, girls and teams of four horses; so do thou speak to him thus, "O Vedvoist! Auharmazd demands from thee a hundred youths of vigour, girls and teams of four horses, if thou dost not give to him evil destiny is thine.' Then Zaratust walked on to Vedvoist of the unsanctified and asked. And that Karap shouted in reply to Zaratust thus, 'For me there is no more from thee, I am more of a divinity and am more forward in opulence than even Auharmazd.'

One marvel is this with which, too, he who was Zaratust became aware from revelations about the vileness and perverted religion of Zak of the deadly Karaps who were at the residence of Vistasp, their combination for the death of Zaratust and influencing Vistasp for his death by command of Vistasp which extends to awful imprisonment and punishment. His uttering, on the horse course of Vistasp, a reminder of the power and triumph of Auharmazd as he invited Vistasp to the religion of Auharmazd. But thereupon, too, before the words of Zaratust were fully heard by him, owing to the demonizing of the deadly Zak, spoken out with slanderous knowledge to Vistasp about Zaratust, there and then occurred his consignment of Zaratust to the confinement and punishment as stated in the words of Zaratust thus, 'I have spoken about their three enquiries and I am bound by thirty. I, with thirty-three fetters of murderers, wicked one and Daeva worshipper.'

(Dinkard. Book VII, Chapter IV)

The passage shows that Zoroaster first approached the king of Turan. He has been named Aurvaita-dang the Tur. Apparently, he is the same as Arjasp of the *Shahnama*. The nobles and the priests of his court were offended at his views and wanted to kill him. They were restrained by the king, who after listening declined to accept his propositions and said that 'thou shalt not attract me to this evil in which thou art'. The next person mentioned is Vedvoist. This name in Sanskrit would be Ved Vashist. Evidently, he is Rishi Vashist. In Indian traditions, Ved is not prefixed to the name of Rishi Vashist. It is prefixed to the name of Rishi Vyas only, but it seems that in Persia, either it was prefixed to all Rishis or was so with some of them other then Rishi Vyas alone. Vashist was one of the seven Angiras Rishis, who, led by Bhrigu, had started the new religious practices in Arjika, which led to all the trouble. The Vedic Aryans had a tradition of gurukuls or teacher families, which used to run ashrams, which can loosely be translated as schools or seminaries. Students lived in these ashrams for about twenty years and learnt the *Veds* under the guidance of the guru. On completion of studies, many took over the name of the gurukul instead of their family name. The person named in the Dinkard appears to be the head of the Vashist gurukul of the time. This appears from the demand of a hundred youths of vigour by Zoroaster, though girls mentioned thereafter creates confusion, because the ashrams were exclusively for boys. The demand appears to be just a way of expressing that Zoroaster had approached Vedvoist. He would have approached to convert him. As this attempt has been mentioned along with those on the part of Zoroaster to convert the sovereign authority, Rishi Vashist appears to have had a major influence in the Persian court, apart from being the head of a gurukul. He appears to be an important royal priest, if not the chief priest of Persia. This emerges from the accounts of the *Veds* also. The last person approached is Vistasp, the king of Persia. The writers of the Dinkard had the compulsion of being careful about him, because he later accepted the religion of Zoroaster and was the main pillar of strength for him. Much of the spread of Zoroastrianism was because of his patronage and adoption of a state policy of suppressing the religion of the Dev worshippers and the promotion of Zoroastrianism. It is for this reason that they have laid the entire blame for the imprisonment of Zoroaster on the deadly Zak and the rest of the Kigs and Karaps, who were evidently nobles and priests of his court. This does not seem reasonable, as Vistasp was the king. His word was law. Zoroaster could not have been put in confinement without his orders.

In his initial attempts to convert the king, Zoroaster was put in prison in Persia. The other references from the *Avesta* show that in course of time, Vistasp changed his mind and was converted to Zoroastrianism and became its first sovereign supporter with a state policy to promote it. There are a large number of references which speak of this. Some are given here.

1. Unto her did the holy Zarathustra offer up a sacrifice in the Airyana Vaegah, by the good river Daitya. He begged of her a boon saying, 'Grant me this, O Ardvi Sura Anahita that I may bring the son of Aurvatasp, the valiant Kavi Vistasp to think according to the law, to speak according to the law, to do according to the law.'

                                                          (Aban Yast XXIV)

2. That clave unto king Vistasp so that he thought according to the law, spake according to the law, and did according to the law; so that he professed the law, destroying his foes and causing the Daevas to retire. Who, driving the Drug before him, sought wide room for the holy religion; who made himself the arm and support of this law of Ahur. Vistasp, conquered all enemies, Tathravant of the evil law, Peshana the worshipper of the Daevas and the fiendish wicked Aregatasp and the other wicked Hvyaonas.

                                                          (Zamyad Yast XIV)

3. Thus said Ahur Mazda unto the holy Zarathustra, and thus again

did Zarathustra say unto the young king, Vistasp, 'Have no bad priests or unfriendly priests. For bad priests or unfriendly priests will bring about much harm and though thou wish to sacrifice, it will be to the Amesha Spentas as if no sacrifice had been offered.'

(Vistasp Yast II)

4. Auharmazd spoke to Zaratust thus, 'That root of a tree which thou sawest and those four branches are the four periods which will come. That of gold is when I and thou converse and King Vistasp shall accept the religion and shall demolish the figures of the demons.'

(Bahman Yast Chapter I)

5. That the prayer has been answered, that Ahur Mazda might grant him those boons. And may Kavi Vistasp, and the Zarathustrian Spitama, and Frashaostra too with them, offer propitiation to Mazda in thought, word and deed.

(Yasna LIII)

6. The creator Auharmazd sends the archangels on to Kai Vistasp as evidence about Auharmazd, and a reminder of Spitaman Zaratust of the pure goodness of the Mazda-worshipping religion and of the command for the ruler Vistasp as to its triumph on accepting the religion from Zaratust. The envoy's explanation of Auharmazd's message to Vistasp and the accepting of the Mazda-worshipping religion by the obedient king, Vistasp.

(Dinkard. Book VIII, Chapter XI)

7. Vistasp, the king when he became relieved from the war with Argasp, sent to the chief rulers about the acceptance of the religion, 'and the writings of the Mazda-worshipping religion and also the tongue of the Magian Man, it is expedient you should send therewith.'

(Dinkard. Book IV)

These passages confirm the adoption of the religion of Zoroaster by Vistasp. The sixth passage shows that this was an act of God. Vistasp received divine inspiration to accept his faith. Once he had accepted the religion, the second passage states that he became the arm and support of the law of Ahur and made wide room for the holy religion by destroying the foes and causing the Daevas to retire. It is evident that Vistasp made it a state policy and took up the spread of his newly accepted religion in his kingdom with the use of the state machinery. The religion of the Devs was declared to be false and steps were taken to stamp it out. It was a complete change of fortune. Zoroaster, who had been put in prison when he approached the king earlier, was accepted by Vistasp as a Prophet now. The priests of the earlier religion, which was the religion of Dev worshippers, would have been removed and the followers of their religion would have been put to difficulties. The seventh passage shows that Vistasp took on the task of the spread of Zoroastrianism not only within his kingdom, but also amongst chieftains over whom he had influence. A royal edict was issued to this effect.

Though the Zoroastrian scriptures show that it was divine inspiration that led to the conversion of Vistasp, he had enough political reasons to do so. The Manavs had a close affinity with Turan as can be seen in their treatment of Turvayan and his defeat at the hands of Sushravas. Despite the kings of Iran being their patrons, Turvayan's defeat has not been mentioned. So long as Iran and Turan were friendly neighbours it did not make a difference, but by the times of Vistasp the situation had changed and they had already fought, not just once but twice and on each occasion the king of the losing side had been killed. The possibilities of Turan launching an attack to avenge the killing of Turvayan were always there. For a king, a situation wherein the people of his kingdom follow a religion, the priests and leaders of which are sympathetic to a hostile neighbour, cannot be said to be comfortable. Vistasp's decision could have been guided by political considerations to wean the people away from the religion, the leaders of which would have always remained more favourably disposed to Turan because of their ethnic affinity. Though Zoroaster was also a Magi, his religion had more or less faded away in the Magi homeland and for all practical purposes presented a rival to the religion being patronized by Turan. The intensity with which the Persian kingdom went about in suppressing the Dev worshippers also points to a political rather than a religious agenda, because Devs and Asurs had been fighting for long but this had not led to a situation as followed after the conversion of Vistasp, wherein the Devs did not have the choice of even leaving the place. As would emerge ahead, it seems to have been just abjuration or death. The reasons for this sudden change of mind on the part of Vistasp would have remained a mystery for the people as no new development had taken place. Zoroaster had presented his case and had not only failed to convince Vistasp but had given enough reasons to order his imprisonment. Thereafter, he was called out of the prison to be the chief priest while his rivals were not only removed from their position but were subjected to the worst possible persecution and their religion declared false. Due to their failure to comprehend the reasons for this decision of Vistasp, the people imputed divine intervention and the stories of miracles would have been woven in the scriptures.

The reverses of the Dev worshippers can be seen from the *Avesta*. Some passages are given here.

1. Yea, I will speak forth, hear ye now listen, yea who from near and yea who from afar have come seeking (the knowledge). Now ponder ye clearly (that concerns) him. Not for a second time shall the false teacher slay our life. The wicked is hemmed in with his faith and his tongue. Yea, I will declare the world's two first spirits, of whom the more bountiful thus spake to the harmful, 'Neither our thoughts nor commands, nor our understanding, nor our beliefs, nor our deeds, nor our consciences, nor our souls are at one.'

    Thus, I will declare the world's first (teaching) that which the all-wise Ahur Mazda hath told me. And they, among you, who will not fulfil and obey this Mathra, as I now shall conceive and declare it, to these shall the end of life in woe.

    (Yasna XLV)

2. (Him would we magnify and praise) who hath despised the Daeva gods and alien men, them who before held Him in their derision. For different are (these) from him who gave Him honour.

    (Yasna XLV)

These passages show that the Dev worshippers had been removed from positions of authority and their religion had been declared to be a deceit. The accounts of Zoroaster, the conversion of Vistasp and the removal of priests of the Vedic religion, as they emerge from the *Avesta*, are confirmed by the *Veds*. This was a reversal for them, therefore, in the usual style, the mention is cryptic. Yet it confirms what had happened in Persia. Here are the Richas that mention Zoroaster.

1. Consume, Agni, all enemies, with the same flames with which you have consumed Jaruth, drive away febrile disease.

    (*Rig Ved.* M-7, S-1, R-7)

2. Agni verily has protected Jaratkarna, he has consumed Jaruth with his flames; Agni rescued Atri in the hot fissure; Agni furnished Nrimedh with progeny.

    (*Rig Ved.* M-10, S-80, R-3)

These Richas have been composed after the death of Zoroaster, as they express satisfaction on his demise. Zoroaster was killed about forty years after the conversion of Vistasp. The Indo-Aryans, who were called Dev worshippers in Central Asia, facing the wrath of the opponent religion would have left Persia much earlier. They would have received this information in India, which shows that lines of communication had remained alive. The Rishis, in these Richas, have mentioned nothing about what Jaruth had done, but their silence speaks of their discomfiture at his hands. It is evident that whatever has emerged from the *Avesta* is true that the Vedic people had lost their position in Iran.

The next mention is that of Vistasp. He has been called Ishtashwa in the *Veds*. 'Ashwa' in Sanskrit and 'asp' in the *Avesta* language, both mean horse. Ishtashwa means a person whose wished for thing was a horse. Ishtashwa was the name of Vistasp in Sanskrit, can be said not only because of the similarity of the names but also because there is a passage in the *Avesta* which states that Vistasp had wished for a horse. Perhaps he got his name because of it. The said passage is stated here.

Before whom the worshippers of Mazda stand. The Hvovas did worship her, the Naotaras did worship her. The Hvovas asked for riches, the Naotaras asked for swift horses. Quickly was Hvova blessed with riches and full prosperity, quickly became Vistasp, the Naotaride, the lord of the swiftest horses.

(Aban Yast XXII)

Ishtashwa is mentioned in only one Richa of the *Rig Ved*, which does speak of hostility. The same is here.

We rejoice that for the satisfaction of the ten (organs of sense), the (priests) bearing the twice five (ladles of) the sacrificial food proceed (to the altar). What can Ishtashwa, (what can) Ishtarashmi, (what can) those who are now lords of the earth achieve (with respect) to the leaders of men, the conqueror of their foe?

(*Rig Ved*. M-1, S-122, R-13)

This Richa explicitly states that the sovereign power is hostile to the Manavs. It is questioning what those who are now lords of the earth can achieve. Evidently, the Manavs are no longer the lords of the earth. The sovereign authority is no longer favourably disposed to them. Ishtashwa has been projected as being hostile, though a certain amount of bravado is displayed by saying what he can do. The other name, Ishtarashmi, cannot be recognized, but possibly he is someone close to Ishtashwa, and could be a prince.

Another Richa names some more kings or chieftains who were hostile. These are perhaps some of the subordinate chieftains or ruler of principalities, who adopted the religion of Zoroaster in accordance with the directions of Vistasp. The names cannot be recognized, but a closer comparison with the names in the *Avesta* may bring out the links. The Richa mentioning them is given here.

The four (silly) sons of Masharshar, the three of the victorious monarch Ayavas (annoy) me. Let your spacious and bright-rayed chariot, Mitra and Varun, blaze (before them) like the sun (filling them with fear).

(*Rig Ved*. M-1, S-122, R-15)

Apart from the mention of Vistasp and some other kings who were hostile to the Manavs, the *Rig Ved* mentions instances where the Vedic priests were removed and replaced by Zoroastrian priests. Though the commentators have taken them to be a case of rivalry between two priests, they are referring to the removal of a Vedic priest and his replacement by a Zoroastrian priest and not just a simple rivalry between two priests of the same religion. The said Richas are stated here.

1. I do not regard it as worthy of heaven or of earth as (fit to be compared) with the sacrifice (I offer) or with these (our) sacred rites, let then, the mighty mountains overwhelm him. Let the employer of Atiyaj be ever degraded.

2. Maruts, may the energies of that man be enfeebled, may heaven consume that impious adversary who thinks himself superior to us and who pretends to depreciate the worship that we offer.

3. Why have they called you Som, the protector of pious prayer? Why (have they called you) our defender against calumny? Why do you behold us subjected to reproach? Cast your destroying weapon upon the adversary of the Brahman.

(*Rig Ved*. M-6, S-52, R-1 to 3)

These hymns have been ascribed to Rishi Rijishwa Bhardwaj. Evidently, he was the priest of someone eminent. He has been removed and in his place Atiyaj has been appointed. Atiyaj is not a Vedic priest, because Rishi Bhardwaj has stated that he is an impious adversary who considers himself to be superior and 'pretends to depreciate the worship that we offer'. In the third Richa he has been called an adversary of the Brahman. Such a statement could not have been made for a rival Vedic priest, because he himself would have been a Brahman. This Richa also states that the Rishi was being subjected to reproach. It is a priest of a rival religion who has declared the rituals and practices of the earlier priest to be incorrect and fit to be rejected.

There are some Richas from Rishi Vashisht Maitravaruni which show that he was also in difficulty. He appears to be the same person who has been mentioned in the *Avesta* as Vedvoist. There, he was in a position of command. In these Richas from the *Rig Ved*, he seems to be at the receiving end.

1. The ends of the earth are beheld laid waste: the clamour has
    ascended, Indra and Varun to heaven: the adversaries of my people
    approach me: having heard my invocation come for my defence.

    (*Rig Ved.* M- 7, S- 83, R- 3)

2. Indra and Varun, the murderous (weapons) of my enemies distress
    me: foes from the Malignant (assail me): you two are sovereigns
    over both (celestial and terrestrial) wealth: protect us therefore on
    the day of battle.

    (*Rig Ved.* M-7, S-83, R-5)

3. Desirous of beholding you, Varun, I inquire what my offence is. I
    have gone to make inquiry of the wise, the sages verily have said
    the same thing to me—Varun is displeased with you.

4. What has the great wickedness been, Varun, that you should seek
    to destroy the worshipper, your friend? Insuperable, resplendent
    Varun, declare it to me, so that freed from sin, I may quick
    approach you with veneration.

5. Relax (the bonds) imposed by the ill deeds of our forefathers and
    those incurred (by the sins) which we have committed in our
    persons. Liberate, royal Varun, like a calf from its tether, Vashist,
    like a thief nourishing the animals (he has stolen).

    (*Rig Ved.* M-7, S-86, R-3 to 5)

After these initial Richas from Rishi Vashist there are some more
which show that he has been removed from his position and his religion
has been declared a deceit. He has been called a liar. What the Rishi
had to say in such a situation comes out from these Richas.

1. Indra and Som, fall upon the destructive (Rakshas) and the
    performers of unprofitable acts, so that, consumed (by your wrath)
    he may perish like the offering cast into the fire. Retain implacable
    hatred to the hater of the Brahmans, the cannibal, the hideous,
    the vile.

2. Indra and Som, disperse from heaven your fatal (weapon), the
    extirpator from the earth of the malignant. Put forth from the

clouds the consuming (thunderbolt) wherewith you slay the increasing Rakshas race.

3. Come with rapid steeds slay the oppressive, mischievous Rakshasas. Let there be no happiness, Indra and Som to the malignant, who harasses us with his oppression.

4. May he who with false calumnies maligns me, behaving with a pure heart; may such a speaker of falsehood, Indra, cease to be like water held in the hand.

5. If I am one following false gods, if I approach the gods in vain, then Agni (punish me). If (we be not such then) why, Jatved, are you angry with us? Let the utterers of falsehood incur your chastisements.

6. May I this day die if I am a spirit of ill, or if I have ever injured the life of any man. May you be deprived of your ten sons, who have falsely called me by such an appellation.

7. May Indra slay with his mighty weapon him who calls me a Yatudhan, which I am not. The Rakshas, who say (of himself) I am pure, may he the vilest of all beings, perish.

8. Stay Maruts, amongst the people, desirous (of protecting them) seize the Rakshas, grind them to pieces, whether they fly about like birds by night or whether they have offered obstruction to the sacred sacrifice.

9. They advance, accompanied by dogs, desirous to destroy him; they assail the indomitable Indra; Shakra whets his thunderbolt for the miscreants, quickly let him hurl the bolt upon the fiends.

10. Slay Indra, the Yatudhan, whether in the form of a man or of a woman doing mischief by her deceptions, may those who sport in murder perish dissipated, let them not behold the rising sun.

(All from *Rig Ved*. M-7, S-104)

These Richas throw light on who the adversaries were, that are being cursed with so much of anguish. The first Richa calls them the performers of unprofitable acts meaning that their mode of sacrifice is not correct. It also states that they are the hater of Brahmans. The second Richa says that the Rakshas race is increasing, a statement to the effect that more and more Manavs were getting converted. The third Richa calls the Rakshasas oppressive, who are harassing them with their oppressions. In the fourth Richa Rishi Vashisht says that false calumnies have been brought against him. The fifth Richa is significant as it states that Rishi Vashist has been accused of worshipping false gods and his religious practices have been declared to be in vain. Indra was the most important of the gods amongst the Manavs. The Asurs had all along refused to acknowledge him as a divinity. This is an accusation from the Asurs. In the next two Richas, Rishi Vashist has been accused of being an evil spirit and a Yatudhan, a term appearing in the scriptures of both sides for an unknown evil creature. The eighth Richa reflects that the sacrifices being performed by the Manavs had been obstructed. The ninth Richa says that they assail the indomitable Indra. The adversaries being cursed are none other than those who do not accept Indra as a god. Though Jaruth has not been named, it is evident that it is Zoroaster and his people who are being referred to, as the adversary. They establish that the scenario has changed completely. From a position of dominance, overnight the Manavs have been reduced to a position wherein they are being oppressed and prevented from conducting the sacrifices as per their practices. The tenth Richa shows that some of them were also killed.

Apart from Rishi Bhardwaj and Rishi Vashist, the *Veds* show Prayaswan Atrigan, who would have been from the Aitarey Gurukul of the time, also complaining of the same fate. They too are praying for the destruction of the adversary in these Richas.

1. Who have disunited my people from the cattle? Was there not for them an invincible protector? May they who have seized upon that (people) perish, for he who knows (our wishes) approaches to (protect) the cattle.

2. Enemies have secreted among mortals, the king of living beings, the asylum of men: may the prayers of Atri set him free; may those who revile be reviled.

3. You have liberated Shunahshepa from a thousand stakes, for he was patient in endurance: so Agni free us from our bonds, having

sat down here (at our sacrifice), intelligent offerer of oblations.

(*Rig Ved.* M-5, S-2, R-5 to 7)

4.   May those prosperous men who do not offer oblations to you
     become destitute of great strength, and may (the followers) of the
     other observances incur (your) enmity and punishment.

(*Rig Ved.* M-5, S-20, R-2)

Three gurukuls of the time have reported the same thing. The adversary,
who follows different observances is prosperous and is oppressing
them. The *Veds* thus confirm what has been stated in the *Avesta*, that
Zoroaster took the wheel from the hands of the Devs. There can be
no doubt about the version of the *Avesta* on how the events unfolded.
The *Veds*, in their style of mentioning adverse things only obliquely,
accept the entire version by these limited references.

What happened after Vistasp was converted and adopted a policy
for the promotion of the religion propounded by Zoroaster and
suppression of the religion of the Dev worshippers, has been described
very elaborately by Firdausi. Apparently he had access to some earlier
recorded history because of which his account matches very accurately
with that of the *Avesta* till he reaches Asfandyar's deeds, when again
his imagination has run riot. He has stated that the Devs sought the
intervention of Turan to stop what was happening in Iran. Arjasp, the
king of Turan, sent a letter to Vistasp to stop his evil ways or face war.
Iran's response was on expected lines, whereafter a fierce war was fought
in which two of Vistasp's sons were killed. His third son, Asfandyar,
finally defeated the Turanian army, after which Arjasp retreated. War
being over, Vistasp and his son took up the task of enforcing the religion
vigorously. The *Avesta* confirms that the Devs sought the intervention
of Turan. The passage which shows this is stated here.

(That rival monarch) for whom some are plotting to secure the
sovereignty, and who, once in power, would deliver over our
home to ruin, is active in his efforts and offering the devotions
of his false religion to accomplish his ends. His lord-kinsman
will pray and his (fellow) Daeva worshippers. O Ahur! May
we be, may we hold back those who hate and who offend You.

(Yasna XXXII)

Firdausi has given an account of the letter written by Arjasp to Vistasp
on this occasion. The contents of the letter give a fair picture of what
had happened. The same is here.

> 'This letter as a king I do indite,
> As it towards a king both fit and right,
> To hero Gushtasp of the land the king.
> Of kings Lehrasp the elder, chosen son,
> This from Arjasp, who China's heroes led.'
> In Turki letters with the royal pen,
> He wrote a letter full of praise then,
> And said, 'Of the world's king O famous son.
> I hear thou goest on destruction's way.
> An old deceitful man has come thee near,
> And thy heart sowed evil seeds as well.
> Him and his faith both dost thou now accept,
> His way and laws hast with due favour kept.
> The customs of thy kings didst thou forswear,
> Of earth the great one who before thee were.
> Ere thou from thy old faith didst loose thy hold,
> Before, behind, why didst thou not behold?
>
> Thou through an old magician now hast strayed.
> Now when the news of this came to my ear,
> In bright day did the stars to me appear.
> A friendly letter to thee now I send.
> When this thou readest, wash thy head and feet
> Off from thy loins do thou these bands undo.
> Cast not the rites of thine own kings away,
> Earth's noble ones that were before thy day.
> If thou accept this counsel wise from me,
> The Turkomans shall do no harm to thee.
> I give thee all the treasure without bound.
> But this my counsel shouldst thou not accept,

In iron fetters shall thy feet be kept.
After this letter in a month or two,
Thy country will I ravish through and through.'

This letter from Arjasp shows that he had received information of
Vistasp forsaking the religion of his forefathers under the influence
of someone who has been called evil and a magician. He has sent an
appeal to return to the old ways and enjoy his friendship. There is also
a threat that if the same is not done, he would attack Iran and destroy
it. The Dinkard mentions that an envoy had been sent by Arjasp on this
occasion with a message, as has been stated by Firdausi. Iran's response
was to accept the challenge and go for war. There are several stray
references in the *Avesta* which speak of this war and the crucial victory
of Vistasp. Firdausi in his account has projected Asfandyar, the son of
Vistasp, who has become Gushtasp with him, as the hero from Iran's
side. The *Avesta* does not mention him and gives the entire credit of the
victory to Vistasp. This was a very crucial war and has been called the
War of Religions in the Zoroastrian scriptures. Its result changed the
course of the history of Iran for several centuries and that of India for
ever. It was fiercely fought and Arjasp was defeated, though not killed.
The passages about it from the Zoroastrian scriptures are given here.

1. Unto her did the tall Kavi Vistasp offer up a sacrifice behind Lake
    Frazdanava. He begged of her a boon saying, 'Grant me this, O
    Ardvi Sura Anahita! that I may overcome Tathravant of the bad
    law and Peshana the worshipper of the Daevas and the wicked
    Arejat asp in the battles of this world.'

    (Aban Yast XXV)

2. Unto her did Zairi-vairi, offer up a sacrifice behind the Daitya
    river. He begged her of a boon saying, 'Grant me this, O Ardvi
    Sura Anahita, that I may overcome Pesho Kangha the corpse
    burier, Humayaka the worshipper of the Daevas and the wicked
    Arejat asp in the battles of this world.'

    (Aban Yast XXVI)

3. Unto her did Arejat asp and Vandaremani offer up a sacrifice by
    the Sea Vouru Kasha. They begged her of a boon saying, 'Grant

us this, O Ardvi Sura Anahita! That we may conquer the valiant
Kavi Vistasp and Zairivairi, that we may smite the Aryan people.'
Ardvi Sura Anahita did not grant them that favour though they
were entreating that she would grant them that favour.

(Aban Yast XXVII)

4. To her did the tall Kavi Vistasp offer up a sacrifice behind the
    waters of the Daitya river, 'Grant me this boon, O Drvaspa! That I
    may put to flight Asta-aurvant, the son of Vispa-thauro-asti, that
    I may put to flight the Hvyaona murderer, Arejat asp, that I may
    put to flight Darsinika, the worshipper of the Daevas; that I may
    smite Tathravant of the bad law, that I may smite Spinguaruska,
    the worshipper of the Daevas, and that I may bring unto the good
    law the nations of the Varedhakas and of the Hvyaonas; and that
    I may smite of the Hvyaona nations.'

(Gos Yast VII)

5. From the same Padashkhvargar mountain unto Mount Kumis,
    which they call Mount Madofryad (come to help)—that in which
    Vistasp routed Arjasp is Mount Miyan-i-dast (mid-plain), and was
    broken off from the mountain there. They say, in the war of the
    religion, when there was confusion among the Iranians, it broke off
    from the mountain and slid down into the middle of the plain. The
    Iranians were saved by it and it was called 'Come to help' by them.

(Bundahis. Chapter XII)

These passages give an account of the war. Arjasp of Firdausi is Arejat
asp in the *Avesta* language. Though defeated with several warriors
killed, he has fled. The fourth passage states that I may put to flight
the Hvyaona murderer Arejat asp. The fifth passage gives the place of
the war. It is called Mount Madofryad or the 'Mount Come-to-help'.
It says that in the war between Vistasp and Arjasp, it slid off from
the mountain down into the middle of the plain because of which the
Iranians were saved. Apparently, the war was closely fought and a
natural disaster, like a landslide, took place which gave an advantage
to the Iranians leading to their victory, though the account is very brief
to give a clear picture of the events. The mountain, however, would be

known in Iran, if not by the same name.

The war between Iran and Turan on this issue and the defeat of Arejat asp is confirmed by the *Veds* by a single Richa of the *Atharv Ved*, which is stated here.

> O horses of Ajashrava! You are employed for all appropriateness.
> Your glory is more increased when you hold Lord Indra who
> is worth saluting very first.
>
> (Kand 20, Sukt-128, Richa-16)

Arejat asp of the *Avesta* is Ajashrava of the *Veds*. This was a defeat for the Vedic people, a very significant defeat. In their usual style adverse matters are ignored, but the effort of Ajashrava was very great and had to be acknowledged. They have done so by blessing his horses and saying that they had been employed for the right cause. The second half of the Richa shows that the effort had not been successful as on this occasion the horses were not carrying Lord Indra, who, being the god of war, symbolizes victory. They simply state that the glory of the horses would have been more had they been victorious. It is a sad lament for the defeat. Though a very oblique reference, this single Richa provides what is needed as a testimony for the full story as has emerged from the *Avesta* and the *Shahnama*.

This Richa, like several others quoted before, is from the twentieth Kand, which is the last Kand of the *Atharv Ved*. Sayan has considered this Kand to be spurious and has refrained from commenting on it. Most commentators have agreed with him. This Kand is not spurious but is only superfluous to the *Atharv Ved*. Something different seems to have happened. The entire text that forms the four *Veds* was a single common text for a very long time. At that stage it must have been in order of the time of composition, because people must have first memorized whatever was already there and thereafter added the newly composed hymns, which would have come at the end. At some stage someone took up the task of arranging the text into four different books. This must have been a stupendous exercise, not only because of the bulk of the text, but also because it was in an oral tradition. The text had to be brought out from memory, classified to its place in the new arrangement and memorized again according to the new order. In Indian traditions, this was done by Rishi Krishna Dwaipayan Vyas, also called Ved Vyas. The word Vyas means compiler or arranger, which confirms this. It seems that he could not complete the work. The reason cannot be known, but possibly he died midway and the work remained incomplete as his successors were perhaps not confident enough to proceed with it. As a result, whatever was the text that remained they put at the end. This is visible in the *Rig Ved* also.

The pattern in which the *Veds* have been arranged shows that Rishi Vyas first separated the text dealing with prayers and hymns addressed to various divinities from that concerning medicines and charms, etc. Essentially, matters relating to God were separated from those relating to human life. The text that dealt with medicine and charms etc. was put in the *Atharv Ved*. Though some exceptions are there, which could be because of error, this is the general pattern of the *Atharv Ved*. The text relating to prayers and hymns addressed to various divinities were further divided into three parts on the basis of the style of composition. Accordingly, what was verse was put in the *Rig Ved*, lyrics in the *Saam Ved* and that which was close to being called prose in the *Yajur Ved*. The pattern in which the *Rig Ved* is arranged, shows that the first Mandal consists of hymns that Rishi Vyas thought were of very old origin. The next six Mandals are each devoted to hymns composed by an individual Rishi Kul. The eighth Mandal has hymns composed by several Rishis the numbers of each of which are not large enough to justify a separate Mandal. The ninth Mandal is devoted to hymns addressed to Som. In this pattern, it can be seen that the first Mandal and the ninth Mandal have been compiled on considerations different from the rest. The first is based on antiquity, while the ninth is for an exclusive divinity. Anybody arranging the Mandals in such an order would have placed the two Mandals based on a different consideration, either in the beginning, or at the end or one in the beginning and one at the end. It seems that Rishi Vyas had decided to place one at the beginning and one at the end. The ninth Mandal, in his scheme of arrangements, would have been the last Mandal, even if it had to be shifted to accommodate a Mandal or more before it. It seems that, in arranging the *Veds* into separate books, he adopted the logical method of first trying to reduce the size of the bulk of the text. Accordingly, he first separated and compiled, the *Saam Ved*, the *Yajur Ved* and the *Atharv Ved*. He was left with the text to arrange the *Rig Ved*, which is the biggest of the *Veds*, into Mandals. When he died leaving the work incomplete, he had before him the text of the *Rig Ved*, which he would have placed in the Mandals before the ninth Mandal. In case of requirement, he would have created another Mandal or two before the ninth Mandal and would have accordingly shifted the Mandal dealing with hymns addressed to Som to whatever position would have been as the last. As the work stopped and the people after him could not take it to its logical conclusion, they decided to put all the remaining text at the end. Whatever they thought could come in a Mandal, they put at the end of the *Rig Ved* as its tenth Mandal and what was still left, was decided to be put at the end of the *Veds*. As the *Atharv Ved* is the last Ved, that is where they have put it, making it the twentieth Kand of the *Atharv Ved*. Sayan has arrived at his conclusions by viewing the *Atharv Ved* in isolation. From that point of view, he is correct. The twentieth Kand does not match with the rest of this Ved, which appears to have ended with the nineteenth. But this is genuine Vedic text. The way it has been placed also speaks of its authenticity, as only a person doing so in complete innocence could have placed it at the end of the *Atharv Ved*, where even a casual observer can notice that it does not match with the rest of the work. If someone had created this as a spurious text and had tried to bring it into the *Veds*, he would have incorporated it at a place where it would have been difficult to find, may be, somewhere in the *Rig Ved*, with which it matches in style and content. It would be a great mistake to consider this Kand to be spurious. It is a part of the text that was before Rishi Vyas for being arranged into the *Rig Ved*, when he died leaving the work incomplete. At this stage when the *Veds* were being arranged into separate books, it also appears that some Richas were lost, because of which there are some Saams in the *Saam Ved*, which do not have corresponding Richas, in the *Rig Ved* or in the *Atharv Ved*.

10
Exodus from Iran

THE SITUATION IN IRAN IN general and the Persian capital in
particular would have become very difficult for the Manavs
with Vistasp getting converted to Zoroastrianism and the Manavs
unsuccessfully seeking Turan's intervention. After Arjasp launched
an attack on Iran and was defeated, Vistasp adopted a state policy
to promote Zoroastrianism. This evidently would have been possible
only with the suppression of the religion of the Dev worshippers. The
religion of the Manavs was hence declared to be false. Their gods, too,
were declared to be false and their religious leaders were declared to
be liars. For the leaders there would have been an additional danger
as they could have been suspected of being responsible for causing
Turan to attack Iran. They were also the people who would have been
held responsible for giving wrong advice to the king for which he had
ordered the imprisonment of Zoroaster earlier. In the backdrop of
this danger and the difficulties in pursuing their own religion, some
Manavs, particularly the religious leaders, fled Iran. One of the places
where they went was India. History has called them the Indo-Aryans
and has painted a totally different picture than what they actually were.
Coming to India, they have called themselves Arya and Manav became
a term meaning human being.

There cannot be an iota of doubt about the identity of the Indo-
Aryans in the backdrop of their history in Central Asia, as emerges
from the *Veds* and the *Avesta*. They belonged to an Aryan group that
has been called Magi or Mede in Central Asia, a group with which the
history of that region is very well acquainted. Apart from the common
history, the *Veds* and the *Avesta* have further evidence to show that

the Indo-Aryans were the Magis of Central Asia. The Vedic Aryans have used the term Panch Jan or Panch Janya very frequently when they wanted to say 'all of us'. Panch Jan means five people. It refers to five clans or five tribes. Some of the references where this term has been used are given here.

1. Aditi is heaven, Aditi is sky, Aditi is mother, father and son, Aditi is all the gods, Aditi is five classes of men (Panch Jan), Aditi is generation and birth.

    (*Rig Ved.* M-1, S-89, R-10)

2. Indra, object of many rites, I regard the organs of sense that exist in the five races of beings dependent on you as yours.

    (*Rig Ved.* M-3, S-37, R-9)

3. When the five kindred sacrificing races, desirous of accomplishing pious rites, honour the sustaining (Som) with their praise.

    (*Rig Ved.* M-9, S-14, R-2)

The meaning of Panch Jan was lost to the Aryans after a certain stage. They have been found making speculations on this point in the *Aitarey Brahman*, which shows that even at that stage the term had become obscure and could not be understood. The passage from the said Brahman on this is stated here.

> The Visvadev Shastra belongs to the five classes of beings. It belongs to all the five classes of beings viz. gods, men, Gandharvs and Apsaras, serpents and manes.
>
> (*Aitarey Brahman.* Book III, Chapter I)

Here Panch Jan has been defined as gods, men, the Gandarvs and Apsaras, serpents and manes. At another place it has been defined as the four castes of Brahman, Kshatriya, Vaishya and Shudra and the non-Aryans. These speculations are not correct, though Sayan has accepted the second definition. These speculations being off the mark is proved by two things. Firstly, the third Richa above calls them kindred, as well as sacrificing races. In the first explanation of the *Aitarey Brahman*, the five include serpents and manes. Serpent was the term used for the Asurs. The entire fight with them was over the

mode of sacrifice in which both sides used to consider the sacrifice of
the other to be falling short of being called so. The Asurs therefore
cannot be one of the five sacrificing races, though they were kindred.
The manes have their own status. They have not been shown to be
offering sacrifices in the *Veds*, instead oblations are offered to them.
The second definition includes non-Aryans. Again, according to the
above Richa, they can neither be kindred nor sacrificing. The second
point which proves these interpretations to be wrong is that after a
certain stage, perhaps after reaching India, these Panch Jan have been
deified. There are references in the *Veds* where blessings are being
sought from Panch Jan. Neither of the two interpretations of Panch
Jan above can stand the test of deification. The Richa that shows their
deification is stated here.

> May they, Indra, (the) Earth, Pushan, Bhag, Aditi and the five
> orders of beings (Panch Jan), give increase to our habitations;
> may they be to us granters of happiness, bestowers of food,
> guides to good, our gracious defenders and preservers.
>
> (*Rig Ved.* M-6, S-51, R-11)

It is obvious that Panch Jan means something different. It refers to
some other social identity, the meaning of which had been lost. We
get the answer to it from this passage of the *Avesta*.

> To five do I belong, to five others do I not; of the good thought
> am I, of the evil am I not; of the good word am I, of the evil am
> I not; of the good deed am I, and of the evil, not. To obedience
> am I given, and to deaf disobedience, not; to the saint do I
> belong, and to the wicked not; and so from this on till the
> ending shall be the spirits' parting. (The two shall here divide)
>
> (Yasna X)

It is evident from this Yasna, that the Magis had ten social sub-units,
which could be called clans. While five of these adopted the religion
propounded by Bhrigu and called themselves Devs, the remaining five
opposed it and were called Asurs by them. The term Panch Jan used
repeatedly in the *Veds* by the authors for themselves and their entire

social group, means these five clans of the Magis that had become Devs. It was the only way in which they could have distinguished themselves from the remaining five clans that had become Asurs, apart from the term Asur itself. All other identifications like Arya etc. would have been equally applicable to the other side also. There is a faint indication in the *Rig Ved* that the clans of the tribe were ten. The following Richa seems to say so.

> He desires not (association in) enterprise with five or ten; he associates not with the man who does not present libations; and cherishes not (his dependents), the terrifier (of foes) punishes him or slays him, but places the devout man in a pasturage stocked with cattle.
>
> (*Rig Ved.* M-5, S-34, R-5)

This has a reference of five, as well as ten. Evidently, this is because the split of five clans each seems to have been based only on broad parameters, as the divide was not so clean. People from the same family have been found to have gone separate ways with the father blinding his son for having adopted the rival religion. Manu and Yam were from the same ancestor, Vivasvat, which would have made them from the same clan. The two sides, in defining the five clans of their own, seem to have gone by the broad majority of people from one social unit going to either side and counted that clan to be with one or the other.

The next evidence on the Indo-Aryans being Magis comes from the priestly class of the Zoroastrians. On the Vedic side Aitarey was a very important school. Some of the Brahman literary works are ascribed to them, which contain some of the earliest speculations about the meaning and the manner in which various rituals connected with the sacrifice were to be conducted. They claim their origin from Atri, who was one of the seven Angiras Rishis and has found mention earlier, as one of the persons who had survived torture at the hands of Val in Arjika, when the new religious practices had been introduced. He had been kept bound in a pit close to fire for several days. Even today in India some of the Brahmans use this name. The *Avesta*, too, speaks of people with the same name. One such passage is here.

And to us Mazdayasnians who are likewise offering sacrifice,
do ye grant to us, Aethrapaitis and Aethryas, for the
overwhelming of malice in the raids of the invader, and in
the face of foes who hate.

(Yasna LXVIII)

The other case is of Manuskihar, who finds mentions in the Dinkard.
Most of the prominent priests of the Zoroastrian religion claimed their
descent from him. Even Zoroaster has been stated to be his descendant.
Some of the passages relating to him are here.

1. Here is an enumeration of the worthy lineage of Zaratust:
    Zaratust was the son of Porushaspo, son of Padiragtaraspo,
    of Urugadhasp, of Haekadaspo, of Kikhshnus, of Paetrasp, of
    Aregadharsn, of Hardhar of Spitama, of Vaedist, of Nayazem, of
    Airik, of Durasrobo, of Manuskihar, monarch of Iran, of Mansus-
    khurnar, of Manus-khurnak, whom Neroksang implanted in
    Vizak, daughter of Airyak, son of Thritak, of Bitak, of Frazusak,
    of Zusak, of Fraguzak, of Guzak, daughter of Airik, son of Fridun,
    monarch of Khvaniras, son of Purtora, the Aspigan, of Nevak tora,
    the Aspigan of Kardar the Aspigan, of Gefar tora the Aspigan, of
    Ramak tora the Aspigan, of Vano fravism the Aspigan, of Yim
    monarch of the seven regions, son of Vivangha, of Ayanghad, of
    Ananghad, son of Hoshang, the Peshdadian monarch, of the seven
    regions, son of Fravak of Siyamak, of Masya, of Gayomard, the
    first man.

    (Dinkard. Book VII, Chapter II)

2. The Avarethrabau, too, is an organizer whose righteous guardian
    spirit we reverence, and in the memory of Manuskihar, the well-
    destined, and a progenitor of Aturpad, it says that 'only from
    him comes Avarethrabau,' and then also arises this one of the
    adversaries of the religion, the apostate of apostate, whom they
    have even called the Mazdag-like.

    (Dinkard. Book VII, Chapter VII)

There are several difficulties with the personality of Manuskihar. In the first passage, wherein the lineage of Zoroaster is traced, he has been stated to be the monarch of Iran and a forefather of Zoroaster. The monarchs of Iran were Persians, while Zoroaster was a Magi. Both were different Aryan tribes. Then before him Fredun is mentioned, the monarch of Khvaniras. The word Khvaniras is in the Pahlavi language, what was Karshvares in the *Avesta* language. Fredun is in the Pahlavi language what Thraetaona was in the *Avesta* and Shambar in the *Veds*. He was the Kavi who had beheaded Dadhich or Dahak and so has to be the immediate successor of Yam, who had been converted by Dadhich to the religion of the Devs. The list has several names between Fredun and Yim. The second passage declares Manuskihar to be the progenitor of Aturpad, a very important religious personality of the Zoroastrians in the Middle Ages. In addition, the *Dadistan-i-Dinik* of the ninth century is ascribed to a Dastur of Faras and Kirman, who had the name Manuskihar. The biggest difficulty with Manuskihar, who has been stated as the king of Iran and a forefather of Zoroaster as well as Aturpad and after whom the author of the *Dadistan-i Dinik* has his name, is that, apart from the Dinkard, he does not find mention anywhere. In the *Avesta* there is a one-line mention of Manuskithra. This line is given here.

> We worship the Fravashi of the holy Manuskithra, the son
> of Airyu.
>
> (Farvardin Yast XXIX)

Here he has not been mentioned as a king, while several others after him have the word before their name. Apart from this single mention in the Farvardin Yast where the Fravashis of a very large number of people are being worshipped, it is only the Dinkard which not only mentions him but also gives him prominence. It appears that he is the same as Manu of the *Veds*. Evidently, the priests who traced their descent from him belonged to families that were Dev worshippers for a very long time. They called themselves Manavs or the descendents of Manu. At a stage, they were converted to their new religion, but continued to remember Manu as their progenitor. With them the image of Manu was of a king and when they brought Manu into the

Zoroastrian myths, the lineage of Zoroaster was drawn, bringing him into it. A very long time had passed by then and it was forgotten that Manu was already there, two times over, deified as Indra by one side and vilified as Angra Mainyu or Ahriman by the other. It is with this group that the Vedic idea of the Ribhus not being one but three and having something to do with agriculture also appears to have come into the books of the Zoroastrians because it is only in the Dinkard that Vaegered has been mentioned as the brother of Hoshang and that he provided to the world the law of husbandry or cultivation. In the entire *Avesta* Haoshyangha, the Paradhata, is mentioned alone as is Hoshang in all other Pahlavi works. It is evident that the entry of Vaegered as the brother of Hoshang and his association with agriculture is the work of people who had the legend of the Ribhus with them. These were the same people who claimed their descent from Manuskihar.

The view that the priestly class amongst the Zoroastrians belonged to families which were the descendants of Manu, matches with what emerges from the political history of Iran of the time. Once Vistasp and his successors adopted a state policy for the promotion of Zoroastrianism and the suppression of the Dev worshippers, their main target would have been the priests of the other religion. The common people follow the priests and religious leaders and if priests and religious leaders of the religion have either been converted or driven away, the masses have no option but to follow those left. Apparently, the priestly class of the Manavs became the priestly class of the Zoroastrians and as Manu was a much venerated forefather for them, they carried him along.

Interestingly, the going away of some of the Manavs from Iran to India was known to the Zoroastrians. This emerges from this passage.

By the united power of knowledge of the religion and by the writings explaining of the religion, I am saved from the many doubts and follies of sects, especially from those of the deceivers and empty-skulled Manicheans, whose religion is deceitfulness and whose teaching is folly and intricate secret proceedings. Zaratust came alone on a true mission to the

lofty portal of Kai Gustasp and the religion was taught by
him with a powerful tongue to Kai Gustasp and the learned
through the speech of wisdom and through presentation of
the visible testimony of the archangels, together with many
miracles. And Kai-Spenda and Zargar and other royal sons
instigating the many conflicts and shedding the blood of
those of the realm, accepted the religion as a yoke, while they
even wandered to Arum and the Hindus, outside the realm,
in propagating the religion.

(Sikand-Gumanik Vigar. Chapter X)

This is a reference to what happened at the time of Zoroaster, as it
mentions his coming to the court of Vistasp and the acceptance of the
religion by the king and further bloodshed thereafter. However, the
Manavs have been called Manicheans. Though the reference is about
the Indo-Aryans leaving Iran and coming to India, it is necessary
to know about Mani, Manichaeism and what the Zoroastrians in
general and the authors of the *Sikand-Gumanik Vigar* in particular
thought Manicheans were, to remove every possible doubt that may
occur because of the use of this term for the Manavs, because the
Zoroastrian scriptures have given a very important information here.
They have stated, that 'they wandered to Arum and the Hindus outside
the realm in propagating the religion'. Arum has been used for Greece
in the Pahlavi works. The passage is saying that the Manicheans who
fled when Zoroaster introduced the religion to Vistasp, went in two
directions, one group went to India and the other went to Greece.
This is an extremely significant piece of information, which would
help in understanding many things found common in ancient Indian
and Greek thought, worth leaving our story as it emerges from the
Veds and the *Avesta*, for a while and going to Mani and Manichaeism.

Mani was born in AD 216 in Babylon. His father Patik, was an
Arsacid prince who lived in Hamadan, the capital of Media and later
moved to Seleucia-Ctesiphon, the capital of the Parthian Empire. A
recently discovered Greek papyrus shows that Mani belonged to a
little known Gnostic sect called Elkesaites. Information about him

comes also from the Firhist and Turfan texts. It appears that at the age of twelve he received a revelation from a celestial being, who he has called his 'Twin' or his higher ego. When twenty-four, he is reported to have been visited anew by this heavenly being, though in between he received a series of visions and auditions through which were communicated to him the doctrines that he was ordered to preach. In a fragment of his autobiography it is stated that he set out to preach at the close of King Ardashir's reign and went to India. In Shapur's reign, he took up missionary activity in the provinces of Asuristan, Mah and Parthav. King Shapur was favourably disposed to him and granted that his doctrine, which had met resistance from the Iranian authorities, should be freely preached in his empire. In his personal preaching activities Mani confined himself to the Sasanian Empire and did not go beyond. Iran did not have a state religion then as Zoroastrianism had not regained its status, though the process had begun with Karter, an important priest, leading it. Perhaps, both Mani and Karter cherished the ambition of having their religion as the state religion of the empire.

After some time Mani decided to propagate his doctrines outside the Sasanian empire as a world religion. To the west he sent Addai and to the east Mar Ammo. Their success is testified by the hate-filled reporting by contemporary Christians. Within the empire, Mani gained strong support in the northwestern Iran which was a centre of Mithra worship. He is reported to have closely associated himself with Mithraism. He was also an accomplished painter and is reported to have created several pieces of art during this period, though surprisingly he has not used any Zoroastrian motifs but instead has painted Hindu deities, particularly Ganesh.

Tolerance from the king ended for Mani with the accession of Bahram I. In AD 276, he ordered Mani to be arrested and kept in fetters, though allowing him to meet his disciples. Mani survived for less than a month and died in prison that year at the age of sixty.

Mani's doctrines were in a collection of his own writings, though only fragments of them survive. However, with information from secondary sources his system can be reconstructed. One of the fundamental ideas of Manichaeism is regarding creation, wherein it believes in the existence of 'the Two Principles', God and Matter. They are uncreated and exist from eternity, being classified as 'natures', 'substances' and 'roots'. The two principles, though both uncreated and defined as diametrically opposed to one another, as Good and Evil, Truth and Lie, Light and Darkness, nevertheless do not exist at the same level. The turning point in the evolution of the universe comes when the two are intermingled. This mixed state must return to its own unmixed existence, when God and Matter would be separated to mingle and to separate again and again. With each mingling the universe is created and with each separation it ends. This idea is central to both, Manichaeism and Zurvanism. While Mani takes Zurvanism as the basis of his system, he appears as its reformer. Zurvanism had its centre in Media where Mani had his most faithful supporters. In Mani's system the substance of the highest God is light. God is rather a principle than a person, a concept fully in conformity with the Zurvan idea of the highest deity, which is more abstract than concrete.

The Manichean eschatology next has the concept of salvation, which is a Zurvanite, but not a Zoroastrian notion. Man has to seek salvation from this world, which has been painted in a negative and pessimistic manner, making it a desired goal for the particles of light to get away from it. For it divine Wisdom has to be obtained. This Wisdom was to be received by 'the eye of the soul', which is opened in order to behold the light of the heavenly glory. Mani was of the opinion that his Wisdom is both the sum and the perfection of all previous religious wisdoms. He accepts his predecessors but sees his superiority to them in the fact that he himself wrote his Wisdom in books. As his predecessors, Mani acknowledged the Buddha in India, Zoroaster in Persia and Jesus in the West, while he proclaimed himself the Apostle of the God of Truth. Of his predecessors, Mani, at least in his later days, considered himself closely connected with Jesus. In his correspondences, Mani introduces himself as 'Mani, Apostle of Jesus Christ'. In Middle Persian texts Mani calls himself, 'the Apostle of Jesus Aryaman'. Here Jesus is identified with Aryaman who is a Zurvanite figure and a representative of Nous, the Great Mind.

Mani's congregation was organized in a twofold way, the Elect and the Hearers, or the righteous and the hearers according to Middle Iranian terminology. Two distinct ways of life were followed by these groups of believers and the demands made upon them were different. While the Elect had to devote themselves to the redemption of their souls, the Hearers had to undertake all acts forbidden to the Elects, but necessary for the maintenance of life. Thus, the Hearers had to furnish the Elect with their essential necessities. They led a normal life but observed Sunday as a special day of fasting. An entire month of fasting was observed prior to the great Bema festival also which marked the death anniversary of Mani.

The spread of Manichaeism is reported by the Cambridge History of Iran. It states that in the West, it had reached Syria, Palestine and Egypt in Mani's lifetime. In AD 300 Alexander of Lykopolis, a philosopher of Egypt had composed a treatise against Manichaeism showing their substantial presence there. From Egypt it spread to northern Africa and Spain while from Syria it went to Asia Minor, Greece, Illyria, Italy and Gaul. In the Roman empire it met with violent persecution. Emperor Diocletian issued his famous edict in AD 297 ordering their books to be burnt and followers punished with loss of life and property. Several emperors after him renewed this edict for the next two hundred years making the penalties all the more severe. Once the Christian Church received the patronage of the Roman state it went after the Manicheans with both weapons, spiritual and secular. It is not known how long Manichaeism survived in the west but by AD 1000 it had certainly become extinct there.

In the East, Manichaeism had reached and crossed the present Amu Dariya, in Mani's times and had Sogdiana as a base for its missionary activities. It had reached China where the Chinese emperor issued an edict against it in AD 732. Its greatest success was amongst the Turkish Uyghur tribe which lived in the Xinjiang province of western China. Uyghur rulers declared it to be the state religion. Here and elsewhere in the east, Manichaeism leaned heavily on Buddhism, though the Buddhists vigorously opposed it, specially Mani's claim that he was an incarnation of Buddha. In AD 840 the Uyghurs lost power to the Kirghiz and only two Uyghur pockets remained in Kansu and Turfan which provided a home to Manichaeism till the thirteenth century when the Mongols overran them. Much of the Manichean literature that has survived is from these two places.

In Iran and its adjoining region to the west, Manichaeism soon faced the emergence of Islam. They were in a better position under the Umayyad Caliphate which was tolerant to them. As the Abbasid Caliphate tried to revive the Sasanian spirit, its establishment unfortunately meant a revival of persecution for the Manicheans. They, however, seem to have survived till AD 1000 as Ibn al-Nadin has reported in his book that he personally knew a few hundred of them in Bagdad.

This account of Manichaeism, as taken from the *Cambridge History of Iran*, shows a distinct error in what has been understood to be Manichaeism. According to this, Mani died in AD 276. It has been stated that in Mani's lifetime Manichaeism had reached Syria, Palestine and Egypt and later from Syria went to Asia Minor and from there to Greece, Illyria, Italy and Gaul. Yet we find that the Roman Emperor Diocletian promulgated his edict against it in AD 297. In just decades it could not have spread to an extent to become such a serious threat. Still more it remained strong enough to require the Romans to renew the edicts for the next two hundred years. In the East also, the success of the religion has been shown to be remarkable during the lifetime of Mani and soon thereafter. Evidently, something is wrong in understanding what got termed as Manichaeism because no founder of a religion has been able to spread his religion in such a vast area within his lifetime and no religion, even with state support, has been able to spread so rapidly, while Mani had no support of the state. He had only been tolerated by Shapur I and had been allowed to preach. There has to be an earlier well-established religion to which Mani belonged and to which he gave a new face with reforms and books, which thereafter got named after him, just like the old religion of the Asurs got named after Zoroaster. As a result, the said religion carried his name and after a certain period was called so, even when being referred to a time before Mani and in areas where Mani may or may not have had any influence. Emperor Diocletian in AD 297 would have been targeting people who may not have had any influence of Mani, but they have been called Manicheans. This religion could have been none other than what has been called the Vedic religion in India. It can be said without hesitation, that people who have been termed as Zurvanites, followers of the Mithra cult and Manicheans were all followers of the same religion. Historians cannot be blamed for making an error on this point because it has always been felt that Zoroastrianism was the only surviving Aryan religion in Central Asia. It has always been believed that the other version, that had the older Indo-Iranian beliefs, had gone to India. This is not true as only a small complement of people who were being persecuted in Iran had fled to India, but the religion was spread over a much wider area, as it had undertaken missionary activities from very remote times.

Manichaeism was the name acquired by the religion of the Dev worshippers is established by three things; one, the doctrines propounded by Mani; two, the identity of the Arsacids, the people from whom Mani had descended; and three, the areas where his supporters were in dominance. So far as his doctrines are concerned, he has given his views on the creation of the universe, wherein he believed in the existence of 'the Two Principles', God and Matter. They are uncreated and exist from eternity. Though the term God has been used, it has been clarified that God is rather a principle than a person. The evolution of the universe comes about when the two principles are intermingled. This mixed state returns to its own unmixed existence when the universe ends. This doctrine of Mani, which is fundamental to his system, is identical with the Sankhya doctrine of the *Veds*. It is propounded in full in the Sankhya Karika and in the *Veds* is indicated by Dyau and Prithvi, the two eternal entities, the parents of everything. In Sankhya, the two eternal principles are Purush and Prakriti or Consciousness and Matter. The evolution of the universe comes about when the two come together and ends when the two are separated. God in the conventional sense has no place in the scheme of things and the philosophy, to a certain extent, can be termed as atheistic. The element of eternal and all-pervading consciousness, however, brings in theism in a different light, different from a God who is basically a benefactor. The concept of Purush or Consciousness has undergone a transition in Sankhya in India. The form in which the doctrine emerges in the *Veds* has only one Purush, the all-pervading consciousness. In the *Gita* also, while speaking of Sankhya, Purush has been treated as a single entity. With Sankhya Karika, however, each individual soul has been treated as a separate entity, making Purushs innumerable. This is evidently a later development of the original idea. Sankhya as seen in the *Veds* and the *Gita* has the Purush in the same form as we find with Mani.

The next doctrine of Mani is of salvation. This concept is necessarily linked to the doctrine of rebirth. It cannot be associated with any doctrine that believes in one birth, one life and thereafter a wait of the soul for the Day of Judgment, when all souls would rise and receive rewards or punishments for their deeds in heaven or hell. The theory of rebirth is the theory of Karm. It says that human life is one in which the individual is equipped with senses to reason out right and wrong. In this birth, he acquires Karm by his good and bad deeds, based on which his next births are determined. It takes him through a series of births and deaths till he is back in human form with some residual Karm, which determine what he gets as his destiny in human life. There is no heaven or hell, but for the soul it is possible to get out of this cycle of births and deaths and merge into Eternal Consciousness. This going out of the soul from the cycle of births and deaths is called Moksh or salvation, a purely Vedic concept. According to Mani, the path to salvation is wisdom, which has to be received with the eye of the soul. This, too, is a Vedic concept of Gyan Marg or the Path of Knowledge. The *Veds*, while mentioning two more paths, of Devotion and Action or Conduct, give prime importance to the Path of Knowledge. It appears that Mani, like Buddha, focused on this path only.

So far as the Arsacids are concerned, they ruled for almost five hundred years and traced their origin from a nomad confederacy known as the Dahae Confederacy. They are listed amongst the nations in the 'Daeva Inscription' of Xerxes at Persepolis as neighbours of a Scythian group, the Saka Haumavarga. The habitat of this Saka group was around the delta of Syr Darya. Amongst the various tribal groups included in the confederacy of the Dahae, the most prominent were the Parni from whom the dynasty of the Arsacids drew their origin. They are also called the Parthians. Dahae gave its name to the province on the eastern shore of the Caspian Sea, which throughout the Middle Ages retained the name Dihistan.

Arsacid rule was established in Parthia in 247 BC with the Parthians revolting against the Seleucids under the leadership of two brothers, Arsaces and Tiridates, and Arsaces becoming the king. The Seleucids tried to regain their position but because of troubles in the west, had to leave the Arsacids alone, giving them the crucial time to consolidate their position. Several capable rulers followed who extended the kingdom to include Media and Babylon, taking it to the level of a world empire by 171 BC. By 70 BC, the expanding Roman power started impinging on its frontiers. In 53 BC, the Romans led by Crassus attacked the Arsacids. This army was completely destroyed by the Parthians in the battle of Carrhae. It was a massive Roman army, but the compound bow of the Parthians was far more powerful than the lighter European bow and was able to pierce the Roman armour, because of which, what followed was a massacre and not a battle. Mark Antony tried to avenge the defeat of Crassus with an army twice as big in 39 BC but was defeated. Augustus, on becoming emperor, sought to settle the issue by negotiations because of which a treaty was signed in 20 BC, which led to peace for about fifty years. During this period the Greek philosopher Apollonius of Tyana journeyed across Babylon, who has given a vivid account of the Parthian palace life and a lavish horse-sacrifice.

Trouble between the two sides renewed again with the Romans taking advantage of conflicts of succession in the Arsacid dynasty. Armenia became a bone of contention by Nero's time who sent a large army against Vologeses, the Arsacid emperor. After several inconclusive battles, the two sides agreed to negotiate and it was agreed that Tiridates, the brother of Vologeses would be the king of Armenia for which he would receive the diadem from Nero's hands. Tiridates undertook an elaborate land journey to Rome as his priestly scruples as a Magian priest prevented him from travelling by sea, and received the diadem from the hands of Nero in AD 64. Vologeses remained the

Parthian king of the east with his capital in Babylon. Friction over Armenia arose again for which the Roman emperor Trajan led an expedition in person in AD 113, which succeeded in overrunning the Parthian territory and reach Babylon. Throughout the second century the Romans made several expeditions into the Parthian empire with varied results, but finally it was not the Romans, but the new Iranian dynasty of the Sasanians that brought an end to the Arsacid rule. Its founder, Ardshir I collected troops from the neighbouring pricipalities and after defeating the Arsacids in three battles established the Sasanian dynasty in AD 224.

In this account of the Arsacids, there are several elements that indicate that these were the people who constituted the main body of the Aryan group from which the Indo-Aryans branched off to India. The first is the information about their origin. They have been stated to be from a nomad confederacy known as the Dahae Confederacy and have been named in the list of nations in the 'Daeva Inscriptions' of Xerxes at Persepolis, which states that they were the neighbours of a Scythian group, the Saka Haumavarga, which had its habitat around the delta of Syr Darya which is close to the delta of Amu Darya the homeland of the Magis. The tribal group Dahae gave its name to the province on the eastern shore of the Caspian Sea, which throughout the Islamic Middle Ages retained it as Dihistan. The area that is being referred to was a part of the kingdom of Turan under Turvayan, as well as Ajashrava, who were both defeated at the hands of Sushravas and Vistasp, respectively. It is apparent that the word Dahae is the corrupted version of the Sanskrit word Dev. The word Dahaestan or Dihistan is what has become of the original Devsthan. This can be said not just because the words are similar, but also because there was an Asuristan, which retained its name till very late. *The Cambridge History* has stated that the Iranian rulers applied the name Asuristan to the province, which the Western historians have called Babylonia. It is evident that these places acquired their names in the times when the two sides of the Magis gained predominance in different areas. The province having Dev dominance was called Devsthan and that of the Asurs, Asuristhan. With the expansion of the Persian Empire under

Darius, Turan as an independent political entity had ceased to exist. Later, when the control of the Persians and after them, the Greeks had slackened, new independent principalities would have emerged which felt a threat from a common enemy because of their past experience and formed a confederacy, which they called the Dev Confederacy. As the history of Turan and that area is generally hazy, they have been called a nomad confederacy. There is mention of a Dahi country in the *Avesta* also. It is here.

> We worship the Fravashis of the holy men of the Dahi countries.
>
> (Fravardin Yast XXX)

The next element that emerges to support the hypothesis is that Parni has been stated to be the most prominent group in the said confederacy and that the Arsacid dynasty drew their origin from it. This name is very close to Pani, a name that occurs in the *Veds*. The Panis were the immediate neighbours of the Devs and Asurs in Arjika. They have been called cattle thieves. Evidently, they were another Aryan tribe which had been moving along with the Magis. In some passages of the *Veds* they have been confused with the Asurs and the name Pani is found interchangeable with Asur. A few such passages are here.

1. The Panis, Indra, fled with hundreds from the sage, your worshipper in battle; neither did he (Indra) suffer the deceptions of the powerful Shushna to prevail over his weapons nor did he (leave him) any of his sustenance.

   (*Rig Ved*. M-6, S-20, R-4)

2. Determined (to recover) the cattle hidden in the mountain associated with the animated by (their) veracious (praise), this (Indra) fractured the infrangible rock of Val and overwhelmed the Panis with reproaches.

   (*Rig Ved*. M-6, S-39, R-2)

These references are of a later period by when details had been lost and Panis who were only cattle thieves, were confused with the Asurs, because in the instance of Val, the Asurs had also taken away the cattle of the Devs. There is, however, a distinction in the two situations. Val was the Kavi and so during his time when the cattle of the Devs were taken away this was in compliance with the orders of the sovereign authority. It amounted to confiscation and not stealing, because of which the cattle taken away by the Asurs would have been kept in an enclosure right in front of the Devs and would not have been hidden. Over time, this distinction was lost and because in both cases cattle had been taken away, the Asurs and Panis were believed to be the same. The passage which shows that Panis were thieves and not custodians of confiscated state property is given here.

1. (The Panis) With what intention has Sarama (a bitch of the Devs) come to this place? Verily, the way was long and difficult to be traversed but the persevering. What is the motive of your coming to us? What sort of wandering was yours? How have you crossed the waters of the Rasa?

2. (Sarama) I come, the appointed messenger of Indra, desiring, Panis, your great hidden treasures. Through fear of being crossed the (water) helped me, thus I passed over the waters of the Rasa.

3. (The Panis) What is Indra like, O Sarama? What is the appearance of him as whose messenger you have come to this place from afar? (They then say to one another) Let her approach, let us make friends with her, and let her be the lord of our cattle.

4. (Sarama) I do not believe that he can be subdued, he as whose messenger I have come to this place from afar. (He) subdues (his enemies), the deep rivers do not conceal him, you, Panis, slain by Indra, will sleep (in death).

5. (The Panis) These are the cows which you, auspicious Sarama, coming to the extremities of the heaven, demand. Who will give them up to you without a combat? And our weapons are sharp.

6. (Sarama) Your words, Panis, are not in the place of armies, your sinful bodies will not be equal to arrows. Let your path be difficult to follow, let Brahaspati show no favour to either (your words or your persons).

7. (The Panis) This treasure, Sarama, secured in the mountains is

composed of cows, horses and riches. The Panis protect it, who are good watchers. You have come to this lonely spot in vain.

8. (Sarama) Excited by the Som, the Rishis, the Angiras of the nine months' sacrifice, headed by Ayasya, will come hither, they will partition this herd of cattle, then the Panis will retract their words.

9. (The Panis) You have indeed come hither, Sarama, constrained by the Devs, we will make you our sister, do not return, we will share the cattle with you, auspicious one.

10. (Sarama) I recognize not fraternity nor sisterhood, Indra and the terrible Angiras know (my kindred); my (masters) desiring the cattle overshadowed (my kindred) when I came. Depart hence, Panis, to a distant (spot).

                                        (*Rig Ved.* M-10, S-108, R-1 to 10)

This dialogue shows that the cattle which were with the Panis were not the ones that had been kept under the orders of the sovereign authority. They had been stolen and so were concealed in the mountain. The Devs sent a bitch, Sarama, to locate them. As she was able to find them, the Panis tried to bribe her, offering a share in the booty. She had her pups left behind, which the Devs had assured to look after and so she told them that her kindred were left behind. This is a normal situation of two people living side by side, with thefts and disputes taking place at regular intervals. If the Panis had written something, their literature would have contained similar allegations for their neighbours. However, as cows were involved, the difference between the stories of Val and the stories of the Panis was lost and so the later hymns give an impression that the Asurs and the Panis were the same. A few Richas are there which show that the two were different. Some are mentioned here.

1. The waters, the wives of the destroyer, guarded by Ahi, stood obstructed, like the cows by Panis, but by killing Vritra, Indra set open the cave that had confined them.

                                        (*Rig Ved.* M-1, S-32, R-11)

2. Agni and Som that prowess of yours, by which you have carried off the cows that were the food of Pani, is (well) known to us.

You have slain the offspring of Brisya and you have acquired the one luminary (the sun) for the benefit of many.

(Rig Ved. M-1, S-93, R-4)

It appears that with the Magis splitting into two mutually inimical groups, the Panis joined the Devs in their religion and very soon developed a common identity with them. They seem to have been driven out along with the Devs from Arjika by Yam and had come along to the banks of Amu Darya, which became their common homeland. After a stage, the name Tur appears to have been used for them and not Pani. Though not in the *Veds*, but in the Brahman text some Turs are credited to be the authors of parts of the Vedic literature. Some passages which show this are given here.

1. This portion was told by Tur, the son of Kavash to Janamejay, the son of Parikshit; thence to Bhim Vaidarbha and Nagnajit.

    (Aitarey Brahman. Book VII, Chapter II)

2. And Shandilya once upon a time said, 'Tur Kavasheya once built a fire altar for the gods at Karoti. The gods asked him, "Sage, seeing that they declare the building of the fire altar not to be conducive to heaven, why then hast thou built one?"'

    (Shat Path Brahman. Kand IX, Adhyay 5, Brahman 2)

3. Now the line of succession (of teachers). The same as far as Sanjiviputra. Sanjiviputra (received it) from Mandukayani, Kusri from Yagnavachas, Yagnavachas from Tur Kavesheya, Tur Kavesheya from Prajapati, Prajapati from Brahma. Brahma is the self-existent.

    (Shat Path Brahman. Kand X, Adhyay 6, Brahman 7)

These references from the Brahman literature show that the Turs were involved in the process of formulation of Vedic rituals and possibly, hymns. These Turs were the people who have been called Panis at an earlier stage and the Parnis in history. They ruled over Turan and had their share of wars with Iran, which have been mentioned earlier being the people from whom the Dev worshippers in Iran had sought assistance, when Vistasp was converted by Zoroaster, which led to war and the fleeing of the Indo-Aryans from Iran. Arejat asp, the king of Turan, has also been called Tur-i Badr Vaksh or the Tur of Badr Vaksh in Zoroastrian literature. Strabo has at one place called the Devs, who have been spelt Daae by him, Scythians and he has stated that some of them were called Aparni. The relevant passage is here.

> On the left and opposite of these people are situated the Scythians or nomadic tribes. Now the greater part of the Scythians, beginning at the Caspian Sea, are called Daae, but those who are situated more to the east than these are named Massagetae and Sacae, whereas all the rest have the general name Scythian, though each people is given a separate name of its own. And as for the Daae, some of them are called Aparni, some Xanthi, and some Pissuri.
>
> (Strabo. Geographica. Book XI. Chapter 8. Para 2)

Strabo gives further information about the Parthians which confirms their indentification with the Magis.

> And then Arsaces, a Scythian, with some of the Daae (I mean the Aparnians, nomads who lived along the Ochus), invaded Parthia and conquered it. They say that the Aparnian Daae were emigrants from the Daae above Lake Maeotis, who are called Xandi or Pari. But the view is not altogether accepted that the Daae are a part of the Scythians who live about Lake Maeotis. I shall omit discussion of that subject here, though I shall mention this alone, that the Council of the Parthians, according to Poseidonius consists of two groups, one that of kinsmen, and the other that of wise men and Magis, from both of which groups the kings were appointed.
>
> (Strabo. Geographica. Book XI. Chapter 9. Para 3)

This passage has the name Magi, apart from Dev, as spelt by him. It also states that the Magis were a part of the ruling council of the Parthians from which the kings were appointed.

The next element that emerges from the history of the Arsacids to establish that they were of the same religion that was called the

Vedic in India, is the account of the Greek philosopher Apollonius of Tyana who journeyed through Babylonia during the reign of Vardanes between AD 38-45. He has described the episodes of palace life and a lavish horse-sacrifice. The sacrifice mentioned by Apollonius is the Ashwa Medh Yagya of the *Veds*, which is a very important sacrifice, restricted to be performed only by the kings.

The last element from the history of the Arsacids on this point is the case of Tiridates, the brother of Vologeses. It has been reported that he was deterred from going to Rome by sea to receive the diadem of Armenia from the hands of Nero, because of his religious rituals as a Magian priest. Tiridates has been called a Magian priest. Zoroastrianism was a well-established religion by then and was known by that name. This has not been used with reference to Tiridates. It is obvious that it is a religion of the Magis different from Zoroastrianism that is being referred to. As the fact that the Vedic religion was the other religion of the Magis has been lost to the history of Central Asia, it has been mentioned as a Magi religion. However, this was the religion of Tiridates, the rituals of which were inhibiting him from going to Rome by sea.

Apart from the various points emerging from the history of the Arsacids to establish that they were the followers of the Vedic religion, the attitude of the ancient Iranian scholars and historians towards them also goes to prove the same point. This is what the *Cambridge History* has to say on this issue.

'Arsacid history was almost passed over altogether in the Khwaday namag. Consequently, the account of these kings is very brief in all the Islamic sources. Firdausi states that he has heard only their names, and winds up their entire history in 20 lines. This period was regarded as one of disunity and chaos when a number of petty kings ruled and the fortunes of the Iranians were at low ebb. Hamza practically declares it to be the dark age of Iranian history, when no one cared to acquire knowledge or wisdom until Ardashir arose. The "Letter of Tansar" in a spiteful indictment of the Arsacids calls their period a time when the world was full of fiends and beasts in human shape, and when nothing but corruption and ruin emerged. This disparagement is set in contrast to a glowing picture of Ardashir's well-organized and cohesive empire.'

The Arsacids were facing the Roman Empire in the West and the Kushan Empire in the east. Despite family bickerings, they gave a fairly good account of themselves, giving Rome some of her most humiliating moments. With such achievements, the Khwaday namag ignoring them and Hamza declaring it to be the dark age of Iranian history can only be because of a very strong bias. Islam came much later and the Muslim historians would have had only the information passed over by their predecessors, the Zoroastrians. Terms like fiends and beasts in human shape were compliments exchanged by Devs and Asurs for a very long time by then. 'The Letter of Tansar' seems to be echoing the same spirit.

The Arsacids were from an ethnic group with the same heritage as the Indo-Aryans emerges also from names of their kings. These are what the Greek and the Roman historians have given us. Their originals have to be different and something closer to Sanskrit. This is revealed by the fact that Arsaces, the name of the founder of the Parthian Empire, is also reported to be the name of a minor king in India in another Greek work. While recording the events in India after Alexander had decided to return, Arrian has recorded the following statement.

> At this time Arsaces, the ruler of the land bordering on that of Abisares, and the brother of the latter, with his other relations, came to Alexander.
> (Arrian. Anabasis of Alexander. Book 5. Para 29)

The third point to establish that Manichaeism was the name acquired by the Vedic religion was its predominance in areas which were evidently inhabited by people who had their origin from the Vedic stock. Three areas emerge in this regard, Media, Sogdiana and Xingjian in western China, the Uyghur country. The flow of migration of the Parthians from the Amu Darya westward was to the east coast of the Caspian Sea, which got named Devsthan or Dahaesthan and then southward to Media and Babylonia, before turning west again to Armenia. The predominance of Manichaeism in Media can be treated as an extension of its predominance in Sogdiana, as people from the same stock had migrated to it. Sogdiana is very significant as it is the region of the Amu Darya, the homeland of the Magis after they came from Arjika. Though the last port of call of the Indo-Aryans in Central Asia was the Persian capital, Iran was not their homeland. Their homeland was Sogdiana, where Mani had his strongest support base. It had to be so because that was the religion of the people from times immemorial to which Mani had given a new face and a new name.

The Uyghurs in western China present a very interesting study. According to *The Cambridge History*, the Uyghur chief was converted to Manichaeism in AD 762 and with him the said religion became the State religion of the Uyghurs till the fall of the Uyghur Empire in the ninth century. Manichaeism survived amongst the Uyghurs as its last pocket. The point of interest is the language of the people in the region. Khotan was an important centre in the south of this region. From here coins of the first century have been found bearing Chinese legends on the obverse and Indian Prakrit in the Kharosti script on the reverse. It is also known that Prakrit was the administrative language of the nearby kingdom of Shan-Shan in the third century AD as is seen from the discovery of Kharosti documents at Niya. One of these documents gives the name of the king as Vijida Simha, a Sanskrit name. Other kings from the Khotanese documents are Vis Sambhav, Vis Sur and Vis Dharm. In the Tibetan 'Prophecy of the Li Country', the list of the kings named for this kingdom are Bijay Sangram, Bijay Bikram, Bijay Dharm, Bijay Sambhav and Bijay Bohan Chenpo. Even the name Khotan in the earlier documents is found to be Gostan. Huan Tsang too has mentioned that the language he found people speaking in India was very close to the language spoken by certain people in western China. The Uyghurs spoke a language that was close to Prakrit and used it for their administrative purposes till their empire was overrun by the Mongols in the ninth century. Use of chaste Sanskrit names for the kings and of Prakrit by the people has been explained by historians as the impact of Buddhist monks. This explanation is unlikely because Buddhist monks were preaching religion and not spreading language. Apart from this, Buddhism had spread over a very large area, but such a phenomena is not to be seen anywhere else. What seems likely is that Sanskrit reached there, not from India but directly, either from the Ili delta or the Amu Darya region and followed the same course of corruption to become Prakrit as it did in India, but independently. It seems that the people of this area were from the Vedic stock and they carried the *Veds* with them, which remained at the centre of their language for the educated class, as happened in India. Because of this, the same pattern followed, with Sanskrit remaining the language of the educated class, while the language of the masses got corrupted to be something like Prakrit in India.

We had digressed to Mani and Manichaeism because the *Sikand-Gumanik Vigar*, though speaking about the departure of the Dev worshipping Aryans from Iran in the times of Vistasp, had called them Manicheans. The issue is very important because it has stated that they had not only gone to India to be called the Indo-Aryans, but also to Greece. On this point more important is what the Zoroastrians in general and the authors of *Sikand-Gumanik Vigar* in particular, thought Manicheans were. Their opinion on what Manichaeism was would be extremely significant, because they were their immediate neighbours and rivals for several thousand years and would have known them the best. In the *Sikand-Gumanik Vigar*, fortunately, an entire chapter is devoted to the repudiation of the Manichean doctrines. This gives a picture of who they were and is given below.

Again about the delusion of Mani, for I am not unrestrained as to writing more fully of the delusion of Mani and the Manicheans. Now you Mazda-worshippers for Zaratust should know that the original statement of Mani was about the unlimitedness of the original evolutions, the intermediate one about their mingling, and the final one about the distinction of light from dark. Again he states this, that the worldly existence is a bodily formation of rudiments of Aharman. He confined life and light in the body and made them prisoners. Again about the difference of nature of life and body. Again they say this that those two original evolutions are perpetually remaining and existed as contiguously as the sun and shadow and no open space and demarcation existed between them. What produced all those within them and where is it, when the two original evolutions have been in an undisturbed position? If a nature that is always unlimited can become limited, that certainly implies that it can become nothing, and that which they say about the unchangeableness of a nature is strange.

(Chapter XVI)

This passage gives the views of Mani on the creation of the universe, where he speaks of the two eternal principles, a concept identical with the Sankhya philosophy of the *Veds* which has been discussed earlier. It is evident that the *Sikand-Gumanik Vigar* means the Dev worshipping Aryans when it speaks of Manicheans, even if it is a reference to a time several centuries before Mani was born. This work was written after the middle of the ninth century AD, about six hundred years after Mani, by when Manichaeism as the name for the said religion would have been well-established and it made no difference whether the event relating to it was before or after Mani. This passage, apart from disclosing who the Zoroastrians meant by Manicheans, also gives information on two more things—one, the Sankhya philosophy had been developed before the Indo-Aryans left Iran and two, the Dev worshippers existed in Iran at least up to the ninth century AD despite everything, including the claims of Xerxes in his famous Daeva inscription of Persepolis of the fourth century BC which reads as follows.

Xerxes, the king says: By the favours of Ahur Mazda these are the countries of which I was king: Media, Elam, Arachosia, Armenia, Drangiana, Parthia, Aria, Bactria, Sogdiana, Chorasmia, Babylonia, Assyria, Sattagydia, Sardis, Egypt, Ionians, those who dwell by the sea and those who dwell across the sea, men of Maka, Arabia, Gandara, Sind, Cappadocia, Dahae, Amyrgian Scythians, Pointed-Cap Scythians, Skudra, men of Akaufaka, Libyans, Carians, Ethiopians.

Xerxes the king says: When I became king, there is

among these countries which are inscribed above (one) was in commotion. Afterwards Ahur Mazda bore me aid. By the favour of Ahur Mazda, I smote that country and put it down in its place. And among these countries there was where previously Daevas were worshipped. Afterwards, by the favour of Ahur Mazda, I destroyed that sanctuary of the Daevas, and I made proclamation, 'The Daevas shall not be worshipped.' Where previously the Daevas were worshipped, there I worshipped Ahur Mazda and Arta reverently.

The Magis, while fleeing from Persia at the time of Vistasp had gone not just to India, but also to Greece, is brought out by another passage of the Zoroastrian scriptures, which is given here.

Shahpuhar, King of kings, again brought together also the writings distinct from religion, about the investigation of medicine and astronomy, time, place and quality, evidence and other records and resources that were scattered among the Hindus and in Arum and other lands, and he ordered their collocation again with the *Avesta*, and the presentation of a correct copy of each to the treasury of Shapigan and the settlement of all the erring upon the Mazda-worshipping religion, for proper consideration was effected.

(Dinkard. Book IV)

This account is of the efforts of the Sasanian kings to reconstruct the *Avesta* as it had suffered damage at the hands of Alexander. The efforts of Shahpuhar show that for topics which were distinct from religion, like medicine and astronomy, he looked for records and resources that were scattered among the Hindus and in Arum and other lands and ordered their collocation again with the *Avesta*. Shahpuhar was not creating a new document. He was reconstructing the *Avesta*, for which he knew that information concerning the subjects which were in the *Avesta*, were also there in the scriptures of their rival religion, as both people had descended from the same stock and had inherited the same knowledge. He was looking for the *Veds*, though not under that name, and for that he sent people to the Hindus, to Arum and other lands. The passage shows that he found them there as he ordered the collected information to be collocated again with the *Avesta*. The other lands remain vague, but Arum is clear. It shows that the Zoroastrians were aware that the *Veds* had gone to India and Greece, a fact that matches with the information provided by the *Sikand-Gumanik Vigar*. Shahpuhar, here appears to be Shapur III, the son of Ardashir II, who reigned from AD 383 to 388.

This is an extremely significant information in the Zoroastrian scriptures, that the Aryan group that fled Iran to come to India to be called the Indo-Aryans, had in fact split into two, one of which went to Greece. This fact does not appear to have been noticed by historians so far. The question then emerges that the *Veds* should have been found in Greece. Apparently, Shapur III had found them at the end of the fourth century AD though now there is no trace of them whatsoever. But for that matter there is no trace of any scripture or religious literature of the pre Christian period in Greece, Rome or elsewhere in Europe despite so much of other literature surviving. Greece and Rome could not have been cultures without scriptures. Credit needs to be given to the efficiency of the Roman Empire in destroying them as edicts to that effect had been issued.

The account of Julius Ceasar of the religious practices of the Gauls in the region which falls in modern France gives an impression that the *Veds* were there in the first century BC. The account of a seminary from him, can be mistaken to be of a Vedic ashram in India. The same is here.

> The Druids do not go to war, nor pay tribute together with the rest; they have an exemption from military service and a dispensation in all matters. Induced by such great advantages, many embrace this profession of their own accord, and (many) are sent to it by their parents and relations. They are sent there to learn by heart a great number of verses; accordingly some remain in the course of training twenty years. Nor is it lawful to commit these to writing, though in almost all other

matters, in their public and private transactions they use Greek characters. That practice they seem to me to have adopted for two reasons; because they neither desire their doctrines to be divulged among the mass of the people, nor those who learn, to devote themselves the less to the efforts of memory, relying on writing. They wish to inculcate this as one of their leading tenets that souls do not become extinct, but pass after death from one body to another, and they think that men by this tenet are in a great degree excited to valour, the fear of death being disregarded. They likewise discuss and impart to the youth many things respecting the stars and their motion, respecting the extent of the world and of our earth, respecting the nature of things, respecting the power and majesty of the immortal gods.

(Julius Ceasar. Gallic Wars. Book 6)

These were, however, too accomplished a group of people for their footprints to be lost, even if the *Veds* got destroyed. It gets reflected in so many similarities in ancient Indian and Greek thought. Much of this can be called incidental with two groups of people speculating on the same subject and arriving at the same conclusions. There is, however, one significant element in astrology common in both Greece and India, which cannot be a coincidence and corroborates the information that a common group of people went to both countries and carried their common knowledge base to both of them. There is no sign of astrology in Homeric Greece. The literature at that stage shows that future was attempted to be known by oracles. Then astrology emerges which is so close to Indian astrology that an inconclusive debate has raged on who influenced whom.

The *Veds*, as well as the *Avesta*, show a very accurate knowledge of astronomy of these people, as well as the use of astrology in predicting future. The Richas from the *Rig Ved* on the subject are given here.

1.   I have beheld the Lord of Men with seven sons, of which delightful and benevolent (deity), who is the object of our invocation, there

is an all-pervading middle brother, and a third brother well fed with (oblations of) ghee.

2. They yoke the seven to the one-wheeled car, one horse named seven, bears it along; the three-axle wheel is undecaying, never loosened, and in it all these regions of the universe abide.

3. The seven who preside over this seven-wheeled chariot (are) the seven horses who draw it; seven sisters ride in it together, and in it are deposited the seven forms of utterance.

4. Immature (in understanding) undiscovering in mind, I enquire of those things which are hidden (even) from the gods; (what are) the seven threads which the sages have spread to envelop the sun, in whom all abide?

5. Ignorant, I enquire of the sages who know (the truth), not as one knowing (do I enquire), for the sake of (gaining) knowledge, what is that one alone, who has upheld these six spheres in the form of the unborn?

(All from *Rig Ved.* M-I, S-164)

6. All beings abide in this five-spoked revolving wheel, the heavily loaded axle is never heated; its external compact nave is never worn away.

(*Rig Ved.* M-1, S-164, R-13)

7. Of those that are born together, sages have called the seventh the single-born; for six are twins, and are moveable and born of the gods, their desirable (properties) placed severally in their proper abode are various informed, and revolve for that which is stationary.

(*Rig Ved.* M-1, S-164, R-15)

8. Those which (the sages) have termed descending, they have also termed ascending. Those they have termed ascending, they have also called descending; and those (orbits) which you, Som and Indra, have made, bear along the worlds like (oxen) yoked to a cart.

(*Rig Ved.* M-1, S-164, R- 19)

9. One stationary sustains six burdens. The rays spread through that true and extensive; three revolving spheres are severally above, two

of which are placed in secret, and one is visible.

(*Rig Ved.* M-3, S-56, R-2)

10. By Indra, the constellations were made stable and firm and stationary, so that they could not be moved by any.

(*Rig Ved.* M-8, S-14, R-9)

11. Whereby you have made Jyotish (astrology) manifest to Ayu and to Manu, and rule rejoicing over this sacred rite.

(*Rig Ved.* M-8, S-15, R-5)

These Richas have a mixture of philosophy and astronomy in them with an occasional hint of astrology. Five planets are visible to the naked eye and so these are the ones mentioned in the astrology, as well as astronomy of the time when telescope was not there. To these five are added the sun and the moon. As the earth was also known to be revolving around the sun, it adds to the number, when the sun is taken out of the count. A remarkable thing here is the indication that they knew that the sun was stable and it is the earth and the planets that revolve around it. The third Richa hints at astrology as it is assigning to each of the seven some presiding entity which is responsible for whatever is bestowed. Astrology is a well-established stream of knowledge of ancient India. These Richas indicate that it is as old as the *Veds*, if not more. The last Richa in this regard is significant, as it names Ayu earlier to Manu, to whom astrology was made manifest. This establishes that the knowledge is of a time before the two sides split in Arjika, a fact corroborated by the existence of the same in the *Avesta* also. The *Avesta* has several references of consultations of astrologers, apart from passages which show their knowledge of astronomy. Some passages which show their knowledge about astronomy are stated here.

1. We sacrifice unto Tistrya, the bright and the glorious star, whose rising is watched by men who live on the fruits of the year; they watch him, as he comes up to the country for a bad year, or for a good year.

(Tir Yast VIII)

2. First he produced the celestial spheres, and the constellation stars are assigned to it by him, especially those twelve whose names are

Varak (the Lamb), Tora (the Bull), Do-patkar (the two figures or Gemini), Kalakong (the Crab), Ser (the Lion), Kushak (Virgo), Tarazuk (Balance), Gazdum (Scorpion), Nimasp (the Centaur or Sagittarius), Vahik (Capricornus), Dul (the Waterpot) and Mahik (the Fish).

(Bundahis. Chapter II)

3. Again, the year dependent on the revolving moon is not equal to the computed year on this account, for the moon returns one time in twenty-nine and one time in thirty days. Whoever keeps the year by the revolution of the moon mingles summer with winter and winter with summer. And the sun comes from the sign of Aries, into which it proceeded in the beginning, back to the same place in three hundred and sixty-five days and six short times (hours), which are one year.

(Bundahis. Chapter XXV)

4. Two dark progeny of the primeval ox move and are made to revolve from far below the sun and moon, and whenever during the revolution of the celestial sphere, they make one pass below the sun or below the moon, it becomes a covering which is spun over the sun and it is so when the sun or moon is not seen. Of each of those two progeny of the primeval ox, one is called the head and one the tail.

(Dadistan-i Dinik. Chapter LXIX)

5. And those are the five planets that rush below them in the shape of stars and they keep them enveloped in light, which are Saturn, Jupiter, Mars, Venus and Mercury. And those two fiends that are greatly powerful, who are the opponents of the planetary sun and moon, move below the splendour of those two luminaries.

(Sikand-Gumanik Vigar. Chapter IV)

These passages show their knowledge of astronomy, especially about the sun and the stars that are linked to seasons. The first passage shows that they made use of their knowledge about the stars for knowing the season of the year. This is important because for a community wanting to know about seasons on the basis of natural features there are two options, one from the position of the sun in its annual north-south movement and the second to know of it from a particular star or constellation that is visible in the sky at a particular time of the year. Normally, it is easier to know of the season from the position of the sun, as this can be done by watching it at sunrise and noticing its position with reference to natural features on the horizon. It can be very easily fixed what season would be when the sun rises from a particular point on being observed from a fixed position. To know of the same from the stars requires a long and more detailed observation. The stars have to be observed for the entire year and their rise has to be linked to the seasons to know which particular star would be visible in which season. That they opted for the more difficult option gives an impression that the time when this knowledge originated, they did not have the luxury of knowing the seasons by observing the sun. It appears to be of the Arctic days, though at that time the records of the stars linked to particular periods of the year would have been for the completely dark months only, but once a beginning had been made on a particular line, it would have been taken to its logical conclusion in due course.

The knowledge of these Aryans at such remote times that the sun was stable and the earth revolves around it also gives an impression that it was acquired in the Arctic region. There are several reasons for this. Firstly, in any other area, the sun is not a rarity to be longed for. Though life depends on it everywhere, the bounty is available every day without asking. The only thing an agricultural community needs to know about is seasons, because it determines their agricultural activities. For this it is not even necessary to know that seasons depend on the position of the sun. In such a situation the people outside the Arctic Circle do not have a pressing necessity to know about it. On the other hand, in the Arctic Circle, the sun disappears for six months. Though it is not dark for all these six months as there are several weeks of dawn and evening twilight, yet there are a few months which are completely dark. Life comes to a standstill during this period and there would be a continuous urge to know when the sun would reappear to bring back activity to a dormant life. This would make the knowledge about the sun a pressing necessity. Secondly, in all other areas, people after a day's labour retire to sleep. It would be odd for them to be out in the night to observe stars. The knowledge that the sun is stable while the earth, with the rest of the planets, revolves around it is acquired by observing the stars. In the Arctic Circle, stars are visible continuously for several months, during which the people would have had precious little to do but to gaze at them. Thirdly, it is far easier from the Polar regions to know that the sun is stable and the earth revolves around it, than anywhere else. In all areas outside the Polar regions, the sun and the stars are seen moving in the same pattern, east to west, the sun during the day and the stars at night. This leads to the first impression that the earth is fixed and the sky revolves around it, in which on one side is the sun and on the other the stars. It is only after a prolonged effort to observe the stars that it emerges that the pattern of the stars in the sky changes and keeps changing till the same pattern comes after a year. This leads to an understanding that the sky appears to move in two ways, one on a daily basis in which it appears to revolve around the earth and two on an annual basis in which the entire canvas of the sky appears to move forward to come back to the same point, which shows that it is moving in a circle. It is only when the sky is seen moving in two ways at the same time that it is concluded that the sky is not moving, because it is not possible for a canvas spread around in the manner of the sky to move in these two directions at the same time. That leads to the next logical conclusion that the surface on which we are standing is moving and has two movements at the same time, one rotational and the other forward, which ultimately forms a circle. Since these two movements at the same time are possible for this object, everything else falls in place. It becomes evident that the sun is fixed and the earth moves around it with two patterns of movement, which cause the day and the year. In the Arctic Circle, to start with, this first impression does not emerge because the stars and the sun do not complement each other in their movement to complete one daily circle around the earth. The stars are visible for six months in which every twenty-four hours, with the rotation of the earth, the sky would appear rotating like a wheel. The sun, on the other hand, rises on the southern horizon, when it is over the Equator and starts circling. It moves in its slow six-monthly journey in which it appears to come closer till it is on the Tropic of Cancer and recedes back to set in the south. The sun during the period of its visibility is seen revolving around the earth every twenty-four hours. With these two different patterns of movement being observed in the sky, the initial impression that the earth is fixed, while the sky is revolving, does not emerge and the observer starts from a neutral ground, instead of an incorrect notion.

The Aryans in the Arctic, with all the time in the world to observe the stars and a pressing necessity to know when the sun would appear and end their six-monthly annual ordeal with darkness and cold, would have applied themselves totally to this task for six months each year. Apparently, they initially tried to do so with reference to the moon cycles, because they had divided the sky into twelve houses of thirty degrees each. Taking the sun to be at the centre, the sky is like a huge football from the inside, in which the twelve houses are formed by lines similar to longitudes on the earth. They emerge like twelve pieces of an orange. Each house was named, though possibly later, after a constellation that happened to be in it, making that to be the sun sign. The effort now would have been to know in which house the sun is, so as to know how many more houses have to be crossed before a particular constellation would be visible. Very soon they would have found that the moon's cycle led to inaccurate predictions. This would have led them to look for the next alternative, which were the stars. They would have seen the pattern of the stars change. In this change, they would have noticed that the movement of this change is in a linear direction. The sky has two movements, one rotational, like a wheel, every twenty-four hours and the other forward, would have been noticed by them at that stage itself, with all its logical conclusions that the canvas spread above cannot have two movements like that and the only thing possible was for the earth to be doing so. Once it was known that the sun was fixed and the earth was moving in a linear direction to pass through six months without the sun and six months with it, to be followed by the same darkness and the same pattern of stars, things would have been clear. As they were also able to observe the five planets and their movements, they would have seen the complete orbits of the two planets that orbit inside the earth's orbit within a single six-monthly night and would have seen that they were orbiting around the point, where their calculations showed the sun was. This would have provided a further confirmation of their understanding. It does sound incredible that Galileo almost lost his life just a few centuries ago for this theory, that these people had such a detailed knowledge of thousands of years earlier at a time when they did not know even to write. This is what necessity can achieve.

The point, common to both India and Greece, that had been mentioned to establish the authenticity of the information emerging from the Zoroastrian scriptures that the Magis fleeing Iran went to India, as well as Greece, related to astrology and not astronomy. Loosely, astrology can be called applied astronomy which is the application of astronomical knowledge to predict future. It is based on long-term observations, in which it is noticed that when a planet is in a particular house, it is the time when good things happen and when it is in some other house bad things happen. When this is seen repeatedly, it is considered to be a pattern and it is deemed that in future also when the planet would be in that position, it would be time for good or bad occurrences. For an individual, a chart is prepared based on the position of the planets in the twelve houses at the time of birth. This is called the birth chart. Depending on the house in which a planet is and what effect that position gives, the planet is taken to be favourably disposed or otherwise to the person. However, being based on observations, the process of updating the understanding with fresh observations, has to be steady and continuous, because even the concept of good and bad changes with time, due to which something that had been recorded as good on the basis of a certain understanding may be its opposite in a different scenario. For instance, in an agricultural economy, if a person had plenty to eat, spent a lot of time with his family, had no necessity to travel and was not pursued by people, it would be deemed that the time is good and he has had a good crop. On the other hand, if he has inadequate food, is away from the family, or has to leave his home in search of survival and is being pursued by people who would be either creditors or enemies, the times are bad. On the other hand, in present times, if a person does not have time even for food, he is somehow picking up a sandwich and eats while he drives, has no time for the family, travels all the time around the world and people don't leave him in peace, with the phone ringing even in the bathroom, he is on top of the world. If he is in peace with plenty of food and the family, he has just lost his job or an election.

Both Greek and Indian astrology have the same basic principles. They have the twelve houses and five planets, to which have been added two more heavenly bodies, the sun and the moon to make them seven. Up to this point, it could have been a coincidence as all these are there and two different people observing them could have arrived at the same conclusions, but what follows cannot be a coincidence. Both have added two more planets to make them nine and these two do not exist, but are only positions in the sky. Apart from the twelve houses for which twelve lines have been drawn like longitudes, to have a reference point, one line has been drawn across which can be treated to be at par with the Equator. This runs through the two points of the equinox of the earth on its orbit. The two opposite nodes of this line have been included as planets in both systems. In the Indian system they are called Rahu or the head of the Asur and Ketu, the torso of the Asur, while in the Greek they are Dragon head and Dragon tail. They have also been mentioned in the passages of the Zoroastrian scriptures as the head and tail of the primeval ox. Treating two positions in the sky as planets cannot be a coincidence because existence is being given to non-existent entities. To do so, exactly in the same manner, has to be due to the common origin of both.

Many more instances could be found in ancient Indian and ancient Greek thought to establish the point. This, however, is not to say that the two cultures did not influence each other and everything common is because of the common origin of some people who went to both the places. Apart from Alexander's invasion, the two sides knew each other from much earlier times through trade, but exposure through commerce would be of a shallower level and can be distinguished from deeper imprints.

The works of Greek and Roman writers bring out evidence in several ways to show that these people went to Greece and nearby places also, apart from coming to India. A passage on this is here.

> The only men of whom I can hear who dwell beyond the Ister are those who are said to be called Sigynnai, and who use the Median fashion of dress. Their horses, it is said, have shaggy hair all over their bodies, as much as five fingers long; and these are small and flat-nosed and too weak to carry men, but when yoked in chariots they are high-spirited; therefore the natives of the country drive chariots. The boundaries of this people extend, it is said, to the parts near the Enetoi, who live on the Adriatic; and people say that they are colonists from the Medes. In what way, however, these have come to be colonists from the Medes I am not able for my part to conceive, but everything is possible in the long course of ages.
>
> (Herodotus. *The Histories*. Book 5. Para 9)

This is an unambiguous statement from Herodotus that the people settled close to the Adriatic Sea were colonists of the Medes. They were having their dresses too in the Median fashion. He could, however, not get a clue how and when they came there.

An interesting feature noticeable in the Greek traditions is that like the Seven Rishis of the *Veds*, the Greeks too had a myth about the Seven Wise Men. Their names do not match the names of the Vedic Rishis but the statements about them are significant. Some are here.

1. And he cites Choerilus also, who in his 'The Crossing of the Pontoon-Bridge' which was constructed by Dareius, says "the sheep-tending Sacae, of the Scythian stock; but they used to live in wheat-producing Asia; however, they were colonists from the Nomads, law-abiding people." And when he calls Anacharsis 'wise', Ephorus says that he belongs to this race, and that he is considered also one of the Seven Wise Men because of his perfect self-control and good sense.

    (Strabo. Geographica. Book 7. Chapter 3. Para 9)

2. These, I affirm, though they have not personally governed the state, are worthy of our consideration, because by their investigations and writings, they exercised a kind of political magistracy. As to those whom the Greeks entitle 'the Seven Sages', I find almost all conversant with public business. Nor indeed is there anything in which human virtue can more closely resemble the divine powers, than by establishing new states or in preserving those already established.

(Cicero. The Commonwealth. Book 1)

3. There are two inscriptions at Delphi which are most indispensable to living. These are 'Know Thyself' and 'Avoid Extremes' for on these two commandments hang all the rest.

(Plutarch. Consolation to Apollonius)

4. After the tables had been cleared away and garlands distributed by Melissa, and we had poured libations, and the flute-girls had withdrawn, then Ardalus, addressing Anacharsis inquired if there were flute-girls among the Scythians.

(Plutarch. The Dinner of the Seven Wise Men)

Plutarch has named these seven sages as Thales, Bias, Pittacus, Solon, Chilon, Cleobulus and Anacharsis. The first and the fourth passages here mention, that Anarcharsis was a Scythian, a term found used also for people coming from the area where the Vedic people lived in Central Asia. For these Seven Wise Men it has been stated that they presented two tablets to the Oracle of Delphi on which were inscribed 'Know Thyself' and 'Avoid Extremes'. As mentioned earlier, the *Veds* had two distinct streams of followers, one were the adepts for whom the objective was the realization of God, while the other were the common worshippers who followed the ritualistic side of the religion. For those who had God realization as their objective and for whom the Upnishads are the guiding books, 'Know Thyself' is the crux of the teachings. For the common worshippers, exercising moderation was the teaching for their day-to-day life.

In Greek and Roman writings throughout, the understanding of the universe is that the earth is stable while the sky, with the stars and the sun, revolves around it. However, at an undated time there was a person named Aristarchus, who stated the opposite. This is reported by Plutarch in the following passage.

> Thereupon Lucius laughed and said, 'Oh Sir, just don't bring a suit against us for impiety as Cleanthes thought that the Greeks ought to lay an action for impiety against Aristarchus the Samian on the ground that he was disturbing the hearth of the universe, because he sought to save the phenomenon by assuming that the heaven is at rest while the earth is revolving along the ecliptic and at the same time is rotating about its own axis.'
>
> (Plutarch. On the Face of the Moon)

Aristarchus is reported to have stated the correct phenomenon, though the Greeks and the Romans did not believe him. This was the knowledge that the Vedic Aryans had from the Arctic days and Aristarchus had evidently carried it to Greece. He has been reported to be from Samos, the island that was the birthplace of Pythagoras also. The views of Pythagoras were very close to the Upanishadic teachings. These views were foreign to Greece and Rome, because of which Pythagoras and his followers were persecuted and his books were burnt. This emerges from the following passages.

1. After the Pythagorean societies throughout the different cities had been defeated by the revolutionaries and driven out, and after partisans of Cylon, heaping fuel about the house where the society that still held together at Metapontum was in session, and setting fire to it, had destroyed them all in the conflagration except Philolaus and Lysis, who forced a way through the flames, Philolaus escaped to Lucania and from there reached in safety to our remaining adherents, but for a long time no one knew what had become of Lysis.

   (Plutarch. De Genio Socratis)

2. When in the district of Italy, then known as Greater Hellas, the club-houses of the Pythagoreans were burnt down, there ensued, a general revolutionary movement, the leading citizens of each city

having then unexpectedly perished, and in all the Greek towns of
the district murder, sedition and every kind of disturbance was rife.

(Polybius. *The Histories*. Book 2. Para 10)

3.   In the same year, some workmen in the farm of Lucius Petillus,
     while digging the ground discovered two stone chests with
     inscriptions in Greek and Latin letters, one signifying that therein
     was buried Numa Pompilius; the other that therein were books of
     Numa Pompilius. In it were found two bundles, tied round with
     waxed cord, and each containing seven books, not only entire, but
     apparently quite fresh. Valerius Anitas adds, that they contained
     the doctrines of Pythagoras. Quintus Petillus, the city praetor, on
     reading the principal heads, perceived that they had the tendency
     to undermine the established system of religious doctrines and
     so he was determined to throw those books into the fire. The
     Senate decreed that the praetor having offered his oath ought to
     be deemed sufficient evidence that those books should be burned
     in the comitium. The books were burned in the comitium in the
     view of the people.

(Titus Livy. History of Rome. Book XL. Para 29)

Apart from being a philosopher, Pythagoras is known for his theorem
of geometry proving the square of the hypotenuse of a right angle
triangle to be equal to the sum of the squares of the remaining two
sides. This theorem is found in Vedic mathematics also under the
name of Baudhayan's theorem, though the method of proving it is
different.

The migration of the Vedic Aryans to Greece is borne out also
by a statement of Aristophenes, the most famous comic dramatist of
ancient Greece, who lived between 445 BC and 375 BC. He speaks of
'a yogi sleep' and calls it Median. The dialogues of the play mentioning
this are here.

Sosias. How goes it with you, poor Xanthias?
Xanthias. I am teaching myself to take this all-night stint easy.
I would just like to lull myself a little.
Sosias. Take your chances, then. My own eyes too are sweetly

suffused with drowsiness.

Xanthias. You are crazy or a dervish.

Sosias. No, but it is a yogi sleep coming over me.

Xanthias. You worship the same foreign Bacchus I do.
A Median host.

(Aristophenes. Wasps)

The reference is to meditation and Aristophenes has mockingly called it 'a yogi sleep'. This, however, goes to prove that Yog had reached Greece with the Medes before the fifth century BC. It also establishes that the Aryans had developed Yog before they left Persia.

11

India, Then

◦❦◦

W HEN THE VEDIC MAGIS WERE fleeing Iran in the face of
reverses in the reign of Vistasp, the Indus Valley Civilization
was flourishing in India. It was in the western region of the country,
which has been called the Sapt Sindhu or the Land of Seven Rivers
in the *Veds*. The *Avesta* is acquainted with this land as can be seen
from this passage.

> The fifteenth of the good lands and countries which I, Ahur
> Mazda, created was the Seven Rivers.
>
> (Vendidad. Fargard I)

Though no literature has survived to provide information about
the Indus Valley Civilization and even the limited written material
available on the numerous seals found has not been understood because
the script has not been deciphered yet, a lot of archeological finds are
there which provide glimpses of this culture. So far, about a thousand
sites have been identified to be of this period and quite a few have been
excavated. More than half of them are along the dried up river bed of
Saraswati. Unlike the Egyptians or Mesopotamians, the Indus people
did not engrave inscriptions on stone or build tombs for their dead in
which things connected with the life of the person were kept. This was
a city culture of which remains of almost complete cities have been
found. One major city has been found at Harappa, on the bank of the
Ravi river and the second is Mohenjo Daro on the bank of the Indus.
Apart from these two cities, several small towns and a large number
of village sites have been found, including a port at Lothal in southern
Gujarat. The area covered is more than a thousand and five hundred

kilometres from north to south. The pattern of the civilization is so uniform that even the bricks were usually of the same size and shape from one end to the other.

There is no indication of the Harappan people having migrated to the Sapt Sindhu from some other place. They were people of the area and had lived there long before they planned and built their cities, which remained unaltered at least for a thousand years. Though a precise date cannot be fixed for the beginning of this civilization yet it cannot be later than 3,000 BC. Except for a small citadel in the cities, no fortifications and very few weapons have been found. No building can be said to be a palace or a temple. The citadel appears to have been used for both religious and governmental purposes. The streets show a well-planned layout of the cities and towns. They are all straight and cross each other at a right angle, creating blocks within which were houses with lanes criss-crossing. This feature is common in all urban sites, making it distinctive of the culture. Another striking feature was its intense conservatism. The site at Mohenjo Daro has nine strata of buildings. Evidently, as the ground level rose for whatsoever reason, new houses were built exactly at the same site of the old, with minor variations, if at all, in the ground plan. Because of this, the street plan of the cities remained unchanged for a thousand years or more. Even the script remained totally unchanged throughout their long history. This continuity of over a thousand years is unparalleled anywhere else in the world.

The city plans of Harappa and Mohenjo Daro, which are similar, have some interesting features. To the west is the citadel, which is an oblong platform about 30 feet high. It is about 400 yards long and 200 yards wide and is defended by walls. Public buildings are erected on the platform. Below it is the town with the main streets as wide as 30 feet. No stone building has been found anywhere. Standardized baked bricks were the building material for dwelling houses as well as public buildings. The dwelling houses were often of two or more storeys. Though they varied in size, their layout plan was the same with a square courtyard in the middle and several rooms around it. The entrance opened into the alley but there were no windows facing the streets. The houses had bathrooms with drains leading to public drains under the main streets which took the water to soak pits. Throughout their length, these were covered by large brick slabs. Such a drainage system, unparalleled in its time, would have required an efficient municipal system to maintain. The average size of the ground floor house was about 30 by 30 feet, though some were much bigger. Another category of houses seem to be dwellings of workmen. These are parallel rows of two-roomed houses with an area of 20 by 12 feet each. Of the public buildings, the most striking is the public bath in the citadel area of Mohenjo Daro. This is an oblong pool 39 by 23 feet and 8 feet deep, constructed of bricks and made waterproof by use of bitumen. It could be drained by an opening in a corner. The largest building excavated is at Mohenjo Daro, which has a superficial area of 230 by 78 feet. This could have been the seat of administration. At Harappa, a granary has been discovered to the north of the citadel. This is a raised platform of 150 by 200 feet divided into storage blocks of 50 by 20 feet each.

The main crops were wheat, barley, peas, sesame and cotton. There is no evidence of the cultivation of rice or use of irrigation, though both are possible. The main domesticated animals were cow, buffalo, goat, sheep, pig, donkey, dog and fowl. The elephant was known and may also have been tamed, but the horse does not seem to have been with them. The bullock was the usual beast of burden along with the donkey. They had a thriving agricultural economy in which enough surplus were produced for trade to create urban occupations for so many people living in towns. The people lived in comfortable houses and even workmen had two-roomed brick-built quarters.

The Harappan culture extended right up to the mouth of the Indus and Saraswati, while a port has been found in Lothal, which shows their association with the sea and the possible link of their prosperity to it, though remains of ships have not been found. The products of the Harappan people were reaching Mesopotamia, certainly and Egypt, possibly. This can be said because a number of seals and a few other objects of the Indus Valley Civilization have been found in Sumer at levels dating earlier to 2,000 BC. Indian exports would have been foodgrains and cotton, for which Indian merchants had some of their people actually residing in those areas. There is no evidence of any Indian import from the Sumerians or Egyptians. The trade was therefore not on barter. It would be of immense interest to know how a medium of trade emerged. The later developments show that it was based on precious metals, but what made the Harappan farmers and traders part with a shipload of foodgrains or cotton for a few kilograms of metals like gold and silver for which they had no real use to start with, would perhaps remain a mystery.

An idea of the economic activities, the agricultural surplus, volume of trade and the distribution of wealth can be had from the archeological remains, especially from the cities. There cannot be cities only for the habitation of people as urban occupations have to be there for people to earn their livelihood. As evidence is there only of commerce and not industry, it can be safely concluded that trade was the only urban occupation and that this was a commercial economy. The size of the cities and towns would show the number of people living and thriving on trade. Apart from the city, traders would have been in rural areas also and some farmers could be trading alongside. Based on this, the volume of trade and agricultural surplus that would emerge would be very significant. Along with farmers and traders, there would have been a very well-organized system of transportation because the items of trade were very bulky. For this there would have been a class of seafarers, who would have been plying hundreds of ships between the Indian cities and the Middle East for centuries. But for the sea route such a volume of bulky trade material could not have been transported or traded. The ships were perhaps not very large as they seem to have been coming up the rivers at both ends to pick the cargo and deliver it. Their passage does not seem to be confined to the sea, as except for Lothal, no other port has been found. It would also be logical because at both ends the destinations were on rivers and larger ships would have remained in the sea, requiring a lot of effort and expenditure in carrying the goods and loading them by some other means and repeating the exercise at the other end. As a large number of sites of these ancient towns and villages have been found along the

Indus and the dried up river bed of the Saraswati it shows that these two rivers were the main trade routes. A larger number have been found on the Saraswati, which shows that of the two, the Saraswati basin contributed more to the production and export. Another exit point was Lothal in southern Gujarat, which would have had its own catchment area. The *Veds* mention of sea trade and of it being a major source of generation of wealth. The reference is here.

> His adorers, bearing oblations, are thronging round (him), as
> (merchants) covetous of gain crowd the ocean (in vessels) on
> a voyage, ascend quickly with a hymn to the powerful Indra,
> the protector of the solemn sacrifice, as women (climb) a
> mountain.
>
> (*Rig Ved.* M-1, S-56, R-2)

The wealth generated from this trade would have been substantial, as the entire civilization was based on it. However, there would have been a very fair and equitable distribution of wealth among the different partners of its generation—the farmers, the traders and the seafarers. This is evident, not only from the fact that there were no disturbances and things remained unchanged for more than a thousand years, but also from the pattern of the archeological remains. More than a thousand sites have been identified so far, of which only a few are cities and towns. The rest are villages. These villages follow the basic pattern of the cities, as their houses are built of the same material and follow the same design because of which they have survived all these years. The only thing missing is the city planning with its drainage system. As the villages, too, had similar houses, it is evident that the farmers received a fair share of the profit and it was not cornered by the traders alone. The seafarers also had their share. The rows of two-roomed houses which have been said to be houses of workmen in Mohenjo Daro and Harappa have to be the houses for families of these seafarers, as no other occupation had emerged which could have had workmen, except brick kilns, which could not have been in towns and so their workmen would not be living there.

The political and administrative set-up of the people also emerges from the surviving ruins. The archeological remains of monarchies have a certain pattern. This is essentially because all resources of the state are at the disposal of the monarch, who is often not very secure of his position and is constantly in need of protection. There are, therefore, buildings used for residential purposes, which are usually huge on one side and have protective fortifications on the other. These palaces, castles and forts stand apart from everything that is around as nobody can match the grandeur of the royal quarters. The next category of buildings associated with monarchies are commemorative structures, which could be tombs, temples, towers, arches or anything that can stand the test of time for people to remember the monarch and his achievements even after he is gone. People want to be remembered and appreciated, and monarchs are no exception. They have the resources to use the most easily available durable commodity, stone. Hence, all over the world monarchs have left monuments as a mark of their glory and achievements. Another distinctive feature of buildings connected with monarchies is art. An artist produces something which is time-consuming to make and therefore expensive, yet it has little or no use though it is beautiful. Artists producing large artifacts therefore need patrons, who would appreciate the beauty of their product and would not be concerned about its utility. The monarch, with the resources of the state at his disposal, not only is in a position to patronize artists, but finds them useful for his own ambitions of being remembered by posterity. As a result, a lot of art remains associated with monarchies. Common people have more stress on utility. Their artistic tendencies find expression in limited ways and often such creations do not survive the test of time. The remains of the Indus Valley Civilization reveal that they did not have a monarchy at any stage. There is no building that can be said to be a palace or a commemorative building or structure. The citadels are too small to be the dwellings of kings of such a flourishing civilization. Apparently, they were the seat of government, which has to be there irrespective of the political system. Entire towns and villages have survived with the houses of common people. These buildings and town planning have remarkable features from the point of utility, like drains, but art is missing. The walls are of brick, which may have had a plaster when the houses were in use. This plaster could have had paintings but nothing has survived. The voice from these remains is loud and clear. They had a democratic system in place, the efficiency of which is only matched by its long survival.

It also appears that they did not face any real crisis for a very long time as democracy survived all those centuries. When a crisis did come and the civilization came to an end with the people moving to the Gangetic plains, democracy gave way to monarchy. Being democratic, they could not have had large political units. Though a striking similarity is noticeable in all the archeological remains of the Indus Valley Civilization, to the extent that even the size of the bricks is the same, this has to be due to some other reason and not because the entire area was a single political unit, because such a political unit would make it an empire spread over a very large area that survived for more than a thousand years without an army, as few weapons have been found. Evidently, they had small autonomous political units, but had a lot of interaction with each other due to trade. Perhaps their inter-dependence for commerce and thereby prosperity, made them very reasonable people, for they could resolve their disputes through civilized means for such a long time without the need to resort to war. This would have made life very comfortable and peaceful on the one hand and history very dull and boring on the other, as there would be no Indra killing Vritra or Sudas killing Shambar or Yam defeating Ushana to talk of. But this is what emerges from the ruins of a civilization that was prosperous and survived for over a thousand years without even changing the position of the houses of people. They grew a lot of wheat and cotton, far more than they needed, had an efficient water transport system to carry it to markets far away, where they traded them for gold and silver and with that wealth made comfortable dwellings for themselves and lived in peace with each other at a time when life in all other parts of the globe was much more difficult and had all the stresses of survival.

Seals are an important source of information about the people of Harappa. Over 2,000 of them have been found. They have an emblem, often of a religious character with a brief inscription in a script that has not been deciphered. The standard seal was a square or oblong plaque, usually made of a soft stone called steatite, which was delicately engraved and hardened by heating. Generally, they depict animals such as the bull, buffalo, goat, tiger and elephant, or what appear to be scenes from a legend. Their brief writings, usually of less than ten symbols, are the only examples of their script to survive. This script has about 270 characters, which are pictographic in origin. Surprisingly, the most striking similarities it has are with the symbols used until not very far back by the natives of Easter Island, in the eastern Pacific. The distance and time gap between the two, however, makes it difficult to claim any connection.

Though the Harappan people did not produce works of art on a large scale, small specimens have survived and have been found in the excavations. The engravings on the seals are very artistic and the animals have been delineated very accurately. Equally notable are some human figures. The torso of a man in red sandstone is impressive for its realism. Another is a bust of a man in steatite which seems to be an attempt at portraiture. It seems to be that of a priest with eyes half-closed in meditation. The most notable is the bronze figurine of a girl, who has been called 'the Dancing Girl of Mohenjo Daro'. She is unclad but for a necklace and a series of bangles that almost cover one arm, with her hair dressed in a complicated coiffure. The Harappan people also made naturalistic models of animals, especially tiny monkeys and squirrels, used as pinheads and beads. For children, they made cattle with moveable heads and monkeys that would slide down a string and little toy carts, all of terracotta. In terracotta, they also made statuettes of women which appear to be icons of the Mother Goddess, because they have been found in large numbers. They seem to have been kept in every home.

Apparently, they still made use of stone tools, though implements of copper and bronze had been introduced. Iron was not in use. So much of progress in agriculture had been achieved without this mighty metal, which shows that they would have used fire to clear the lands for their farms. Even their copper and bronze tools were technologically very inferior. Their knives were flat and could be easily bent while the axe head did not have a hole for the shaft to pass through. It had to be tied onto the shaft. Only their saw was superior as it had undulating teeth for the dust to escape. This must have been an important tool for use in ship-building. Their pottery was plain and well made though lacking in artistry.

The men wore robes which left one shoulder bare and the garments were often richly patterned. Men and women alike had long hair and the women had elaborate hair dresses. Jewellery is seen depicted in the figures which show their fondness for bangles, large necklaces and earrings. Beads of semi-precious stones have been found which must have been used in some of them.

The religion of the people seems to have had a number of features common with later Hinduism. The Mother Goddess seems to have been a very important, if not the most important, divinity. Her figurines in terracotta outnumber any other image. There are some figures in terracotta of nude bearded men with coiled hair in a posture rigidly upright with legs slightly apart and arms held parallel to the sides of the body but not touching it. They closely resemble the Jain saints in the meditating posture as portrayed in later times. The most striking deity is the horned god found depicted on the seals. He has been found sitting on the ground in padmasan, a yogic posture. He has a pair of horns and in the largest seal, has four animals surrounding him, an elephant, a tiger, a rhinoceros and a buffalo, with two deer below. Historians have called him the Proto Shiv or Pashupati, the Lord of Beasts. It is possible that the two horns got replaced by the crescent of the moon on the side of Shiv's head in course of time, by reducing their size and changing the position. Phallic worship was also an important part of their religion. Many objects have been found, which are certainly a representation of the phallus. Several animals and trees were also sacred to them. The bull seems to be the most important of these as a large number of seals portray it. At this stage, however, it does not appear to be associated with Shiv as it is not one of the animals depicted on the Pashupati seal. It could have been an independent cult figure. Of the trees, the pipal seems to have been held in very high regard. One seal depicts a horned goddess in a pipal tree being worshipped by a figure also wearing horns, with a human-headed goat watching the ceremony.

How the Indus Valley Civilization came to an end has remained a mystery. From the archaeological remains it can be seen that towards the end all the town planning and good governance were severely eroded. The signs are not of a well-functioning administration with prosperous cities and towns having been overrun and destroyed by enemy, but of decay. At Mohenjo Daro, large rooms were divided into smaller ones and mansions became tenements, potters' kilns came up within the city boundaries and one even in the middle of a street. The street plan was no longer maintained and a lot of jewellery was buried. Evidently, the city received a very large number of people and got over populated to an extent that it could not be managed in its earlier ways. Law and order could not be maintained and the city elders could not maintain the age-old pattern of the city culture. In Mohenjo Daro, it seems that when the end came, most citizens had already abandoned it. In the excavations of Mohenjo Daro at the level which is of the stage when the town was at this decay, a fine copper axe has been found with a strong shaft hole and an adze blade opposite that of the axe. This tool can be adapted for both war and peace, and is superior to any tool or weapon found anywhere in the Harappan sites. It does not, however, appear to be of invading Aryans as it is still of copper while the Aryans had been using iron for their weapons for a very long time. At Harappa, the cemeteries on the higher level have fractional burials in pots of men with short-headed Armenoid skulls. At Chanhu Daro, on the lower Indus, the Indus valley people living in planned houses were replaced by squatters living in small huts.

This was the India to which Indo-Aryans were coming on fleeing from Iran. The Indus Valley Civilization, in all its glory, was known to the Magis in Iran as the *Avesta* mentions it. Hundreds of ships were sailing between the two lands, which would be returning empty from the Persian Gulf after off-loading their cargo. A number of Indian traders and ship captains would be visiting Iran and a few could have been having their agents in several cities of Mesopotamia and Iran. The Magis, being priests, traders and officials in the employment of the government, would have certainly known many of them. Though even the land route along the sea was possible, the most logical thing would have been to board the ships, especially when the fleeing people were not hardy soldiers and farmers, but priests, traders and possibly officials. It was also safer in case of a pursuit as all danger would have ended once the ships were in the open sea. This is exactly what the Indo-Aryans did in their journey to India. They travelled by Indian trade ships. This is borne out by the pattern of their initial settlement on arrival in the Sapt Sindhu, as is reflected in the *Veds*. In them, of the Indian rivers, the Saraswati finds frequent mention. Thereafter are references of the Indus. The remaining five find only a fleeting mention. This shows that the main concentration of the Indo-Aryans was along the Saraswati river and some were in the Indus basin. They were not along the rest of the five rivers. The Indus and Saraswati were two independent trade routes of ships sailing between India and the Middle East, of which more trade was from the Saraswati basin as a larger number of archeological sites have been found there. The Indo-Aryans, coming by ships, would have alighted at these places and would have settled down there. Had they come by land, travelling along the sea coast, they would have first reached the delta of the Indus river and then moved inland. In this process, they would have been found settled more along the Indus and then with a gradual movement to the other five rivers to the east, before reaching the Saraswati, which was the easternmost of the seven rivers. Their skipping the five in between totally and being less along the Indus and more along the Saraswati goes to show that the mode of their arrival and the pattern of their settlement and spread was not the land route. There is evidence in the *Rig Ved* also to show that they came by sea in Indian ships. The Richas that say so are stated here.

1.   May that best beloved Brahaspati, who is desired of all, sit down in our hall of sacrifice; may he gratify our desires of riches and of male posterity, transporting us (at present) embarrassed, uninjured beyond (the assaults of enemies).

(*Rig Ved*. M-7, S-97, R-4)

2. The divine heaven and earth, the parents of the deity have by their might, given growth to Brahaspati. Magnify, friends, the magnifiable, and may he render (the waters) easy to be crossed and forded for (the attainment of) food.

3. This praise has been offered as prayer to you both, Brahmanaspati and Indra, the wielder of the thunderbolt, protect our ceremonies, hear our manifold praise, annihilate the assailing adversaries of your worshippers.

                            (*Rig Ved.* M-7, S-98, R-8 and 9)

4. When (I, Vashisht) and Varun ascend the ship together; when we send it forth into the midst of the ocean, when we proceed over the waters with swift (sailing vessels), then may we both undulate happily in the prosperous swing.

5. So Varun placed Vashisht in the ship and by his mighty protection made the Rishi a doer of good works. The wise Varun placed his worshipper in a fortunate day of days, he extended the passing days, the passing nights.

                            (*Rig Ved.* M-7, S-88, R-3 and 4)

6. May he your unvarying kin, who was ever dear, though committing offences against you, still be your friend; adorable Varun, offending you, let us not enjoy (happiness); but do you who are wise, bestow on your worshipper a secure abode.

                            (*Rig Ved.* M-7, S-88, R-6)

7. May I never go, royal Varun, to a house of clay. Grant me happiness possessor of wealth, grant me happiness.

8. When, Varun, I am throbbing as if (with awe) like an inflated skin, grant me happiness, possessor of wealth, grant me happiness.

9. Thirst distresses (me) your worshipper in the midst of the waters, grant me happiness, possessor of wealth, grant me happiness.

                            (*Rig Ved.* M-7, S-89, R-1,2 and 4)

These Richas are ascribed to the same Rishi Vashisht, who had been earlier found replaced as the priest of the Persian King Vistasp. In the first Richa, he is praying to be transported away, uninjured beyond the assaults of the enemies. It also mentions that at the present place they are embarrassed. The third Richa too is a prayer for protection and the annihilation of the adversaries. The second Richa hints of the route he is about to take to get out of the place. He is praying that the waters may be easy to cross and that they may be able to ford them. The fourth and fifth confirm this. The fourth gives an account before the ship has been boarded. It says that when Varun and I shall ascend the ship and send it forth to the middle of the ocean, we will proceed swiftly and undulate happily in the prosperous swing. Evidently, Rishi Vashisht is looking forward to the sea journey. He seems to have never sailed before and has only seen a ship rocking from the shore. He feels that the swing would be very joyful and is not aware that it causes sickness of the most irritating kind. In the fifth Richa, Vashisht has boarded the ship and has come out into the open sea. He is now out of danger from the royal persecutors. He is saying that his life has been extended by Varun. The sixth and seventh Richas are his apprehensions on board. He does not know how he would be received and how he would be treated on reaching India. In the sixth, he is praying for a secure abode and in the seventh that he may not have to live in a house of clay. Evidently, the Rishi was used to living in proper houses in the Persian capital as the priest of the king. He was now a refugee and did not know what awaited him. He is praying for a secure and decent abode in his new home. The eighth Richa shows the Rishi sick on board. Sea sickness has hit him and there is possibly nothing that could be done but to pray. He would have never before had the feeling and is scared. The last Richa shows that the ship has run short of drinking water and the Rishi is thirsty in the midst of the sea. This shows that the ships were not equipped to carry so many passengers. They were cargo vessels and would have had arrangements of water only for the limited crew. Food could have been loaded for the additional numbers, but containers for water would have been limited and the results are evident.

Journey by sea has been mentioned by Rishi Kutsa Angiras also, which is given here.

Do you convey us in a ship across the sea for our welfare; may our sins be repented of.

(*Rig Ved.* M-1, S-97, R-8)

Apart from providing information about the manner in which the Indo-Aryans came to India, these Richas also show the change in the role of Varun. These Aryans had last encountered the sea in the Caspian with Bhujyu, the son of Tugra, going in for a journey and having his ships wrecked in a storm, to survive alone and be rescued after four days. Though Varun, as a god, had emerged with the Ribhus, the divinity protecting Bhujyu was not Varun but the Ashwins. Varun then was a god of waters, but this was limited to waters needed for agriculture. He had not yet emerged as the god of the sea, a role he has acquired by the time the sea had to be crossed this time to reach the Sapt Sindhu.

This departure of Rishi Vashisht from Iran was apparently because of grave risk to his personal safety. He seems to have been in danger and had escaped in the dead of night. The Richas from him that say so are here.

1. Protector of the dwelling, remover of disease, assuming all (kinds of) forms, be to us a friend, the granter of happiness.

2. White offspring of Sarama, with tawny limbs, although barking you display your teeth against me, bristling like lances in your gums, nevertheless, go quietly to sleep.

3. Offspring of Sarama, returning (to the charge) attack the pilferer or the thief, why do you assail the worshipper of Indra? Why do you intimidate us? Go quietly to sleep.

4. Do you rend the hog, let the hog rend you, why do you assail the worshipper of Indra? Why do you intimidate us? Go quietly to sleep.

5. Let the mother sleep, let the father sleep, let the dog sleep, let the son-in-law sleep, let all the kindred sleep, let the people (who are stationed) around sleep.

6. The man who sits, or he who walks, or he who sees us, of these we shut up the eyes, so that they may be as unconscious as the mansion.

7. We put men to sleep through the irresistible might of the bull with a thousand horns, who rises out of the ocean.

8. We put to sleep all those women lying in the courtyard in a litter

on the bed, the women who are decorated with holiday perfumes.

(*Rig Ved.* M-7, S-55, R-1 to 8)

Apart from Rishi Vashisht saying so several other Rishis were faced with a similar situation. There was a threat to their life and they fled the place in secret, staying away from the sight of their adversaries, who seem to be keeping an eye on them. Rishi Kanav Ghaur has stated this.

1. Pushan, convey us over the path, remove the wicked (obstructor of the way). Son of the cloud deity go before us.
2. If a wicked (adversary), Pushan a robber, or one who delights in evil, points out to us, do you drive him from the path.
3. Drive him far away, apart from the path, the hinderer of our journey, a thief, a deceiver.
4. Lead us past our opponents; conduct us by an easy path; know Pushan, how to protect us on this (journey).
5. Lead us where there is abundant fodder; let there be no extreme heat by the way; Pushan, know how to protect us on this (journey).

(All from *Rig Ved.* M-1, S-42)

It appears that several of the religious leaders of the Manavs were imprisoned, of whom some seem to have escaped to reach India to record their tale in the *Veds.* These Richas say so.

1. Who have disunited my people from the cattle? Was there not for them an invincible protector? May those who have seized upon that (people) perish, for he who knows (our wishes) approaches to (protect) the cattle.
2. Enemies have secreted among mortals, the king of living beings, the asylum of men; may the prayers of Atri set him free; may those who revile us be reviled.
3. You have liberated the fettered Shunah Shepa from a thousand stakes, for he was patient in endurance; so Agni, free us from our bonds, having sat down here (at our sacrifice), intelligent offerer of oblations.

(*Rig Ved.* M-5, S-2, R-5 to 7)

4. Open, Vanaspati, like the womb of a parturient female; hear

Ashwins my invocations; set Sapt Vadhri free.

5. Ashwins, by your devices sunder the wicker-work (for the liberation of the) terrified, imploring Rishi Sapt Vardhri.

(Rig Ved. M-5, S-78, R-5 and 6)

The most detailed account of a Rishi having been imprisoned and fettered, who somehow escaped to come to India, comes from the legend of Shunah Shepa. The story is found in the Brahman literature and has also been mentioned in the *Ramayan,* wherein it has been portrayed as a case of a proposed human sacrifice, with Shunah Shepa as the victim. As the story is very long, an abridged version is given here.

> Harish Chandra, the son of Vedhash of the Ikshavaku race, a king, did not have a son. Narad told him, 'Go and beg of Varun, that he might favour you with a son (promising him at the same time) to sacrifice to him this son when born.' He went to Varun, praying, 'Let a son be born to me; I will sacrifice him to thee.' Then a son, Rohit, was born to him. Varun said to him, 'A son is born to thee, sacrifice him to me.' Harish Chandra delayed it for one reason or other till the child was a youth. Varun then said, 'He has now received the armour, sacrifice him to me.' After having been spoken thus, he called his son and told him, 'Well, my dear, to him who gave thee unto me, I will sacrifice thee now.' But he said, 'No, no,' took his bow and absconded into the wilderness. After he had roamed for about a year, Varun seized Harish Chandra and his belly swelled.
>
> Rohit wandered in the forest for six years. He met the Rishi Ajigart, the son of Suyavash, who was starving in the forest. He had three sons, Shunah Puccha, Shunah Shepa and Shunah Langula. He told him, 'Rishi! I give thee a hundred cows for I will ransom myself from being sacrificed with one of these (thy sons).' They agreed upon the middle one, Shunah Shepa. He then gave for him a hundred cows, left the forest, entered the village, and brought him before his father, saying, 'O my dear father! By this boy I will ransom myself from being

sacrificed.' He then approached Varun the king and said, 'I will sacrifice him to thee!' He said, 'Well, let it be done.' At the sacrifice they could not find a person willing to bind him to the sacrificial post. Ajigart said, 'Give me another hundred cows and I will bind him.' They gave him a hundred cows and he bound him. They could not find a slaughterer. Ajigart said, 'Give me another hundred and I will kill him.' They gave him another hundred and he whetted the knife. Shunah Shepa then got aware that they were going to butcher him like an animal. 'Well,' said he, 'I will seek shelter with the gods.' As he repeated one verse after the other, the fetters were falling off, and the belly of Harish Chandra became smaller. And after he had done repeating the last verse, all the fetters were taken off and Harish Chandra restored to health. The priests now said to Shunah Shepa, 'Thou art now only ours (thou art a priest like us).' From that time he was Devrat, Vishwmitra's son. Ajigart said, 'Come son we will call you. Thou art known as a seer of Ajigart's family.' Vishwmitra said, 'Do not become his son again, but enter my family as my son.'

(*Aitarey Brahman*. Book VII, Chapter 3)

It appears that the authors in the *Aitarey Brahman* had the compulsion of explaining why Shunah Shepa was in fetters, despite being a worshipper of Indra and Varun. By then the memory of what had happened in Iran had been lost. It was not remembered why the Rishi had been fettered and all that could be speculated to explain it is what has been given in the story. In the *Rig Ved*, the Richas coming from Shunah Shepa do show that he was fettered, but they do not say that this was for offering him as a victim in a sacrifice. What emerges from them is, in fact, just the opposite. The relevant Richas from Shunah Shepa on this are here.

1. Of whom, or of which divinity of the immortals, shall we invoke the auspicious name? Who will give us to the great Aditi, that I may again behold my father and mother.

2. Let us invoke the auspicious name of Agni, the first divinity of

the immortals, that he may give us to the great Aditi, and that I may behold my father and mother.

(Rig Ved. M-1, S-24, R-1 and 2)

3. Praising you with (devout) prayer, I implore you for that which the institutor of sacrifice solicits with oblations; Varun, undisdainful, bestow a thought upon us; much-lauded, take not away our existence.

4. This your praise they repeat to me by night and by day; the knowledge speaks to my heart; may he whom the fettered Shunah Shepa has invoked, may the royal Varun set us free.

5. Shunah Shepa, seized and bound to the three-footed tree, has invoked the son of Aditi, may the regal Varun, wise and irresistible, liberate him; may he let loose his bonds.

6. Varun, loosen for me the upper, the middle, the lower band; so son of Aditi, shall we through faultlessness in the worship become freed from sin.

(Rig Ved. M-1, S-24, R-11 to 13 and 15)

7. Loose us from the upper bonds, untie the centre and the lower, that we may live.

(Rig Ved. M-1, S-25, R-21)

8. Cast asleep (the two messengers of Yam); looking at each other, let them sleep, never waking; Indra, of boundless wealth, enrich us with thousands of excellent cows and horses.

9. May those who are our enemies, slumber, and those, O hero who are our friends, be awake; Indra, of boundless wealth, enrich us with thousands of excellent cows and horses.

10. Indra destroy this ass, (our adversary) praising you with such discordant speech; and do you, Indra, of boundless wealth enrich us with thousands of excellent cows and horses.

(Rig Ved. M-1, S-29, R-3 to 5)

These Richas show that Rishi Shunah Shepa is in danger. He is praying that he may be able to see his parents again. The Richas four and five show him fettered and tied to a tree. This is all that has come from him in recalling his tale of horror. The authors of the *Aitarey Brahman* have taken the clue from these and have proceeded to weave a story of a proposed human sacrifice. This is an incorrect understanding, not only because human sacrifice was never practised by the Aryans as neither the *Veds* nor the *Avesta* mention it, but what has been stated in the Richas here would contradict this proposition. In the eighth Richa the Rishi is praying that the people around him should fall asleep. In the next, he is praying that the enemies should slumber and the friends should be awake. It is obvious that he is amidst enemies, but also has some well-wishers. If it had been a situation as portrayed in the *Aitarey Brahman*, there would not have been a necessity for him to flee in secret, once Varun had removed his fetters and had set him free. That would have been an amicable end wherein the sacrificer as well as the victim would have been happy as the god had refused to accept a human as an offering. The story of the *Aitarey Brahman* presents a happy ending as Shunah Shepa has been shown to have been accepted as a priest and admitted to the family of Vishwmitra as his son. His father, too, was keen to take him back, but this has not been agreed to by Shunah Shepa. He had all the reasons to complain of the conduct of his father who had not only sold him but had fettered him when no one else was willing to do so, and was also ready to immolate him like an animal when again no one else was prepared to do so. This would contradict the first two Richas wherein Shunah Shepa is praying that he may be able to see his father and mother again. This would not have been necessary as per the story of the *Aitarey Brahman* as his father was right there fettering him and whetting a knife to immolate him. Considering this legend to be a case of a proposed human sacrifice, is an evident error on the part of the *Aitarey Brahman*. From these Richas it is evident that he has been fettered by an enemy and with the help of some well-wishers is running away from confinement. Who the enemy was, gets revealed in the tenth Richa, which says that 'he praises you with a discordant speech.' Though Indra has been referred to in this Richa, it appears to be a reference only to God. In the *Veds*, the Asurs have been called 'babblers', an indication of their language not having remained chaste Sanskrit, something that has been mentioned earlier. The enemy with a discordant speech is none other than the

Asurs. It is a case of persecution in Iran after the conversion of Vistasp and the adoption of a state policy to suppress the religion of the Dev worshippers. Shunah Shepa has been lucky to escape. The case of Mani shows that Persia had the tradition of keeping prisoners in fetters, often till death. Shunah Shepa seems to be in a similar situation and had all the reasons to be thankful to Varun to have survived.

Subandhu was not as lucky as Shunah Shepa. The legend about him says that there were four brothers, Bandhu, Subandhu, Srutbandhu and Viprabandhu, all of whom were priests of Raja Asamati. The Raja having dismissed them appointed two others who were Magavins. At this, the four brothers were offended and instituted ceremonies for the destruction of the Raja. Hearing this, the Magavins put Subandhu to death on which the other three brothers have composed Sukts of the *Rig Ved* praying for his return and their own safety. This legend can be said to have retained the original position accurately. It states that the Vedic priests were dismissed by a king and replaced by Magavin priests whereafter for performing some Vedic ritual Subandhu was killed. The use of the word Magavin in it is significant as it is very close to Magi. It is noteworthy here that though the historians have called this entire Aryan tribe Magi, the *Veds* have not used this term anywhere. The word is of the Avesta language and is the corrupted form of the Sanskrit word 'Margi'. The word 'marg' in Sanskrit means a path and 'margi' means a person who follows the path. It is only in the *Avesta* that it is found to have been used by the composers for themselves wherein it does not include the Manavs or the Dev worshippers in the Magi identity. It appears that to start with, only the Asurs called themselves Magi as distinct from the Dev worshippers. The passage from the *Avesta* that shows this is given here.

> Let not our waters be for the man of ill intent, of evil speech, or deeds, or conscience; let them not be for the offender of a friend, not for an insulter of a Magian, nor for one who harms the workmen, nor for one who hates his kindred.
>
> (Yasna LXV)

A few Richas from the hymns ascribed to the three surviving Bandhu brothers that speak of Subandhu's fate are mentioned here.

1. Let us not depart, Indra, from the path; let us not (depart) from the sacrifice of the offerers of the libation; let not our adversaries remain (in our place).

    (*Rig Ved.* M-10, S-57, R-1)

2. We call upon the spirit (of Subandhu) with the Som appropriated to the progenitors, with the praises of the Pitras.

3. May (your) spirit (Subandhu) come back again to perform pious acts; to exercise strength; to live; and long to see the sun.

    (*Rig Ved.* M-10, S-57, R-3 and 4)

4. Although your spirit has gone far away to Yam, the son of Vivasvat, we bring back that (spirit) of your to dwell here, to live (long).

    (*Rig Ved.* M-10, S-58, R-1)

5. Give not us up, Som, to death; may we long behold the rising sun; may old age brought on by passing days be happy; may Nirriti depart far off.

6. Asuniti, give us back the (departed) spirit; extend our life that we may live (long); establish us that we may (long) behold the sun; do you cherish the body with the ghee (that we have offered).

    (*Rig Ved.* M-10, S-59, R-4 and 5)

7. May the earth restore the (departed) soul to us; may the divine heaven, may the firmament (restore it); may Som restore the body to us; may Pushan restore to us speech, which is prosperity.

8. May the great heaven and earth, the parents of sacrifice, (grant) happiness to Subandhu; heaven and earth, remove all iniquity; let heaven and earth (take away) iniquity; may no ill ever approach you.

    (*Rig Ved.* M-10, S-59, R-7 and 8)

9. This (Agni) your mother, this your father, this the giver of life to you, has arrived; come back Subandhu, to this your (body) that is capable of motion. Come forth.

    (*Rig Ved.* M-10, S-60, R-7)

The first Richa is significant as in it the three surviving brothers are praying 'let us not depart from the path; let us not depart from the sacrifice of the offerer of the libations; let not our adversaries remain in our place.' This shows that the composers of the hymns were under pressure to leave their religious practices, which were of offering oblations in a sacrifice. Their adversaries had occupied their place because of which they were feeling intimidated and seeking protection from the gods. The remaining Richas confirm that Subandhu has been killed as has been stated in the legend about him.

The migration of the Indo-Aryans could have continued for centuries, till at least trade between the two countries was flourishing. This was not only because it was so easy to reach, but also because they would have remained in contact with each other through traders and seamen. This was perhaps the easiest leg of the journey from the North Pole. After the first exposure, when Rishi Vashisht was apprehensive about the kind of reception he would get, they would have known how comfortable life would be and how hospitable the people were. In the Sapt Sindhu, they settled down in cities and towns. It is tragic that history books say that the Aryans invaded India and destroyed the Indus Valley Civilization. They were not kings or military commanders. They had neither an army nor weapons. They were priests, traders and people engaged in other urban occupations in Iran, fleeing in the face of religious persecution. They travelled in Indian trade ships and were brought to Indian cities by Indian traders and sailors. Not only was their coming not an invasion, even the migration was not without the consent of the people of the Sapt Sindhu. The towns and cities of Sapt Sindhu were very well-administered. This is evident from how they were maintained for such a long time. It would not have been possible for anyone to come and settle down without the consent of the government in such well-administered units and there is evidence to show that the Indo-Aryans, on arrival in India, settled down in the cities only. The circumstances in which these Aryans came to India show that they were aware that they would be welcome. For them, fleeing from Iran was a compulsion, but coming to India was a choice, as they had several options before them. They could have gone to Turan, where Ajashrava was the king and patron of people of their religion. He continued to rule for several decades after the war with Vistasp as he is reported to have killed Zoroaster when the latter was seventy-seven years old. They could have gone to Egypt, which was a flourishing civilization and was closer. They could have gone to Greece, where some of them had gone. Amongst these options, which were easier, they chose Sapt Sindhu, a choice that reveals that they felt that it was the best for them. Evidently, they were in contact with a few prominent traders from India who welcomed their coming and offered assistance. It is only in this scenario that they could have settled down in the towns and cities of the Sapt Sindhu. This peaceful arrival in India of a highly accomplished group of people has been portrayed in history as an invasion by hordes of semi-literate, blood-thirsty tribes on horseback with iron weapons, who considered cities to be the creation of demons and so destroyed them, while the civilized people of the Sapt Sindhu were too perplexed at the very sight of such uncivilized behaviour that they not only got beaten but left the place and moved away.

There is evidence in the *Veds*, as well as that external to them to establish that the Indo-Aryans did not invade India, but came with the consent of the Harappan people. First, the evidence from the *Veds*, which have these Richas composed shortly after their arrival in the Sapt Sindhu.

1. Who, Agni, among your (followers) are the imprisoners of foes who among them are the protectors (of men) the splendid distributors of gifts. Who among them defend the assertion of untruth? Who are the encouragers of evil deeds?
2. These your friend, Agni, everywhere dispersed, were formerly unhappy, but are again fortunate. May they who, with (censorious) words, impute fraudulent (practices) to me, who pursues a straight path, bring evil upon themselves.

(*Rig Ved.* M-5, S-12, R-4 and 5)

These Richas are ascribed to Rishi Sutambhar Aitarey. Evidently, he is a first-generation migrant. He has seen Iran and has gone through the turbulent times. In the first Richa he is speaking of the two sides. On one side are those who imprison their foes and protect fellow beings and on the other are those who defend the assertion of untruth and encourage evil deeds. The Rishi is remembering the bad days that are over. The second is significant. It shows that the Indo-Aryans on arrival were dispersed. This indicates that the settlement of the arriving population had been managed by the administrative machinery of the towns and cities of Sapt Sindhu. The entire population concentrating in one place would have made the municipal services collapse and cause difficulties. They spread the people over the place to ensure that no single town or city gets over burdened with the additional population. This, not only speaks of the efficiency of the governance of Sapt Sindhu, but also shows that they had accepted and assimilated the new population from the very beginning. The arriving population being dispersed also goes to prove that they were not invaders. In an invasion, the invaders are unsure of their position and feel the threat of being attacked by the local population, to counter which they stick together and often make protective structures for themselves, like forts. The Aryan population felt no such necessity and was secure even though dispersed. The Richa proceeds to say that they were formerly unhappy, but are fortunate again, an indication that the Rishi who composed it had himself come to Sapt Sindhu and was not a descendant of one of the migrants. As he is remembering the earlier unhappy times and is grateful to be fortunate again, it is not a situation in which refugees fleeing Iran had somehow found a place to survive, but a situation in which the host has made an effort to make them comfortable. The Richa concludes with the Rishi cursing the people who had censured him and had imputed fraudulent practices to him. This reveals the identity of the people because of whom these friends of Agni were formerly unhappy.

Apart from these Richas which directly speak of what the Indo-Aryans received on arrival, there are several passages in the *Veds* which show that they were living with the Harappan people. In some of them they appear to be in their cities. A few such passages are given here.

1. I repeat with a (willing) mind, the unreluctant praises of Bhavya, dwelling on the banks of the Sindhu, a prince of unequalled

(might), desirous of renown, who has enabled me to celebrate a thousand sacrifices.

2. From which generous prince, soliciting (my acceptance), I Kakshivat, unhesitatingly accepted a hundred nishkas, a hundred vigorous steeds, a thousand bulls, whereby he has spread his imperishable fame through heaven.

3. Ten chariots drawn by baysteeds and carrying my wives stood near me, given to me by Svanay and a thousand and sixty cows followed. These, after a short interval of time, did Kakshivat, deliver (to his father).

4. Forty bay horses (harnessed) to the chariot, lead the procession in front of a thousand (followers). The Pajras, the kinsmen of Kakshivat, rub down the high-spirited steeds, decorated with golden trappings.

5. I have accepted a prior grant (kinsmen) for you; three and eight harnessed chariots and cattle of incalculable value, may the kindred Pajras, like well-disposed relations, be desirous of acquiring renown by their abundant offerings.

(*Rig Ved.* M-1, S-126, R-1 to 5)

6. Is it Indra who has given to the donor (of the oblation) so much affluence? Is it the auspicious Saraswati (who has given) the treasure? Or Chitra, is it you?

7. Verily, Raja Chitra, giving his thousands and tens of thousands, has overspread (with his bounty) those other petty princes who rule along the Saraswati, as Parjanya (overspreads the earth) with rain.

(*Rig Ved.* M-8, S-21, R-17 and 18)

8. The Sindhu is rich in horses, rich in chariots, rich in clothes, rich in gold ornaments, well-made, rich in food, rich in wool ever fresh, abounding in Silama plants, and the auspicious river wears honey-growing (flowers).

(*Rig Ved.* M-10, S-75, R-8)

The first five Richas have the name and clan of the Rishi who composed them. Rich and influential persons with the names Bhavya and Svanay living on the banks of the Sindhu have given him very expensive gifts, to be shared with his kinsmen. He has called them princes, which could have been titles in the democracy of the time. These gifts he has received on behalf of his father to whom he delivers them. His kinsmen, the Pajras, are following the gifts in a procession as this grant has been received by him on their behalf. This shows that in each city or town where they settled, the administrative unit gave a grant to them collectively, to start life anew. It was left to the clan elder to distribute it amongst the members. An exaggeration of what was received is apparent, but still it shows the generosity of the hosts. The sixth and the seventh Richas speak of a grant given by Raja Chitra, who lived on the banks of the Saraswati river. The seventh provides additional information that Sapt Sindhu was not a single political unit, but had small independent political entities, as it speaks of several other petty princes who, it says, rule along the Saraswati. The last Richa is a description of a city on the Indus, most likely Mohenjo Daro. It has been called 'well-made', an appreciation of the town planning and the amenities provided in it. This is not a description by someone who was part of a marauding tribe, which had come and destroyed the civilization. Nor is it a description of a city which has been ravaged and destroyed by an invader. It does not match with the descriptions of Indra destroying the 'Purs' of Asurs. It is the description of a city in all its glory with different articles of trade and luxuries. The Rishi who composed it is appreciative of the place and is, in all likelihood, an inhabitant there. The word 'nishka' appears here. It seems to be the name of the currency of the time.

Though after some time people of the Sapt Sindhu called themselves Aryans, there is a reference in the *Rig Ved* which shows that even initially when the distinction of Aryan and non-Aryan was there, the non-Aryans had adopted Aryan religious practices and were inter-marrying. These Richas from the *Rig Ved* speak of it.

1. I, the sage, accepted the hundred from the Das Balbutha, the cowherd. We here are yours, O Vayu. Those who have Indra and the gods for protection rejoice (through your favour).

2.   This tall maiden, adorned with gold, is led towards me, Vash, the son of Ashwa.

(*Rig Ved.* M-8, S-46, R-32 and 33)

Balbutha is a non-Aryan and has been called a Das, a term earlier applied to Asurs, but evidently continuing to mark a distinction between the Aryans and non-Aryans now. Perhaps he has given the priest a dakshina or a gift for conducting religious rituals. This is something which could not have happened in Central Asia because there the Devs and the Asurs were of the same Aryan stock. The difference was due to the differences in the mode of sacrifice. As soon as someone from one side gave up the practices of that side and switched over to those of the other, he became a follower of that side and terms like Das, Dasyu, Ahi and Vritra ceased to be applicable to him. An Asur became a Dev or vice versa. In this case, Balbutha is a non-Aryan and though he has offered a sacrifice in which a Vedic priest has been engaged, he has still been called a Das. This is an indication that the Indo-Aryans were not only living with the people of the Sapt Sindhu, they had become their priests, as the people had started adopting their religion. Very soon this distinction faded away and everyone became an Aryan and the Vedic religion merged with the religion of the people. By the time Sapt Sindhu was abandoned and the centre of the Indian civilization shifted to the Gangetic plains, all people claimed themselves to be Aryans. The second Richa shows that the Rishi, who has given his name as Vash is getting married, apparently to a non-Aryan maiden. There is no mention in this Richa whether the maiden is an Aryan or a non-Aryan, but several Richas before this, speak of gifts received by the priest from people who appear to be non-Aryan and the Richa just before names the donor as Balbutha and calls him a Das. The Sukta is apparently an account of the Rishi's interaction with non-Aryans in which he received a lot of gifts and finally, a wife.

Apart from the evidence from the *Veds* showing a very comfortable arrival of the Indo-Aryans in Sapt Sindhu and the warm welcome received by them, the theory of invasion gets disproved by the fact that no account of war is left in these scriptures that could be said to have been fought in India in the process of such an invasion. All wars that have been described in the *Veds* and are quoted for the said invasion, with Indra destroying the strong cities of Asurs and killing Vritra and others had already been fought and are accounted for in Central Asia. All Asurs who have been named like Shambar, Pipru, Chumuri, Dhuni, etc. had already been killed much before the Indo-Aryans came to India. The only war that is left unaccounted in the *Veds* is that which is said to have been fought between Indra and Krishna. In this, the error in understanding it as a separate war is evident. The account from the *Rig Ved* of this war is given here.

1. For him the dawns prolonged their risings; for Indra the nights uttered auspicious voices by night; for him the waters, the mothers, the seven rivers, stood offering an easy passage for men to cross over.

2. By him the thrower, unaided, were pierced asunder the thrice seven tablelands of the mountains heaped together neither god nor mortal could do what he, the showerer, in his full grown strength has done.

3. When, Indra, you grasp in your arms your pride humbling thunderbolt to smite Ahi, when the mountain clouds loudly roar and the cows loudly bellow, then the Brahmans offer their worship to Indra.

4. All the gods who were your friends forsook you, flying away at the snorting of Vritra; O Indra, let there be friendship to you with the Maruts, then do you conquer all these hostile armies.

5. These sixty-three Maruts were worthy of sacrifice who were nourishing your vigour like cows gathered together; we come to you, do you grant us our portion; so will we produce strength in you by this offering.

6. Send forth your praise to mighty Indra who is borne by the hymns, as (a sailor sends a traveller) in a ship across the rivers; bring to me by your rites that wealth which belongs to him, the renowned and beneficent; may he speedily give much wealth.

7. The swift-moving Krishna with ten thousand (demons) stood on the Anshumati; by his might Indra caught him snorting (in the water); he benevolent to man, smote his malicious (band).

8. I have seen the swift-moving (demon) lurking in an inaccessible place, in the depths of the Anshumati river; (I have seen) Krishna standing there as (the sun) in a cloud; I appeal to you, showerer, conquer him in battle.

9. Then the swift-moving one shining forth assumed his own body by the Anshumati, and Indra with Brahaspati as his ally smote the godless hosts as they drew near.

10. As soon as you were born, Indra, you were an enemy to those seven who had no enemy. You recovered the heavens and earth when concealed (in darkness); you cause joy to the mighty worlds.

11. Thunderer, you, the resolute one, did smite that unrivalled might with your bolt; you destroyed Shushna with your weapons you recovered the cows, Indra, by your wisdom.

12. You, showerer, were the mighty destroyer of the hindrances of your worshippers; you did set free the rivers that were obstructed; you did win the waters which the Dasyus had mastered.

13. He who noble in his exploits rejoices in the Som libations, he whose wrath cannot be repelled and who is wealthy as the days, he who alone performs the rites for his worshipper, he the slayer of Vritra, men say, is a match for all others.

14. Indra is the slayer of Vritra, the cherisher of men, let us invoke him worthy of invocation, with an excellent hymn; he is Maghvan, our protector, our encourager, he is the bestower of food that brings fame.

15. As soon as he was born, he, Indra, the slayer of Vritra, the chief of the Ribhus, was worthy to be invoked; he performing many sacred acts for men, is worthy to be invoked for his friends like the quaffed Som juice.

(All from *Rig Ved.* M-8, S-96)

It was necessary to quote more Richas from the Sukta because this is quoted at some places as a reference in the *Veds* of Indra's war with

Lord Krishna, just because the name Krishna is there in the seventh and eighth Richas. It is deemed to be the Vedic version of the fight between Lord Krishna and Indra, as distinct from their quarrel as is found in the *Purans*. This is incorrect as can be seen from reading the other Richas. Even otherwise this cannot be a reference to Lord Krishna because first of all, the Anshumati river cannot be the Yamuna, the river on the banks of which Lord Krishna spent his childhood. Yamuna was a new river and had got her name from the beginning. She has been mentioned by that name in the *Veds* also. Secondly, Lord Krishna, when he lived on the banks of the Yamuna was neither a king nor a military commander. He was a village boy tending cattle, who could not have had an army of ten thousand men. This is an account of Indra's war with Vritra in Arjika that has been retold by a much later composer according to his perception. The entire description matches with what had happened on that occasion and Vritra, as well as Shushna are mentioned in other Richas. It is apparent that Vritra has been called Krishna in these two Richas. This shows the perception of the Aryans about the Asurs after they had spent quite some time in India. By then their acquaintance with the Asurs was only from the scriptures, wherein they have been painted in black. The Rishis would have thought that the Asurs must have been dark-skinned as that is the image that emerges from the accounts about them. Krishna means black and this is all that is meant by the word in the two Richas where it finds mention. It does not refer to Lord Krishna and is not an account of a new war fought on Indian soil by Indra, who, in any case, had ceased to be a war god and was a rain god. The Indo-Aryans in any case had come to believe that the Asurs were dark-skinned and when they saw dark-skinned people around them, they must have believed that the Asurs were their forefathers. The following Richa shows this.

> Going to the battle, marching with easy gait, desiring the spoil, he set himself to the acquisition of all (wealth). Invincible, destroying the phallus worshippers, he won by his prowess whatever wealth (was concealed in the city) with the hundred gates.
>
> (*Rig Ved*. M-10, S-99, R-3)

Here Asurs have been called phallus worshippers, a reference to the people of Sapt Sindhu. It is evident that the dark skin of the people and all the descriptions of Asurs as the very embodiment of evil and darkness led to this misconception, as a very long period had elapsed from the time when any of them had seen an actual Asur. It is this same misconception that had led to the use of the word Krishna in the other Richas.

For the sake of argument, even if it is admitted that this war took place, it cannot be an evidence of the Aryans invading India because the location of the Anshumati river, even if it is not the Yamuna, would be outside the Sapt Sindhu. In that case, the war would have been fought deep inside Indian territory and centuries after the arrival of the Aryans because they stayed in Sapt Sindhu for several centuries before moving east to the Gangetic plains. A war fought as a part of an invasion should have been fought close to the Indian borders and on arrival of the invaders or soon thereafter.

Apart from the evidence emerging from the *Veds* to show that the Aryans did not invade India and did not destroy the Indus Valley Civilization, there is evidence, external to them, to establish the same. The first is the Varn Vyavastha and the manner in which it took shape, as distinct from what it originally was, which is reflected from the *Avesta* and subsequent Zoroastrian scriptures. Varn Vyavastha is translated as the caste system, though that is not a correct rendering of the term. Varn means colour and so a truthful meaning of it would be 'the colour scheme'. It is evident that the Indo-Aryans were losing the most distinctive part of their identity in India, the complexion of their skin, due to inter-marriages with the people of the host country. They were no longer the white race that they had been, but were different shades of white by then. The Varn Vyavastha was a desperate attempt on their part to save whatever was left of the white complexion. The Magis had the system of the four classes from very remote times. This is evident as it is found in the *Avesta* also, making it older than the time when the two sides split. However, this was based on profession and not on birth. The Indo-Aryans, as they were trying to save their complexion, aimed at preventing inter-marriages between people of different Varns and restricting marriage to the same Varn. This obviously led to the tragic consequence of Varn getting based on birth and not on the profession of a person. The passages from the Zoroastrian scriptures that give an idea about the original concept of the four classes and the identity of the professions of these classes follow.

1. And this saying, uttered by Mazda belongs to four classes (of men as its supporters).
   (Question) With what classes of men?
   (Answer) The priest, the charioteer (as the chief of warriors), the systematic tiller of the ground, and the artisan.

   (Yasna XIX)

2. The four twigs are the four classes of the religion, which are priesthood, warriorship, husbandry and artisanship. As unto the head is priesthood, unto the hand is warriorship, unto the belly is husbandry and unto the foot is artisanship.

   (Sikand-Gumanik Vigar. Chapter I)

3. And it came at another time for the conference with Auharmazd to Yim; and owing to his accepting the four classes of the religion, which are priesthood, warriorship, husbandry and artisanship, and thereby the world was improved, extended and developed.

   (Dinkard. Book VII, Chapter I)

The four classes were based on profession and these have been given as priests, warriors, farmers and artisans. The second passage declares the priests unto the head, the warriors unto the hands, the farmers unto the belly and artisans unto the foot. This concept is not seen anywhere in the *Avesta*, but is identical with the Purush Sukta of the *Rig Ved*. The book from which it has been taken, *Sikand-Gumanik Vigar*, is of the ninth century AD, several centuries after Shapur III took up the task of re-constructing the *Avesta* for which he had sent people to India and Greece to collect those parts of the *Avesta* that were not related to religion. It is possible that this concept has gone from the Purush Sukta of the *Rig Ved*, which is given here.

1. Purush, who has a thousand heads, a thousand eyes, a thousand feet, investing the earth in all directions, exceeds (it by a space) measuring ten fingers.
2. Such is his greatness and Purush is greater than even this. All beings are one-fourth of him; his other three-fourths (being) immortal (abide) in heaven.
3. When the gods performed the sacrifice with Purush as the offering, then Spring was its ghee, Summer the fuel, and Autumn the oblation.
4. They immolated as the victim upon the sacred grass Purush, born before (creation), with him the deities who were Sadhyas and those who were Rishis sacrificed.
5. When they immolated Purush, into how many portions did they divide him? What was his mouth called, what his arms, what his thighs, what were his feet called?
6. His mouth became the Brahman, his arms became the Rajanya, his thighs became the Vaishyas, the Shudra was born from his feet.
7. The moon was born from his mind; the sun was born from his eyes, Indra and Agni from his mouth, Vayu from his breath.

(All from Rig Ved. M-10, S-90)

The information from the *Avesta* shows that the four classes were priests, warriors, farmers and artisans, while the Vedic Varns of Brahman, Kshatriya, Vaishya and Shudra get translated as priests, warriors, merchants and artisans. There is a crucial difference in the third Varn which reveals the story of what was intended and what happened. The word Vaishya comes from the root 'vish', which means people. It was intended to mean the rest of the people, after the three other classes had been classified. In Central Asia, the farmers were the people left, after the other three classes had been given a distinct identity and so it was they who have been named in the *Avesta* in the class where the rest of the people had to be. In course of time, the original intention was lost and as the remaining three classes were named after the professions of the people, this class got named as the class to which the farmers belonged. The same thing was done by the Indo-Aryans in India. Here, the rest of the people turned out to be merchants. The farmers would have constituted more than 80 per cent of the population even in the commercially vibrant Sapt Sindhu. No social order can be formed ignoring such a huge proportion of a society. Farming, as a profession, has no place in the Varn Vyavastha, which would have been an impossibility if the farmers had been taken into account when the system was being introduced in India. This shows that it was only the urban population that was being considered and the rural population had been kept out of its ambit, as a result, the rest of the people, were found to be merchants, who got classified as Vaishyas instead of what had happened in Central Asia. It goes to show that the Indo-Aryans were only in towns and cities of the Indus Valley Civilization and it was only here that they had inter-married and were now faced with the problem of salvaging their complexion, in which they fought a losing battle. The Varn Vyavastha remained limited to urban areas for a sufficiently long time for the term Vaishya getting identified with merchants and merchants alone, losing its original meaning as rest of the people, as a result, when the system got extended to the entire population, perhaps when the people moved to the Gangetic plains or after the end of the cities, the farmers were not in its ambit. The consequences were disastrous, as the entire farming population, except those who had already acquired a Varn and so retained it even after becoming farmers, got classified as Shudra by sheer default, a tragedy unparalleled in history, as the population that was the backbone of India's glorious achievements and constituted more than 80 per cent of the people, became Shudra without that being the intention of the people who introduced it, and suffered all the consequences that followed because the system was based on birth instead of profession due to the intention of the Indo-Aryans to prevent inter-marriages and retain the shades of white that had remained by then in their complexion. Though there are a few references in the *Purans* that have put farmers in the Varn Vaishya, in place of merchants, this never really happened in the country. As firmly fixed social groups emerged in water-tight compartments, they endeavoured to increase their privileges, all of which went in favour of the Varns higher in the order, leaving the farmers of the Indus Valley Civilization in a state where they were deprived even of the basic dignities of life as they had fallen in the Varn lowest in the order. No framer of a social order could have done such a thing. The Rishis who had initiated it in Central Asia would have shuddered at the evil consequences of the system, which got distorted due to the changed objectives and limited focus of the people who introduced it in India and its expansion to cover the entire population with changes that were detrimental to those lower down in the hierarchy. This, however, shows where the people who introduced it in India were, what the population was that was being covered, and what was the population that was not their concern—the towns and cities of the Indus Valley Civilization and nothing beyond the municipal limits. A clear evidence that on arrival in India, the Indo-Aryans settled in cities and urban areas of Sapt Sindhu and got assimilated with the local population, while their religion, language and social systems found a firm footing and became predominant. Perhaps their heritage of war and victory as contained in their holy texts was fascinating for the people of Sapt Sindhu who had a colourless history of peace and prosperity which made them want to be the inheritors of such a rich and colourful past and claim that they were Aryans, due to which, despite such a small population coming to India, by the time Sapt Sindhu was left, everyone was believed to be an Aryan.

The next evidence that emerges to establish that the Aryans did not invade India and destroy the Indus Valley Civilization comes from the fact that the institutions of the Harappan culture survived the entire period that is believed to be the time of Aryan invasion, spread and dominance. The survival of the Harappan institutions is visible most prominently in Vaishali of the Licchavis in the sixth century BC. For India, history begins with the sixth century BC, as multiple sources of information from the Buddhist and Jain scriptures also emerge for cross-checking facts, which so far were only from a single source, the Hindu scriptures. At that time north India had sixteen Janpads, which can be called independent states. Amongst them, Vaishali is unique where the institutions of the Harappan culture can be seen in a functional state. The first institution that is seen in Vaishali is the political system of the Indus Valley Civilization. All other Janpads had a monarchy while Vaishali stands alone as a republic. As a concept, democracy comes naturally to people of a small community, because all members of the community are stakeholders in its fortunes and wish to have a say in the decision making process. However, for it to evolve, to be able to handle the affairs of a state, it needs a long period of existence in which it is not required to face emergencies which are better handled by monarchies. Sapt Sindhu had been fortunate to have this peace and evolve democratic institutions. The same cannot be said for Vaishali, because in a scenario wherein all the other fifteen Janpads went through the stress that led to monarchies, Vaishali could not have been an exception. Its republican character marks its success in retaining the original political system that the people had. Even in other Janpads, the emergence of monarchies appears to be a transition from democracy as in Sanskrit, the word for the king's court is Rajsabha, which means a king's assembly. There used to be a Sabha or an assembly in the early days of the monarchies. It had Sabhasads as members, which means members of the assembly and not courtiers. Though all decisions were to be taken by the king, he was expected to take those of importance after a discussion in the Rajsabha, where he was expected to honour the wishes of the members. It is apparent that the Sabha was an institution of the days before the monarchy and when the Sabha decided to have one of its members to be always available to take decisions and face emergencies, it had a chief amongst equals. As a result, the king was there and so was the Sabha and in decision-making, both had an active role. All major issues came before the Sabha with the king at its head, though the king had the freedom to take decisions in the absence of the Sabha that could be deliberated upon in it later. However, as time passed, the king became powerful, while the Sabha faded away but the word for a king's court remained the same. The king's position became autocratic and people before him became courtiers and not Sabhasads. The chief amongst equals became the chief.

Vaishali was not a monarchy and was a functional republic in the sixth century BC. It cannot be called a democracy but only an oligarchy, as all the people were not involved in the power structure, but that was perhaps the structure of the political system of the Indus Valley Civilization also. A group of prominent merchants forming the power structure was replaced by a group of prominent Kshatriyas doing so. Individually they were also called Raja, a term used for the king in other states, but there were several of them who together did what the king alone did elsewhere. Unfortunately, Vaishali's existence was wiped out by the expanding Magadh Empire just as history had started to emerge in India, otherwise it would have given an idea about the functioning of the political institutions of the Harappan people. The republic of the Licchavis at Vaishali was not just a mere state somehow trying to cope with the changing times and situation but was a powerful entity, as powerful as Magadh with which it had several encounters before finally going down. The early decades of Magadh's imperial ambitions were more or less devoted to the subjugation of the Licchavis in which the republic was able to resist its intrusions for a very long time. Its power is a testimony of the efficiency of the democratic institutions running its affairs. Evidently, the institutions were deep-rooted and had a long tradition behind them because of which they were as efficient as the monarchies of the time. Though Vaishali was the only republic big enough to be counted in the sixteen Janpads, there were several smaller ones in the region north of the Ganga, including that of the Shakyas to which Buddha belonged. All these functional democracies that are seen in the sixth century BC represent the political institutions of the Harappan people. Magadh did finally consume all of them, as it consumed the monarchies also, in the process of becoming an empire.

The next institution of the Indus Valley Civilization that is seen in Vaishali is the Jain religion, which was very strong there. Lord Mahavir was born in a princely family of the Licchavis and the religion had Vaishali as a very important centre for a long time. Many scholars believe that Mahavir was the founder of the Jain religion, though the Jains themselves do not subscribe to this view. They believe that he was the twenty-fourth Tirthankar, a word that can be translated as the founding saint of the religion. Apart from the terracotta figures found in the Harappan sites which are in a posture in which the later Jain saints have been portrayed, the interaction of Buddha and Mahavir shows that Mahavir was not the founder of Jainism and it was a much older religion. The meeting of Buddha and Mahavir at Rajgrih is reported in the Sutta Pitak, wherein Buddha has addressed Mahavir as Niganth, a Pali word for the Sanskrit Nirgranth, which means without a book or without scriptures. Buddha could not have called Mahavir, Niganth, if he had been the founder of the religion, because till then even Buddhism, of which Buddha was the founder, was without books or scriptures, as the earliest Suttas were recorded in the First Buddhist Council, which was held shortly after his demise. A religion may or may not have a book of its teachings during the lifetime of its founder, but normally over a period of time it does have them. The Jain religion was called a Nirgranth religion as they had a tradition of not recording scriptures. Teachings of saints were passed down from generation to generation but not in the form of a fixed text. When the Jains finally recorded their scriptures they are in Prakrit, due to which it is often believed that while Buddha preached in Pali, the language of the Buddhist canonical works, Mahavir preached in Prakrit, the language of their scriptures. Here an important point is missed that both Buddha and Mahavir were contemporaries and preached in the language of the people. The area in which they were preaching was the same. It was the same Rajgrih, the same Vaishali, the same Shravasti, where both were active. The people of the same area could not have had two different languages at the same time. It is obvious that the language in which both were preaching was Pali, as that is the language in which the initial Buddhist scriptures are. The Jain scriptures were recorded in the Third Jain Council held at Vallabhi in AD 453, about 980 years after the death of Mahavir. Till then, the teachings would have been passed down from generation to generation wherein, there being no fixed text, the language would have been of the current teacher. As centuries moved on, the language of the people changed and so would have been the language of the teachers, without anyone realizing it. By the time the scriptures were recorded, almost a thousand years after Mahavir, the language of the people was Prakrit and not Pali, because of which that is the language that has been used.

Even the language of the later Buddhist scriptures shows that Pali had ceased to be the language of the people, because their later literature is in Sanskrit. This difference in the language of the Buddhist and the Jain scriptures goes to establish that people were justified in calling the Jains Niganth or Nirgranth. They were really without books, but this trend did not start from Mahavir but was much earlier, to justify Buddha addressing him as Niganth.

No religion can acquire its identity with the name Niganth if it is developing in isolation. This name can emerge only in a situation wherein it is developing alongside some other religion, which had books. This was the Vedic religion which had the *Veds*, though still in an oral tradition, but as a fixed text. The Jain religion was being practised by the people parallel to the Vedic religion for which it acquired the name Nirgranth and Niganth. The Indo-Aryans and the *Veds* were coming from the Saraswati and the Indus basins and so would have to be the Jain religion, which is seen to have a very strong centre in Vaishali.

The third thing amongst the Licchavis of the sixth century BC which appears to be a legacy of the Indus Valley Civilization is the legend of Amrapali, the Nagar Vadhu or the city bride of Vaishali. Amrapali was the most beautiful girl of her time. The Council of the Licchavis decided that as the most beautiful girl is married to the king and in a republic as all of them were kings, she has to be married to all of them. As a result, she was made a courtesan, an absolutely outrageous act, which went unprotested, as well as uncondemned. The fact that the literature of the time treated it as nothing out of the ordinary, shows it to be an established custom. It has to come from somewhere. On the other hand, in the finds of the Indus Valley Civilization there is a bronze statuette, which has been named 'the Dancing Girl of Mohenjo Daro'. The same girl, in the same posture, has been found sketched on a terracotta tablet, a repetition which means that this is not a stray creation of an artist, but is picturing an event of significance. The girl has a story to tell which has to be listened to. She has her right arm resting on her hip, while the left is hanging loosely by her side and her left leg is moved a little forward as she holds her head up. She wears an elaborate hair dress and a necklace with bangles on her arm, but is unclad. By no stretch of imagination can this be called a dancing pose and she has unjustly been named a dancing girl, just because she is naked. The pose in which she stands, is a posture which people take when quarrelling, especially with a group. The girl has evidently been depicted quarrelling. As she is quarrelling in a state of undress, the cause of the quarrel has to be related to it. It cannot be a case where she was unclad and an intruder barged in because of which she is fighting with him, because in such a situation she would have first covered herself before coming out to sort out the person. A significant thing in this figurine is that the girl is wearing a lot of ornaments and her hair has been done very meticulously, as if it was an occasion. A lady normally does not put on ornaments and make her hair before wearing clothes, she normally first puts on clothes. As this girl has her hair done and has ornaments on, it can be said that she was clothed when she came out of her house, but is now without them. The reason for her being upset is, therefore, apparent. She has been disrobed.

In between Amrapali and the lady of Mohenjo Daro, there is a third case in India's past having similarity, that of the disrobing of Draupadi in the *Mahabharat*. This is a case wherein the Pandavs, the rulers of Indraprasth, were invited to a game of dice by Duryodhan, their inimical cousin and crown prince of Hastinapur. The Pandavs lose in gambling whatever they had, their kingdom, as well as their personal freedom. At the end they lose their wife Draupadi. Duryodhan orders her to be brought to the court and to be disrobed, while his father, King Dhritrashtra, grandfather Bhishm, teacher Dronacharya and Prime Minister Vidur were present. There are two things that call for attention, one, how could such an outrageous thing come to Duryodhan's mind and two, how could King Dhritrashtra and others remain silent spectators to the daughter-in-law of the family being dishonoured. They were all righteous people and were not powerless either, as at the end of the day they ensured that the Pandavs got back what they had lost, on condition of living in a forest for twelve years and incognito for one year. There has to be something which stopped them.

The lady of Mohenjo Daro seems to have suffered the fate of both

Amrapali and Draupadi. It seems that like Amrapali she was the most beautiful girl of her time and was called to the Council, where she went in her best attire, to be told of the decision of the Council. It could either be a custom, or the act of a few rowdy elements that she was disrobed. She felt outraged but was strong enough to fight back, which is what she is doing in the moment that has been frozen in time by the two artists. Despite being unclad in front of an assembly of men she holds her head high, because it is only people who have done wrong that hang their head in shame. The people of the assembly would have done so on hearing her words. The self-esteem that can be seen in the manner in which she holds her head and the fact that this incident had so much of an effect on the people that two artists of a culture which did not have much of an art, have immortalized the occasion, go to show that she did not abide by the decision of the Council and exercised the only other option left to her, of ending her life. The incident had enough effect to ensure that such a thing was not repeated as Amrapali did not suffer this fate, but did not wipe out the custom. It is evident that the royal court of Hastinapur was aware of it and it is this that had held back King Dritrashtra and others, as the law was on Duryodhan's side and it was left to Lord Krishna to save Draupadi.

Apart from Vaishali where several institutions and customs of the Indus Valley Civilization emerge, the religious beliefs of the Harappan people survived all over the country. The images of the Mother Goddess have been found in a very large number from the Indus Valley Civilization. She emerged as the Shakti Cult later though more prominently in the eastern region of the country. For almost a thousand years after the decline of the Harappan culture, there is virtually no reference to the Mother Goddess, but this could be because of an absence of literature from the areas in which this cult was more popular. Proto Shiv and Pashupati emerged as Shiv and became one of the most prominent divinities. Phallus worship also got associated with him as did the bull, though it cannot be said whether they were a part of the identity of Proto Shiv in the Indus Valley Civilization. The Vedic influence on these deities can also be seen, but by and large, they appear to have retained their original character in the later period also.

12

Withering Away of the Indus Valley Civilization

P EOPLE CANNOT BE BLAMED FOR concluding that the Aryans
destroyed the Indus Valley Civilization, because that is the first
impression that emerges from the scenario, as the Harappan culture
was an urban civilization, while in the Veds the Aryans introduce
themselves as rural people and in the sequence of things the urban
civilization is followed by a rural culture in the history of India. From
the history of the Indo-Aryans in Central Asia, it can be said that the
people who came to India were not rural people by the time they came
to this country. Yet that is the impression they give. In fact, if the
accounts of the *Veds* are taken as the only source to know about them,
they do not appear to be practising even agriculture properly. They
give an impression of being pastoral nomads always praying to Indra
to give them cattle and protection from the Asurs who deprived them
of cows. This was their style. They have taken the art of camouflage
to perfection. They have expressed the most subtle philosophical
thoughts, yet they want the reader not acquainted with their system
to feel that they are simple hymns in praise of a deity to be used in
rituals of a semi-literate race. They have fought wars and killed not just
fellow humans, but their own brothers and have given an account of it
in their scriptures, yet they would like the reader to believe that they
were wicked demons, that had been killed by Indra, Agni, Vishnu,
anyone but them, as they were innocent people praying for protection,

a harmless group sitting in front of fire chanting hymns. The same thing appears on this point also. They had been practising agriculture from the days of the Ribhus and had perfected it with irrigation when at Arjika. They lived in the luxuries of the Persian capital with all the wealth that the king and others would have given for their services as priests, yet when it came to giving an account, they show themselves in such poor light. The deception here has been caused by the use of the word 'cow'. But for a few places, they do not appear to be meaning the four-footed animal when they use this word. It seems to be meaning prosperity, well-being, progress, virtually everything good and desirable and not the animal that it denotes. The *Avesta*, too, gives a picture that the cow was meant in this sense amongst the Asurs also. As the same idea is found in the *Avesta*, it can be said that the trend of treating the cow as a symbol of prosperity pre-dates the break-up. It is earlier to the *Veds* because of which it is seen from the beginning. The passages from the *Avesta* which show this are stated here.

1. In the ox is our strength, in the ox is our need, in the ox is our speech, in the ox is our victory, in the ox is our food, in the ox is our clothing, in the ox is tillage that makes food grow for us.

    (Bahram Yast XX)

2. His is Grehma! And to (oppose) Thee he will establish the Kavis and (their) scheming plans. Their deeds of power are but deceits since they have come as an aid to the wicked and since he has been (falsely) said (to be set) to conquer the kine.

    (Yasna XXXII)

3. This I ask Thee, O Ahur! tell me a right. For whom has Thou made the mother kine, the producer of joy.

    (Yasna XLIV)

4. (And if Thy guardian is verily to save our wealth) how shall he obtain that joy creating-kine who is the living symbol of our peace? How shall that man obtain his wish who shall desire to see her provided with pastures for (the welfare of) this land?

    (Yasna L)

5. It is the tiller of the earth who asks this of Thee, O Ahur! striving to discover how he may gain to himself the sacred kine (and with

all wealth in herds beside).

(Yasna LI)

6. And to Thy good Kingdom, O Ahur Mazda! May we attain forever; and a good kine be Thou over us.

(Yasna XLII)

These passages that show the cow as a symbol of prosperity and its bestower, have their counterparts in the *Veds*, which are here.

1. May the divine cows, and the waters, supply you with the (sacrificial) food, for the prosperity of the people whom you favour; and may (Agni) the former protector of this (our patron), be the donor (of the oblation); eat (of the butter and curds), drink of the milk of the kine.

(*Rig Ved*. M-1, S-153, R-4)

2. What objection (can be offered) to this my assertion, that they affirm that the milk of the kine which (the milkers) obtain like water, is placed in concealment (by Vaishwanar) and cherishes the excellent and valued expanse of the wide earth.

3. I recognize this adorable assemblage of the great (deities) which from old the milk-shedding cow affects, shining above the region of water (the firmament) in secret, swift gliding, swift moving.

(*Rig Ved*. M-4, S-5, R- 8 and 9)

4. (She who is) the mother of the Rudras, the daughter of the Vasus, the sister of the Adityas, the home of ambrosia, I have spoken to men of understanding, kill not her, the sinless inviolate cow.

5. The divine cow, who herself utters speech and gives speech to others, who comes attended by every kind of utterance, who helps me for my worship of the gods, it is only the fool who abandons her.

(*Rig Ved*. M-8, S-101, R-15 and 16)

6. Which did you milk? This cow Vishw Ayu (all-life-containing). This Vishw Karma (all-effecting). This Vishw Dhaya (all-supporting). You, Indra's share with Som do I curdle. Be you the protector of the oblation, Vishnu.

(*Yajur Ved*. Adhyay I, Yajush 4)

These passages make it evident that the cow does not necessarily mean the animal that the name denotes. At many places, it means prosperity in general and at others it has a philosophic and mystic symbolism. A Rishi seeking a cow from Indra could be meaning something very different and in no way connected to the humble animal, which gives a picture of pastoral nomads for the composers of these writings. He may not be having anything to do with worldly desires and cravings and may be in search of the Ultimate, yet his hymns would not reveal this to anyone not acquainted with the code that he is using, leaving the lay worshipper happy with what he was doing. If understanding of the word cow is changed to mean general prosperity or having a mystic symbolism, the image of the Aryans as presented by the *Veds* would change. They would not appear to be pastoral nomads and would emerge in their true light, an accomplished group of people who came to India as refugees and not invaders. Without this understanding, the history of Aryans gives a picture that the country had an urban civilization, which vanished and was followed by a rural culture, while around the same time a group of people came from outside, called the Aryans, who were pastoral nomads. As the literature thereafter shows that the people believed themselves to be Aryans, the natural conclusion would be that the nomadic Aryans destroyed the urban civilization and drove away its people to settle in their place, but with a rural culture, as they were too ignorant to understand cities and did not use them even after taking them over by defeating their occupants.

The story would look incomplete with just stating that the Aryans did not destroy the Indus Valley Civilization. A word is necessary on what possibly happened. There have been difficulties in understanding this point because what has happened is very different from what has been found to have happened elsewhere in the world. In the process of development, normally the beginning is made with an agrarian economy, as to start with that is the only occupation people can have to sustain themselves. Over time, improvements lead to an agricultural surplus. This surplus is a source of strength and can be used for any purpose. Some may use it for trade to generate more wealth, some may bring out men from farms to create an army and embark on military ventures, some may build monuments while some may use the spare time to produce pieces of art. As culture is based on economy, all civilizations start as rural civilizations and gradually emerge to have small towns for the seat of governance or centres of trade. The road from villages to even small unplanned urban hamlets is very long, as only that many people can be sustained in an urban habitation as can be provided with urban occupations. The process of growth of urban occupations has been very slow, because the process of the growth of technology has been very slow till the Industrial Revolution. In the absence of technology, industries remained limited to very few areas and that too on a very small scale. In the absence of industries to create urban occupations only trade and services relating to governance were there for it. Trade had limitations because of the absence of a proper transport system and the buying capacity of people. As a result, urban habitations used to be few and far between, with only the essentials for being called urban, but without proper planning or municipal services. In structure, they could be called over-grown villages with people pursuing occupations other than agriculture. Above all, there were the fledgling institutions of governance, which were neither efficient enough to protect people able to generate wealth, from marauding raids of those who had not succeeded in doing so, nor were benevolent enough to leave them with their money. As a result, whoever made a little money faced two dangers as the money could be taken away either by robbers or by the king. As a result, money was not left at the disposal of those few who had the capacity to make more even in that difficult situation. Consequently, the journey from small unplanned urban habitations to well-planned cities with amenities for its citizens was again a long and agonizing wait. Even in civilizations, which have left very impressive monuments and palaces, these parameters of development were not met. The kings lived in a different world, the remains of which have survived, while the common people only made their contribution towards their greatness.

India unfolds a totally different picture. Before the time from when the history is known, India had a civilization that would be placed far ahead in the scale of human development but there is an absence of information about it and its links with the culture of India later. It had been long forgotten with virtually no trace even in the available literature, till its remains were found about a century ago in archaeological excavations. The picture that emerges from its ruins is astonishing. At a time when people elsewhere were somehow trying to meet their requirements, these people were producing massive agricultural surpluses. At a time when most people were either nomads or did not venture out of their homes, these people had built ships to venture into the sea to carry this surplus to lands that were prepared to buy it. At a time when most people knew nothing about trade except a little barter, these people had developed a medium of trade with which they generated wealth for the country. At a time when most people lived in houses which were nothing beyond shelters from rain and wind, these people had houses of bricks in well-planned cities, which not only had good and straight roads, but also drains. At a time when most parts of the world did not even have a proper agrarian economy, these people had a commercial economy. To top it all, they had governance efficient enough to ensure peace and continuity for such a long period that their cities survived without much of a change for over a thousand years. They may not have left behind pyramids and palaces, but the level of development that the inartistic and utilitarian brick houses of Mohenjo Daro and Harappa show, is unparalleled in the ancient world.

Though information about these people starts from the commercial civilization of Indus valley, it has to be preceded by a rural civilization of an earlier period, because the process can start only with an agrarian economy. There is not even the slightest trace of this period, but it has to be assumed that there was a long period of agricultural buoyancy, because without that what is seen could not have been possible. Before the dawn of the urban civilization, these people would have made substantial progress in at least three spheres, as they are the foundations of what followed, agriculture, which in their case was without iron, ship-building with which trade became possible and political institutions which ensured the progress to be well-planned and trade to flourish without molestation from robbers. Ship-building is very significant at this early stage as they had built sea-worthy ships to sail to the Middle East. This involves an important technological breakthrough. Normally boats are made with a flat bottom. A ship made on the same design does not survive in the sea because waves rock the ships. In this rocking, the front and the rear of the ship are alternately raised above the water. Whenever an end of the ship rises, the raised portion does not get the support of water and becomes a free lever and the point in the body of the ship which holds its weight becomes the fulcrum. If the sea is violent, the ship gets rocked violently and a longer portion of its ends rises above the water. In a flat-bottomed ship, this longer portion raised above the water would be horizontally at a greater distance from the fulcrum. This increased horizontal distance of the weight from the fulcrum increases the load on the fulcrum and as the structure of the ship is not designed to withstand this load, the ship breaks from the middle. In a sea-worthy ship, the bottom is curved instead of being flat, because of which the ship rocks on the sea like a ball. The end of the ship, instead of rising forward rolls and rises upward, due to which, even when the sea is violent and the ship is rocked violently, the raised end is at a vertically increased distance from the fulcrum and not horizontally. As a change in the vertical distance does not affect the load on the fulcrum, this rocking does not break the ship. Though modern ships do not follow this principle, as they are too large and heavy for the sea to rock them hard enough to make the ends rise above the water, if a similar situation emerges, it has the same result. The sinking of the *Titanic* is an example, as after bruising its nose with a hit on an iceberg, when water started seeping from the front, the front became heavier and the rear started rising above the water till it reached a point when the load on the fulcrum was more than what the structure could sustain and such a massive liner split into two like a matchstick before going down. In what remote antiquity, these people mastered this design cannot be said, but without it nothing that followed could have been possible. Handling the sails was the other part of seafaring, which they would have learnt by experience.

Having reached this level of human development, the urban

civilization of India just disappeared, as if in thin air and the country is seen again at the initial stages of development with an agrarian economy and a rural culture with no signs of the commercial civilization and urban habitations. It is as if the past had been wiped out and the country had to move on the path of development once again. Wherever in the world, civilizations have been destroyed, in most cases it has been because of invasions. In such cases often the invaders have occupied the same habitations because of which the remains of the earlier civilizations have survived around the same locations. The same was thought for India, and as the Aryans were found to have come from outside, the blame went to them which got reinforced by they giving their introduction as village people always on the lookout to destroy 'Purs', which were understood to be the cities of the Indus Valley Civilization. As it is seen that the Indo-Aryans were neither invaders nor village people nor were the 'Purs' in the *Veds* the cities of the Indus Valley Civilization, the theory of invasion has to be given up and the reasons for the end of the Indus Valley Civilization have to be searched on the basis of the available facts. As all we know about this civilization is from its ruins, the causes of its end have to be found only from them.

From the location of the sites of the remains, it is seen that of more than a thousand sites, over half are along the dried up river bed of the Saraswati, much more than the number found on the Indus and its five tributaries or elsewhere. This shows that while Indus and Saraswati were the two waterways for trade, Saraswati basin contributed a major share. This was the main production area and had more than half of the total population of Sapt Sindhu. Though the two best made cities of Mohenjo Daro and Harappa were on the banks of the Indus and Ravi, the Saraswati basin was the heartland of Sapt Sindhu and perhaps the original core area of the civilization. Better cities could be a mark of a new creation where the accumulated knowledge was given an expression. As the basin of the Saraswati was the main production area for exports it was the foundation of the commercial economy of Sapt Sindhu. The Indus Valley Civilization thus had Saraswati as a major factor of its origin, growth and existence. This river is not to be seen now. It has not been heard of as flowing at any time in the known history of India. What happened to it is expressed in Sanskrit by using the word 'lupt', which means disappeared. The Saraswati river, at some point of time, disappeared and with it the very factor on which the Indus Valley Civilization depended for its existence, disappeared.

A view has been expressed in certain quarters that there was never a river with the name Saraswati and that it is the name of only a goddess. The Indian Space Research Organization had conducted a study a few years back to trace the river bed of the Saraswati, using remote sensing satellite imageries. They found it to be descending from the Shivaliks, flowing along the dry bed of the Ghaggar river near Chandigarh and flowing into Rajasthan along all the sites of the Indus Valley Civilization to finally fall in the Rann of Kutch. The evidence from the *Veds* about the Saraswati matches these findings. A few passages from the *Veds* that tell about Saraswati are here.

1. Saraswati, best of mothers, best of rivers, best of goddesses, we are as it were, of no repute; grant us mother, distinction.
    (*Rig Ved*. M-2, S-41, R-16)
2. With impetuous and mighty waves she breaks down the precipices of the mountains, like a digger for the lotus fibres; we adore for our protection, the praises and with sacred rites, Saraswati, the underminer of both her banks.
3. Destroy, Saraswati, the revilers of the gods, the offspring of the universal deluder, Brshaya; giver of sustenance, you have acquired for men the lands (seized by the Asurs), and have showered water upon them.
4. May Saraswati, who has seven sisters, who is dearest amongst those dear to us, and is fully propitiated, be ever adorable.
5. Abiding in the three worlds, comprising seven elements, cherishing the five races (of beings), she is ever to be invoked in battle.
6. She who is distinguished amongst them as eminent in greatness and in her glories; she who is the most impetuous of all the other streams; she who has been created vast in capacity as a chariot, she, Saraswati, is to be glorified by the discreet (worshipper).
    (All from *Rig Ved*. M-6, S-61)

7. May the seventh (stream), Saraswati, the mother of the Sindhu and those rivers that flow copious and fertilizing, bestowing abundance of food, and nourishing (the people) by their waters, come at once together.

(*Rig Ved.* M-7, S-36, R-6)

8. Saraswati chief and pure of rivers, flowing from the mountains to the ocean, understood the request of Nahush, and distributing riches among the many existing beings, milked for him butter and water.

(*Rig Ved.* M-7, S-95, R-2)

9. Thou chantest, Vashisht, a powerful hymn to her who is the most mighty of rivers, worship Vashisht with well-selected praises, Saraswati, who is both in heaven and earth.

(*Rig Ved.* M-7, S-96, R-1)

These Richas leave no scope for doubt that Saraswati was a river, apart from being a goddess. At places they seem to show that she was the biggest of the seven rivers. This cannot be taken at face value because at another place in the *Rig Ved*, the Indus has been said to be the biggest river. Calling her the mother of Sindhu, the chief, best and the most mighty of the rivers could perhaps be an allusion to its importance in the Sapt Sindhu rather than the flow of the water. The location and the course it followed are given in the seventh and eighth Richas. The seventh calls it the seventh stream, which shows that it was to the east of the remaining six rivers of the Sapt Sindhu. The eighth says that it flows from the mountains to the ocean, which shows that it was an independent river and did not meet the Indus like the remaining five. This description matches the findings of the Indian Space Research Organization, as that is the only passage left in the western drainage basin of the north Indian plains for an independent river to flow. The last Richa creates a doubt as, while speaking of a mighty river in the beginning it says that the Saraswati is both in heaven and earth. In the *Veds*, Arjika is referred, at places, as the heaven. It cannot be said whether the reference to Saraswati being in heaven, is a reference to the goddess in heaven or a stream in Arjika. Hints of the references meaning that Arjika had a river with the name Saraswati come from Richas at two to seven. The second mentions Saraswati in the hills, while the habitations of people in Sapt Sindhu were in plains. Several Richas also speak of a situation of conflict with the Asurs. This could have been possible only in Arjika. The possibility of one of the streams in Arjika having the name Saraswati is reflected also from a pressing desire that the Aryans had to give a river this name in India. Though they finally did name a river so, they seem to have at one stage unsuccessfully tried to name the Indus as Saraswati. The passage that shows this follows.

Five rivers flowing on their way speed onwards to Saraswati.
But then became Saraswati, a fivefold river in the land.
(*Yajur Ved*. Adhyay 34, Yajush 11)

This is a reference to the Indus with five rivers joining it, but the name given is Saraswati, showing this attempt. There is no other reference in the *Veds* to indicate that a stream in Arjika too was named Saraswati, but it looks likely. There can, however, be no doubt of it flowing in the Sapt Sindhu and that too, as a mighty river at the centre of trade activities in its most productive and populous part. As the bulk of the trade was from Saraswati basin and the river was the source of its prosperity, the disappearance of the Saraswati river has to be the cause of the end of the prosperity and, therefore, the end of the Indus Valley Civilization.

All that tradition says is that the Saraswati as a river disappeared. It does not elaborate how it happened. A river as big as what the Saraswati has been described to be, does not dry up. It only changes its course. If the course of the river, as found by the Indian Space Research Organization is examined, it would be noticed that the river enters the plains at a point very close to where the eastern drainage basin and the western drainage basin of the north Indian plains meet. Though the north Indian plains appear as a single unit, for the flow of water, it is divided into two. There is a line running across, east of Chandigarh that divides these plains into two. Water on the east of it flows east to fall in the Bay of Bengal, while that on the west flows southwest to fall in the Arabian Sea. The Saraswati used to descend onto the plains at a point very close to this, as can be seen from the dry bed of the Ghaggar river near Pinjore. A river descending onto the plains a little west would flow into the western drainage basin to become the Saraswati, while descending a little east, would flow into the eastern drainage basin to become the Yamuna. Evidently, the mishap happened in the hills. Due to natural reasons, whether an earthquake, landslide or high floods, a stream from the Saraswati found another channel in the hills, which gradually became wider and deeper, till the channel of the Saraswati became higher than it and so the water flowing into the Saraswati gradually got reduced till it became totally dry. There is a Richa in the *Rig Ved* that gives a hint that the water of the river reduced gradually. It is given here.

> When the bright fertilizing rivers flow with diminished waters, then take the overflowing Som for Indra to drink.
> (*Rig Ved*. M-8, S-69, R-10)

With no reference to the Saraswati, as a general prayer for any river, it seems to be in the backdrop of the diminished flow of water in the said river. It cannot be a reference to the diminished flow of water in a river during dry season because that is a natural and expected occurrence. Prayers are offered to ward off unnatural and unexpected occurrences. Though not in the *Veds*, there are references elsewhere which show that the Yamuna was a new river. For her it has been said that she was wayward in the beginning till Yam, her brother, drew a path for her with his plough, whereafter she follows the same path, an allusion to the time when the course of the river had not been settled. Even today at Allahabad on the confluence of the Ganga and the Yamuna, it is believed that it is not the confluence of two, but of three rivers, Ganga, Yamuna and Saraswati. It is apparent that when the belief started, the people knew that the Yamuna was carrying not only her own water, but that of the Saraswati also.

Confirmation for the existence and drying up of the river Saraswati along the hundreds of archaeological sites of the Indus Valley Civilization in Rajasthan, comes from a very unexpected source,

Aristobolus, a Macedonian General who accompanied Alexander to India. Like several other military commanders, who came on that expedition, Aristobolus also wrote an account of Alexander's campaign, and like all others, his account has also been lost. However, several writers in the centuries that followed have quoted him extensively. This is what Strabo has quoted from him.

> Aristobolus, comparing the characteristics of this country that are similar to those of Aegypt and Aethiopia, says that when he was sent upon a certain mission he saw a country of more than a thousand cities, together with villages, that had been deserted because the Indus had abandoned its proper bed, and had turned aside into the other bed on the left that was much deeper, and flowed with the precipitous descent like a cataract, so that the Indus no longer watered by its overflows the abandoned country on the right, since that country was now above the level, not only of the new stream, but also of its overflows.
>
> (Strabo. Geographica. Book XV. Chapter 1. Para 19)

Alexander spent several months in Punjab after deciding to return to Greece. During this period he sent several exploratory missions. It appears that Aristobolus was sent to the south from Punjab and he reached the abandoned river bed of the river Saraswati in Rajasthan, where hundreds of archaeological sites are presently located. His observations are significant, as apart from showing that the dried up river bed was visible at least up to the fourth century BC, Aristobolus by mistaking it to be that of Indus, indicates its size. He would have been acquainted with all the rivers of Punjab, including Satluj, which he would have crossed while moving to this location. He has not confused it to be the abandoned river bed of any of the other rivers, but of Indus, showing that the river bed was comparable with that river, a fact which is borne out from the descriptions of the river Saraswati as found in the *Veds*. He has also thrown light on the manner in which the Indus Valley Civilization came to an end. He did not notice signs of destruction caused by an enemy attack, but only of being deserted as the river had abandoned its course and no longer watered the area.

The change of the course of the Saraswati river to become the Yamuna was the greatest catastrophe to have struck ancient India. It did not just change the course of a river, it changed the history of the country. With it, the Indian civilization, which at that point was far ahead in the scale of human development, had to die to be reborn again and start the entire process afresh. A process which most people in the world went through once, India had to go through a second time, for such a small thing as a few boulders giving way to a small stream to leave its course and flow in a different direction. In the history of the world, there may not be any other instance where such a small and insignificant occurrence had such a devastating impact on the lives of so many people. The effect of this on the course of the history of India has not received the attention it deserves from historians. As a single factor, it is the most important of all those that have shaped the way things turned out to be. Yet, if it is ever mentioned, it is just in passing as a river that dried up, without really appreciating what it caused.

If the impact of the change of course of the Saraswati on the economy of the Sapt Sindhu is analysed, it will explain what has been noticed in Mohenjo Daro and Harappa in their decaying stage. The reduced flow of water would have, in the beginning, led to a situation wherein floods would have ceased to occur in the Saraswati basin and water levels would have been low in the waterway. Both would have had an immediate impact on the economy. Low water levels in the waterway would have made it difficult for ships to travel up the river to the stations from where they picked cargo. The production of foodgrains would have begun to fall, not only because of shortage of water for irrigation but also due to the absence of the fertilizing effects of floods. With the water level falling below a critical level, plying of ships would have become impossible and the Saraswati would have ceased to be a waterway for exports, though this would not have caused any problem because there would have been nothing to export. The agricultural surplus would have been wiped out and the entire

Saraswati basin would have gradually moved from a region surplus to one deficient, till it became a desert. The Indus basin would have had no effect on the availability of water due to the drying up of the Saraswati, but its economy would have collapsed with the collapse of the Saraswati basin. To start with, the fall in food production in the Saraswati basin would have required the surplus of the Indus basin to go to the Saraswati basin to meet the deficiencies there, instead of being available for exports. This would have happened up to a point, after which the difficulties of transport and the absence of means of livelihood in the Saraswati basin would have led to a large-scale migration of people from there into the Indus basin in search of alternatives. This would have led to over-crowding of the Indus region and the consumption of the entire food production by the people, leaving nothing for exports.

It has to be kept in mind that the Saraswati basin was the main area of habitation of Sapt Sindhu and so the majority of the population had either moved to or was dependent on the production of an area which had lesser people and lesser production. The signs of this overcrowding are visible in the remains of Mohenjo Daro, where, towards the end, large rooms are found divided into smaller ones and mansions becoming tenements with the city administration collapsing with not even the road plan being maintained. The signs of this decay have been attributed by historians to an invasion, which is not supported by any evidence. This decay was because of the collapse of the economy of the Saraswati basin, leading to an influx of people into the Indus basin at a scale which could not have possibly been handled by the smaller population and lesser production of that area. The impact of the gradual decline in the water flow and thereby prosperity in the Saraswati basin and the resultant effect on the Indus basin would have been different on different segments of the population. The first thing to get affected would have been exports, as very soon no surplus would have remained either in the Saraswati basin or in the Indus basin, while one of the waterways would not have remained navigable any longer. The only area remaining unaffected would have been southern Gujarat, which may not be having a volume of trade big enough to be viable alone. The Indian exports would have collapsed very soon, if not immediately. Two segments of the population of Sapt Sindhu were an integral part of this business, the traders and the seafarers. The traders were on land and had more resources, while the seafarers were on ships and could not have been rich enough to sustain unemployment for long. Though it is possible that some of them may have left the ships to look for employment on land, this is unlikely, because the failure on the part of the farmers from the Saraswati basin to get alternate means of sustenance would have kept them on board. This segment of the population of the Sapt Sindhu could be responsible for some of the puzzles of the history of the world as they were very experienced seafarers and could have gone to any part of the globe to emerge out of the deep blue sea. They would have left the Indian shores soon after the Saraswati changed its course, to find an alternate location to be able to live off their ships. Two possibilities are there on the likely course that could have been adopted by the seamen and both could have been exercised by different people amongst them, as the group was large. They were already moving directly to Mesopotamia and Egypt, and to Greece with a changeover, for centuries. They could already have had stations in these areas. Some of them would have certainly gone to these areas and could have even switched over to the Mediterranean Sea where there was maritime activity already. Another group may have tried to explore the possibility of continuing the trade of foodgrains with the Middle East. The market and its requirements were known to them, they had to look for people who had a surplus and were prepared to sell it. As in those days, sailors did not venture into the open seas and sailed along the coast only, they would have moved in the opposite direction along the Indian coast and beyond. They would not have known that what they were looking for was a near impossibility, because even if they found people with surplus foodgrains and willing to part with it, the medium of trade would not be there. Those people would not have understood why these people were trying to take away a ship load of food in return for a few kilograms of shining metals, whether yellow or white, for which they had no use. Their destiny could have taken them anywhere along the coasts of peninsulas and islands, till either their spirit or their boats gave way, when they would have got down onto land, leaving the sea to which they thought they always belonged, bringing with reverence the images of the protecting god which each ship carried, to a place somewhere for their continued protection in their new and unknown homeland. No distance could be too long for them. The only silver lining in getting to know that it was these people, is that at that time it was the Indians alone who were out there in the sea, because everything is based on necessity and it was only the Indians who had developed a condition wherein it was necessary for them to be out there. For no other people, even if they had progressed substantially in other fields, was a sea journey of much relevance, except for the Greeks, whose history and movements are more or less known. During this time, if any part of the globe has reported of people coming by the sea from an unknown place and settling down, it is very likely that they would be the seafarers of the Indus Valley Civilization.

The second segment of the population connected with exports was of traders. They would have had different compulsions to stay on where they were in the hope of better days. They were rich and had the resources to survive much longer than others. Being rich they would also be having more fixed assets, which would be lost if they were to leave the place. Due to the combination of both these factors, they are the people who would have stayed on the longest and would have left only when it became impossible to stay on in the towns and cities, either because of the breakdown of the city administration and with it the municipal services or the necessity of looking for an alternate source of livelihood, this time in agriculture as urban occupations were no longer there. Traders from the Saraswati basin would have certainly left that area like all others, but the same may not be true for the Indus basin. They would have left the towns certainly, but may not have moved to the Gangetic plains. They could have exercised the option of returning to farms in the Indus basin itself.

Apart from the two segments of the society directly connected with exports, there were the farmers and a few artisans, mainly in brick kilns. They were the people with limited resources and limited stakes in the place, as their assets would not have been much. In this segment, the farmers of the Indus basin would not have been affected at all, initially, as their agricultural production would have remained unaffected because they were not dependent on the Saraswati. Despite the breakdown of exports, there would not have been any problem in the sale of the surplus production as the internal demand was there. However, once the people of the Saraswati basin would have left the Sapt Sindhu and moved to the Gangetic plains, they would have felt the impact. By then, the entire infrastructure of export would have broken down as the seafarers would have left the Indian shores while the traders would have left their business to find alternate means of livelihood. The traders could have emerged in a short time, but restoring the transport system would not have been easy. As a result, the surplus production of the Indus basin would not have found a market. The farmers would have been compelled to reduce production and return to an agrarian economy instead of being a vital link of a commercial economy. This would have been a great loss, but out of all the people, the farmers of the Indus basin were the people who would have suffered the least in this calamity. They would have had the compulsion of neither leaving their land nor their profession for survival, but could continue where they were, doing what they were, but with a difference. The farmers of the Saraswati basin were the people who would have been the first to receive the blow of this catastrophe. Their income would have fallen almost immediately and very soon they would have been struggling for survival. Their lands would have become uncultivable, leaving them with no option but to abandon the place. The overcrowding of the cities of the Indus basin shows that that is where they initially went. This would have been the natural reaction, as the towns of the Saraswati basin would have given a dismal picture with no hope of getting employment, while the Indus basin would have remained an area of hope. It would have been a situation wherein they would not have known what to do, but were only struggling for survival and moving to cities in the hope of finding employment. They would have been disappointed as, with the breakdown of trade with the Middle East, these urban centres would have been left with no urban occupations and even people who were already engaged in them would have been feeling the strain and leaving for alternate occupations. However, their numbers and the compulsion to stay on in towns, even if they had to beg or steal for survival, would have been enough to give a blow to the tottering urban institutions, strong enough to ring their death knell.

The migration out of the Sapt Sindhu would have started after the farmers of the Saraswati basin had failed to find means of livelihood in the cities of the Indus basin. It is not clear why these farmers opted to move to the Gangetic plains instead of settling down in the Indus basin itself, even if the cities had failed them. Their number was not such that the Indus with its five major tributaries could not have been able to accommodate. It is possible that some of them went looking for where the water had disappeared and found the Saraswati flowing in the other direction as the Yamuna. This may have led them to move to the same direction as by then a lot of their religious beliefs were associated with the Saraswati. However, once in the Gangetic plains, they preferred to settle more along the Ganga rather than the Yamuna, which may have been due to the initial unpredictable nature of that river and in course of time, all the sanctity associated with the Saraswati got transferred to the Ganga. Whatever may have been the reason, this is a crucial turning point in the history of India because with it started the process by which the Gangetic plains became the centre of activity of north India instead of the Sapt Sindhu. It would have been a very painful phase after centuries of well-being, in which the entire population of a region had to move to a new and unknown area to start the process of civilization afresh, leaving behind their past to decay and die. The urban civilization of the Sapt Sindhu, which these people had been able to create in such remote times, had to die because no urban occupations were left to support an urban population. Though the natural calamity had struck the Saraswati basin, it took with it the infrastructure of the Indus basin also, because of which even the Indus basin could not bear the impact and could not re-establish itself. The failure on the part of the Indus basin to restore exports after the migrant population had left, shows that these people remained in

338 HARSH MAHAAN CAIRAE

that area for a sufficiently long time to destroy all the institutions and the infrastructure completely, leaving them to start from scratch again, something which could not be achieved, especially because the ships had vanished along with the men who knew about them.

Though evidence from the *Veds* is of their migration to the Gangetic plains only, it is likely that this migration took place towards South India also. However, as none of the rivers or other natural features of the area in that direction have found mention, nothing on this point can be said on the basis of these scriptures.

Apart from having the requirement of starting the development process again from an agrarian economy, the shifting of the population and with it the centre of activity from the Sapt Sindhu to the Gangetic plains, had other implications which have moulded the history of India. So long as it was the Sapt Sindhu Indian trade routes were opening into the Arabian Sea as that is where the rivers were going. From the land borders also the other centres of civilization were close by, though the land routes to them were not very frequently used. As trade relations had been established with Mesopotamia, Egypt and Greece, India was integrated for the purposes of flow of information with these centres of civilization. This was important, as not only information about new developments reached the country, but anything with defence implications would have been known in advance. If the situation as it prevailed in the Sapt Sindhu is seen, it would appear that it had several very vital ingredients that are necessary for spectacular achievements by a race. It had an agriculture in which the farmers were producing a massive surplus, which could be exported and converted into wealth. This meant that they had the incentive to produce as much as they could. It had an urban class which was not only rich, but had the exposure of other cultures and countries. Some of them would have been well-educated and would have been open to new ideas for the improvement of what was being done. It had a class of seafarers who had the experience of thousands of years and could reach virtually any place if required. They had an administrative system which could ensure peace. These are vital ingredients for the development of new ideas and inventions, which could have led to very spectacular achievements by India, far more than what she achieved. The only major element missing was want, which undoubtedly is the strongest driving force forward. Even from the point of view of the defence of the country, this position was far more important. It was close to the western borders from where all the invaders came. Had Sapt Sindhu remained the centre of activity of the country, the importance of defending the Hindukush would have been understood by them. It provided a natural barrier with only two passes, the Khyber and the Bolan. A country conscious of the importance of these natural features in its defence, would have had a totally different strategy. This would have been the place for it to engage the intruders.

The shift to the Gangetic plains changed the scenario altogether. The lands were as fertile as those in the Sapt Sindhu, with a large number of rivers flowing down from the mountains, making agriculture as lucrative as before, but with several vital differences. There were no markets which could absorb the excess production and convert the surplus into wealth. The rivers that flowed were flowing to the east to fall into the Bay of Bengal and the sea was very far from the places in which the initial settlements took place. In the East, the only civilization of the ancient world was China, which was not only very far but was not in need of foodgrains as its lands were equally fertile. Even if the farmers produced a surplus, it would have been very difficult to repeat the feat of Sapt Sindhu, in India's second endeavour. The farmers, therefore, did not have the incentive to produce beyond what was required by them or what limited amount of foodgrains could be locally sold. As the scope of trade was also limited to whatever could be sold locally, the possibilities for the growth of urban occupations became very limited. It was, therefore, not only a situation in which the country had to begin a second time in its struggle for development, but to do so without the conditions which were primarily responsible for the achievements of the Indus Valley Civilization. Perhaps, if the farmers of the Saraswati basin had settled down in the Indus basin itself, instead of trying to follow the waters of the Saraswati, the story may have been different, because then it would have only been a question of coming out of the impact of the blow received from

the natural catastrophe that had struck them, with all other factors
remaining more or less the same except the departure of the seafarers
from Indian shores. It would have been a far easier situation to deal
with as compared to what they faced in the Gangetic basin. This shift
also meant that India got disconnected from the other civilizations of
the ancient world. Not only the breakdown of trade but the change
of focus towards the East, led to a situation wherein India went into
isolation. It is difficult to assess the impact of this factor, but whatever
new developments took place in other parts of the world, took very
long to reach India and the process of growth here did not have the
benefit of what had already been achieved by others. For the defence
of the country too, this had vital implications. On the one hand,
developments in Central Asia with security overtones for the country
were never known in advance and most of the times the invaders took
the people by surprise, on the other, the Hindukush, which provided
a natural barrier from the west, became very far from the heartland,
because of which its importance in the defence of the country was
never really understood. Except for Chandragupt Maurya, who was
active for a long time along the Indus river, because of which he and
Chanakya knew what Hindukush meant to Indian defence, India
does not seem to have appreciated its significance at any stage in her
history. No ruler ever had a plan for this frontier nor was anything ever
done for the two passes that it had, to prevent an unwelcome guest
from coming in. This was a failure on the part of the military strategy
of the country, which did not take into account the most important
natural feature for its defence in the direction from which all invaders
came. To a large extent this was because of the shift of the centre of
activity to the Gangetic plains, because of which most of the empires
that emerged, did not have their boundaries up to this mountain
range. As they were confined to more fertile lands in the east, the less
prosperous areas toward the western borders never seemed to attract
their attention. As a result, the area that was crucial for the defence
of the entire country remained under the control of minor kingdoms,
which could not have been expected to have an imperial outlook and
focus on the Hindukush to make it impregnable. It is unfortunate

that despite so many intrusions, starting from that of Alexander, the necessity of blocking the Khyber and the Bolan passes could never be realized.

A question does emerge about what happened to the urban culture of the Indus Valley Civilization, when all the same people were still there, not only in the Gangetic plains but also in the Indus basin. The planned cities and towns with houses made of baked bricks are the unique features of this civilization, which disappeared totally. Planned cities never appeared in the history of India again, while even baked bricks as a building material were not to be seen for a long time, till Nalanda and Sarnath. Urban centres had emerged due to a growth of urban occupations in the Sapt Sindhu on a very large scale. They could not have survived nor could have new centres come up, once the urban occupations were no longer there. While the Gangetic valley could not develop foreign trade, the exports from the Indus basin could not be restored, because of which urban occupations became a thing of the past. For a very long time, the only urban occupations would have been those related to the affairs of the state and local trade, with a few people engaged in providing services to them. This limited population could not have been able to sustain a township of a reasonable size and even places like Rajgrih, Vaishali, Shravasti and Patliputra, all of which are referred to as big cities in the literature of the time, could not have been very big. To this was added the fact that democracy was replaced by monarchy in the entire country, except Vaishali, by the sixth century BC and even Vaishali perished shortly thereafter. It must be remembered that a major factor for the Indus Valley Civilization having so much concern for its citizens was due to the fact that those very citizens were responsible for their destiny. It was not the contribution of a benevolent monarch that good and comfortable houses were built for all. It was the contribution of an efficient administrative machinery that was run by the people, and so had to provide for the welfare of all the people. For very valid reasons their focus was to have planned cities with wide roads and houses with civic facilities of drainage. For the same reasons they built no palaces or monuments for an individual, which could be compared with the impressive monuments left by other contemporary civilizations. With the emergence of monarchies, there was a complete shift in the priorities of the governing machinery. People no longer had a say in their destiny and all resources of the state were at the disposal of an individual. What he gave to someone was a bounty and this patronage could be extended by him now for whatsoever reason. In this changed situation, providing for the welfare of the entire community could not have been a policy of the government, despite being declared to be so. Such a thing has not happened in a monarchy anywhere in the world and it could not be expected in India either.

The disappearance of baked bricks as a building material is more intriguing than the disappearance of cities. Along the bed of the Saraswati, over five hundred sites of the Indus Valley Civilization have been found. It shows that bricks were used in houses even in villages and their complete disappearance because of the breakdown of trade and the urban civilization is difficult to understand. The blame has to go, perhaps, to the gradual reduction in the flow of the water of the Saraswati river, instead of a sudden drying up, because of which different segments of the society were affected in a manner that meant they had to look for alternate means of livelihood at different times. Of the people living on land the first to be affected would have been the people working in brick kilns, as a general fall in prosperity would have immediately led to a virtual halt to all new constructions and, therefore, a demand for bricks. These would also have been the people in the lower levels of economic well-being, because of which they could not have had the capacity to withstand a situation of unemployment for long and would have been compelled to look for an alternate source of livelihood before any other segment on land. This was a class which would have been affected in both the Indus as well as the Saraswati basin because their existence was dependent on a demand for bricks, which was not an item essential for survival but was required for the luxury of a good house. In a situation of crisis, all resources of people are put in the effort for survival and items of luxury are the last priority. As people of both basins were struggling for survival the brick-makers would have been left with virtually no employment. Once the trend of migration to the Gangetic plains started, these people from both basins would have been amongst the first to move out and go into agriculture for survival, and within a couple of generations the art of brick-making would have been lost. By the time the situation stabilized in the Indus basin with the departure of the excess population the brick-makers would not have been there any longer, even if there had been a limited demand for bricks. The richer segments of the society of the Saraswati basin would have been the last to move into the Gangetic plains. By the time they would have come, much of their prosperity would have been gone and by the time people would have become a little better off, it would have been several generations after the last brick had been made, due to which the art would have been reduced to be a thing of the past. However, just as intriguing is the disappearance of bricks after the Indus Valley Civilization, is their reappearance at Nalanda and Sarnath, to disappear once again. This gives an impression that the art was known all along though it was not put to use, but whenever someone did decide to have bricks on a reasonably large scale, he could always find people who knew how to make them. Houses in the Gangetic plains were built of timber. Even royal quarters were made of timber up to a very late stage, as there is an instance in the time of Chandragupt Maurya to show this. To ensure his safety, Chanakya had prescribed a practice that he slept in a different house every night. Once when he went to inspect a house which was to be used by Chandragupt for a night, he noticed ants carrying food from under the floor. He could sense that there were conspirators under it waiting for the night when Chandrgupt would be there and ordered it to be burnt. The charred bodies of the conspirators were found when the fire had died down. As even the emperor was living in houses made of timber, it appears that the use of timber in place of bricks could have been a matter of preference, as that enabled people to have a raised platform for the floor, which provided a better protection from insects and reptiles.

But for the existence of the Indus Valley Civilization, the history of India before the sixth century BC is not known. For the period between the decline of the Indus Valley Civilization and the sixth century BC nothing is known, as very few archaeological remains have been found. This covers the entire period of the decline of the Harappan culture and the migration of the population to the Gangetic plains. It cannot, however, be said that no literature of this period has survived. The *Rig Ved* mentions the Ganga, the Yamuna, the Gomati and the Saryu. It is evident that the process of composition of hymns of the *Rig Ved* was continuing at least till the people had reached the Saryu river in the process of their migration from the Saraswati basin to the Gangetic plains. It would have to be said that not only the later Vedic literature but even the *Rig Ved* covers the period up to the migration to a point at least somewhere in eastern Uttar Pradesh. One of the Richas that mentions Saryu is of interest. It is stated here.

> You (Indra) have slain those two Aryas at once, Arna and Chitrarath (dwelling) on the opposite (bank) of the Saryu.
> (*Rig Ved*. M-4, S-30, R-18)

Apart from bringing out the fact that the composition of the hymns of the *Rig Ved* had not stopped at least up to this point, this Richa shows a number of things. It speaks of killings, which shows that war and violence were still an important subject for their compositions. Secondly, it says that two Aryans, Arna and Chitrarath, have been killed. The *Veds* all along had a tradition of not mentioning reverses. Here reverses of two Aryans is being reported, which shows that the issue was no longer relevant as everyone was considered to be an Aryan. There was no other side. The winning side was an Aryan and so was the losing, because of which it did not make a difference in mentioning specifically that the two persons killed were Aryans. The *Rig Ved* covering the period of migration at least up to the Saryu means that the most crucial period of this change was seen by the *Rig Ved*, because once the trend had started and had got stabilized, it was only a question of taking it forward by proceeding along the Ganga.

Despite the Vedic literature being available for this very crucial period of the history of India, no history is to be found in this literature for this period. This was the literature which had all along been open to record history, though in its own style. Perhaps it would have to be said that no history was being created. Normally, history is looked at as a story of war and violence. Poets and artists, too, are inspired by significant things to reflect them in their creations. Peace seems to be the most uninspiring and colourless thing around. It appears that India had peace even in those days of turbulence and disorder. There does seem to have been a degree of strife as the people gave up democracy and switched over to monarchy in most of the places of the country, but this appears to have been more on the economic side and did not lead to too much of bloodshed or at a scale that could inspire poets and artists. The Indians seem to have been a race of very tolerant people, who could go through all the turmoil that was involved in the process of starting the process of development for a second time, without much of violence. It does not appear to be a case wherein the literature of the time did not record history, but one wherein history was not created.

The tolerance of the people of the time is reflected in the case of Ajeet Keshkamblin, more frequently called Charvak. He preceded Buddha by a few centuries and is said to have propounded a philosophy of hedonism. He is reported to have held the view that there is nothing before or after this life, which emerges with the right elements coming together in the right manner and ends when the critical level of this correctness is lost because of which the entire composition gets dissolved. There being nothing before and nothing after means that there was no scope for rebirth or heaven and hell. As there was no system in place for divine punishment there was no need to lead a good, disciplined life. He is reported to have propounded a theory that life should be enjoyed even if one has to borrow or steal for it. Unfortunately, the Brahaspatya Sutra, which is said to be the original document of this school, is not available and all that is known of his doctrine is from what has been quoted of him by his critics for rebutting his views, or from the *Sarva Darshan Sangrah*. The *Sarva Darshan Sangrah* or the compendium of all philosophies is a work of the fourteenth century AD of Madhavacharya, different from the Madhav who had propounded the Dwait philosophy. This is Madhav Vidyaranya who is reported to be the brother of Sayan, the famous Vedic commentator. Being a work as late as the fourteenth century AD, it cannot be said whether Madhavacharya had access to the Brahaspatya Sutra or his information was also based only on the extracts of Ajeet Keshkamblin that had been quoted by his critics in their works. The critics cannot be expected to have given a correct presentation of his doctrines. They would have quoted in a manner that suited them in their effort to prove him wrong. He may also have been quoted out of context to give a meaning totally different from what was intended. His doctrines, as they emerge from what has been quoted by his critics, appear to be very shallow, which does not seem probable in view of the fact that for about two thousand years every philosopher of the country found it expedient to take note of them, though only to disagree. Ajeet Keshkamblin was a staunch opponent of the Vedic philosophy and religious practices, which by then were the predominant practices of India. He refused to accept the *Veds* as an authority and questioned the rationale of rituals, especially those related to sacrifice, which formed the central theme of the Vedic religion. In the Vedic system it was believed that the animal that was killed for sacrifice went straight to heaven. This could have emerged to mollify the feelings of people who witnessed the slaughter of the helpless animal. The idea had, however, come in very early as can be seen from these Richas.

1. Let not your precious body grieve you, who are going verily (to the gods); let not the axe linger in your body; let not the greedy and unskilful (immolator) missing the members, mangle your limbs needlessly with the knife.

2. Verily at this moment you do not die; nor are you harmed; for you go by auspicious paths to the gods. The horses of Indra, the steeds of the Maruts shall be yoked (to their ears), and a courser shall be placed in the shaft of the ass of the Ashwins (to bear you to heaven).

(*Rig Ved.* M-1, S-162, R-20 and 21)

It has been reported that Ajeet Keshkamblin had raised a question that if it was so, don't the people conducting the sacrifice want their father to have a place in heaven? It was not a simple objection of why waste food by consigning it to fire, when it can be eaten or given in charity. It was far more fundamental. If such an easy passage to heaven had been found, was there not a better claimant than this poor animal, which had not expressed a wish to go there, at least not so soon. It was, however, equally objectionable for the people on the other side. It can be termed to be offensive and if someone had felt offended by it to take Ajeet Keshkamblin to task he could not have been blamed. A thousand reasons may have been brought forward to prove him wrong, but during his lifetime neither he, nor his followers, were ever prevented from preaching their philosophy or attending conferences of learned men who used to assemble to debate on philosophy and religion. Shashtrarth, as it was called, remained open to Ajeet Keshkamblin all through his life and he attended them with all his rhetoric trying to prove his doctrines. Nobody ever thought of binding him in order to throw him in a pit, with fire burning around and leave it to the Ashwins to protect if they wished to, or to cut his limbs and throw the torso in a river and blame it on Indra.

It was this spirit of tolerance of the people of Sapt Sindhu which was responsible, more than anything else, for the long survival of the Indus Valley Civilization, so much so that even the cities of Mohenjo Daro and Harappa remained unchanged for a thousand years. It is this same spirit of tolerance which is responsible, more than anything else, for the nightmare of historians that they are not able to find history. It is not just the period after the fall of the Indus Valley Civilization upto the sixth century BC but also several centuries during the time when the Indus Valley Civilization was flourishing that the Indo-Aryans were in the Sapt Sindhu and the *Veds* were being composed. The *Veds* and the Vedic literature can be deemed to be the literature of the Indus Valley Civilization from the time the Indo-Aryans came to India. There is no history that emerges from them of the days of prosperity either, except a confirmation of the fact that things were good and they were comfortable. The country was not creating history. It was living in peace.

13
India in the Mediterranean Sea

RETURNING TO THE QUESTION OF the places outside India, where the people of the Indus Valley Civilization could have migrated to, the Phoenicians present a very interesting study. Also referred to as the Tyrians, Sidonians and Carthagians, they are believed to have come from an unknown place by sea and made tremendous contributions to the culture and knowledge of the area. They were neither white like the Europeans nor black like the Africans. The earliest cities established by them were Byblos, Sidon and Tyre on the Mediterranean coast in an area that falls in Lebanon today and was called Phoenicia in earlier times. Herodotus has recorded the founding of Tyre at 2,750 BC. Archaeological findings confirm this. The earliest Phoenician city, however, was not Tyre but Byblos. It had developed into a town of small houses by 4,500 BC and by 3,200 BC was a bustling city with a massive city wall. Some fishhooks and other implements found at Byblos are as old as 6,000 BC. Evidence on the activities of the Phoenicians in very early times comes from Egypt. In the ancient Egyptian city of Hierakonpolis, archaeologists have unearthed an old temple built in 3,500 BC in which four huge cedar pillars were added to form an impressive front. These have been dated at 3,200 BC. As Egypt has no wood except palm and acacia, these have been identified as the cedar of Lebanon. Measuring thirty-six feet in length and three feet in diameter, these logs were transported by sea from Lebanon to the mouth of the river Nile and from there taken to the temple by the river. As Egyptians were not seafaring people it is evident that this was done by the Phoenicians who were in Lebanon and who are reported in the *Bible* to have delivered cedar logs to David and Solomon also.

The passages from the *Bible* on this are here.

1. Now Hiram king of Tyre sent messengers to David, and timber of Cedar, with masons and carpenters, to build him a house.

    (1 Chronicles: 14. 1)

2. And Solomon sent to Huram the king of Tyre, saying, As thou didst deal with David my father, and didst send him cedars to build him a house to dwell therein, even so deal with me. Behold, I build a house to the name of the Lord my God, to dedicate it to him. Then Huram the king of Tyre answered in writing, which he sent to Solomon. And we will cut wood out of Lebanon, as much as thou shalt need: and we will bring it to thee in floats by sea to Joppa: and thou shalt carry it up to Jerusalem.

    (2 Chronicles: 2. 3, 4, 11 and 16)

With evidence showing that they were traders and seafarers from such remote times, the Phoenicians had interactions with all cultures of the area and contributed a lot to them. They dominated the sea trade for over three thousand years and opened up new areas for trade and commerce. In the process, they established several small colonies along the trading routes, which initially emerged only as supporting stations for their vessels and often were at a distance of a day's journey from each other. In 1,200 BC something dramatic happened which changed the nature of the Phoenicians. It has been termed as 'the invasion of the Sea Peoples'. Though it has been called an invasion, there is no sign of violence in the archaeological remains of the Phoenician cities of the period. A large population of people came from an unknown place, as they had been forced to leave their homeland by a natural calamity, and mingled with the people of these cities on the Mediterranean coast, whereafter the Phoenicians emerge with a new face having interest in land also, instead of only in the sea. Archaeological findings show signs of destruction in the surrounding areas of the Phoenician cities, which shows, that to begin with, these areas were taken over from others by the 'Sea Peoples' who took up agriculture as an occupation. The colonization process of even far flung areas became rapid and instead of just having supporting stations for the mariners, regular colonies came

up. Gades (modern Cadiz) in Spain was established in 1,110 BC, while
Utica in Africa was founded in 1,101 BC. Crete had been a very old
Phoenician station. Its ancient Minoian culture had deep Phoenician
imprints with Minos, its legendary founder being believed to be the son
of a Phoenician princess, Europa, the sister of Cadmus. Cyprus, Malta,
Sicily, Sardinia and Tangier were other major Phoenician settlements,
apart from a few in southern France and Spain. Carthage was founded
in 814 BC which became a centre more important than the cities of
Phoenicia for several centuries. As it came in conflict with Rome, a lot
of its history is known from Greek and Roman sources.

Before this name was coined by the Greeks, the Phoenicians were
called the Canaanites. Mention of them from the *Bible* is here.

> And Canaan begat Sidon his first born, and Heth,
> And the Jebusite, and the Amorite, and the Girgasite,
> And the Hivite, and the Arkite, and the Sinite,
> and the Arvadite, and the Zemarite and the Hemathite:
> and afterwards were the families of the Canaanites spread
> abroad.
> And the border of the Canaanites was from Sidom, as thou
> comest to Gerar, unto Gaza; as thou goest unto Sodom,
> and Gumorrah, and Admah, and Zeboim, even unto Lasha.
>
> (Genesis : 10.15 to 19)

All the different people known to the *Bible* have been stated by it to
be the descendants of Noah, as everyone except his family has been
said by it, to have perished in the floods. Canaan has been stated to be
a grandson of Noah. As apart from Sidon from whom the Sidonians
were born, several sons of Canaan have been reported, including Heth,
a name in the *Bible* used for the Hittites, it cannot be said whether
only the Phoenicians were called Canaanites or the name included
some other races also.

Phoenicia being on the crossroad of trade routes, it came in the
way of several empires, because of which the Phoenician cities often
faced pressures for their existence. These were all independent city
states, which had a mechanism of coordination, but being a mercantile

community, had hardly anything by way of military strength. As a result, at different times, they were subjugated by the Egyptians, Assyrians, Persians, Macedonians and Romans. Despite being a subject of these empires the Phoenician cities maintained a certain degree of autonomy for themselves and their seafaring capabilities were at times used by some of these empires for building a navy for themselves. They suffered the worst at the hands of Alexander, who, after defeating the Persian Emperor Darius in the battle of Issus, turned towards Phoenicia to subjugate the Phoenicians, before proceeding further on in Asia, as the Phoenicians were in charge of the Persian navy and had the control of the sea. If he had proceeded further without subjugating them, the sea would have remained in hostile hands and his supply line from Greece would not have been safe. All Phoenician cities surrendered voluntarily but a problem arose at Tyre, where Alexander expressed a desire to enter the city to offer prayers at the temple of Heracles. The Tyrians did not agree to this and closed themselves in the city. Alexander laid a siege and took it after a few months, but was exceptionally cruel to the place, as he killed all the leading citizens and razed the city.

Politically, the Phoenicians had better luck in Carthage as they proceeded to establish an empire there which included not only large parts of Africa but also Portugal, Spain and Sardinia. They came in conflict with the Roman Empire over the possession of Sicily, which led to three long drawn wars known as the Punic Wars. In these emerged great military commanders like Hamilcar Barca, after whom the Spanish city of Barcelona is named, and his son Hannibal. The career of Hannibal marks the high watermark of the military achievements of the Phoenicians, as he ravaged Italy for eighteen years and defeated Rome in several engagements.

So far as the Indian links of the Phoenicians are concerned, the evidence from Greek and Roman writers needs to be examined. To start with, the statements of these writers on the place from where these people came to the Mediterranean are mentioned here.

1. Those of the Persians who have knowledge of history declare that the Phoenicians first began the quarrel. These, they say, came from

that which is called the Erythraian Sea to this of ours; and having settled in the land where they continue even now to dwell, set themselves forthwith to make long voyages by sea. And conveying merchandize of Egypt and of Assyria they arrived at other places and also at Argos.

(Herodotus. *The Histories*. Book 1. Para 1)

2. These Phoenicians dwelt in ancient times, as they themselves report, upon the Erythraian Sea, and thence they passed over and dwell in the country along the sea coast of Syria; and this part of Syria and all as far as Egypt is called Palestine.

(Herodotus. *The Histories*. Book 7. Para 89)

3. The larger island according to Timaeus is known as Potimusa from its wells, but our people call it Tartesos and the Punic name is Gadir, which is Carthaginian for a fence; it was called Erythea, because the original ancestors of the Carthaginians and the Tyrians, were said to have come from the Red Sea.

(Pliny, the Elder. Natural History. Book IV. Para 22)

The first passage is the opening sentence of *The Histories of Herodotus*. The quarrel he has referred to and blamed the Phoenicians, is the siege of Troy, as they have been blamed for the first incident of abduction of a woman of a different ethnic group, that led to a series of such abductions and finally to that of Helen. In this passage, he has stated that the Persians have reported that the Phoenicians came to the Mediterranean Sea from the Erythraian Sea and forthwith started making long sea voyages and trading. Apart from stating that these people came from the Erythraian Sea, this statement shows that they already were seafarers and traders, because they took up these activities immediately on moving to the new location. The second passage, also from Herodotus, reports a statement from the Phoenicians themselves, that in ancient times they dwelt on the Erythraian Sea and from there moved to the Syrian coast. Here they have stated that they not only came from the Erythraian Sea but also dwelt there. The third passage is from Pliny the Elder, who, while describing Cadiz has stated that the Phoenicians came from the Red Sea.

At present no sea has the name Erythraian, while the sea between Saudi Arabia and Africa is called the Red Sea. This, however, does not seem to have been the understanding in earlier times. To understand the location of these seas as per the perception of these writers their works have to be examined. The following passages from Herodotus are relevant.

1. Babylon then was walled in this manner; and there are two divisions of the city; for a river whose name is Euphrates parts it in the middle. This flows from the land of the Armenians and is large and deep and swift, and it flows out into the Erythraian Sea.

   (Herodotus. *The Histories*. Book I. Para 180)

2. Now when Cyrus on his way towards Babylon arrived at the river Gyndes, of which river the springs are in the mountains of Matienians, and it flows through the Dardanians and runs into another river, the Tigris, which flowing by the city of Opis runs out into the Erythraian Sea.

   (Herodotus. *The Histories*. Book 1. Para 189)

3. Now there is in the land of Arabia, not far from Egypt, a gulf of the sea running in from that which is called the Erythraian Sea, very long and narrow, as I am about to tell.

   (Herodotus. *The Histories*. Book 2. Para 11)

4. Now in the place where the journey is least and shortest from the Northern to the Southern Sea (which is also called Erythraian), that is from Mount Casion, which is the boundary between Egypt and Syria, the distance is exactly a thousand furlongs to the Arabian Gulf.

   (Herodotus. *The Histories*. Book 2. Para 158)

5. The Persians inhabit Asia to the Southern Sea, which is called the Erythraian.

   (Herodotus. *The Histories*. Book 4. Para 37)

6. The land of the Persians stretches along to the Erythraian Sea, including Persia and next to it Assyria, and Arabia: and this ends at the Arabian Gulf.

   (Herodotus. *The Histories*. Book 4. Para 39)

These passages show what Herodotus meant by the name Erythraian Sea. The first two passages state that the rivers, Euphrates and Tigris, flow into the Erythraian Sea, which would be the Persian Gulf. The remaining passages show that the entire sea south of the coast of Persia and Arabia was called the Southern Sea or the Erythraian Sea. The sea beyond had no other name. This would mean the Arabian Sea. The Persian Gulf and the Red Sea being inlets of this sea have been included under the same name. The present Red Sea has been called the Arabian Gulf in these passages. It is evident that the statement of Herodotus that the Phoenicians came from the Erythraian Sea and that they dwelt there earlier means that they came from the Persian Gulf.

Pliny the Elder has stated that the Phoenicians came from the Red Sea. His understanding of the Red Sea emerges from the following passages.

1. Moreover in this region the sea then makes a double inroad into the land; the name given to it by our countrymen is the Red Sea, while the Greeks call it Erythrum, from king Erythras. However, this sea is divided into two bays. The one to the east is called the Persian Gulf. Opposite is Arabia and on its other side Arabia is encompassed by the second bay, named the Arabian Gulf.
    (Pliny the Elder. Natural History. Book VI. Para 28)
2. Persians have always lived on the shore of the Red Sea, which is the reason why it is called the Persian Gulf.
    (Pliny the Elder. Natural History. Book VI. Para 29)

These passages show that there is no difference in the statements of the two authors regarding the place from where the Phoenicians came. What has been stated as the Erythraian Sea by Herodotus has been called the Red Sea by Pliny. He too has named the present Red Sea as the Arabian Gulf, while the Red Sea remains the Arabian Sea including the Persian Gulf. Strabo and Arrain too have stated that the Persian Gulf was called the Red Sea also. It is evident that both authors have marked the Persian Gulf as the point of arrival on land within their known geographical area. It could also mean that they came from the Arabian Sea, beyond the Persian Gulf.

Though Herodotus has stated that the ancestors of the Phoenicians dwelt upon the Persian Gulf, this could have been only a stay in transit. It could not have been their place of origin, as the Phoenicians had spread and colonized a very large area for which a large population base is required. The Persian Gulf could not have provided such a mass of people. It has to be beyond, where the Indus Valley Civilization flourished. Traders and seafarers from India would have developed their trading stations in the Persian Gulf to start with. After a time when they decided to move over to the Mediterranean Sea, they would have moved over from there. The stations in the Persian Gulf were places of stay in transit only and not their place of origin is borne out also by the fact that the Phoenicians considered Tyre in Phoenicia as their mother city despite knowing that they had stayed in the Persian Gulf before that and that there were cities with the same name in the said Gulf. The passages that show the presence of Phoenician cities with the same names in the Persian Gulf are mentioned here.

1. On sailing further, one comes to other islands, I mean Tyre and Aradus, which have temples like those of the Phoenicians. It is asserted, at least by the inhabitants of the islands, that the island and cities of the Phoenicians which bear the same name are their own colonies.

    (Strabo. Geographica. Book XVI. Chapter 3. Para 4)

2. When the poet says, 'I came to Aethiopians and Sidonians and Erembians,' historians are entirely at loss to know, in the first place, in regard to the Sidonians whether one should call certain people who dwelt in the Persian Gulf, from whom Sidonians in our part of the world were colonists, just as they speak of Tyrians there islanders, as also of Aradians, from whom they say those in our part of the world were colonists, or whether one should call them the Sidonians themselves.

    (Strabo. Geographica. Book XVI. Chapter 4. Para 27)

3. The city of Tyre sending Alexander, by the hands of a deputation, a golden crown of great value, as a token of congratulation, he

received their presents kindly, and told them that 'he intended to visit Tyre to pay his vows to Hercules.' The deputies replying that 'he would do that better at Old Tyre, in the more ancient temple;' he was so provoked with them, because they evidently deprecated his visit, that he threatened their city with destruction.

(Justin. Philippic History. Book XI. Para 10)

The first two passages are from Strabo. He is describing the Arabian coastline of the Persian Gulf, where he mentions two islands with the name Tyre and Aradus, both of which were names of Phoenician cities in the Mediterranean also. The people of those islands claimed that Phoenician cities with the same names in Phoenicia were their colonies. In the second passage he mentions the same thing for the Sidonians. The third passage is from Justin where he is describing the incident that led Alexander to besiege Tyre and destroy it. On his request to visit the city to pay his vows to Hercules, the Tyrians advised him to go to Old Tyre where there was a more ancient temple. It is evident that not only Phoenician settlements with the same names were there in the Persian Gulf, but the Phoenicians were aware of their existence and of they being of an earlier time. Despite this they treated Tyre in Phoenicia as their mother city and not the Tyre in the Persian Gulf. The passages which show this are mentioned here.

1. Alexander gave an amnesty to all those who fled for refuge into the temple of Hercules; among them being most of the Tyrian magistrates, including King Azemilcus, as well as certain envoys from Carthaginians, who had come to their mother-city to attend the sacrifice in honour of Hercules, according to an ancient custom.

    (Arrian. Anabasis of Alexander. Book 2. Para 24)

2. Next Tyre, once an island separated from the mainland by a very deep sea channel 700 yards wide, but now joined to it by the works constructed by Alexander when besieging the place, and formerly famous as the mother-city from which sprang cities of Leptis, Utica and the great rival of Rome's empire in coveting

world-sovereignty, Carthage and also Cadiz, which she founded outside the confines of the world.

(Pliny the Elder. Natural History. Book V. Para 17)

3. The fourth is the son of Jupiter and Asteria, the sister of Latona, and is worshipped principally at Tyre, the mother city, according to tradition of Carthage. The fifth belongs to India, and is called Belus.

(Cicero. On the Nature of Gods. Book III. Para 20)

4. Finding a Carthaginian ship that had carried sacred offerings anchored at the mouth of Tiber, he hired it. Such ships were specifically selected at Carthage for the conveyance of the traditional offering of first-fruits to their gods that the Carthaginians sent to Tyre.

(Polybius. *The Histories*. Book 31. Para 12)

These passages show that the Phoenicians treated Tyre in Phoenicia as their mother city and had a custom of sending their envoys with offerings to the temple of Heracles each year. It goes to show that the places with the same names in the Persian Gulf, though known to them as their earlier places of stay, were of no emotional value and were not considered to be their place of origin. It is evident that these were only places of stay in transit and the original homeland was beyond, which had been lost. Since the original homeland could not be reached and perhaps its location was no longer known, they were treating Tyre in Phoenicia as their mother city.

Another point of relevance on this issue is the manner of the Phoenician migration. They had been traders and seafarers for several thousand years in the Persian Gulf as well as the Mediterranean Sea. It was in 1,200 BC that a large population migrated into Phoenicia. By then the cities in Phoenicia were already thriving and the migration from the cities of the Persian Gulf would have been a matter of the remote past. This new population would have migrated straight to the Mediterranean shore and would not have stayed longer than necessary in the Persian Gulf, as with the breakdown of trade with India there would not have remained much of an economic activity there.

The arrival of the 'Sea Peoples' in large numbers in 1,200 BC is also indicative of the Phoenicians being Indians. These people had been uprooted from their homeland due to an unknown natural calamity and had migrated by sea in a number large enough to be called an invasion. As there was no conflict and as these people were readily accepted by the existing Phoenician cities, it shows that they were of the same stock and were in contact with each other. Migration is a part of human history and people from very remote times have been doing it but such migrations have been by land, while this was by sea. Only people with the means of undertaking a sea journey can do this. It has to be from a place where human development had reached a level that people in such large numbers could travel by sea and reach those places. A natural calamity should have occurred in an area of civilization to trigger such an exodus. This was India with its flourishing Indus Valley Civilization that had a major trade with West Asia at least, if not beyond, and which faced a natural calamity of the river Saraswati changing its course to a new direction, leaving the population bereft of its lifeline. The date of this event is not known but as the 'Invasion of the Sea Peoples' took place in 1,200 BC, the change of its course by the river Saraswati has to be around the same time.

It is also of interest that they were called the 'Sea Peoples'. It is generally believed that this was because they came by the sea from an unknown place. There is, however, another possibility for the origin of this name. India at that time was known as the 'Sapt Sindhu'. We now translate it as the Seven Rivers as we know that it is a reference to the seven rivers, but the word 'Sindhu' does not mean river but sea, and so the correct translation of the name 'Sapt Sindhu' would be Seven Seas. Unlike plain names like Rome and Egypt etc. this name was descriptive in nature and would have been liable to translation in the language of the people wherever it went. 'Sapt Sindhu' itself is a Sanskrit name, which the Aryans would have given by translating it from the original language of the Indus Valley Civilization, which must have had the name Seven Rivers, as that is the name found in the Avesta at a time just about when the Indo-Aryans came to India. As the Aryans used a hyperbole the name underwent a change. The

Indians telling the name of their country would have been understood by people unacquainted with the facts, to be a reference to a sea. If the manner in which this name got transformed is examined, it would emerge that the word 'Sapt' got dropped somewhere along the way and the land was known only as 'Sindhu' and became 'Hind' in West Asia, which is the name found used in early Persian works. This in Greece became 'Ind' and got Hellenized as Indes and India. At these stages, it became specific and ceased to be descriptive in nature. In this background the Indians, when they named their country, would have been understood as the people from the sea, and as Seven Seas were being spoken of, they were thought to be from seven different seas, because of which they have been called the 'Sea Peoples' and not just 'Sea People'. Such confusion about them can be seen in the following passage.

> Like them are writers who tell of Sidonians on the Persian Gulf, or somewhere else on Oceanus, and who place the wanderings of Menalaus, and likewise place the Phoenicians out in Oceanus. And not the least reason for not believing them is the fact that they contradict one another. For some of them say that even the Sidonians who are our neighbours are colonists from the Sidonians on Oceanus, and they actually add the reason why our Sidonians are called Phoenicians, namely, because the colour of the Persian Gulf is red; and the others hold that the Sidonians on Oceanus are colonists from our Phoenicia.
>
> (Strabo. Geographica. Book I. Chapter 2. Para 35)

Strabo has not given the names of the writers whose opinion he found difficult to believe. These writers had stated that the Sidonians were on the Persian Gulf or somewhere else beyond in the ocean and those of them who were neighbouring Greece were colonists of the Sidonians of the ocean. Strabo had valid reasons for disbelieving the statement because man is a land animal. It could not have been known to him that the ocean which was being spoken of did not mean the water that surrounds land, but the land which was called the sea, the Seven Seas.

The name Sapt Sindhu and what the people of the land explained about it to foreigners created the impression that there were seven seas, can be seen from Chinese sources also. A passage from Huein Tsang is mentioned here.

Around this there are seven mountain ranges and seven seas, between each range; a flowing sea of eight peculiar qualities. Outside the seven golden mountain ranges is the salt sea.
(Huein Tsang. Record of the Western Region. Book I)

Huein Tsang had visited India and would have crossed all the rivers, except Saraswati, which made up the seven rivers of Sapt Sindhu. Here, he is describing India as per the perception prevalent in his country. The seven seas have been called flowing seas by him and distinct from the salt sea, yet Huein Tsang has not understood them to mean rivers and continues to call them seas. It is evident that a similar confusion was there in the west, which is reflected in the passage from Strabo, because of which Indians have been called the 'Sea Peoples'. The invasion of these people into Phoenicia in 1,200 BC should be understood to be the migration of Indians on a massive scale from Sapt Sindhu, triggered by the collapse of the economy of the Indus Valley Civilization, because of the change in the course of the river Saraswati.

The next evidence that emerges to prove the link of the Phoenicians with the Indians is the similarities in their economic activities. The Indus Valley Civilization was a commercial civilization in which foreign trade was primarily based on agricultural products. The seafarers and the traders would have been the segments of the society having an interface with foreign countries while the farmers would have been the backbone of the economy. In all these three fields, the Phoenicians show a remarkable level of skill and knowledge. To start with, it was the traders and seafarers who had made their appearance in the Mediterranean. The passage from Herodotus as already mentioned shows that as soon as they reached the Mediterranean coast, they took up long sea voyages and trading, reflecting their existing proficiency in these fields. Their achievements on sea are unbelievable, but they have left evidence to prove them. An astounding feat reported by Herodotus is here.

> And this fact was shown by Necos king of Egyptians. He when he had ceased digging the channel which goes through from the Nile to the Arabian Gulf, sent Phoenicians with ships, bidding them sail and come back through the Pillars of Heracles to the Northern Sea and so to Egypt. The Phoenicians, therefore, set forth from the Erythraian Sea and sailed through the Southern Sea; and when autumn came, they would put to shore and sow, wherever in Libya they might happen to be, and then waited for the harvest: and having reaped they would sail on, so that after two years, in the third they turned through the Pillars of Heracles and arrived again in Egypt. And they reported a thing which I cannot believe, but another man may, namely that in sailing round Libya they had the sun on their right hand.
>
> (Herodotus. *The Histories*. Book 4. Para 42)

Herodotus uses the name Libya for Africa. He has reported that in the reign of Necos the Phoenicians sailed around Africa. This is Neco II, who ruled from 610 BC to 595 BC. An unbelievable feat for the time, but the evidence that it is true is in the statement itself. Herodotus has refused to believe what the sailors reported that in sailing around Libya they had the sun on their right hand. Which direction is meant by the right hand cannot be said, but it can be said with certainty that it means that the position of the sun that they saw while sailing around Libya was the opposite of what is seen from the Mediterranean Sea at a particular time of the year. Because of the tilt of the earth's axis, the position of the sun in its north-south annual movement is diametrically opposite in the northern and the southern hemispheres throughout the year, except on the equinoxes, when it is the same. Being sailors they would have been well acquainted with the stars and known what month of the year they indicated. It is evident that in particular months of the year these people observed the position of the sun in its annual north-south movement to be opposite of what they had all along known by viewing it from the northern hemisphere. Thus they have gone deep down in the southern hemisphere to see the opposite position of the sun at particular times of the year, a proof that they went around the cape, which had Vasco da Gama as its next known visitor.

Reports of sea journeys by the Phoenicians have been made by Pliny and Strabo also. Their statements are mentioned here.

1. Also when the power of Carthage flourished, Hanno sailed round from Cadiz to the extremity of Arabia and published a memoir of his voyage, as did Hamilcar when despatched at the same date to explore the outer coast of Europe.

    (Pliny the Elder. Natural History. Book II. Para 47)

2. Again the maritime supremacy of Minos is far-famed, and so are the voyages of the Phoenicians, who, a short time after the Trojan War, explored the regions beyond the Pillars of Heracles and founded cities both there and in the central parts of the Libyan seaboard.

    (Strabo. Geographica. Book I. Chapter 3. Para 2)

Hanno and Hamilcar were brothers. Pliny has reported that both of them led expeditions at the same time, Hamilcar to the north and Hanno to the south from Cadiz. For Hanno, he has reported that he circumnavigated Africa and reached Arabia, and published a memoir of his voyage. How far Hamilcar went has not been reported, but it has to be beyond Britain as the Phoenicians were already operating tin mines there. Hanno's memoir of his voyage around Africa has not been found. Account of another voyage from Hanno has been found in which he reached somewhere around the middle of Africa. In this account he does not mention that his brother had, at the same time, led an expedition to the north. The objective too of that voyage, was not exploration but settlement of colonies. The voyage mentioned by Pliny appears to be different from the one for which Hanno's account is available. The said account, as engraved on tablets hung in the temple of Cronos is mentioned here.

The Carthaginians decided that Hanno should go past the Pillars and found Carthaginian cities. He set sail with sixty ships carrying thirty thousand men and women with provisions and other necessities. After passing the Pillars of Heracles and setting sail for two days beyond them we founded the first city, which was named Thymiaterion. Around it was a large plain. Next we went on in a westerly direction and arrived at the Libyan promontory of Soloeis, which is covered with trees; having set up a shrine of Poseidon, we set sail again towards the rising sun for half a day, after which we arrived at a lagoon close to the sea covered with many tall reeds. Elephants and large number of other animals were feeding on them. Leaving this lagoon and sailing for another day, we founded the coastal cities named Carion Wall, Gytte, Acra, Melitta and Arambys.

Leaving this place we arrived at a great river Lixos which comes from Libya. On the banks nomads like the Lixites were feeding their flocks. We stayed for some time with these people and made friends with them. Upstream from them lived the unfriendly Ethiopians whose land is full of wild beasts and broken up by high mountains where they say that about these mountains dwell the strange-looking Troglodytes. The Lixites claim that they can run faster than horses. Taking Lixite interpreters with us we sailed alongside the desert in a southerly direction for two days, then towards the rising sun for one more day. We then found at the far end of an inlet a little island five shades in circumference. We named it Cerne and left settlers there, judging by our journey we reckoned that we must be opposite Carthage, since we had to sail the same distance from Carthage to the Pillars of Heracles as from the Pillars of Heracles to Cerne. From there, sailing up a big river named the Chretes, we arrived at a lake in which there were three islands, all larger than Cerne. Leaving these islands, we sailed one day and came to the end of the lake, which was overshadowed by high mountains full of savages dressed in animal skins that threw stones at us and thus prevented us from landing. From there we entered another river, which was big and wide, full of crocodiles and hippopotamuses. Then we retraced our journey back to Cerne.

From there we sailed south along a coast entirely inhabited by the Ethiopians, who fled at our approach. Their language was incomprehensible even to the Lixites, whom we had with us. On the last day we disembarked by some high mountains covered with trees with sweet smelling multi coloured wood. We sailed round these mountains for two days and arrived in a huge bay on the other side of which was a plain; there we saw fires breaking out at intervals on all sides at night, both great and small. Having renewed our water supplies, we continued our voyage along the coast for five days, after which we arrived at a huge inlet, which the interpreters called the Horn of the West. There was a big island in this gulf and in the island was a lagoon with another island. Having disembarked there, we could see nothing but forest by day; but at night, many fires were seen and we heard the sound of flutes and the beating of drums and tambourines, which made a great noise. We were struck with terror and our soothsayers bade us leave the island. We left in haste and sailed along by a burning land full of perfumes. Streams of fire rose from it and plunged into the sea. The land was unapproachable because of the heat. Terror-stricken, we hastened away. During the four days of sailing, we saw at night that the land was covered with fire. In the middle was a high flame, higher than the others, which seemed to reach the stars. By day, we realized that it was a very high mountain, named the Chariot of the Gods. Leaving this place, we sailed along the burning coast for three days and came to the gulf named the Horn of the South. At the end of it was an island like the first one, with a lake in which was another island full of savages. The greater part of these, were women. They had hairy bodies and the interpreters called them Gorillas. We pursued some of the males but we could not catch a single one because they were good climbers and they defended themselves fiercely. However, we managed to take three women. They bit and scratched their captors, whom they did not want to follow. We killed them and removed their skins to take back to Carthage. We sailed no further, being short of supplies.

(Periplus of Hanno)

This account of Hanno is of immense interest, as apart from stating how he went around in his voyage, it discloses the mind of the Phoenicians and the manner in which they functioned despite being a democracy. Without having any compulsion to move out, they could send a large population out to colonize new areas along the coast, perhaps to have supporting stations to open up a maritime highway and to find new economic avenues. These people could be left in the middle of nowhere to fend for themselves with no protest from any quarter. Perhaps this spirit, more than anything else, was at the base of their success in such rapid expansion and control of the sea. Hanno seems to have gone as far as Congo where there are gorillas, because he seems to have come across real gorillas which he thought were humans. This can be said because firstly, he has said that the greater parts of these were women, which shows that it was a herd of animals in which there is a dominant male and just a few peripheral males, and secondly, there is no human race in which the women are so strong that several men together cannot overpower a single of them.

This does not, however, appear to be the voyage mentioned by Pliny, as he had stated that Hanno took four months to reach Arabia. In this voyage, Hanno has not maintained his journey on the coast alone but has gone inland, too, in rivers and does not seem to have sailed for four months. This account, however, does leave a possibility that Hanno undertook an expedition before this one, circumnavigating Africa, as has been reported by Pliny, because no prudent person can go out with such a large population to settle colonies on an unknown coast. He would first survey it and get a broad idea before taking thirty thousand people along. It seems likely that Hanno undertook an exploratory voyage first, which has been reported by Pliny, but of which the memoir has been lost.

There is no account of the places that the Phoenicians reached sailing north from Gibraltar. They used to sail along the coast and there are indications that they had reached America. They may possibly have sailed north till they reached the ice and then sailed along it to the west. A study of Phoenician coins by Mark MacMenamin suggests that gold coins minted in Carthage between 350 and 320 BC depict a map of America. Apart from this some first century BC Peruvian pottery have a very close resemblance with Phoenician pottery. To top it all, wreckage of Phoenician ships and a rock inscription found in Brazil mark their visit to the place. Phoenician ships were unique in their design and cannot be mistaken. They were not curved bottom boats, as the Phoenicians had found a totally new solution to the problem of increased load on the structure of the ship caused due to it being rocked by the sea. They had come across cypress and cedar trees in Lebanon which grew straight to a great height and were strong with a thick girth. They used to join these logs in a straight line for making the keel of the ship. This was chiselled from the outside to give the desired shape, but from the inside only as much was dug out as was necessary to fix the hull and the superstructure. Thus, this keel of solid cedar or cypress logs took the load caused by the rocking of the ship and was strong enough to withstand it. The Phoenicians were thus able to make flat bottom sea-worthy ships.

Being a commercial civilization, trade was the main occupation of the people of the Indus Valley Civilization. The Phoenicians too excelled in this. References of they being very enterprising merchants are replete in all accounts about them but Pliny has reported that trade was introduced by them. His statement on this is here.

> Erichthonius of Athens, or according to others Aeacus, discovered silver; mining and smelting of gold was invented by Cadmus, the Phoenician at Mount Pangaeus;...trade by the Phoenicians.
>
> (Pliny the Elder. Natural History. Book VII. Para 56)

Pliny is enumerating the achievements of different people wherein he has given the credit of introducing trade to the Phoenicians. Strabo has made a similar statement about them which is here.

> Now in former times it was the Phoenicians alone who
> carried on commerce for they kept the voyage hidden from
> everyone else.
>
> (Strabo. Geographica. Book III. Chapter 5. Para 11)

Evidently along with sea voyages, the Phoenicians were the people who introduced trade in the Mediterranean amongst the Greeks, Egyptians and others. Homer calls them 'the profit seeking Phoenicians'. Herodotus has given an account which is a testimony to their enterprising nature. It is mentioned here.

> The Carthaginians say also this, that there is a place in Libya
> and the men dwelling there, outside the Pillars of Heracles, to
> whom when they have come and have taken the merchandise
> forth from their ships, they set it in order along the beach
> and embark again in their ships, and after that they raise
> a smoke; and the natives of the country seeing the smoke
> come to the sea, and then they lay down gold as an equivalent
> for the merchandise and retire to a distance away from the
> merchandise. The Carthaginians upon that disembark and
> examine it, and if the gold is in their opinion sufficient for
> the value of the merchandise, they take it up and go their
> way; but if not, they embark again in their ships and sit there;
> and the other approach and straightaway add more gold to
> the former, until they satisfy them: and they say that neither
> party wrongs the other; for neither do the Carthaginians lay
> hands on the gold until it is made equal to the value of their
> merchandise, nor do the others lay hands on the merchandise
> until the Carthaginians have taken the gold.
>
> (Herodotus. *The Histories*. Book 4. Para 196)

This reference is to trade with people in Africa along the Atlantic coast. They lived in isolation to the extent that they did not even interact with the people from whom they were buying commodities, yet the Phoenicians had found a way to trade with them. An idea about the volume of their trade and the spirit of enterprise can also be had from the colonies and settlements that they had established, as emerges from the accounts of various writers. Here are some of them.

1. The whole of this (of Spain) coast was thought by Marcus Agrippa to be of Carthaginian origin; but beyond the Guadiana and facing the Atlantic Ocean is the territory of the Bastuli and Turduli. Marcus Varro records that the whole of Spain was penetrated by invasions of Hiberi, Persians, Phoenicians, Celts and Carthaginians.

    (Pliny the Elder. Natural History. Book III. Para 1)

2. As for the people of the west, Homer makes plain that they were prosperous and that they lived in a temperate climate, doubtless having heard of the wealth of Iberia, and how in quest of the wealth, Heracles invaded the country, and after him the Phoenicians also, the people who in earliest times became masters of most of the country.

    (Strabo. Geographica. Book I. Chapter 1. Para 4)

3. In the first place, the expeditions of Heracles and of the Phoenicians, since they both reached as far as Iberia, suggested to Homer that the people of Iberia were in some way rich and led a life of ease. Indeed these people became so utterly subject to the Phoenicians that the greater number of the cities in Turdetania and of the neighbouring places are now inhabited by the Phoenicians.

    (Strabo. Geographica. Book III. Chapter 2. Para 13)

4. Carthage was founded by Dido, who brought a host of people from Tyre. The colonization proved to be so fortunate an enterprise for the Phoenicians, both this Carthage and that which extended as far as Iberia—I mean the part outside the Pillars as well as the rest of it—that even to this day the best part of continental Europe and also the adjacent islands are occupied by the Phoenicians; and they gained possession of all that part of Libya which men can live in without living a nomadic life. From this dominion they not only raised their city to be a rival of Rome, but also waged three great

wars against the Romans. When they began to wage this war they had three hundred cities in Libya and seven hundred thousand people in their city.

(Strabo. Geographica. Book XVII. Chapter 3. Para 15)

5. After the rule of kings was at an end, the Carthaginians were the first that made themselves masters of the country, for when the Gaditani according to the directions which they received in a dream, had removed the sacred things of Hercules from Tyre, whence also the Carthaginians had their origin, into Spain, and had built a city there, the neighbouring people of the country, being jealous of the rise of this new city, and in consequence attacking the Gaditanis in war, the Carthaginians sent them succour as being their kindred. The expedition being successful, they both secured the Gaditani from injury, and added the greatest part of the province to their dominions.

(Justin. Philippic History. Book 44. Para 5)

6. The Carthaginians had not only reduced Libya to subjection, but a great part of Spain besides, and that they were also in possession of all the islands in the Sardinian and Tyrrhenian Seas.

(Polybius. *The Histories*. Book I. Para 10)

These passages show the extent of Phoenician control of the western Mediterranean. The entire North Africa, Spain and Portugal were under their control along with all the islands. Cadiz had come up on the Atlantic coast in Spain in 1,110 BC and Utica in Africa in 1,101 BC, within a century of the arrival of the 'Sea Peoples' in Phoenicia. They are reported to have had three hundred cities in Africa, and Carthage, their Megalopolis, is reported to have had a population of seven lakhs. They were trading on the Atlantic coast also and were mining tin in Britain. Herodotus has referred to this mining, though he has named the place as 'Tin Islands' and has not named the Phoenicians as the miners, but it has to be them as nobody else was venturing out into the sea. The said passage is here.

These are the extremities of Asia and in Libya; but as to the extremities of Europe towards the West, I am not able to speak

with certainty: for neither do I accept the tale that there is a
river called in the Barbarian tongue Eridanos, flowing into
the sea which lies towards the North Wind, whence it is said
amber comes; nor do I know the real existence of 'Tin Islands'
from which tin comes to us.

(Herodotus. *The Histories*. Book 3. Para 115)

This is believed to be Cornwall, which is at the southwestern tip of
England. Apart from tin, Herodotus has mentioned amber coming
from a place towards the North Wind where a river flows into the sea.
This place cannot be located, though the possibility is that the river
Rhine is being spoken of.

Apart from reaching the extreme west of the Mediterranean Sea,
the Phoenicians had made several inroads into Greece and Italy. It
was Rome that finally uprooted them from most of these places, but
till then not only their presence, but colonization of several areas is
reported by several writers. One from Herodotus is here.

Now at this very same time Theras was preparing to set forth
from Lacedamon to found a settlement. This Theras, who was
of the race of Cadmus, was mother's brother to the sons of
Aristodemos, Eurysthenes and Procles; and while these sons
were yet children, Theras as their guardian held royal power
in Sparta. When, however, his nephews were grown and had
taken the power into their hands, then Theras, being grieved
that he should be ruled by others after he had tasted of rule
himself, said that he would not remain in Lacedemon, but
would sail away to his kinsmen. Now there were in the island
which is now called Thera, but formerly was called Callista,
descendants of Membliaros the son of Poikiles, a Phoenician:
for Cadmus the son of Agenor in his search for Europa put in
to land at this island which is now called Thera; and, whether
it was that the country pleased him when he had put to land
or whether he chose to do so for any other reason, he left in
this island, besides the Phoenicians, Membliaros, also, of his
kinsmen. These occupied the island called Callista for eight

generations of men, before Theras came from Lacedemon.
(Herodotus. *The Histories*. Book 4. Para 147)

Cadmus is a very significant figure in Phoenician migration to Greece and would be examined separately. His time is believed to be 2,100 BC. Here Herodotus is writing of Sparta, where Theras, a Phoenician, held royal power on behalf of his young nephews and on their reaching maturity, moved to a nearby island which too was a Phoenician settlement and got its name from him. The main settlement by Cadmus, in Greece, was Thebes, which is adjoining Athens. The area was also called Cadmea and the people, Thebans as well as Cadmeans. Gephyraians, is another name used for a group of Phoenicians. They had occupied the neighbouring Boetia. References of their settlements are here.

1. Now the Gephyraians, of whom were those who murdered Hipparchos, according to their own account were originally descended from Eretria; but as I find by carrying inquiries back, they were Phoenicians of those who came with Cadmus to the land which is now called Boetia, and they dwelt in the district of Tanagra, which they had allotted to them in that land. Then after the Cadmeans had first been driven out by the Argives, these Gephyraians next were driven out by the Boetians and turned towards Athens; and the Athenians received them on certain fixed conditions to be citizens of their state, laying down rules that they should be excluded from a number of things not worth mentioning here.
    (Herodotus. *The Histories*. Book 5. Para 58)

2. Now it was in the reign of this very Laodamas, the son of Eteocles that Cadmeans were driven out by the Argives and turned to go to the Enchelions; and the Gephyraians being left behind were afterwards forced by the Boetians to retire to Athens. Moreover they have temples established in Athens, in which the other Athenians have no part, and besides others which are different from the rest, there is especially a temple of Demeter Achaia and a celebration of her mysteries.
    (Herodotus. *The Histories*. Book 5. Para 61)

3. I myself too once saw Cadmean characters in the temple of Ismenian Apollo of Thebes of the Boetians, engraved on certain tripods, and in most respect resembling the Ionic letters: one of the tripods has the inscription...

(Herodotus. *The Histories*. Book 5. Para 59)

These passages speak of Phoenicians settling in Boetia, which is on the Isthmus connecting Sparta and is neighbouring Thebes and Athens. Though Herodotus has stated that the Cadmeans were driven out by the Argives, other accounts show that the Argives were defeated in the battle. The cause of the war too was not land as Argos is not a neighbouring state of Thebes or Boetia, but is far away in the Pelopennese peninsula. It does not seem likely that the Cadmeans were driven out as they were completely assimilated amongst the Greeks. Gephyraians, the other Phoenicians, have been reported to have moved to Athens, where they were granted citizenship and had their temples, including one with which mysteries were associated. In the third passage, Herodotus has recorded that he saw some tripods with inscriptions in the Phoenician script in the temple of the Ismenian Apollo of Thebes. He has recorded the inscriptions of three tripods, which have the name of the person dedicating it and a few words of his achievements. Strabo has also written about the Phoenicians settling in Thebes. Passages from him are here.

1. Yet one might say that in ancient times the whole of Greece was a settlement of barbarians, if one reasons from traditions themselves: Pelops brought over peoples from Phrygia to Peloponnesus that received its name from him; and Danaus from Egypt... Cadmea by the Phoenicians who came with Cadmus.

(Strabo. Geographica. Book VII. Chapter 7. Para 1)

2. Then the Phoenicians occupied it, I mean the Phoenicians with Cadmus, the man who fortified the Cadmea and left the dominion to his descendants. Those Phoenicians founded Thebes in addition to the Cadmea and preserved their dominion, commanding most of the Boetians until the expedition of Epigoni. On this occasion they left Thebes for a short time, but came back again. And in

the same way, when they were ejected by the Thracians and the Pelasgians, they established their government in Thessaly along with the Arnaei for a long time, so that they were called Boetians. Then they returned to the homeland at the time when the Aeolian fleet near Aulis in Boetia, was ready to set sail.

(Strabo. Geographica. Book XI. Chapter 2. Para 3)

These statements from Strabo show that some of the city states of Greece were originally Phoenician. Thasos is another Greek island state, which has been reported by Herodotus to have been settled by the Phoenicians. The relevant passage is here.

I myself saw these mines, and by much the most marvellous of them were those which the Phoenicians discovered, who made the first settlement in this island in the company with Thasos; and the island had the name which it now has from this, Thasos the Phoenician. These Phoenician mines are in that part of Thasos which is between the places called Ainyra and Koinyra and opposite Samothrake, where there is a great mountain which has been all turned up in the search of the metal.

(Herodotus. *The Histories*. Book 6. Para 47)

The mines that Herodotus is appreciating were gold mines that the Phoenicians were operating. At a nearby place, they had turned up an entire mountain in search of it. The island bore the name of a Phoenician who had made the first settlement. Crete was another Greek island which was a very old Phoenician settlement and had a unique culture amongst the Greek states, known as the Minoian Civilization. Herodotus has mentioned its Phoenician connection in the following passage.

As to Europe, however, it is neither known by any man whether it is surrounded by sea, nor does it appear whence it got its name or who it was who gave it, unless we shall say that the land received its name from Europa the Tyrian; and if so, it would appear that before this it was nameless like the rest. She, however, belongs to Asia and did not come to this land which is now called by the Hellenese Europe, but only from Phoenicia to Crete, and from Crete to Lykia.

(Herodotus. *The Histories*. Book 4. Para 45)

It has been stated that Europa was a Phoenician and Europe got its name from her. She had gone from Phoenicia to Crete and from there to Lykia. Europa was a princess of Tyre, the daughter of Agenor and the sister of Cadmus. Minos, the legendary founder of Crete was her son.

For Italy the information provided by the writers is primarily about the control of Sicily, which is understandable as it must have been an important station on the maritime highway. The relevant passages are here.

1. Now there sailed with Dorieos others also of the Spartans, to be joint founders with him of the colony, namely, Thessalos and Paraibates and Keleas and Euryleon; and these when they reached Sicily with all their armament, were slain, being defeated in battle by the Phoenicians and men of Egesta.

   (Herodotus. *The Histories*. Book 5. Para 46)

2. The envoys spoke thus, 'Hellenes, a selfish speech is this, with which ye have ventured to come and invite me to be your ally against the Barbarians; whereas ye yourselves, when I in former times requested of you to join with me in fighting against an army of Barbarians, contention having arisen between me and the Carthaginians, and when I charged you to exact vengeance of the men of Egesta for the death of Dorieos the son of Anaxandrides, while at the same time I offered to help in setting free the trading places, from which great advantages and gains have been reaped by you, ye, I say, then neither for my own sake came to my assistance, nor in order to exact vengeance for the death of Darieos; and so far as ye are concerned, all these parts are even now under the rule of Barbarians.'

   (Herodotus. *The Histories*. Book 7. Para 158)

These passages show that Sicily was under the control of the Phoenicians and the Spartans unsuccessfully tried to dislodge them.

The second passage is significant as it shows that the aim of the Spartans was to free the trading places. It appears that centuries after the Phoenicians had begun trading in the Mediterranean, other groups tried to venture into it, but the Phoenicians maintained their monopoly, which led to friction and ultimately war. Geographically, Sicily occupies a very important position in the Mediterranean Sea for ships sailing across its length.

Apart from Portugal, Spain, Italy, Greece and Africa there are references of Phoenician settlements in Egypt, Ethiopia, Armenia and Thrace also. This shows that beginning from their settlements on the Syrian coastline, the Phoenicians had explored the entire Mediterranean Sea and wherever any economic activity was possible they put their enterprise into it. In the process they established colonies all over the place, which despite being independent of each other, had a lot of cohesion leading to their complete control over the area.

The third pillar of the economy of the Indus Valley Civilization was agriculture. Their entire prosperity began with agriculture and was sustained by it. It may seem to be a surprise that the Phoenicians, who have the image of being only traders and seamen, were not just acquainted with agriculture but were masters of the art, to the extent that the earliest work on agriculture has been written by them. Known as *Mago's Treatise*, which was in twenty-eight books, this was the only book of the library of Carthage that the Romans took to Rome after destroying the city. The rest were presented to African princes. The Roman Senate decreed it to be translated into Latin. Cassius Dionysius of Utica had translated it into Greek also. Unfortunately, neither the original Punic version nor the Greek and Latin translations have survived. However, as almost all early writers on the subject in Greek as well as Latin have leaned heavily on Mago, about forty quotations of varying length are available. They deal with a wide variety of subjects covering cereal crops, olives, fruit trees, vegetables, the breeding of horses, mules and oxen, farmyard animals, bee-keeping, wine making and internal organization of the farm etc. Several writers like Diodorus Siculus and Polybius have stated that the Carthaginians were very prosperous in agriculture and looked on its improvement as a real science and that there were several highly renowned works on the subject, other than that of Mago. Unfortunately, there is no trace left of any of them. This deep knowledge of agriculture, in the midst of such a vibrant mercantile economy, points to a very long tradition lost in antiquity.

Just as the economic life of the Phoenicians, reflects their links with India, so do their religious beliefs, as can be seen in the works of ancient Greek and Roman writers. It has to be admitted that the available stories of Phoenician mythology, like the Baal Cycle have nothing similar in Indian mythology. But for that matter, several evidently mythological scenes depicted on the seals of the Indus Valley Civilization have nothing corresponding in the later mythology of the country. Extracts from the writers that tell about the Phoenician religious beliefs are here.

> Then for Dionysos on the eve of the festival each one kills a pig by cutting its throat before his own doors, and after that he gives the pig to the swineherd who sold it to him, to carry away again; and the rest of the feast of Dionysos is celebrated by the Egyptians in the same way as by the Hellenes in almost all things except choral dances, but instead of the phallus they have invented another contrivance, namely figures of about a cubit in height worked by strings, which women carry about the village, with the privy member made to move and not much less in size than the rest of the body: and a flute goes before and they follow singing the praises of Dionysos. As to the reason why the figure has this member larger than is natural and moves it, though it moves no other part of the body, about this there is a sacred story told.
>
> Now I think that Malampus the son of Amytheon was not without knowledge of these rites of sacrifice, but was acquainted with them, for Melampus is he who first set forth to the Hellenes the name of Dionysos and the manner of sacrifice and the procession of the phallus. Strictly speaking indeed, when he made it known did not take in the whole,

but those wise men who came after him made it known more at large. Melampus then is he who taught of the phallus which is carried in procession for Dionysos, and from him the Hellenes learnt to do that which they do. I say then that Melampus being a man of ability contrived for himself the art of divination, and having learnt from Egypt he taught the Hellenes many things, and among them those that concern Dionysos, making changes on a few points of them, for I shall not say that which is done in worship of the god in Egypt came accidently to be the same with that which is done among the Hellenes, for then these rites would have been in character with Hellenic worship and not lately brought in, nor certainly shall I say that the Egyptians took from the Hellenes either this or any other customary observance, but I think it most probable that Melampus learnt the matter concerning Dionysos from Cadmus the Tyrian and from those who came with him from Phoenicia to the land which we now call Boetia.

(Herodotus. *The Histories*. Book 2. Paras 48 and 49)

Herodotus has described a religious belief of the Greeks concerning Dionysos and the phallus worship linked with him. He has also compared it with similar practices of Egypt and has concluded that the said beliefs and practices came to Greece from the Phoenicians. Apart from some other practices a procession of the phallus was taken out. In the archaeological remains of the Indus Valley Civilization a very large number of phallus symbols have been found. Phallus worship is a part of the religious practices of the Hindus even today. Though there is no tradition of taking out of a procession now, it may have been there in the remote past. Plutarch too has mentioned of the phallic procession of Egypt and has stated that it was called the festival of Pamylia which was linked to Osiris. He has also made a brief description of the procession in Greece which is mentioned here.

Our traditional festival of the Dionysos was in former times a homely and merry procession. First came a jug of wine and a vine branch, then one celebrant dragged a he-goat along, another followed with a basket of dry figs, and the phallus-bearer came last.

(Plutarch. On the Love of Wealth)

What has been called a procession seems to be a ritual of each family separately and not a general procession of the city or locality. As members of the family moved in a sequence, carrying different articles, it has been called a procession. In a play Aristophenes too has described a phallic procession, which is mentioned here.

Dicaeopolis (coming out). Keep ye all the holy silence! Now, the basket bearer, go you in front. You, Xanthias, hold the phallus pole erect.

Wife. Sit down the basket, girl, and we'll begin.

Daughter. O mother, hand me here the gravy spoon, to ladle out the gravy on the cake.

Dicaeopolis. 'Tis well. Lord Dionysos, grant me now to show the show and make the sacrifice as thou would'st have me, I and all my house; then keep with joy the Rural Dionysia; no more of soldiering now. And may this Peace of thirty summers, answer to my hopes.

Wife. O daughter, bear the basket sweetly, sweet, with savoury-eating look. Happy the man, whoe'er he is, who weds you and begets kittens as fair and saucy as yourself. Move on! but heed lest any in the crowd should nibble off, unseen, your bits of gold.

Dicaeopolis. O Xanthias, walk behind the basket bearer, holding, you two, the phallus pole erect. And I'll bring up the rear, and sing the hymn, wife, watch me from the roof. Now then, proceed.

(Aristophenes. Acharnians)

The Phoenicians worshipped a goddess also. Herodotus, while describing Memphis in Egypt has made the following statement.

Round about this enclosure dwell Phoenicians of Tyre, and

this whole region is called the Camp of the Tyrians. Within the enclosure of Proteus there is a temple of the 'Foreign Aphrodite', which temple I conjecture to be one of Helen the daughter of Tyndareus.

(Herodotus. *The Histories*. Book 2. Para 112)

In the archaeological finds of the Indus Valley Civilization a very large number of figures of the 'Mother Goddess' have been found. The number gives an impression that she was perhaps the most prominent deity of the people. The Phoenicians, in their settlement in Memphis, have been reported to be having a temple of 'the Foreign Aphrodite'. Evidently, she was not a Greek or Egyptian goddess. As this goddess has not been described by Herodotus, nothing with certainty can be said for linking her to the Mother Goddess of India, but a possibility remains, as she was a part of the Phoenician belief system. Another very interesting god of the Phoenicians has been mentioned by Herodotus, which seems to have links with India. The passage about him is here.

Likewise also he entered into the temple of Hephaistos and very much derided the image of the god: for the image of Hephaistos very nearly resembles the Phoenician Pataicoi, which the Phoenicians carry about on the prows of their triremes; and for him who has not seen these, I will indicate its nature, it is the likeness of a dwarfish man.

(Herodotus. *The Histories*. Book 3. Para 37)

This is significant, as a god is normally conceptualized with all perfections. It is unusual to have the image of a god with perfection lacking. In this case the Phoenician god, who has been named Pataicoi, and the Egyptian god Hephaistos, were believed to be dwarfs. Indian mythology too has a dwarf as a god, Vishnu in his Dwarf Incarnation. This god of the Phoenicians, whose image they used to place on the prow of their ships, appears to have travelled from India.

An interesting observation reflecting the social system of the Phoenicians has been made by Socrates. This is mentioned here.

Nothing new, I replied; only an old Phoenician tale.

How your words seem to hesitate on your lips!

You will not wonder, I replied, at my hesitation when you have heard.

Speak, he said, and fear not.

Well, then, I will speak, although I really know not how to look you in the face, or in what words to utter the audacious fiction, which I propose to communicate gradually, first to the rulers, then to the soldiers and lastly to the people. They are to be told that their youth was a dream, and the education and training which they received from us, an appearance only; in reality during all that time they were being formed and fed in the womb of the earth, where they themselves and their arms and appurtenances were manufactured; when they were completed, the earth, their mother, sent them up; and so their country being their mother and also their nurse, they are bound to advise for her good, and to defend her against attacks, and her citizens they are to regard as children of the earth and their own brothers. Citizens, we shall say to them in our tale, you are brothers, yet God has formed you differently. Some of you have the power of command, and in the composition of these he has mingled gold, wherefore also they have the greatest honour; others he has made of silver, to be auxiliaries; others again who are to be husbandmen and craftsmen he has composed of brass and iron; and the species will generally be preserved in the children. But as all are of the same original stock, a golden parent will sometimes have a silver son, or a silver parent a golden son. And God proclaims as a first principle to the rulers, and above all else, that there is nothing which they should so anxiously guard as of the race. They should observe what elements mingle in their offspring; for if the son of a golden or silver parent has an admixture of brass and iron, then nature orders a transportation of ranks, and the eye of the ruler must not be pitiful towards the child because he has to descend in

the scale and become a husbandman or artisan, just as there
may be sons of artisans who having an admixture of gold or
silver in them are raised to honour, and become guardians
or auxiliaries. For an oracle says that when a man of brass
or iron guards the state, it will be destroyed. Such is the tale;
is there any possibility of making our citizens believe in it?
(Plato. The Republic. Book 3. The Arts of Education)

Socrates is relating the values that were imparted to students by
the Phoenicians, as a part of their education. The first statement is
of their political ethos wherein the basic concept is that the citizen
is for the state and not the other way round. This is visible in the
account of Hanno of his voyage, wherein comfortable settled people
could be asked to leave and go to an unknown location to establish
colonies. It was also the guiding principle of governance of Sparta,
which even otherwise is known to have had Phoenician influence,
as Lycurgus, the framer of the Spartan constitution had gone to
Crete to study their constitution, which in turn had deep Phoenician
connections. The second statement is very significant as it not only
confirms the links of the Phoenicians with India, but also confirms
the manner in which the 'Varn Vyavastha' or the caste system had
been introduced in India.

Socrates has stated that the Phoenicians had a caste system
having three castes, the first was that of rulers and warriors, the
second of auxiliaries and the third of husbandmen and craftsmen.
These were based on birth and it was the paramount duty of the
rulers to anxiously guard that there occurs no mingling of the
castes. The manner in which the caste system had been introduced
in India has already been mentioned earlier. To recapitulate, the
Zoroastrian scriptures show that the Aryans had four classes, the
priests, the warriors, the husbandmen and the artisans. In India,
this got translated to the priests, warriors, merchants and artisans.
The crucial difference was in the third caste wherein the farmers
had been replaced by merchants. The name used for this caste was
'vaishya', a word which is from the root 'vish', which means people.

This category was intended to have the rest of the people, after the remaining three had been segregated on the basis of their profession. In Central Asia the rest of the people were farmers, because of which, in course of time, the four classes in the Zoroastrian scriptures got named as the priests, warriors, husbandmen and artisans. In India, as the system had been introduced only in the cities of the Indus Valley Civilization, the rest of the people there were traders and so this caste came to be known as that of merchants. In India, to begin with, the farmers had no place in the caste system as they were not in cities though they constituted an overwhelming majority of the overall population. At a later stage, when the caste system was extended to cover the entire population and not just the city dwellers, the farmers by default, got included in the lowest caste with the artisans.

The statement from Socrates confirms this process. First of all, the farmers have been placed in the lowest category, being clubbed with artisans, and secondly, the merchants, who constituted the most important segment of the Phoenician society also, have not been named by their profession, but have fallen in a category with a general name of auxiliaries. In India too, they had fallen in the category of the rest of the people, despite being the most important part of the society and had got the name 'vaishya', which to begin with, was a general term and only in course of time came to be associated with merchants alone.

Another significant feature of this statement is, that the highest caste of priests or brahmans is missing. Almost all societies have had some sort of class distinctions, even if they were not water-tight and based on birth. In every society, one class that has been found without exception is that of priests. The Phoenicians had temples and priests, but evidently they did not have a caste of priests. This, further points to their Indian links. Religious injunctions prohibit the brahmans from undertaking a sea journey, except in the face of death. Thus we have had Rishi Vashisht travelling by sea from Persia to India, as he faced death. However, in the Parthian history it has emerged that Tiridates went to Rome by land to receive the diadem from Nero but did not exercise the easier option of travelling by sea, as his priestly scruples prevented him from doing so. It is evident that the brahmans did not migrate out of India with the rest as they could not undertake a sea journey and the Phoenicians maintained the caste system and their individual caste identity as they carried it from India and did give the status of the caste of the brahmans to their priests, though they had temples and, in them, priests. As it was based on birth it could not have been done within the laid down religious norms.

Socrates has made this statement with a lot of hesitation and embarrassment and has concluded by saying that their citizens cannot be made to believe in it. Cadmus had led a Phoenician migration into Thebes from where people had moved to Athens also and acquired its citizenship and had established temples. Despite this, the Phoenician concept of caste has been spoken of as something foreign and absurd. A lot of Phoenician ideas had been adopted by the Greeks from Cadmus. This hesitation of Socrates shows that the caste system was not one of them. Evidently Cadmus represents the pre-Aryan Indian thought and beliefs, while elsewhere the later beliefs and practices had also been mingled.

The comparison of the political system of the Phoenicians with that of ancient India, to bring out their links, has its limitations, as the political system of the Indus Valley Civilization, is known only from indirect sources. It is, however, known with certainty from the archaeological sites that the Indians lived in cities. The design of these cities and the absence of palaces show that they were not monarchies, but were having a democratic system of governance. Despite having a democratic set up, the people in authority were called kings. This can be said because the *Rig Ved* uses this word. It is confirmed also by similar usage in the sixth century BC as the father of Lord Buddha was called King Suddhodhan, though Kapilvastu was a republic. The cities were independent political units is borne out by the *Rig Ved* as it mentions several kings dwelling on the river Saraswati. Thus the overall picture that emerges of the political system of the Indus Valley Civilization is of city states, which had an oligarchy, wherein the oligarchs were addressed as king. The Phoenician system of governance had all these features though a lot more is known about it.

Several writers have written about the Carthaginian constitution and the system of governance of the Phoenicians. In the *Odyssey*, Homer has mentioned a race which he has named the Phaeacians. Odysseus reaches their island at the end of his adventures and narrates much of his story there. Though the name is different, the description about them matches the Phoenicians completely as they are reported to be seafarers and traders. At the end Homer creates a further confusion, as when the Phaeacians have dropped Odysseus at Ithaca, his home, and a little later Athena asks him, how he came, he replies that he came in a Phoenician ship. Homer has given a vivid description of these people and for their political set up their king has made the following statement.

> Here are twelve noble kings who rule among the people, with myself as the thirteenth.
>
> (Homer. The *Odyssey*. Book 8)

Aristotle has briefly written about the Carthaginian constitution in his work the *Politics*. He has stated that the constitutions of Sparta, Crete and Carthage closely resembled each other and had a lot of differences from those of the rest of the states. Like Sparta, Carthage too had common meals for the citizens. It had a board of 104 members like the Ephers of Sparta, but was better as its members were chosen on merit. Their kings and Board of Elders were the counterparts of the Spartan kings and Board of Ephers. The kings were neither drawn from one family alone, nor from any and every family. Election depended on the eminence of a person's family and his worth. The kings, acting in conjunction with the Elders had sovereign power to refer or not to refer a matter to the people, provided they were unanimous, failing which the people had the power of decision. There was a Board of Five, which had supreme control over many important matters including filling up of vacancies in the Board of 104. As it had eminence of a person's family as a deciding factor, along with merit, the appointments and elections were guided by the wealth of the family of the person. Within these parameters they had elections to the highest offices like kings and generals. They also allowed the same person to hold more offices than one. The aim of their constitution was threefold, wealth, virtue and the good of the people. Polybius has made some interesting observations about the constitution of Carthage. These are here.

1. One may say that nearly all authors have handed down to us the reputation for excellence enjoyed by the constitutions of Sparta, Crete, Matinea and Carthage. Some mention also those of Athens and Thebes.

    (Polybius. *The Histories*. Book 6. Para 43)

2. The constitution of Carthage seems to me to have been originally well contrived as regards its most distinctive points. For there were kings and the House of Elders was an autocratic force, and the people were supreme in matters proper to them, the entire frame of the state much resembling that of Rome and Sparta. But at the time when they entered in the Hannibalic War, the Carthaginian constitution had degenerated and that of Rome was better. For as every body or state or action has its natural periods first of growth, then of prime, and finally of decay, and as everything in them is at its best when they are in their prime, it was for this reason that the difference between the two states manifested itself at this time. For by as much as the power and prosperity of Carthage had been earlier than that of Rome, by so much that Carthage had already begun to decline while Rome was exactly at her prime as far as, at least as her system of government was concerned. Consequently the multitude of Carthage had already acquired the chief voice in deliberations; while at Rome the Senate still retained this; and hence, as in one case the masses deliberated and in the other the most eminent men. The Roman decisions on public affairs were superior, so that although they met with complete disaster, they were finally by the wisdom of their counsels victors over the Carthaginians in the war.

    (Polybius. *The Histories*. Book 6. Para 51)

Apart from the economic, religious and political affairs of the Phoenicians pointing to their Indian connections, there are a few isolated elements related to them which support the same conclusions. The elephant is an intriguing link between the two. Like the Indians, the Phoenicians too used it very effectively as an instrument of war. In recognition of its position, some of the Phoenician coins have it embossed on them. Looking at the curvature of its back, it can be said with certainty that these were Indian and not African elephants. Chandragupt Maurya had presented five hundred elephants to Selucus as a part of the peace process after defeating him. These elephants remained with the Selucids and were used by them in wars in Greece and Italy. They had, however, not gone to Carthage. On the other hand Carthage not only had Indian elephants, but Indians were also involved in training and handling them. There is no reference to show how these Indians and Indian elephants reached Carthage, but their presence is brought out by the following passages.

1. Scipio–Thus the Indian or Carthaginian regulates one of these huge animals, and renders him docile and familiar with human manners.
    (Cicero. Treatise on the Commonwealth. Book 2)
2. In consequence they were most of them cut to pieces on the battle-field. Of the elephants six were killed with their drivers and the other four having forced their way through the ranks were captured afterwards alone and abandoned by their Indians.
    (Polybius. *The Histories*. Book XI. Para 1)

In the second passage Polybius is describing the battle fought by Hasdrubal, the brother of Hannibal, with the Romans, after he crossed the Alps and entered Italy to join Hannibal. He has reported that the drivers of the elephants were Indian. Cicero too has reported that the Indians and the Carthaginians trained the elephants. This goes to show that the Phoenicians had maintained links with India much longer than is known.

The next feature of the Phoenicians that links them with India is their acquaintance with the script. They are reported to have introduced this in Greece. The people of the Indus Valley Civilization had a script as can be seen from their seals. It is true that the Phoenician script that has come down to us does not have any similarity with the script found on these seals, but this does not negate the assertion, because the earliest examples of the Phoenician script found are on an inscription at Byblos of the eleventh century BC, known as the 'Ahiram Epitaph'. Also, none of the Indian scripts of later times have their roots in the Harappan script. Though the Harappan script has not been deciphered, but from the little that has been understood of it, the Phoenician script has the similarity with it of being written from right to left and not having any vowels. The fact that they were aware of the concept of framing a script is revealed from their ability to modify it to suit new languages. They had introduced it in Greece is brought out from the following passages.

1. Now these Phoenicians who came with Cadmus of whom were the Gephyraians, brought in among the Hellenes many arts when they settled in this land of Boetia, and specially letters, which did not exist, as it appears to me, among the Hellenes before this time; and at first they brought in those which are used by the Phoenician race generally, but afterwards, as time went on, they changed with their speech the form of letters also.

    (Herodotus. *The Histories*. Book 5. Para 58)

2. The Phoenician race itself has the great distinction of having invented the alphabet and the science of astronomy, navigation and strategy.

    (Pliny the Elder. Natural History. Book V Para 13)

3. Cadmus imported an alphabet of sixteen letters into Greece from Phoenicia and that to these Palamedes at the time of the Trojan War added four characters and after him Simonides the lyric poet added another four.

    (Pliny the Elder. Natural History. Book VII Para 56)

4. But as it is, the sea brought the Greeks wine from India, from Greece transmitted the use of grain across the sea, from Phoenicia imported letters as a memorial against forgetfulness, thus preventing the greater part of mankind from being wineless, grainless and unlettered.

    (Plutarch. Moralia. Is Water or Fire more Useful)

With so many features of the Phoenicians matching those of the Indus Valley Civilization, they confirm the conclusions that emerge about their place of origin as have been referred to by several early writers in their works. Added to this is the fact that the Phoenicians witnessed a sudden increase in their population in 1,200 BC, caused by a natural calamity in an area that was civilized enough that its people could travel by sea in such large numbers and reach West Asia. They all point to India.

14
Cadmus and Greece

CADMUS IS A VERY IMPORTANT link in the Indian connections with Greece. He has acquired a mythological status and is the first Greek hero, the slayer of monsters, before Heracles. The story about him says that his father Agenor was the king of Tyre, who had two more sons—Phoenix and Cilix, and a daughter Europa. Zeus, in the shape of a bull, abducted Europa and took her to Crete. Cadmus and his nephew Thasus, the son of Cilix, were sent out by Agenor to find her, and enjoined not to return without her. On finding that it was Zeus, who was the culprit, Cadmus, either unwilling to go against Zeus or unable to fight him, gave up the quest, but did not return to Tyre. In his wanderings, he went to Samothrace and Thasos, the latter was settled by his nephew Thasus from whom the island got its name. Finally, he reached Delphi to consult the Oracle. He was ordered to give up his quest and follow a special cow which would meet him, and to build a town on the spot where she should lie down exhausted. The cow guided him to Boetia where he founded the city of Thebes. He wished to sacrifice the cow to Athena and sent some of his companions to the nearby Ismenian Spring to fetch water. These were killed by the water dragon who was the guardian of the spring. In turn Cadmus killed this dragon. It being sacred to Ares, Cadmus was made to do penance for eight years, at the end of which Ares gave him his daughter Harmonia as wife. He had a son named Polydorus and four daughters, Agave, Autonoe, Ino and Semele. As king, he started a dynasty in Thebes which continued for several generations. Cadmus abdicated in favour of his grandson Pentheus, and went away with Harmonia to Illyria to fight on the side of Encheleans. Later, he became a king there and founded the cities of Lychnidos and Bouthoe on the east coast of the Adriatic Sea.

Several writers have mentioned Cadmus and his descendants, giving a fair picture of him. Pindar, who lived between 522 and 438 BC, and is one of the nine canonical lyric poets of ancient Greece, was from Thebes and traced his descent from Cadmus. Some of his Odes give an idea of Cadmus and his successors. Extracts from them are here.

1. Under the power of noble joys, malignant pain is subdued and dies, whenever god-sent Fate lifts prosperity on high. This saying applies to the daughters of Cadmus on their lovely thrones: they suffered greatly, but their heavy sorrow collapsed in the presence of greater blessings. Long-haired Semele who died in the roar of the thunderbolt, lives among the Olympians; Pallas is her constant friend and indeed so is father Zeus, and she is loved by her ivy-crowned son. And they say that even in the sea, among the ocean-daughters of Nereus, immortal life is granted to Ino for all time.

    (Pindar. Olympian Ode 2)

2. With these wreaths and garlands of flowers they entwine their hands according to the righteous counsels of Rhadamanthys, whom the great father, the husband of Rhea whose throne is above all others, keeps close beside him as his partner. Peleus and Cadmus are counted among them.

    (Pindar. Olympian Ode 2)

3. They heard the muses of the golden headbands singing on the mountain and in seven-gated Thebes, when Cadmus married ox-eyed Harmonia, and Peleus married the famous daughter of wise Nereus.

    (Pindar. Pythian Ode 3)

4. Daughter of Cadmus, Semele dwelling among the Olympians and Ino Leucothea, sharing the chamber of the Nereid sea-nymphs: come with the mother of Heracles, greatest in birth, to the presence of Melia.

    (Pindar. Pythian Ode 11)

These passages show that not only Cadmus and his wife Harmonia, but even his daughters Semele and Ino were deified by the Greeks. Dionysos was a god in his own right and was believed to be the son of Semele. Pindar has a lot of praise for the past of the city of Thebes. He as well as other writers have called it the seven-gated Thebes. This is of interest as seven gates for a city are unusual. They tempt a conclusion that the number may have had something to do with the seven rivers of Sapt Sindhu. The name Thebes too seems to have had a background for the Phoenicians. There was a city with that name in Egypt, which the Greeks called the hundred-gated Thebes, signifying that it did not have a peripheral wall. Besides cities with this name are reported in Lydia and Armenia, which were all areas of Phoenician influence. Pindar's description of the past achievements of Thebes is here.

> In which of the local glories of the past, divinely blessed Thebes, did you most delight your spirit? Was it when you raised to eminence the one seated beside Demeter of the clashing bronze cymbals, flowing-haired Dionysos? Or when you received, as a snow-shower of gold in the middle of night, the greatest of gods, when he stood in the doorway of Amphitryon, and then went in to the wife to beget Heracles? Or did you delight most in the shrewd counsels of Teiresias? Or in the wise horseman Iolaus? Or in the Sown Men, untiring with the spear? Or when you sent Adrastus back from the mighty war-shout, bereft of countless companions, to Argos, home of horses?
>
> (Pindar. Isthmian Ode 7)

In this Ode, apart from other thing, Pindar mentions of a war with Adrastus of Argos, in which the Cadmeans were victorious. This war, and its causes, has attracted a lot of attention of ancient Greek writers. A few of such these are here.

1. Tydeus did not shrink thus, but was ever ahead of his men when leading them on against the foe. He once came to Mycenae, not as an enemy but as a guest, in the company of Polynices to recruit

his forces, for they were levying war against the strong city of Thebes. The Acheans sent Tydeus as their envoy, and he found the Cadmeans gathered in great numbers to a banquet in the house of Eteocles.

(Homer. *Iliad*. Book 4)

2.   Tydeus was a little man, but he could fight, and rushed madly into fray even when I told him not to do so. When he went all unattended as envoy to the city of Thebes among the Cadmeans, I bade him feast in their house and be at peace, but with that high spirit which was ever present with him, he challenged the youth of the Cadmeans, and at once beat them in all that he attempted, so mightily did I help him.

(Homer. *Iliad*. Book 5)

3.   Be with me even as you were with my noble father Tydeus when he went to Thebes as envoy sent by the Acheans. He left the Acheans by the bank of the river Aesopus, and went to the city bearing a message of peace to the Cadmeans; on his return thence, with your help goddess, he did great deeds of daring.

(Homer. *Iliad*. Book 10)

4.   I am by lineage son to a noble sire, Tydeus, who lies buried at Thebes.

(Homer. *Iliad*. Book 14)

5.   Her did Pegasus and noble Bellerophon slay, but Echidna was subject in love to Orthus and brought forth the deadly Sphinx which destroyed the Cadmeans.

(Hesoid. Theogony)

6.   But when the earth had covered this generation also, grim war and dread battle destroyed a part of them, some in the land of Cadmus at seven-gated Thebes, when they fought for the flocks of Oedipus, and some, when it had brought them in ships over the great sea gulf to Troy for rich-haired Helen's sake.

(Hesiod. Works and Days)

These references show that there was a war between Argos and Thebes, in which before the start of hostilities Tydeus was sent as an envoy by the Acheans, while the rest of the army waited on the banks of the river Aesopus. The peace efforts were unsuccessful and war followed, in which Tydeus and a lot many warriors fell and the Argives were defeated. The passages from Hesiod show that the war was fought for the children of Oedipus and it was the deadly Sphinx which was the cause of the destruction of the Cadmeans. Homer has made a mention of Oedipus. The same is here.

> I saw Epicoste, the mother of Oedipodes. She in ignorance sinned greatly when she let herself be married to her own son; the son who murdered his father, he it was that wedded her. Presently the gods made their state notorious to all men. By their dooming he must linger in distress as king of the Cadmeans in lovely Thebes: whereas she went down to Hades, that strong keeper of the gate of Hell. She tied a running noose to the high beam across her hall and perished, mad with remorse: leaving her son alone to face all the pains and obloquy which avengers of a mother can impose.
>
> (Homer. *Odyssey*. Book 11)

The war fought between Thebes and Argos, the Sphinx causing the destruction of the Cadmeans and the story of Oedipus are interrelated. The complete story emerges from the play *Oedipus Rex* of Sophocles, who lived between 496 and 406 BC. As per this, Laius, a descendant of Cadmus and the king of Thebes, went on a pilgrimage to Delphi. On way, he and his entire entourage, except one, is killed by a band of robbers. The lone survivor brought back the report. As Laius did not have an heir, the Sphinx gave a riddle to the Cadmeans with instructions that whoever solves it should be made the king of Thebes and should marry the queen. Oedipus happened to come that way and solved the puzzle for which he was married to the Queen Iocasta and made the king. Oedipus was the prince of Corinth, where his father Polybus ruled. It had been foretold that Oedipus would kill his father and marry his mother. To save himself from committing such a deed he had left Corinth and had wandered away. Several years later when Oedipus was ruling and had had five children, a severe plague ravaged

Thebes. The priests were consulted and they stated that a sinner, who had killed his father and defiled the bed of his mother, was living in the town and unless he was banished the tempest would not subside. A divinely inspired person is summoned by Oedipus to know the identity of the said person. With some reluctance this person names Oedipus himself. In complete disbelief Oedipus claims his innocence, as his parents were living in Corinth. His wife Iocasta too tells him that he could not have been the killer of her husband, as he was killed on way to Delphi where two roads met. The description of the place where Laius was killed alarms Oedipus, as he had had a quarrel with a group of people at such a location and had killed them. The lone survivor of the incident is summoned to clarify whether it was a band of persons or a single man who had killed Laius and his entourage. As the king and the queen wait for him, a messenger comes from Corinth with the news that king Polybus had died and to request Oedipus to return to his kingdom. Oedipus shows his reluctance, as though with the death of his father the first part of the prophesy could not be fulfilled, the second part still remained as his mother was still alive. The messenger tells him, that if that was the reason for his going into exile, it was useless as he was not a child of Polybus and his wife. The messenger states that Oedipus, as a baby was handed over to him by a person of Thebes and he himself had delivered the baby to Polybus, who, being childless, had adopted him. By then the lone survivor of the incident in which Laius was killed, arrives and the messenger recognises him and says that it was this man who had given the baby to him. The old man discloses that Oedipus was the son of king Laius and Iocasta, who had given the baby to him to be taken away as bad omens had been reported about him. The Queen takes her life while Oedipus blinds himself and moves away from Thebes as a beggar, supported by one of his daughters.

Further story emerges from the plays *Oedipus at Colonus* and *Antigone* by the same author. Oedipus had two sons, Eteocles and Polyneices. As they were young, their uncle Creon became the regent. Once of age, it was decided that the two brothers would alternately be kings for a year at a time. When Eteocles became king, he refused to step down in favour of Polyneices at the end of the year. This led Polyneices to contrive ways and means of regaining the throne. He married the princess of Argos and sought the help of the Acheans in the venture, which led to the war. This war is the subject matter of the play *Seven Against Thebes* of Aeschylus, who lived between 525 and 455 BC. This play was a part of a trilogy of which the other two plays were *Laius and Oedipus*, and *The Sphinx*, which are lost. In the war, apart from several other warriors, both sons of Oedipus died together at the hands of each other. Oedipus died in Colonus near Athens as a beggar. The dynasty of Cadmus thus came to an end with whatever role the Sphinx may have had in it.

It cannot be said how much is fiction, in what has been stated by Sophocles and Aeschylus, as they were writing plays and not history. However, it appears that there is a substantial element of truth in it as Homer, Herodotus and other writers have also referred to it, though fleetingly. From the point of history, apart from giving the story, Sophocles has given an important piece of information. He has the priests tell Oedipus, "For you came to the town of Cadmus and rid us of the tax we rendered to the hard songstress". Though the word tax has been used, it appears to mean rent, as it was not being paid to the state. It appears that Cadmus, on arrival at Thebes, took the area on lease from whoever happened to be the owner of the land. The rent for this lease was paid by the Cadmeans till the time of Oedipus, who seems to have stopped making the payment without making the owner agree to it.

Herodotus has made a statement by which the time of Cadmus can be reckoned. The same is here.

> Now the Dionysos who is said to have been born of Semele the daughter of Cadmus, was born about sixteen hundred years before my time, and Heracles who was the son of Alcmene, about nine hundred years.
>
> (Herodotus. *The Histories*. Book 2. Para 145)

This would place Cadmus around 2,100 BC and about seven hundred years before Heracles. The war of the Cadmeans with Argos has been placed several centuries before the Trojan War. It was perhaps the first major war of Greece, because of which the attention of a lot of writers has been attracted to it. Alexander the Great, however, seems to have had something in his stars against the Phoenicians, because, just as Tyre was singled out by him for exceptionally severe treatment and was destroyed, Thebes was the only Greek city that he razed to the ground.

The contributions made by Cadmus and the Cadmeans to the Greek culture have come up for mention earlier. An additional piece of information comes from Euripides, who lived between 485 and 406 BC. In his play *The Bacchants*, he has described the Bacchic rites and has associated them with Cadmus and his race. Bacchus, also called Dionysos at some places, is reported to be the son of Semele the daughter of Cadmus. He has been reported to have introduced his mysteries and rites in Thebes before any other Greek city. The cult has been stated to have come from Asia and had Cybele, the Great Mother, associated with it. The plot of the play has Pentheus, the grandson of Cadmus as the ruler and strongly opposed to the initiation of people into the Bacchic rites. Dionysos, his cousin, states that he has changed his form from divine to human to introduce these beliefs, bringing them from Asia where they are practiced all over. The play has Cadmus as a character, who comes out to dance for Bacchus. The dialogues from him, as he tries to convince Pentheus to accept them, show that these rites were practiced by the Phoenicians from very remote times as he says, 'Dwell with us, do not break with our old ways.'

The association of the Bacchic mysteries with the Phoenicians has implications of their origin in India, because many of the practices reported in them are very similar to the practices of some of the Tantric sects of India. As Cadmus has called them 'our old ways', they would have been with the Phoenicians from their remote past. They having a common origin with the practices of the Tantrics of India would take Tantra back to the Indus Valley Civilization for its origin. The play also has a statement 'all barbarians celebrate it', making it very widely spread at least in the Mediterranean. Evidently, the practices went all over the place with the Phoenicians.

The Greeks appear to have all along been aware of the Indian links of Dionysus as Commodianus has stated this in the third century AD. His statement is given below.

Ye yourself say that Father Liber was assuredly twice begotten. First of all he was born in India of Proserpine and Jupiter, and waging war against the Titans, when his blood was shed, he expired as one of the mortal men. Again, restored from his death, in another womb Semele conceived him again of Jupiter. From this being twice born he is called Dionysus.

(The Writings of the Early Church Fathers. Vol 4 Commodianus. Against the Gods of the Heathens. Chapter 9)

The migration of the Phoenicians that took place into Greece and its adjoining areas during the times of Cadmus appears to be different in nature from the later migrations. In later times, the Phoenicians maintained their links with their mother cities, Tyre, Sidon, Byblos etc. and retained their Phoenician identity. They had a closer association with fellow Phoenicians, even if they were from a city far away, than they had with their non-Phoenician neighbours. Migrants into Greece who went in the times of Cadmus got completely Hellenized. Though they continued to remember that they came from Phoenicia, they lost their Phoenician identity. They became Greeks and Phoenicia became a matter of their remote past only.

Apart from Cadmus, the influence of the Phoenicians on Greek thought and beliefs emerges from Sanchuniathon. He was a Phoenician priest and writer who compiled the ancient theogonic and historical documents that had reached him either by oral tradition or in writing. Some believe him to be the contemporary of the Assyrian Queen Semiramis, which would place him at 2,000 BC. Others believe him to be of the fourteenth century BC. Sanchuniathon, in turn, had received his records from Hierombolus, the priest of the god Ieuo. The Phoenician history written by him was dedicated to Abibalus, the king of Berytus. His whole work was divided into nine books, of which the first dealt with mythology. Unfortunately, his work has not survived. Philo of Byblos, another Phoenician scholar who lived between AD 64 and AD 141, had translated his work into Greek. This translation too is not available. What has survived of them, are quotes in the works of Eusebius of Caesarea, who lived between AD 260 and 341. Eusebius was a Christian bishop, who wrote for the promotion of Christianity. His focus was thus to demonstrate the fallacy of other beliefs, because of which, he has quoted only the part relating to mythology and has ignored the human history. The mythology stated by him is of little interest, but the preface of Philo and Sanchuniathon recorded by him are of immense importance. These are here.

Philo then, having divided the work of Sanchuniathon into nine books, in the introduction to the first book takes this preface concerning Sanchuniathon, word for word.

'These things being so, Sanchuniathon, who was a man of much learning and great curiosity, and desirous of knowing the earliest history of all nations from the creation of the world, searched out with great care the history of Taautus, knowing that of all men under the sun Taautus was the first who thought of the invention of letters and began writing records, and he laid the foundation as it were, of his history, by beginning with him, whom the Egyptians call Thoyth, and the Alexandrians Thoth, translated by the Greeks into Hermes.' After these statements he finds fault with the more recent authors as violently and untruly reducing the legends concerning the gods to allegories and physical explanations and theories; and so he goes to say:

'But the most recent of the writers on religion rejected the real events from the beginning, and having invented allegories and myths, and formed a fictitious affinity to the cosmical phenomena, established mysteries, and overlaid them with a cloud of absurdity, so that one cannot easily discern what really occurred, but he having lighted upon the collection of secret writings of the Ammoneans which were discovered in the shrines and of course were not known to all men, applied himself diligently to the study of them all; and when he had completed the investigation, he put aside the original myth and the allegories, and so completed his proposed work; until the priests who followed in later times wished to hide this away again, and to restore the mythical character; from which time mysticism began to rise up, not having previously reached the Greeks.'

Next to this he says: 'These things I have discovered in my anxious desire to know the history of the Phoenicians, and after a thorough investigation of much matter, not that which is found among the Greeks, for that is contradictory, and compiled by them in a contentious spirit rather than with a view to truth.'

And after other statements:

'And the conviction that the facts were as he described them came to me, on seeing the disagreement among the Greeks: concerning which I have carefully composed three books bearing the title *Paradoxical History*.'

And again after other statements he adds:

'That with a view to clearness hereafter, and the determination of particulars, it is necessary to state beforehand that the most ancient of the barbarians, and especially the Phoenicians and Egyptians, from whom the rest of the mankind received their traditions, regarded as the greatest gods those who had discovered the necessaries of life, or in some way done good to the nations.'

(Eusebius. Praeparatio Evangelica)

This statement from Philo shows that Sanchuniathon before him had taken up the task of compiling history so as to correct the beliefs that had spread all over, including Greece. Philo has mentioned the same intention on his part. He has also stated that the Phoenicians and the Egyptians established all the traditions that were later followed by the rest of the people. The first book of Philo, out of the nine, is the only one that received the attention of Eusebius. The mythological beliefs have been treated as history, though human history would have followed as there were eight more books in the work. Two Phoenician scholars trying to correct the mythological beliefs of the Greeks show that Greek mythology had its origin from Phoenician mythology.

This is further confirmed by another statement from Philo which is here.

> But the Greeks, surpassing in genius, appropriated most of the earliest stories, and then variously decked them but with ornaments of tragic phrase, and adorned them in every way, with the purpose of charming by the pleasant fables. Hence Hesoid and the celebrated Cyclic poets framed theogonies of their own, and the battles of the giants, and battles of titans, and castrations; and with these fables, as they travelled about, they conquered and drove out the truth.
>
> 'But our ears having grown up in familiarity with their fictions, and being for long ages pre-occupied, guard as a trust the mythology which they received, just as I said at the beginning; and this mythology being aided by time, has made its hold difficult for us to escape from, so that the truth is thought to be nonsense, and the spurious narrative truth.'
>
> Let these suffice as quotations from the writings of Sanchuniathon, translated by Philo of Byblos, and approved as true by the testimony of Porphyry, the philosopher.
>
> (Eusebius. Praeparatio Evangelica)

The Epilogue

JOURNEYS OF PEOPLE DO NOT end, only narratives do. People remain the same, their identities change. Two journeys have emerged, one from the Arctic Circle to India and the other from India to the Atlantic. For the first, the narrative was recorded from the times of lake Balkash and it had its days of tests and trials. Fortunately, one branch came to the peaceful plains of India because of which the narrative survived. The *Veds*, though not with that name, would have been there not only in Central Asia, but all over from the Uyghur country to Spain, as the efforts of Trishok and his successors had led to a situation wherein the Vedic religion was the most widely practised religion of the world. Unfortunately, not even a trace of it has survived anywhere else. If it had not been for the generations of people who kept them safe even as an oral tradition, for such a long time, it would not have been known that there was a group of people, so small as this, which had such spectacular achievements and which had its influence in an area as wide as this, that it may be difficult to assess its impact on humanity. They created neither pyramids nor a wall across mountains for people to marvel, but there was something in their intellectual achievements which makes them a category apart. It would be difficult to assess these people on the basis of our normal understanding about the evolution of man, because from a very early stage they appear to be very intelligent. They were in the Arctic Circle, which had neither trees nor pastures, but by the time they reached the Caspian Sea, they were practising agriculture, they had boats in which they could venture into the sea, though not sustain a storm, they had chariots, they had iron, they had domesticated the cow, horse, goat and sheep. This could not have been a long enough period as should be expected for people to cross so many stages of human development. The knowledge of stars that had been gathered in the Arctic days survived all through, though they did not have even a script. By the time they were in the Ili delta, they knew enough about agriculture, not to be too keen to appease Pushan, a god that had been created to help in the fertility of seeds. Soon they were practising agriculture of a level at which it remained throughout the world till less than a century ago. As they had a system of irrigation, it can be said to be superior to the agricultural practices of many parts of today's world. With this, they had more than what was needed, due to which they could have the luxury of having religious practices in which food was wasted in the name of being offered to gods. People not having enough to afford could not have thought of it. To top it all, they could fight wars over ideas. This is something, which has never been thought of for the ancient world. It was always believed that people at that stage were too involved in their struggle for survival and so, if ever they fought, it was because of reasons of survival only. It was either to gain control of more fertile lands or rivers which provided support to life in many ways. Here is a case where survival was more than ensured and life was as comfortable as could be expected in the given circumstances with plenty of food to eat and Som to drink. There was no enemy who came from outside to deprive them of their land and prosperity, yet they fought with each other over a difference of opinion, which if seen from an impartial position, looks so trivial that at times it seems difficult to believe whether people could really fight over it and for so long. Yet they did and not once, but for generations. Arjika or Airyana Vaego, which was so dear to them that both sides elevated its memory to mythological levels, was lost but the fight did not cease.

A race with this level of intelligence in such remote times had taken up missionary activities for the spread of their religion. Their success in this is evident from what has been believed to be Manichaeism. They had reached Egypt and the entire North Africa till they crossed over to Europe and spread their influence in Spain. The Roman Empire and the Roman Church found them a formidable enemy in Europe. Religion would have been only one aspect of their impact as all their ideas and knowledge would have travelled with them. Even in the field of religion, to be able to give the Upanishadic philosophy at such an early stage is difficult to understand. However, this is evident not only from what has been stated earlier, but also because Ibn Arabi, one of the earliest Sufi saints, whose works are available, hailed from Spain. He lived between AD 1165 and AD 1240. This shows that what was being preached by Trishok and the rest was not just the ritualistic side of religion, but had also its deep mystic core. Till much later, people were debating about monotheism and polytheism, while they had reached a stage to realize that the issue was not relevant. It did not matter what name was being used as it remained only a name. Only when other religions came up and challenged their concepts, did they find it difficult to face the challenge because their main strength became a weakness in these debates. Their strength was in the core Upanishadic philosophy, which would have been appealing only to the class of people that approached religion in search of God and not those who came in search of worldly things through God. As they knew that this was the real meaning of what was being said and the rest was a mere eye-wash for the rest of the people who were looking for a benefactor and not God, what was being said or done on the ritualistic side was of no great concern to them. When it came to a debate with the people who were challenging their concepts, it was only the ritualistic side which could be presented and which had to prove itself to be superior to the concepts of their rivals. The mystic core could not be disclosed even at this stage for a variety of reasons. Firstly, the requirement in the debates was of logic, rhetoric and arguments. The mystic core was not based on logic or arguments, but on realization. It had declared God to be beyond human expression. 'Neti' is all they had to say. Everyone who wanted to come forward to realize Him was welcome to do so, but He could not be described by anybody. On a forum where people from different religions were arguing their case, this would not have been an acceptable argument.

Secondly, the audience that was listening to the debate and deciding which side was more convincing was of people who were looking for a benefactor in God. For them this core philosophy would not have been appealing, as this was not what they were looking for. Thirdly, a disclosure of the core philosophy would have left the followers of their own religion in a state of confusion. They were also the people who were looking for a benefactor and not God. If they had been told that there is no Indra, no Varun, no Agni to give them anything or to protect them from the Asurs and whatever is there was within them, they would have been left in the wood with no one to help. As a result, it was only the ritualistic side which had to face the brunt. This was what had no real meaning to them and so its weaknesses or strength were of no concern. It could have a hundred gods if someone wished to have them. It could have a hundred rituals if that gave any joy to people doing them. It was all the same.

The impact of these Aryans on Greece and Rome would make a very interesting study. A group while fleeing from Iran at the time when the Indo-Aryans came to India had gone to Greece also. This group would have made its contribution in a very direct manner, while for a long time the preachers would have brought their thoughts and ideas in an indirect way. A study of the ancient Greek thought and its comparison with Indian thought would bring out the common features which would give an indication of the contribution of this Aryan group to ancient Greece. Rome, after a stage, made a conscious effort to uproot Manichaeism. Initially, it was out of distrust because of its believed Persian origin at a time when Rome was at war with Persia. Later, when Christianity became the state religion, it was a question of a rival religion. In this conscious effort to eradicate Manichaeism, the Roman emperors kept issuing edicts for centuries, which shows how deeply rooted the religion was. Though ultimately no trace of it was left in Europe, this long association would have left its imprint on the people to survive much after nobody even remembered it. An interesting issue of Manichaeism in the West was its claim that it represented true Christianity. Though a far deeper study would be needed to say something conclusively, it raises questions about the relationship between Christ and the Vedic religion. The arguments that were used to disprove the claim of the Manicheans that they were true Christians were based on their not following the Christian dogmas and cult as they had different views on the origin of the universe and other such things than what was given in the *Bible*. However, all these issues are not a part of the Gospels, which provide information of the life and teachings of Christ. Dogmas and cult-related issues are either in the *Old Testament* or in the *Epistles of St Paul*, which are undisputedly after Christ, while the *Old Testament* is the scripture of the Jews. Christ was certainly born a Jew, but he did not accept the basic principles of Judaism. The words ascribed to Christ have been printed in red in several versions of the *Bible*. These are scattered and so few that the full message of Christ does not emerge very clearly from them. However, his stress on universal love and brotherhood, and the idea that the kingdom of God is within you, are a departure from the Hebrew religion, which was the religion of the chosen few. A study of the *Bible* does not show that Christ, while rejecting the basic principles of Judaism, accepted their dogmas. It cannot be said whether the acceptance of the Jewish dogma was mandated by Christ or by the Church later. This issue becomes critical as it is known that the *Bible* underwent the imperial scrutiny of Rome, before an official version was declared, after which all other versions were as systematically searched and destroyed as were the Manichean scriptures. Christ appears to be totally unconcerned about matters relating to dogma and cult in the Gospels. If it was not Christ but the Church that had introduced the dogmas, the failure of the Manicheans to prove their claim in the absence of this cannot be held against them. Apart from the later Manicheans, Mani himself in his lifetime had claimed that he was the Apostle of Christ. This cannot be taken to be just a ploy on his part to woo the Christians to his religion, because there would not have been very many Christians by then, as Christianity was in its infancy. Moreover, the claim would not have taken him very far if he had been saying something very different from Christ. The Christians contemporary to him did not dispute his claim. It was only the Church which did so later. The claim of the Manicheans that they represented true Christianity, therefore, needs to be examined again looking for the real message of Christ, instead of simply accepting what Rome said it was, because Rome had enough political compulsions to outweigh the necessity of remaining faithful to Christ.

The impact of the Magis on Central Asia would have been in all walks of life. Though in politics their role remained limited, they were the religious leaders of the entire region for a few thousand years. Such a position would have left its imprint on many things. They were the priests of the Persian Empire throughout and in that role were in a position to influence the policies of the state. Much of the other areas of Central Asia had different Aryan tribes, amongst whom the Magis had their position as the priests, an office which included that of a doctor, an astrologer and a counsellor.

In India, where the legacy of the Indo-Aryans survived as a living heritage, the impact can be felt in every walk of life. Their language made a major inroad into Sapt Sindhu. If this issue is examined keeping the linguistic pattern of modern India, it would emerge that Sanskrit is the mother language of all north Indian languages, while south Indian languages have Tamil for their origin, with a distinct impact of Sanskrit in their vocabulary. Sapt Sindhu would have had its original language before the arrival of Sanskrit. The present linguistic pattern of the country could be reflecting the interface this had with the newly arrived language.

By the time they left the area, all people of Sapt Sindhu who moved to the Gangetic plains believed that they were Aryans. The Vedic religion took a very strong hold in the area, though with its spirit of tolerance, there was never an attempt to eradicate any other religion or religious practices. Its impact on later Hinduism is evident with the *Veds* occupying the highest position of reverence amongst all scriptures. The war between the Devs and Asurs is the pivotal theme of Hindu mythology, though many of the wars therein are not related to those that were actually fought by the real Devs with the real Asurs. Even the Mother Goddess of the Indus Valley Civilization, who in all likelihood would have been a fertility deity, emerges in the Shakti Cult as the goddess of war, fighting and killing Asurs. The social order was what the Aryans had prescribed, though with a lot of distortions which crept in because of the situation in which it was introduced and later expanded. Aryan influence and the heritage of the Indus Valley Civilization has become so deeply intermingled that it would be difficult to assess what, in India of the later times, is an impact of the Aryans and what the heritage of the Indus Valley Civilization. In the religion, sacrifice may have been given up a long time ago, but the spirit of the Vedic religion got reiterated in the *Gita*, which formed the foundations of the Hindu thought of later times.

The narrative from *Veds* ends in the middle of the north Indian plains, giving a long account, which began from the freezing winters of the Arctic Circle and went through all the turbulence of a history spread over several thousand years. It survived through times when there was no script or writing material, or when *Veds* were considered to be too sacred to be reduced to paper. Times of affluence and times of distress came and passed away as the journey continued. It has its irony that the people who, while recording the narrative tried to get away from the blame of killing their brothers and succeeded in doing so, got blamed for what they did not do, the destruction of the Indus Valley Civilization. The style of presenting facts makes it difficult to comprehend, but once they start emerging they turn out to be fascinating enough to lead to a deeper study. Identities of people have changed, making it difficult to know what became of those who went west of the Amu Darya, what of those who went east or south and how to link this journey with the journey of man thereafter.

The second journey was equally fascinating. Unlike the first which began to get away from the cold, there were no compelling reasons for this. It was driven by enterprise and continued to remain so for a very long time, till a natural calamity led a large number of people to join it. It is difficult to say when it began and how far it went. Byblos has signs of it having reached there by six thousand BC. How much earlier these people reached the Persian Gulf, Ethiopia and Egypt cannot be said. How far it went is also shrouded in mystery. Whether the limit should be fixed at Brazil or Peru would remain open. Unfortunately no information about it is available from Indian sources, because of which the first leg of it, from India to West Asia remains unknown, making it necessary to bring forward evidence from Greece and Rome to link it with Sapt Sindhu. With the identity as Phoenicians, the activities of these Indians are reasonably well documented. Their contribution to Greek, Roman and world civilization is fairly well acknowledged. Even today there are several areas where people claim descent from the Phoenicians. The search for their roots ends there, because beyond that all that is known is that the Phoeicians came from the sea. It is not known that they came not from the Sea but from the Seven Seas. Their journey however continues, just as that of those who stayed behind but the story, though endless, must end and the storyteller should sit back and say 'Neti'. That is not all.

Bibliography

1. *The Rig Ved*. Translation by H.H.Wilson
2. *The Saam Ved*. Translation by R.T.H.Griffith
3. *The Yajur Ved*. Translation by R.T.H.Griffith
4. *The Atharv Ved*. Translation by W.D.Whitney
5. *The Aitarey Brahman*. Translation by Martin Haug
6. *The Shatpath Brahman*. Translation by Justin Eggeling
7. *The Nighantu and Nirukt of Yask*. Translation by Lakshman Swarup
8. *The Brahm Sutra Bhashya of Shankaracharya*. Translation by Swami Gambhirananda
9. *The Yog Sutra* of Patanjali
10. *The Zend Avesta*. Translation by James Darmesteter and L.H. Mills
11. *The Bundahis*. Translation by E.W.West
12. *The Bahman Yast*. Translation by E.W.West
13. *The Shayast La-Shayast*. Translation by E.W.West
14. *The Dadistan-i Dinik*. Translation by E.W.West
15. *The Din-i Mainog-i Khirad*. Translation by E.W.West
16. *The Sikand Gumanik Vigar*. Translation by E.W.West
17. *The Sad Dar*. Translation by E.W.West
18. *The Dinkard*. Translation by E.W.West
19. *The Nasks*. Translation by E.W.West
20. *The Shahnama of Firdausi*. Translation of Alexander Roger
21. *The Cambridge History of Iran*
22. *The Holy Bible*

23. *The Histories* by Herodotus
24. *The Geographica* by Strabo
25. *The Lives* by Plutarch
26. *The Moralia* by Plutarch
27. *The Iliad* by Homer
28. *The Odyssey* by Homer
29. *The Diwan-e Shams-e Tabriz* by Rumi
30. *The Anabasis of Alexander* by Arrian
31. *The Gallic Wars* by Julius Ceasar
32. *The Commonwealth* by Cicero
33. *The Histories* by Polybius
34. *The History of Rome* by Titus Livy
35. *The Wasps* by Aristophanes
36. *The Acharnians* by Aristophanes
37. *The Natural History* by Pliny, the Elder
38. *The Philippic History* by Justin
39. *The Record of the Western Regions of the Tang Dynasty* by Huein Tsang
40. *The Periplus* of Hanno
41. *The Republic* by Plato
42. *The Politics* by Aristotle
43. *The Odes* of Pindar
44. *Theogony* by Hesiod
45. *The Works and Days* by Hesiod
46. *The Oedipus Rex* by Sophocles
47. *The Antigone* by Sophocles
48. *The Oedipus at Colonus* by Sophocles
49. *The Seven Against Thebes* by Aeschylus
50. *The Bacchants* by Euripides
51. *The Praeparatio Evangelica* by Eusebius of Caesarea
52. *The Writings of the Early Church Fathers*